Marketing Innovations for Sustainable Destinations

T0291269

Editors:

Alan Fyall, Metin Kozak, Luisa Andreu,

Juergen Gnoth and Sonja Sibila Lebe

(G) **Goodfellow Publishers Ltd**

Published by Goodfellow Publishers Limited,
Woodeaton, Oxford, OX3 9TJ
http://www.goodfellowpublishers.com

British Library Cataloguing in Publication Data: a catalogue record
for this title is available from the British Library.

Library of Congress Catalog Card Number: on file.

ISBN: 978-1-906884-05-5

 Design and typesetting by P.K. McBride, www.macbride.org.uk

Printed by Baker & Taylor, www.baker-taylor.com

Cover design by Cylinder, www.cylindermedia.com

Contents

List of figures

List of tables

Contributors

José Luís Abrantes, Universidade Nova de Lisboa, Portugal

Eunice Amissah, University of Cape Coast, Ghana

Francesca d'Angella, IULM University, Milan, Italy

Magda Antonioli Corigliano, Bocconi University, Italy

Maria D. Alvarez, Boaziçi University, Turkey

Luisa Andreu, Universitat de València, Spain

Eli Avraham, University of Haifa, Israel

Rodolfo Baggio, Bocconi University, Italy

Juan José Blázquez, University Of Castilla-La Mancha, Spain

Bruce Braham, Bournemouth University, UK

Enrique Bigné Alcañiz, Universitat de València, Spain

Sara Campo Martínez, Universidad Autónoma de Madrid, Spain

Manuela De Carlo, IULM University, Milan, Italy

Dean Carson, Charles Darwin University, Australia

Jason L. Chen, The Hong Kong Polytechnic University, China SAR

Chris Cooper, University of Nottingham, UK

Antónia Correia, University of The Algarve, Portugal

Rafael Currás Pérez, Universitat de València, Spain

Estrella Díaz, University of Castilla-La Mancha, Spain

Pablo L. De Diesbach, Lausanne Hospitality Research Lab, Ecole Hôtelière de Lausanne, Switzerland

Alain Decrop, Louvain School Of Management, Belgium

Leonardo (Don) A.N. Dioko, Institute for Tourism Studies, Macau, China

Diana Ene, Nottingham University, UK

Peter Erdélyi, Bournemouth University, UK

Águeda Esteban, University of Castilla-La Mancha, Spain

Isabelle Frochot, Cemagref and University of Savoie, France

Isabel Sánchez García, Universitat de València, Spain

Christine Harris, Bournemouth University, UK

Tomaz Kolar, University of Ljubljana, Slovenia

Carmen Lages, ISCTE Business School – Lisboa, Portugal

Metin Kozak, Mugla University, Turkey

Luís Filipe Lages, Universidade Nova de Lisboa, Portugal

Gang Li, University of Surrey, UK

Peter Lugosi, Bournemouth University, UK

David Martín-Consuegra , University of Castilla-La Mancha, Spain

Armelle Maumelat, Enita Clermont-Ferrand, France

Luc Mazuel, Enita Clermont-Ferrand, France

Ishmael Mensah, University of Cape Coast, Ghana

Vivien R. Moinat, University of Lausanne, Switzerland

Tonino Pencarelli, University of Urbino, Italy

Rosária Pereira, University of The Algarve, Portugal

Ruggero Sainaghi, Università IULM, Italy

Doris Schmallegger, James Cook University, Australia

Peter Schofield, University of Salford, UK

Ronaldo Schutz, University of The Algarve, Portugal

Noel Scott, The University of Queensland, Australia

Cláudia Seabra, Instituto Politécnico de Viseu, Portugal

Carla Silva, Instituto Politécnico de Viseu, Portugal

Siu-Ian (Amy) So, University of Macau, China

Simone Splendiani, University of Urbino, Italy

Haiyan Song, The Hong Kong Polytechnic University, China SAR

Andrew Taylor, Charles Darwin University, Australia

Karin Teichmann, Institute for Tourism and Leisure Studies, Austria

Robert Van Der Veen, The Hong Kong Polytechnic University, China SAR

Vesna Zabkar, University of Ljubljana, Slovenia

Andreas H. Zins, Institute for Tourism and Leisure Studies, Austria

About the editors

Alan Fyall is Deputy Dean Research & Enterprise in the School of Services Management, Bournemouth University and Head of Enterprise for the Centre for Research & Enterprise, Bournemouth University. He has published widely in the areas of destination management and marketing, visitor attractions and heritage tourism, and is the author of over 100 articles, book chapters and conference papers as well as ten books including *Tourism Principles & Practice*, one of the leading international textbooks on the subject published by Pearson. Alan has organised a number of international conferences and workshops and sits on the editorial boards of *Annals of Tourism Research*, *Journal of Heritage Tourism*, *International Journal of Tourism Research* and *Tourism Recreation Research* while he is book review editor on *Anatolia*. Alan has conducted numerous consulting and applied research projects for clients across the UK and overseas and currently serves on the ESRC Cluster Advisory Board for Exeter University Business School.

Metin Kozak is Professor of Marketing in the School of Tourism and Hospitality Management, Mugla University, Mugla, Turkey. He holds both Master's and Ph.D. degrees in tourism. He has published over 60 papers in several national and international pure management, tourism and hospitality journals, both in English and Turkish, and presented over 40 papers at various national and international conferences on tourism, hospitality, regional development, international management, and international marketing. He is the author or co-author of eight books. Metin has also an extensive experience in taking part in the organisation of various tourism and hospitality conferences. Following his successful career within the last nine years (since the approval of PhD degree), Metin has received two awards to mark his achievements. His main research interests focus on consumer behaviour, benchmarking, competitiveness, cross-cultural research, destination management and marketing, European tourist markets.

Luisa Andreu is Associate Professor of Marketing, University of Valencia. Bachelor and Doctor of Economics and Business Administration at the University of Valencia (Spain), and Master of Science in Tourism Management and Marketing from the International Centre for Tourism & Hospitality Research at Bournemouth University (United Kingdom). Luisa is the author of several articles published in international and national journals. In particular, she has published research papers in *Annals of Tourism Research*, *European Journal of Marketing*, *Tourism Management*, *Journal of Travel & Tourism Marketing*, *Journal of Services Marketing*, *Tourism Review* and the *International Journal of Culture, Tourism and Hospitality Research*. Member of American Marketing Science (AMS), European Academy of Marketing (EMAC), the Spanish Association of Scientific Experts in Tourism (AE-CIT). She has participated in conferences organized by the Academy of Marketing Science (AMS), European Marketing Conference (EMAC), Tourism: State of the Art II and EuroCHRIE, among others. Luisa was co-chair of the 3rd edition of Advances in Tourism Marketing Conference (ATMC) in 2009. Previously, she was co-chair of ATMC in 2005 and 2007. Her research interests include the analysis of destination marketing, tourist behaviour, tourism networks, corporate social responsibility and online marketing.

Juergen Gnoth is a senior lecturer at the University of Otago, New Zealand. He obtained his PhD in Tourism from the University of Otago. His research interests lie in consumer behaviour, tourism services marketing, place branding and marketing ethics. Juergen is a leading member of the Tourism Research & Place Branding Group and an international and cross-cultural researcher. The main focus of his research lies with the constructs of networks, intentions, expectations, image and satisfaction, but also with understanding and measuring the influence of emotions on consumption behaviour. He deals closely with Tourism New Zealand, and members of the tourism industry, such as hotels, airlines, operators and consultants to keep his teaching up-to-date and relevant. Juergen is a member of a number of editorial boards and Associate Editor- Research Notes of the top journal in tourism, *Annals of Tourism Research*.

Sonja Sibila Lebe is Head of the Tourism Department at the Faculty of Economics and Business, University of Maribor (Slovenia). Additionally to the pedagogic work, she has two advisory jobs: due to maintaining good contacts to the regional tourism industry, she has been appointed as the director of the RAST association (Regional Avio-destination of Slovene Tourism) – an organisation that is concerned to attract airlines to north-Eastern Slovenia. Additionally to this, she is head of the Scientific board of the Multidisciplinary Research Institute Maribor, where she is leading tourism-related projects and her research work in the field of tourism. As the team-leader, she has prepared several strategies for tourism product development on the national level, like: Development of Cultural Tourism in Slovenia or Development of Gastronomy Tourism in Slovenia. Her institute is very active in the field of eco management; Sonja Sibila is involved in advisory and consultancy work as well, e.g. coaching hotels on their way to attain their eco-certificate. Due to her multiple foreign language skills (7 languages), Sonja Sibila has often been invited to act as co-organiser of several conferences and seminars in Slovenia and abroad, where she has also acted as visiting professor. She has written a lot of scientific and expert articles and presented papers in domestic and foreign seminars. She also is co-author and co-editor of books and reviewer in several domestic and foreign scientific journals including *Tourism Management*.

1 Introduction

Luisa Andreu, Universitat de València, Spain; Alan Fyall, Bournemouth University; Metin Kozak, Mugla University; Juergen Gnoth, Otago University; Sonja Sibila Lebe, Maribor University

Introduction

The initial idea for this book originated from papers submitted for presentation at the 3rd Advances in Tourism Marketing Conference (ATMC 2009) held in Bournemouth, United Kingdom, between 6-9 September 2009. Under the conference theme of *Marketing Innovations for Sustainable Destinations: Operations, Interactions, Experiences*, the conference set out to build on the success of the two previous Advances in Tourism Marketing conferences; the first hosted in 2005 by Mugla University in Akyaka (Turkey), and the second hosted in 2007 by the Universitat de València (Spain). With more than 70 researchers and practitioners from more than 15 different countries partaking in the first conference in Turkey, and around 160 researchers and representatives of companies and institutions from five continents partaking at the event in Spain, there is little doubt that the Advances in Tourism Marketing conferences have become a significant event in the academic calendar. As a direct result of the first conference held in Turkey, Kozak and Andreu (2006) published the book *Progress in Tourism Marketing* while in 2009, Kozak, Gnoth and Andreu published the book *Advances in Destination Marketing* which came about in direct response to papers presented at the Valenica conference in 2007. As with the previous two books, the editors of this book, with the assistance of many colleagues who willingly gave their time to serve as reviewers for papers submitted to the conference, selected those papers that successfully navigated the reviewing process and those that neatly dovetailed the overriding theme of the conference. In this regard, the papers selected for the chapters in the book were judged to continue the trend of encouraging critical discussion on a number of contemporary themes relating to innovative marketing operations, interactions and experiences and the means by which each contributes to the sustainable development of destinations.

In its broadest sense, the 3rd Advances in Tourism Marketing Conference explicitly set out to explore, analyze, and evaluate the state of the art in tourism marketing from an international perspective and bring together academic researchers, policy makers and practitioners, and provide a forum for the discussion and dissemination of themes related to the tourism system under a marketing approach. Under the theme of Operations, submissions to the conference were invited that challenged existing paradigms and explored critically current conventions and *modus operandi* and the means by which they remained valid in the changing destination marketplace. The combined forces of growing competition, changing patterns of consumption and slowing economic growth in much of the world, suggest that the next decade will provide a challenging environment for marketing practitioners as well as a stimulating research setting for academics to scrutinise operational practice. In particular, the theme invited submissions that explored the marketing system more broadly and the increasing complexity of its networks, interactions and relationships, and underlying theoretical constructs upon which marketing operations are derived. The second theme, that of Interactions, invited submissions that investigated the dynamic nature of relationships and encounters existing within destinations and the influence and impact marketing operations and practices have on them. Particular attention was drawn to the host community and the role they play in the marketing of destinations generally and their contribution to the destination experience, more specifically via their interaction with visitors. The final theme, that of Experiences, sought to develop further the concept of the *Experience Economy* and aimed to introduce many of the emerging concepts, ideas and practices more common in other sectors to the specific management of destinations. Among other things, this included the design, co-creation and delivery of memorable experiences, the role of destination stakeholders in experience creation, analysis of the elements of the visitor experience, the use of stories, dramas narratives, symbols and meanings and the means by which experiential marketing appeals to the senses, emotions and values.

Despite the themes set for the conference, it is interesting to note that the majority of the papers fell within three slightly different, but equally strong themes, namely: consumer decision making and tourist experiences; destination image, positioning and branding; and, destinations stakeholders and networks. Hence, it is with these three specific themes – within the broader theme of marketing innovations for sustainable destinations – that the remaining twenty-five chapters of the book feature.

Part I: Consumer Decision Making and Tourist Experiences

Tourist Search and Marketing Communications

Tourists usually make use of a variety of external information sources (Moutinho, 2000). These information sources form the basis for trip planning (Snepenger et al., 1990). When searching for tourist information, one must consider the variety of sources used (Beatty and Smith, 1987; Srinivasan and Ratchford, 1991). From both theoretical and practitioner perspectives, it is particularly useful to study the importance of specific information sources that tourists use for selecting services. This book contains three chapters that analyze this topic, covering not only the traditional media but also online search engines and the importance of word of mouth. In the early years, word of mouth (WOM) was defined as face-to-face communication about products or companies between those people who were not commercial entities (Arndt, 1967). Later, Westbrook (1987, p. 261) described WOM more broadly, to include "all informal communications directed at other consumers about the ownership, usage, or characteristics of particular goods and services or their sellers". While Westbrook did not specifically define what constitute "informal communications", his writing clearly indicated that these are the communications of interpersonal relationships, as opposed to those through mass-media channels that pass product knowledge from producers/providers to consumers (Litvin et al., 2008).

Mass media are an important channel of communication for service companies. However, understanding the effectiveness of traditional advertising versus other external sources becomes an interesting issue to provide increase effectiveness in communication campaigns. In Chapter 2, **Baggio et al.** analyze the effect of WOM in comparison to advertising on travel behavior using a modelling approach. A population of 500 individuals was used for the simulations and was considered to interact in a random network. In addition, this chapter analyzes the effect of social networks on WOM amongst a population in the origin prior to travel. By comparing the two communication stimuli, WOM was found to have higher effectiveness and this level is dependent on a moderate cohesion of the target group. The authors suggest that the structural characteristics of a target market be considered in developing marketing campaigns.

Focusing on external tourism information sources in Chapter 3, **Seabra et al.** develop a scale that assesses the importance of these sources to the selection of tourism services. Based on an empirical study of 350 tourists in Portugal, the authors identify five dimensions of this 'Inforsource' scale: media, institutional brochures, commercial brochures, travel agents and the Internet. As the authors suggest, through the Infosource scale, tourism organizations might have a framework to develop and implement strategies that might bring value to their services, as well as to provide some guidance on how to better pursue an information-oriented strategy.

Cyberspace has presented marketers with new opportunities to improve the efficiency and effectiveness of communication (Litvin et al., 2008). Taking advantage of new technologies, the Internet can also enable destinations to enhance their competitiveness (Buhalis, 2000). Developments in search engines, carrying capacity and speed of networks have influenced the number of travelers around the world that use the Internet for the planning and experiencing of their travels (Buhalis and Law, 2008). Focusing on the search engines, in Chapter 4 **Díaz et al.** analyze the presence of 50 European tourism destinations using four Internet search engines. In particular, the authors analyze the general visibility ratio of tourist destinations in each of the search engines, as well as the presence of specific tourist information available in each search engine. The boom of the Internet, especially vis-à-vis search engines, has changed the media tourist companies use for the distribution of tourist information and also the way in which potential tourists search for and consume information for their journey. As the authors suggest, tourist organizations should make sure they are present in a significant number of search engines, but also that they design strategies to increase website visibility in online search engines.

Consumption, Tourist Decision Making and Experiences

More recently, new forms of consumption have appeared such as eco-volunteering, scientific tourism, adventure tourism, etc. that, according to **Moinat and de Diesbach** in Chapter 5, are far removed from the traditional holidays at the beach or in the mountains. To explain these practices, the authors propose an integrative framework of tourism marketing research that allows understanding as to how three approaches – cognitive, emotional and symbolic – constitute a new theoretical framework and are complementary. In the context of consumer decision making (CDM) for budget city breaks, in Chapter 6 **Ene and Schofield** suggest an integrated approach to structure the analysis of tourist decisions by adapting and extending Hansen's (2005) conceptual CDM framework. The original model was extended by incorporating two new variables: repurchase and recommendation, which add a conative dimension to the extant cognitive and affective dimensions. Using qualitative and quantitative research, the findings highlight the complexity of decision making in this product market and confirm the extended version as a viable framework. Both cognitive and affective dimensions influence consumer satisfaction with budget short city breaks and their intention to both recommend these products to others and to purchase similar city breaks. In Chapter 7, **Decrop and Kozak** analyze six decision strategies that are used when making tourism choices: deal proneness, experience-based strategy, maximization, affective strategy, social, and situational rules. Using an empirical study, the authors investigate how such strategies differ across both product (generic, modal, specific) and social (single, couple, family, friendship groups) layers from a multi-level decision making perspective.

In the analysis of tourism behaviour, motivations are an important issue as they are starting points of the travel decision and destination choice processes. Despite wide academic interest in this topic, there are issues that deserve further research. In Chapter 8 of this book, **Silva et al.** develop a 'mountain tourism push motivation' (MTPM) scale that assess the importance of push factors in deciding to travel to mountain tourism destinations. This MTPM scale is a multi-dimensional model that reflects contemporary society changes through three dimensions: adventure/excitement, social/knowledge, and prestige. In the context of cultural heritage, one of the tourist drives is the quest for authentic experiences. There is a growing desire to obtain experiences and products that are original and the real thing, not contaminated by being fake or impure. This movement away from impurity, the virtual, the spun and the mass-produced in a world seemingly full of falseness needs further explanation (Yeoman et al., 2007). With an attempt to operationalize the authenticity concept, **Kolar and Zabkar** in Chapter 9 propose a conceptual model of perceived authenticity. This model consists of ten dimensions (objects, facts, authority, context, self, people, spirituality, cultural frame, experience and offering) that represent various elements of cultural heritage sites through which tourists form their perceptions of authenticity.

In the tourism literature, numerous studies have been devoted to analyzing tourist satisfaction. According to Yuksel and Yuksel (2001), there are three aspects of customer (tourist) satisfaction that are widely debated: the definition of customer satisfaction, the relationship between customer satisfaction and service quality, and the measurement of customer satisfaction. Even though much research has been carried out regarding tourist satisfaction, there is a need to research this important issue on a continuous evaluation system that facilitates the assessment of tourist satisfaction on a regular basis at both sector and destination levels. To fill in the above research gap, **Song et al.** in Chapter 10 create a comprehensive tourist satisfaction index (TSI) system based on the expectancy-disconfirmation framework. Using a pilot study in mainland Chinese tourists visiting Hong Kong, the authors integrate three tourism-related sectors (hotels, retail shops and travel agents) to calculate the tourist satisfaction index. Looking at the negative emotions after a service failure, in Chapter 11 **Bigné et al.** analyze the effects of discrete emotions on tourist negative word-of-mouth and exit. These effects can be either mediated by dissatisfaction or direct depending on the type of emotion. Based on a quantitative study to tourists who had an unsatisfactory experience with a hotel or restaurant (308 for hotels and 358 for restaurants), the findings show that when tourists have a negative experience with a provider, while anger has an indirect effect on negative WOM and exit through regret and dissatisfaction, regret influences post-purchase behavior directly. Additionally, anger and dissatisfaction explain to a greater extent negative WOM whereas regret is the main driver of exit. The final chapter in Part I, Chapter 12 by **Teichmann and Zins**, explores what role travel behaviour has on future destination decisions. Through the use of a self-administered questionnaire, the study found that in general the predictive qualities of the destination horizon concept are rather limited while on a short-to-medium term scope the traditional horizon approach more or less reflects the already known phenomenon of destination loyalty.

Part II: Destination Image, Positioning and Branding

Destination Image

The evaluation and analysis of destination image has been the subject of much attention in related academic literature and has made a significant contribution to a greater understanding of tourist behavior. Hunt (1975) was among the first to demonstrate its importance in increasing the number of tourists visiting destinations. Today there is a general consensus about the significance of the role played by image in the process of decision making, and, by extension, choice (Baloglu and McCleary, 1999). Despite the numerous contributions on destination image, there is a lack of research on certain issues. Three chapters of this book focus on destination image to explore: (i) the destination image in urban destinations; (ii) destination image of non-visitors; and, (iii) the relationship between destination and country image.

Studies on destination image mainly concentrate on leisure tourism, with a focus on pleasure tourist perceptions and the determinants of leisure destination image. In the literature there is a gap of research to study the image of destinations with a business orientation, i.e., where travel for attending meetings, exhibitions and incentive visits. With the aim to fill this gap, **d'Angella and De Carlo** in Chapter 13 offer a case study of Milan to analyze the international image of a business destination. The authors identify nine key dimensions of destination's international image – private transport, accommodation, leisure offer, events, life quality, public transports, tourism communication, city environment and residents' receptiveness. The findings of the study provide destination and firm managers with original insights for the implementation of effective marketing strategies. In the tourist behavior literature, destination image has been the object of intense academic interest over the past decade since it is a critical element in the tourist decision process. As **Frochot et al** point out in Chapter 14, the majority of destination image studies have been conducted on current consumers, and the non-consumers' segment remains relatively unexplored. To bridge this gap, the authors explore further how consumers perceive and describe the image of a destination they have yet not wanted to visit. Using focus groups to analyze the image of non-visitors to the Auvergne region in France, this study suggests that when destinations have a limited image, the organic image can be strongly influenced by repetitive and dominant information.

The majority of destination image studies analyze tourists' perceptions regarding countries as tourism destinations. However, recent literature claims that there is a need to distinguish between the image of the country and as a tourism destination. According to Nadeau et al (2008), country image and destination image are 'two fields of research that have evolved separately through distinct literature and research communities, yet developments in the former can contribute significantly to the latter' (p. 85). Country image can be defined as mental maps or knowledge structures related to countries (Jaffe and Nebenzahl 2001), while destination image is defined as 'an attitudinal construct consisting of an individual's mental representation of knowledge (beliefs), feelings, and global impression about an object or destination' (Baloglu and McCleary, 1999, p. 870). Taking into account the need to treat the image of the country and that of the tourism destination as two different constructs, in Chapter 15 **Campo and Alvarez** conduct research applied to Turkey. The authors suggest that country image is more general, while destination image is related to the evaluation of a place visited. Research findings show that the evaluation of Turkey as a tourism destination is significantly more positive than that of the country. To analyze the determinants of the image of Turkey as a country and as a tourist destination, the authors analyze the influence of the controllable and non-controllable information sources influencing both images. Using an experimental methodology, research findings show that controllable promotional sources of information have a stronger impact on both country and destination image.

Destination Positioning

With thousands of destination marketing organizations (DMOs) now competing for attention, places are becoming substitutable. Effective positioning and branding are mutually beneficial processes to both the consumer and the marketers. This is because positioning is underpinned by the philosophy of understanding and meeting unique consumer needs. For the organization, the value of positioning lies in the link it provides between the analyses of the internal corporate and external competitive environments. This is fundamental to the definitions of strategic marketing, which point to the matching of internal resources with environmental opportunities (Pike and Ryan, 2004). Within a tourism destination there are also geographic regions that increase complexity for destination marketing organizations. While positioned in Australia's outback, **Carson and Taylor**'s research in Chapter 16 offers insights and managerial implications about the challenges of competitiveness for other destinations linked by their location within areas of iconic imagery (i.e., Europe's Alps, the Caribbean's beaches, Africa's savannahs). As the authors explain, Australia has its own formally designated regions labeled 'outback', i.e. Outback Queensland, Outback New South Wales, the Flinders Ranges and Outback South Australia (FROSAT), Western Australia's Golden Outback, Western Australia's North West, and the Northern Territory. The authors analyze the extent to which these six outback tourism destinations have differentiated themselves in their online marketing, and relate evidence of marketing innovation to evidence of economic performance during the current decade.

Acknowledging the importance of destination positioning, **Mensah and Amissah** analyze the prospects and challenges of positioning Ghana as a preferred tourist destination for African American tourists in Chapter 17. The authors describe the attempts by Ghana's government and other stakeholders to position this country as a tourism destination. Recognizing the potential development of this country due to the Ghana' stock monuments and relics of the transatlantic slave trade, the authors discuss the obstacles and challenges that need to be addressed. From a marketing perspective, the authors indicate the need to address public relations campaigns towards correcting the erroneous impressions associated with Ghana. For many destinations events provide a large number of tourists and a high public exposure through extensive media coverage. Sport events can help to enhance the country's image and in its promotion as an international tourist destination. In the context of sport events, in Chapter 18 **Braham** examines the motivations and outcomes of the relationship between motor sport and tourism. This chapter reviews specific examples of motor sport tourism such as the F1 Grand Prix. As the author suggests, many of the tourism benefits of motor sport events imply that tourists are individuals from overseas.

Destination Branding

Although the branding literature commenced during the 1940s, the first publications related to destination branding did not emerge until half a century later (Pike, 2009). Destination branding has been considered a powerful marketing tool (Gnoth 2002; Morgan, Pritchard and Pride, 2004). It is defined as 'selecting a consistent element mix to identify and distinguish [a destination] through positive image-building' (Cai 2002,

p. 722), and has been considered synonymous with (re)positioning, image-building, and image-reconstruction of a destination (Park and Petrick, 2006).

In Chapter 19, **Avraham** focuses on how to restore a place image using the case of Israel. Based on the multi-step model for altering place image, the author analyzes strategies that have been applied to restore Israel's positive image. Findings show three kinds of strategies: source-focused, audience-focused and message-focused strategies. For instance, due to the intensive coverage of the Israeli-Arab conflict in the international media, Israel's marketers worked hard using source strategies to find alternatives to the traditional media (i.e., movies and the Internet, attracting opinion leaders and celebrities, among others). The use of audience strategies to market Israel is also relevant. Destination marketers need to decide on the primary countries in which they want to concentrate their efforts, and to develop a specific campaign for each target audience in those countries. Finally, the author discusses different forms of message-focused strategies to direct handling of the place's negative image (i.e., illustrating the negative stereotype of the place, show how ridiculous it is and thereby nullify it).

The name of a destination has collateral effects like the name of a company selling consumer products (Konecnik and Gartner, 2007). Brands serve several valuable functions. At their most basic level, brands serve as markers for the offerings of a firm. For visitors, destination/firms brands can simplify choice, promise a particular quality level, reduce risk, and/or engender trust. Brands are built on the product itself, the accompanying marketing activity, and the use (or non-use) by customers as well as others. Brands reflect the complete experience that customers have with products. Brands also play an important role in determining the effectiveness of marketing efforts. The value accrued by these various benefits is often called 'brand equity' (Keller and Lehmann, 2006). In the context of the gambling center of Macau, **Dioko and So** analyze the brand equity in both hotels and destinations as co-branded products in Chapter 20. Using a cross-sectional survey of international visitors in Macau, research findings show that the new Las Vegas brand hotels in Macau are attracting visitors with perceived levels of brand equity significantly higher than those found among visitors staying at international brand chain hotels and local Macau hotels. Additionally, findings indicate that the new Las Vegas operators seem to be attracting more business visitors compared to those staying at locally branded hotels and even long-established international branded hotel chains in Macau. Overall, visitors staying at the three hotel categories – international brand chain hotels, local Macau hotels and new Las Vegas brand hotels – are indistinguishable in terms of the level of their perceived destination brand equity. As a consequence, Dioko and So conclude that whatever new visitor segment is being attracted to Macau by the new Las Vegas hotels is likely drawn more by the prospect of experiencing what new entertainment concept they have to offer than they are by the characteristics of the destination.

As tourism destinations become more substitutable due to increasing competition in global tourism markets, destination personality is seen as a viable metaphor for building destination brands (Ekinci and Hosany, 2006). In Chapter 21 **Pereira et al.** review the main approaches and dimensions of the personality construct. Adopting the five factor model of personality, the authors present a survey of practices which aims to clarify the adoption of human personality scales from the psychology field (i.e., agreeableness, extroversion, conscientiousness, openness and neuroticism) to product's brand personality (i.e., sincerity, excitement, competence, sophistication and ruggedness). The current literature about the relationship between an individual and a brand leads to the conclusion that 'since brands can be personified, human personality descriptors can be used to describe them' (Azoulay and Kapferer, 2003, p. 149); however, as suggested by Aaker

(1997), Pereira et al. recommend that an adaptation is required. In addition, the authors suggest future research in this area; for instance, a scale designed to measure brand personality can become a potential and useful market segmentation tool.

Part III: Destination Stakeholders and Networks

Individuals, organizations and firms are not isolated, independent actors separately contributing their piece to the total value created for customers. As suggested by March and Wilkinson (2009, p. 455), 'the quality of the experience offered by a tourist destination is more than the sum of its parts; it depends in important ways on how the organisational parts are interconnected, the way they act and interact and the relations between the actors involved'. In this book there are interesting contributions that are focused on the network approach. From a stakeholder point of view, a destination can be seen as an open-social system of interdependent and multiple stakeholders (D'Angella and Go, 2009). In Chapter 22, **Pencarelli and Splendiani** point out the strong relationship between tourist destination and tourist products due to the fact that tourist products, with highly experiential content, are extremely affected by the location in which they are provided. Using the context of two Italian regions, the authors indicate the need to analyze this relationship to understand the role of destination leader and the opportunities of branding tourist destinations.

Collaboration and networking in tourism destinations seems critical to develop innovative marketing strategies. However, remote regions appear to be fundamentally constrained in the pursuit of networks and clusters by a lack of critical mass, the geographic dispersal and isolation of firms. In the context of a remote destination in South Australia, **Schmallegger** presents a case study of the Flinders Rangers region in Chapter 23. This research proposes a new way of looking at the capacity for innovation in remote destination systems from a different angle. Results of this case study show that recent marketing and product development initiatives in this remote region are based on the creation of a number of different network structures. Drawing on the actor-network theory (ANT), in Chapter 24 **Lugosi and Erdély** analyze how the owners-managers of the rom bar – a particular type of hospitality establishment in Budapest – had to painstakingly assemble for their service concept. According to the authors, the bar's operators managed to survive thanks to a most curious inversion and reflexivity: 'in their struggle to create a marketplace for their new service, they themselves became a marketplace of sort, by providing a space for the outputs of cultural and creative industries'. Accordingly, this research contributes to understanding how different actors interact and are enrolled in the creation of hospitality services and spaces.

Focusing on business stakeholders in tourist destinations, in particular, hotel firms, in Chapter 25 **Sainaghi** aims to analyze the determinants of hotel performance. Using bibliographical research, this study analyzes 67 studies that use performances (operational, financial, organizational dimension) as a dependent variable and some determinants as independent variables. This chapter shows the strong link existing between the type of evidence used, research design, the choice of dependent and independent variables, identifying three different research styles: European, American and Asian styles. Finally, in certain destinations, hawkers are members of the informal sector who sell goods or services (Bromley, 2000). Hawking is one of the earliest forms of retailing that, are part of the tourist landscape (Henderson, 2000). According to **Harris** in Chapter 26, groups such as shopkeepers and local officials often call for the removal of hawkers but this is unlikely to be effective despite the introduction of legislation. In this chapter, a model is proposed to illustrate the relationship between the marketability of the destination and the hawker's long-term future. Using blogs for an ethnographic research, the author explains that consumers' reactions to the hawkers are based on approach and avoidance strategies.

To conclude, with all the chapters comprising this book originating from papers presented at the 3rd Advances in Tourism Marketing Conference (ATMC 2009) held in Bournemouth, United Kingdom, in September 2009, the editors believe strongly that together with the conferences held in Mugla, Turkey in 2005 and Valencia, Spain in 2007, the Advances in Tourism Marketing conferences have very much become a significant event in the academic calendar as have they 'raised the bar' in the exploration, analysis and evaluation of the state of the art in tourism marketing from an international perspective. In turn, the conferences have consistently brought together academic researchers, policy makers and practitioners under one roof for the discussion and dissemination of themes related to the tourism system under a marketing approach

References

Aaker JL. 1997. Dimensions of brand personality. *Journal of Marketing Research* **34**: 347-356.

Arndt J. 1967. Role of product-related conversations in the diffusion of a new product. *Journal of Marketing Research* **4**, 291–295.

Azoulay A, Kapferer JN. 2003. Do brand personality scales really measure brand personality? *The Journal of Brand Management* **11** (2): 143-155

Baloglu S, McCleary K. 1999. A model of destination image formation. *Annals of Tourism Research* **26**: 868–897

Beatty SE, Smith SM. 1987. External search effort: An investigation across several product categories. *Journal of Consumer Research* **14**: 83–95.

Bromley R. 2000. Street vending and public policy: a global review. International *Journal of Sociology and Social Policy* **20** (1/2): 1–29.

Buhalis D. 2000. Marketing the competitive destination of the future. *Tourism Management* **21** (1): 97-116

Buhalis D, Law R. 2008. Progress in information technology and tourism management: 20 years on and 10 years after the Internet—The state of eTourism research. *Tourism Management* **29** (4): 609-623

Cai L. 2002. Cooperative branding for rural destinations. *Annals of Tourism Research* **29**: 720–742

D'Angella F, Go, FM. 2009. Tale of two cities' collaborative tourism marketing: Towards a theory of destination stakeholder assessment. *Tourism Management* **30** (3): 429-440

Ekinci Y, Hosany S. 2006. Destination personality: An application of brand personality to tourism destinations. *Journal of Travel Research* **45** (2):127-139.

Gnoth J. 2002. Leveraging export brands through a tourism destination brand. *Journal of Brand Management* **9** (4/5): 262–280.

Hansen T. 2005. Perspectives on consumer decision making: An integrative approach. *Journal of Consumer Behaviour* **4** (6): 420-437.

Henderson J. 2000. Food hawkers and tourism in Singapore. *International Journal of Hospitality Management* **19**: 109–117.

Hunt JD. 1975. Image as a factor in tourism development. *Journal of Travel Research* **13**: 1–7.

Jaffe E, Nebenzahl. 2001. *National Image and Competitive Advantage: The Theory and Practice of Country-of-Origin Effect*, Copenhagen Business School Press, Copenhagen.

Keller KL, Lehmann DR. 2006. Brands and branding: Research findings and future priorities. *Marketing Science* **25** (6), 740-759

Konecnik M, Gartner WC. 2007. Customer-based brand equity for a destination, *Annals of Tourism Research* **34** (2), 400-421.

Kozak M, Andreu L. 2006. *Progress in Tourism Marketing*. Elsevier: Oxford.

Kozak M, Gnoth J and Andreu L. 2009. *Advances in Destination Marketing*. Routledge: Oxford.

Litvin SW, Goldsmith RE, Pan B. 2008. Electronic word-of-mouth in hospitality and tourism management. *Tourism Management* **29** (3): 458-468

March R, Wilkinson I. 2009. Conceptual tools for evaluating tourism partnerships. *Tourism Management* **30** (3): 455-462

Morgan N, Pritchard A, Pride R. 2004. *Destination Branding: Creating the Unique Destination Proposition*, Butterworth Heinemann, Oxford.

Moutinho L. 2000. Consumer behaviour. In: Moutinho, L. (ed.). *Strategic management in tourism*, CABI Publishing, New York, pp. 41–79.

Nadeau J, Heslop L, O'Reilly N, Luk P. 2008. Destination in a country image context. *Annals of Tourism Research* **35** (1): 84-106

Papadopoulos N, Heslop L. 2002. Country equity and country branding: Problems and prospects. *Journal of Brand Management* **9**: 294–314.

Park SY, Petrick JF. 2006. Destinations' perspectives of branding. *Annals of Tourism Research* **33** (1): 262-265.

Pike S. 2009. Destination brand positions of a competitive set of near-home destinations, *Tourism Management* (in press): 1-10.

Pike S, Ryan C. 2004. Destination positioning analysis through a comparison of cognitive, affective, and conative perceptions. *Journal of Travel Research* **42** (4): 333-342

Snepenger D, Meged K, Snelling L, Worral K. 1990. Information search strategies by destination-naïve tourists. *Journal of Travel Research* **29**: 13–16.

Srinivasan N, Ratchford BT. 1991. An empirical test of a model of external search for automobiles. *Journal of Consumer Research* **18**, 233–242.

Westbrook RA. 1987. Product/consumption-based affective responses and postpurchase processes. *Journal of Marketing Research* **24** (3): 258–270

Yeoman I, Brass D, McMahon-Beattie U. 2007. Current issue in tourism: The authentic tourist. *Tourism Management* **28** (4): 1128-1138

Yuksel A, Yuksel, F. 2001. Measurement and management issues in customer satisfaction research: review, critique and research agenda: part two. *Journal of Travel and Tourism Marketing* **10**: 81–111.

Part I:

Consumer Decision Making and Tourist Experiences

2 Advertising and Word of Mouth in Tourism, a Simulation Study

Rodolfo Baggio, Bocconi University; **Chris Cooper**, University of Nottingham; **Noel Scott**, University of Queensland; **Magda Antonioli Corigliano**, Bocconi University

Introduction

The nature of tourism is that the potential visitor lives at a distance from the place where the consumption of the experience will occur, the destination. This distance may increase the perceived psychological risk of travel due to the cost of the trip and the lack of familiarity with the destination (Law, 2006; Roehl and Fesenmaier, 1992). On the other hand, distance may increase the attractiveness of the destination making it exotic and appealing. These factors have emphasized the importance of marketing as a fundamental activity for a tourism operator (or destination) and an important determinant of success (Govers et al., 2007) as marketing is considered a key variable that managers can influence in their search for customers. In order to better market a tourism destination or resort, marketers study consumer behavior and develop models such as those examining consumer decision making and information search (Moutinho, 1987). A variety of previous studies have used such models to examine how to influence the consumer to travel to particular places.

A number of prior studies have examined the way potential travelers obtain information on which to base travel decisions (Fodness and Murray, 1999; Gitelson and Crompton, 1983; Lee and Sparks, 2007; Rasinger et al., 2007; Zins, 2007). The main approach used is based on individual psychology where visitors are considered active and purposeful agents who seek information useful for their trip. The effect of others is recognized through discussion of social influences on decision making or more specifically the effect of word-of mouth (WOM) (passing information from person to person) but somewhat surprisingly there has been little study of the specific effect of such influences (Murphy, 2001). Recently studies have examined at the effect of a number of individual traveler characteristics that encourage WOM (Simpson and Siguaw, 2008) and have also noted the strong effect of WOM on travel patterns, particularly for the backpacker market (Hanlan and Kelly, 2005). Other studies, have suggested the effectiveness of WOM but always from an individual perspective (Kim et al., 2005; Stokes and Lomax, 2002; Sweeney et al., 2008). WOM is considered to be growing in importance due to the increase in digital social networking. This digital version of WOM is considered to provide a wealth of new opportunities and possibilities to reach market segments that would have been hard to access otherwise (Dellarocas, 2003; Litvin et al., 2008).

This chapter seeks to examine the effect of WOM compared to advertising on travel using a modeling approach. In particular it seeks to examine the effect of social networks on WOM amongst a population in the origin prior to travel. In this chapter the effect of WOM is compared to paid advertising (ADV).

Modeling Advertising and Word of Mouth

There is a long history in marketing of developing models to help address marketing problems with early investigations in the 1950s characterized by use of existing operations research and management science methods (Leeflang and Wittink, 2000). In general, two types of marketing models may be discussed, market response models which try to model market reaction as a function of marketing activities without consideration of intermediate variables and intermediate effects models which consider a consumer decision or aggregate market outcome as the result of a series of, often sequential, processes.

Many authors have studied the effects and the impact of advertising and WOM activities, and numerous models for the process have been proposed (Vakratsas and Ambler, 1999). Formal models regard the process as an information diffusion process, whereby an organization sends consumers advertising messages containing explicit (Goldenberg et al., 2001; Stigler, 1961) or implicit (Milgrom and Roberts, 1986; Nelson, 1974) information about itself or its products. The process is initiated by sending a message to a number of potential customers over an appropriate communication channel (Nelson, 1974; Stigler, 1961). A certain fraction of the potential consumers will acquire the advertising information. After a period of time some of them will have 'disposed of' the piece of information received (because they have forgotten or they are not interested or convinced) and in this case, the customers are considered independent of one another.

Most of the models used to explain the effects and the general behavior of ADV campaigns have attempted to provide analytical expressions for the phenomenon (Bass et al., 2007; Doraszelski and Markovich, 2007). In these studies, the intensity and duration of the campaign memory effects and number of concurrently broadcasted messages are considered as parameters. Recently, simulation models based on techniques derived from different fields (physics, for example) have been used and have provided interesting outcomes (Sznajd-Weron and Weron, 2003). These interdisciplinary works mostly derive from the research on opinion formation models (Castellano et al., 2007) and many also take into account the peculiarities of the distribution of the relationships among the target population.

When WOM is considered, the main communication channel becomes the set of relationships among the potential market actors. Described in this way, the WOM communication process has a striking analogy with an epidemiological infection process (Bettencourt et al., 2006). A population of actors is considered to be susceptible to an 'advertising infection'. During the unfolding of the process, a certain number of actors become infected while some recover and become immune by forgetting the information received (or discarding the information because they are not interested in it). The mathematical models describing an epidemiological infection process are well known (Bailey, 1975; Hethcote, 2000). When we introduce the underlying social network for modeling a WOM phenomenon, these models need to be amended in order to consider the topology of the communication network which has been shown to have a great impact on the whole dynamic of the diffusion (Barthélemy et al., 2005; Iribarren and Moro, 2007; López-Pintado, 2004).

Complex networks have been extensively studied in the last decade. The availability of large samples of data on networked systems (natural or artificial) and the advances in information technology have made possible the rapid development of a whole new discipline which may be termed 'network science' and the discovery of a whole range of models for these systems. A network is described by a number of metrics able to synthesize its topological (structural) features. These have also been found to be important determinants for the behavior of many dynamic processes. The main metrics used to characterize a network are: the statistical distribution of the connections (degree distribution); the density and the pattern local groups assume (clustering); the average number of connections between any two nodes (path length); the possibility to identify dense subgroups (modularity); the efficiency (at a local or global level) with which a process can develop; and the correlation between the number of connections a node and its neighbors have (Boccaletti et al., 2006; da Fontoura Costa et al., 2008; Watts, 2004). It has been found that besides networks with a purely random distribution of links (RN), networked systems exhibit peculiar forms, called small-world (SW) networks where clustering is higher and path length lower than in a random case or scale-free (SF) network where the degree distribution follows a power–law relationship.

Methodology

Numerical simulations are used in this chapter as a means to derive insight into phenomena that are difficult to study for theoretical or practical reasons (Inbar and Stoll, 1972). While the outcomes of a simulation are only one possible representation of the phenomenon under study, researchers consider them as good approximations provided that a reliable conceptual model and good implementation practices are used. No absolute value can be given to such processes, as their value depends on the specific situation or the specific purpose (Küppers and Lenhard, 2005; Law and Kelton, 2000; Schmid, 2005). Nonetheless, even with these limitations, simulation models are considered effective in reproducing different types of complex systems and represent a valuable support to decision making (Tesfatsion and Judd, 2006; Toroczkai and Eubank, 2005).

Advertising (ADV) and WOM are, as described above, different processes and are simulated here using two different models. ADV, in essence, can be described as follows. A message is broadcast to a target population of individuals. The targets receive the message and form an opinion: they can either accept the information content or ignore it (or refuse). Since the work of Weidlich (1971), a number of models have been proposed to explain or simulate the process of opinion formation in a group of individuals. Most of these have been devised by using simplified versions of well known physical models used to describe magnetic properties in a material. The analogy is due to the similarity of the situations: a magnetic material can be seen, in a rough approximation, as an ensemble of elementary magnets, each one having one of the two possible magnetizations (also called spins): positive or negative. The number and the distribution of the spins is influenced by the temperature T of the material and can be influenced by the strength of an external magnetic field H (Feynman et al., 1963: chap. 37).

Among the many possible models (Castellano et al., 2007; Stauffer, 2003) the 'Magnetic Eden Model' (MEM) was chosen for use here. Originally proposed by Eden (1961) to describe the growth of bacterial colonies, it has been generalized by Ausloos et al. (1993) and adapted by Candia and Albano (2008) to a stochastic situation. The model is as follows. Let us assume that a certain number N of elements in a material can be magnetized by assuming a spin ± 1. A randomly chosen element starts the process. At each point in time all the neighbors (elements directly connected to a magnetized one) can be magnetized. The global energy E of a configuration of spins is given by:

$$E = -J\sum_{\langle j \rangle} S_i S_j - H\sum_i S_i$$

where $S_i = \pm 1$ indicates the orientation of the spin for magnetized element, $J > 0$ is a coupling constant (representing the strength of the interaction between neighbors), $H > 0$ is the external magnetic field, and $\langle ij \rangle$ indicates that the sum is taken over all pairs of magnetized elements. The probability for a new spin to be added to the set of magnetized elements is proportional to $\exp(-\Delta E/T)$, where ΔE is the total energy change involved and T is the absolute temperature of the material. At each step, all perimeter elements are considered and the probabilities of adding a new spin (either up or down) to each site must be evaluated. This is done by employing a Monte Carlo simulation method: all probabilities are first computed and normalized then the new element and the orientation of the new spin determined. The process ends when all the elements of the material have been magnetized. A characteristic of this model is that once a spin is set, it is 'frozen' and cannot change.

Applying this model to an advertising process it is relatively straightforward to interpret the whole process as a single campaign (at the end a certain number of target individuals will have 'absorbed' the message), the magnetic field H is a measure of the intensity of the campaign, and the temperature T is a measure of the social cohesion of the target group (or responsiveness to advertising messages), a spin $S = +1$ means an individual has accepted the advertising message, $S = -1$ means that the message was ignored (or refused). Once the campaign is ended, the opinions of the target population are set and we may assume that they remain stable until the next campaign.

A population of 500 individuals was used for the simulations and were considered to interact in a random network (in the case of a 'traditional' advertising process links between target individuals are ignored) with 1000 links. The simulation were performed by using a modified version of the software implemented by Candia and Albano (2008). Several measurements can be used to represent the effectiveness of an ADV process. In what follows, the fraction of spins up (individuals accepting the advertising message) is used.

WOM was studied by using an epidemiological diffusion model (Hethcote, 2000). This was built by considering the infection cycle in an individual (actor). The actor is first considered susceptible (*S*), i.e. able and ready to receive a piece of information. Then, if reached by a message it becomes 'infected' (*I*) and is considered as such for a certain period of time. Finally, the individual can recover (*R*) by forgetting what he received (or discarding the information). The mathematical treatment is well known and consists of a system of differential equations that can be solved and produce curves describing the results of the infection. These are mostly s-shaped curves belonging to the family of logistic curves. Traditionally a perfect mixing is assumed: that is, all individuals are equally able to infect all others, the contacts between them are ignored or, better, considered as having a random distribution. When dealing with WOM, however, the diffusion process develops by using the relationships among the social network formed by the individuals (potential tourists in our case) as infection channels.

Recent advances in the study of complex networks have allowed a reconsideration of epidemic diffusion models to take into account the effects of non-homogeneous network topologies (Balázs et al., 2005; López-Pintado, 2004; Watts and Dodds, 2007). These effects are quite important. For example, 'standard' epidemiological diffusion models show a clearly defined threshold condition for the spread of an infection which depends on the density of the linkages between the different elements of the network (Kermack and McKendrick, 1927). If the distribution of connections is not of a random nature, but has some structured, non-homogeneous characteristics, this threshold may disappear. The diffusion process, once started, unfolds over the whole network (Pastor-

Satorras and Vespignani, 2001). The formulation of an epidemiological model leads to the layout of a system of differential equations which can be solved in standard way. In this chapter we approach the problem by using computerized numerical simulations (Castellano et al., 2007; Stauffer, 2003).

As a substrate for the simulation, we should use a real social network, formed by a population of potential tourists. Classic ways for obtaining it are surveys among people which ask them how many and what relationships they have with other individuals. The construction of such a network, however, can be quite difficult and resource-intensive, with a number of well known issues associated with the reliability of the answers and the size of the sample used (Killworth and Bernard, 1976; Kossinets, 2006; Lee et al., 2006; Marsden, 1990).

An interesting and useful suggestion to overcome these problems comes from a recent paper by Ormerod (2007). The author provides a method to simulate the topology of the social network in a specific country or geographical area by using available empirical evidence on the behavior of the members of the community. Knowing that that evidence is heavily influenced by the social connections among the individuals he builds a series of synthetic networks with different topologies and uses an agent-based model to derive a distribution of the characteristics. These are then compared with the empirical data. This allows the author to choose the topology that better reproduces the observed patterns.

The country used in Ormerod's paper is the United Kingdom for which he shows that a SW network with an average clustering coefficient $C \approx 0.26$ is the best approximation. 'We can think of it as implying that people are mainly influenced by those closest to them, such as family members, but with a number of more long range connections, as it were, across their network of friends' (Ormerod, 2007: 51). For the sake of brevity and simplicity we use his results and consider this layout for the simulation of a WOM process. In other words we simulate a situation in which a tourism operator (a hotel, for example) wishes to understand the possible effectiveness of traditional advertising as compared to word-of-mouth for promoting the services offered to a UK market.

The network used has 500 nodes and 1000 links (density = 0.008), and a small-world structure (by construction) with a clustering coefficient = 0.25 and an average path length = 5.9. The algorithm employed is the following:

♦   A single node is initially infected;

♦   At each time step, with probability p_I each of the infected nodes, transmits the infection to its first neighbors;

♦   At each time step a fraction p_R of infected nodes recovers 'forgetting' the infection;

♦   The simulation is run until a stable configuration is reached, i.e. a situation in which no more changes in the number of infected or recovered nodes are recorded; and

♦   At the end, the peak number of infected nodes is used as a measure of the effectiveness of the process.

In both cases (ADV and WOM), the size of the network used is non-influential for the aims of the simulations, the actual size used here was chosen for the capability of providing meaningful statistical outcomes while minimizing computational efforts. All simulations were run by using 10 different seeds and run 100 times each. The results presented are the average values. We assume that the proportion of people forgetting or refusing to accept the piece of information (the fraction of recovered actors in the epidemic process) is 10%. All simulations were implemented as Matlab (2004) scripts.

Results

The results for the ADV process simulation are shown in Figure 2.1. For different values of H (ADV campaign intensity) the fraction F_{UP} of individuals who accepted the message is shown. Different temperatures T corresponding to different levels of cohesion in the social group (or responsiveness to advertising messages) were used.

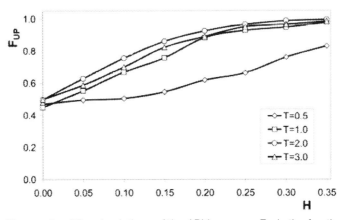

Figure 2.1: The results of the simulations of the ADV process. F_{UP} is the fraction of elements with spin=+1, H is the external magnetic field, T is the temperature

As expected, the fraction of people convinced by the advertising message has a clear dependency on the intensity of the advertising campaign and on the level of social cohesion (temperature T) in the target group. It must also be noticed that the effect of cohesion is higher than the one due to the campaign intensity, at least up to a certain level. If cohesion is very high (cohesion is low, see the curve for $T=3$), it lead to a 'randomization' of the target group opinions and to a lower effectiveness of the advertising efforts.

The simulation of the WOM process is depicted in Figure 2.2. The curve represents the fraction of informed individuals (F_{IN}) at each time step (t_{STEP}).

In this case, in a relatively short period of time (10 steps) the number of informed individuals reaches a maximum of 74%. Then the number decreases (individuals 'forget'). In the WOM process no external intensity field is taken into account, the process is almost independent from the efforts of the informing organization and depends only on the set of relationships between the members of the social group. In other words, once a suitable medium is chosen (an Internet social network, for example) only a minimum effort is needed to start the process and to achieve a good result.

By comparing the two situations (ADV and WOM) we can better understand the two methods and the higher effectiveness, at least in the short term, of WOM. In fact, a very intense advertising effort is needed to reach the same (74%) level of informed people, and this level is dependent on a moderate cohesion of the group. If the cohesion is very high (or responsiveness is low, T=0.5) this proportion is attained only with a very high expenditure of resources (very high H intensity).

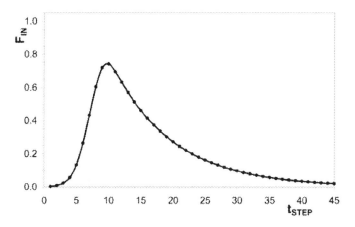

Figure 2.2: The simulation of the WOM process. The curve represents the fraction of informed individuals (F_{IN}) at each time step (t_{STEP})

Conclusion

This chapter set out to examine the effect of WOM compared to advertising on travel using a modeling approach. Moreover, the effect on WOM of the structure of the social networks amongst a population in the target market was examined. By comparing the two situations, WOM was found to have higher effectiveness and this level is dependent on a moderate cohesion of the target group. If the cohesion is very high ($T=0.5$) this proportion is attained only with a very high expenditure of resources. These results are in line with the prior research that notes the effectiveness of WOM (Hogan et al., 2004) compared to advertising but provides in addition a means of including the effect of cohesion and relationship topology on WOM transmission. This effect has been noted before in the diffusion of innovation literature (Rogers, 1983) where the effect of diffusion through a connected social system has been studied although the connection between group cohesion and WOM in the context of advertising and especially new digital media has not been discussed.

This study is an initial exploratory study and the results are indicative of a need for further research. As also stated previously, the validity of the results presented here cannot be extended beyond the specific case analysed, but the methods adopted are of general validity and increasingly researchers are using them to model different phenomena in the social world. More outcomes are expected which will be able to refine the models and to take into account less 'elementary' interaction patterns.

Clearly this is an area of potential interest and suggests that the structural characteristics (such as cohesion) of a target market be considered in developing marketing campaigns. It may also be useful in the study of viral marketing programs. In this area there has been some recent work on modeling the effect of size of a person's network but not on its cohesiveness (Smith et al., 2007). Further research in this area, examining the effects of social and digital networks appears to be promising, in particular by improving the calibration of the model with better estimates of the cohesiveness and the topology of the target populations.

Acknowledgements

The authors wish to thank Julian Candia for the software provided and the help in applying the modifications needed.

References

Ausloos M, Vandewalle N, Cloots R. 1993. Magnetic Eden Model. *Europhysics Letters* **24**: 629-634.

Bailey N. 1975. *The Mathematical Theory of Infectious Diseases and its Applications* 2nd edn. Griffin: London.

Balázs K, Hastings M, Korniss G. 2005. Diffusion processes on power–law small-world networks. *Physical Review Letters* **95**: art. 018701.

Barthélemy M, Barrat A, Pastor-Satorras R, Vespignani A. 2005. Dynamical patterns of epidemic outbreaks in complex heterogeneous networks. *Journal of Theoretical Biology* **235**: 275-288.

Bass F, Bruce N, Majumdar S, Murthi B. 2007. Wearout effects of different advertising themes: A aynamic Bayesian model of the advertising–sales Relationship. *Marketing Science* **26** (2): 179–195

Bettencourt, LMA, Cintrón-Arias A, Kaiser DI, Castillo-Chávez C. 2006. The power of a good idea: Quantitative modeling of the spread of ideas from epidemiological models. *Physica A* **364**: 513-536.

Boccaletti S, Latora V, Moreno Y, Chavez M, Hwang D. 2006. Complex networks: Structure and dynamics. *Physics Reports* **424** (4-5): 175-308.

Candia J, Albano E. 2008. The Magnetic Eden Model. *International Journal of Modern Physics C* **19** (10): 1617-1634.

Castellano C, Fortunato S, Loreto V. 2007. *Statistical physics of social dynamics*. Retrieved October 2007, from http://arxiv.org/abs/0710.3256.

da Fontoura Costa L, Oliveira Jr. O, Travieso G, Rodrigues F, Villas Boas P, Lucas Antiqueira L, Viana M, Correa da Rocha L. 2008. *Analyzing and Modeling Real-World Phenomena with Complex Networks: A Survey of Applications*. Retrieved June 2008, from http://arxiv.org/abs/0711.3199.

Dellarocas C. 2003. The digitalization of word-of-mouth: promise and challenges of online reputation mechanisms. *Management Science* **49** (10): 1407-1424.

Doraszelski U, Markovich S. 2007. Advertising dynamics and competitive advantage. *RAND Journal of Economics* **38** (3): 557-592.

Eden M. 1961. A two-dimensional growth process. In *Proceedings of the Fourth Berkeley Symposium on Mathematical Statistics and Probability Held at the Statistical Laboratory University of California, June 20–July 30 1960* Neyman J (ed.). University of California Press: Berkeley; vol. IV: 223-239.

Feynman R, Leighton R, Sands M. 1963. *The Feynman Lectures on Physics*. Vol. II. Addison Wesley: Reading, MA.

Fodness D, Murray B. 1999. A model of tourist information search. *Journal of Travel Research* **37**: 220-230.

Gitelson, R. J., Crompton, J. L. 1983. The planning horizon and sources of information used by pleasure travellers. *Journal of Travel Research* **32** (3): 2-6.

Goldenberg J, Libai B, Muller E. 2001. Talk of the network: A complex systems look at the underlying process of word-of-mouth. *Marketing Letters* **12**: 209-221.

Govers R, Go F, Kumar K. 2007. Promoting tourism destination image. *Journal of Travel Research* **46**: 15-23.

Hanlan J, Kelly S. 2005. Image formation, information sources and an iconic Australian tourist destination. *Journal of Vacation Marketing* **112**: 163.

Hethcote H. 2000. The mathematics of infectious diseases *SIAM Review* **42** (4): 599-653.

Hogan J, Lemon K, Libai B. 2004. Quantifying the ripple: word-of-mouth and advertising effectiveness. *Journal of Advertising Research* **44** (3): 271-280.

Inbar M, Stoll C. 1972. *Simulation and Gaming in Social Science*. Free Press: New York.

Iribarren J, Moro E. 2007. *Information diffusion epidemics in social networks*. Retrieved October 2007, from http://arxiv.org/abs/0706.0641.

Kermack W, McKendrick A. 1927. Contributions to the mathematical theory of epidemics, part 1. *Proceedings of the Royal Society of London A* **115**: 700-721.

Killworth P, Bernard H. 1976. Informant accuracy in social network data. *Human Organization* **35**: 269-296.

Kim D, Hwang Y, Fesenmaier D. 2005. Modeling tourism advertising effectiveness. *Journal of Travel Research* **44**: 42-49.

Kossinets G. 2006. Effects of missing data in social networks. *Social Networks* **28** (3): 247-268.

Küppers G, Lenhard J. 2005. Validation of simulation: patterns in the social and natural sciences. *Journal of Artificial Societies and Social Simulation* **8** (4): retrieved March, 2006, from http://jasss.soc.surrey.ac.uk/8/4/3.html.

Law A, Kelton W. 2000. *Simulation Modelling and Analysis* 3rd edn. McGraw-Hill: New York.

Law R. 2006. The perceived impact of risks on travel decisions. *International Journal of Tourism Research* **8**: 289–300.

Lee S, Sparks B. 2007. Cultural influences on travel lifestyle: A comparison of Korean Australians and Koreans in Korea. *Tourism Management* **28** (2): 505-518.

Lee S, Kim P, Jeong H. 2006. Statistical properties of sampled networks. *Physical Review E* **73**: art. 016102

Leeflang P, Wittink D. 2000. Building models for marketing decisions: Past, present and future. *International Journal of Research in Marketing* **17** (2-3): 105-126.

Litvin S, Goldsmith R, Pan B. 2008. Electronic word-of-mouth in hospitality and tourism management. *Tourism Management* **29**: 458-468.

López-Pintado D. 2004. *Diffusion in Complex Social Networks*. Working Papers No. AD 2004-33: Instituto Valenciano de Investigaciones Económicas, S.A.. Retrieved December 2005, from http://www.ivie.es/downloads/docs/wpasad/wpasad-2004-33.pdf.

Marsden P. 1990. Network data and measurement. *Annual Review of Sociology* **16**: 435-463.

MATLAB. 2004. *MATLAB Version 7, R14*. Matworks: Natick, MA.

Milgrom P, Roberts J. 1986. Price and advertising signals of product quality. *Journal of Political Economy* **94**: 796-821.

Moutinho L. 1987. Consumer behaviour in tourism. *European Journal of Marketing*, **21** (10): 5-44.

Murphy L. 2001. Exploring social interactions of backpackers. *Annals of Tourism Research* **28** (1): 50-67.

Nelson P. 1974. Advertising as information. *Journal of Political Economy* **82**: 729-753.

Ormerod P. 2007. Extracting deep information from limited observations on an evolved social network. *Physica A* **378**: 48-52.

Pastor-Satorras R, Vespignani A. 2001. Epidemic spreading in scalefree networks. *Physical Review Letters* **86** (14): 3200-3203.

Rasinger J, Fuchs M, Hopken W. 2007. Information search with mobile tourist guides: A survey of usage intention. *Information Technology Tourism* **9** (3/4): 177-194.

Roehl W, Fesenmaier D. 1992. Risk perceptions and pleasure travel: An exploratory analysis. *Journal of Travel Research* **30** (4): 17-26.

Rogers E. 1983. *The Diffusion of Innovations* 3rd edn. Free Press: New York.

Schmid A. 2005. What is the truth of simulation? *Journal of Artificial Societies and Social Simulation* **8** (4). Retrieved June, 2006, from http://jasss.soc.surrey.ac.uk/8/4/5.html.

Simpson P, Siguaw J. 2008. Destination word of mouth: The role of traveler type, residents, and identity salience. *Journal of Travel Research* **47** (2): 167-182.

Smith T, Coyle J, Lightfoot E, Scott A. 2007. Reconsidering models of influence: The relationship between consumer social networks and word-of-mouth effectiveness. *Journal of Advertising Research* **47** (4): 387-397.

Stauffer D. 2003. Sociophysics simulations. *Computing in Science and Engineering* **5** (3): 71-75.

Stigler G. 1961. The economics of information. *Journal of Political Economy* **71**: 213-225.

Stokes D, Lomax W. 2002. Taking control of word of mouth marketing: the case of an entrepreneurial hotelier. *Journal of Small Business and Enterprise Development* **9** (4): 349-357.

Sweeney J, Soutar G, Mazzarol T. 2008. Factors influencing word of mouth effectiveness: receiver perspectives. *European Journal of Marketing* **42**: 344-364.

Sznajd-Weron K, Weron R. 2003. How effective is advertising in duopoly markets? *Physica A* **324** (1-2): 437-444.

Tesfatsion L, Judd K. 2006. *Handbook of Computational Economics, Volume 2: Agent-Based Computational Economics*. North-Holland: Amsterdam.

Toroczkai Z, Eubank S. 2005. Agent-based modeling as decision-making tool. *The Bridge* **35** (4), 22-27.

Vakratsas D, Ambler T. 1999. How advertising works: what do we really know? *Journal of Marketing* **63** (1): 26-43.

Watts D. 2004. The 'new' science of networks. *Annual Review of Sociology* **30**: 243-270.

Watts D, Dodds P. 2007. Influentials, networks, and public opinion formation. *Journal of Consumer Research* **34**: 441-458.

Weidlich W. 1971. The statistical description of polarisation phenomena in society. *British Journal of Mathematical and Statistical Psychology* **24**: 251-266.

Zins A. 2007. Exploring travel information search behavior beyond common frontiers. *Information Technology Tourism* **9** (3/4): 149-164.

3 Infosource Scale: a Measure to Assess External Tourism Information Sources' Importance

Cláudia Seabra, Instituto Politécnico de Viseu; Luís Filipe Lages, José Luís Abrantes, Universidade Nova de Lisboa

Introduction

Research in the marketing field indicates that consumers search for external information before taking the initiative of acquiring or using a service (Midgley, 1983). Within this stream of research, several models have been developed to explain how consumers search for information (e.g., Beatty and Smith, 1987; Murray, 1991; Parasuraman and Zinkhan, 2002). From a theoretical perspective, research in consumer behaviour becomes essential to decode all the activities used to develop, communicate and sell services. The optimization of services marketing activities depends on a better understanding of which sources consumers use to take their decisions before selecting and using a service. Similarly, from a practitioner perspective, marketers need to identify which information sources are preferred or rejected by consumers. In such way, it will be possible to influence consumers' choices through use of information.

When researching consumer behaviour issues in a services context, this becomes a very complex task due to the intrinsic characteristics of services, such as intangibility, inseparability of production and consumption, heterogeneity, and perishability (Zeithaml et al., 1985). Tourism is a services area of extreme importance from both public policy and managerial perspectives. The tourism activity is of extreme importance from the point of view of nations and firms. From the point of view of national governments, tourism activity is crucial because it contributes to the economic development of nations. Additionally, tourism enhances societal prosperity and helps national industries to develop, improve productivity and create new jobs, while shaping public perceptions of national competitiveness and improving the standard of living and quality of life. At the firm level, tourism provides an opportunity for national firms to become less dependent on the domestic market. By serving foreign customers, firms may also explore economies of scale and achieve lower production costs while serving clients more efficiently. Additionally, the firm may use the experience with international customers to become a stronger competitor at home.

Comprehension of consumer behaviour in the tourism arena is particularly complex because the acquisition process has an emotional component. For instance, vacation buying is the culmination of a long process of planning, choice, evaluation and assessment of alternatives. The final decision to purchase and select a tourist service presents unique aspects. The acquisition is generally prepared and planned over a considerable period of time by a large number of the people involved. Moreover, the tourist will make selections without expectations of material and economic return. It is an investment with an intangible index of return where the final selection is exclusively associated with intangible satisfaction (Moutinho, 1987). More important, in service selection situations, the intangibility of services creates uncertainty and perceived risk in the consumer's mind. Since services are much more difficult to evaluate than goods, it is natural to expect that consumers of services acquire more information for risk reduction than when selecting goods (Hugstad et al., 1987; Zeithaml, 1981).

Consumers will evaluate services in a distinctive way and, necessarily, will need more information about services that have a strong component of complexity, such as tourism (Murray, 1991). Tourism uncertainty is even greater as it often takes an individual from a comfortable-known environment to one that is unusual or even unknown. In this situation, consumers are expected to use different types of information sources, in order to reduce uncertainty and reduce the risk of selecting an unfamiliar service (Dodd et al., 1996; Murray, 1991).

Within this context, information search becomes essential at two different levels. At the internal level, information is acquired in the subject's memory, which is formed by consumer experiences. At the external level, information is sought in the environmental context (Bettman and Park, 1980). The external information search is a conscious and motivated decision to acquire information from the consumer's environment. Despite the number of risks associated with service selection, this information search is limited because consumers select a limited number of information sources (Midgley, 1983; Murray, 1991).

In the case of tourism services, information search is typically external. Information sources used by tourists are the basis of any trip planning (Snepenger et al., 1990). The information is collected in the consumer's environment involving active processes and a variety of information sources (Moutinho, 2000). Previous research investigates external information sources in terms of the number of sources used and the amount of information search in each source (e.g. Beatty and Smith, 1987; Srinivasan and Ratchford, 1991). However, from both a theoretical and practitioner perspective, recent research suggests that this type of approach might not be the most useful. Research should now focus on assessing the importance of specific information sources to service selection (see: Brucks, 1985; Fodness and Murray, 1999; Murray, 1991). This is the focus of our paper. It is our aim to develop a scale that assesses the importance of information sources to the selection of tourism services. We are seeking to understand how far those sources are simultaneously used during the information search process in order to select specific activities, such as, the route to the final destination, selection of accommodation, and selection of activities at the destination.

This chapter is organized into three sections. First, an overview of the current literature is offered. The conceptual framework is then tested via a survey of 350 tourists, and the five dimensions of the INFOSOURCE scale are presented. Implications for theory and managerial practice, limitations of the research and future directions are then considered.

The Infosource Scale

In order to assess the importance of information sources we use five of them: media, institutional brochures, commercial brochures, travel agents, and the Internet. One or more of these are essential when selecting tourism services, such as choosing routes, accommodation, and activities to develop at the destination (Filiatrault and Ritchie, 1980; Jenkins, 1978; Perdue, 1985; Shoemaker, 1984).

Information from Mass Media

Media are an important channel of communication for the service companies, such as tourism firms (e.g. hotels and restaurants). They present publicity and advertising messages emphasizing the immediate benefits that tourists can achieve by selecting a specific service (Zeithmal et al., 1985).

A media information source is considered a formal (Raitz and Dakhil, 1989) and impersonal source. The type of information presented by media includes, for example, information presented by consultants and journalists (articles and reports on TV, radio, press and magazines) and advertising. Information provided from impersonal sources, such as media, are especially important in high-risk purchase situations such as tourist services (Hugstad et al., 1987). Consumers are particularly willing to spend time and effort seeking information from print media, because this search provides them with a greater variety of information to reduce risk. This explains why consumers obtaining information from print media will typically spend more time and effort than when obtaining information from other sources (Dodd et al., 1996).

In a recent study about information sources, the authors (Bieger et al., 2000) argued for the importance of media information sources. Media in the form of newspaper articles, travel guides, and books are a valuable basis of information, particularly when planning long trips, regarding groups on package tours and individually organized tours. Gitelson and Crompton (1983) also demonstrated that media information is essential for young people.

Information from Brochures

In line with previous studies (Fodness and Murray, 1999; Raitz and Dakhil, 1989), we make the distinction between institutional and commercial brochures. Although researchers often analyse information provided in brochures from a broad perspective, this distinction is essential because while commercial brochures are controllable by tourism service organizations (e.g. hotels, restaurants), the same does not apply to institutional brochures.

Information from Institutional Brochures

When planning their trips, tourists tend to use informative travel brochures as a key source of information. These sources are very informative and reliable due to their institutional nature, namely due to the fact of being provided by the tourism destinations and associated institutions (Nolan, 1976). Many authors have included these sources in their studies. For example, Snepenger and colleagues (Snepenger, 1987; Snepenger et al., 1990) reported that group tourism travelers use institutional brochures during their information search. This is also confirmed by other studies, which reveal that institutional brochures are considered to be a major source of trip-planning information (Raitz and Dakhil, 1989), and tend to be used by travelers with high income (Fodness and Murray, 1999).

Information from Commercial Brochures

Much of the travel and tourism industry relies on commercial brochures. For example, as early as a decade ago, British commercial operators alone were spending an estimated £200 million on printing approximately 200 million commercial brochures to yield an estimated 15 million bookings per year (Hodgson, 1993). Tourism services use brochures as a privileged advertising channel. For example, travel agencies and operators typically use these sources to provide their clients with concrete information about different themes (e.g. hotels, destinations, recreation parks). Commercial brochures tend to be very effective because the consumer pays nothing for these expensive publications, and they help consumers to avoid risk perception. Just very recently, Bieger et al. (2000) demonstrated that commercial brochures from hotels and tourist operators are regularly used as key information sources to select a tourism destination.

Travel Agents

Travel agents are used as a key communication channel with consumers. This occurs because service consumers tend to have a great preference for personal sources of information, especially when acquiring a complex service, such as a touring excursion (Murray, 1991). Through their sales force, travel agencies can constitute one of those personal sources. As do other services firms, tourism agencies might use their sales force (i.e. the travel agents) to create a favorable image (see: Zeithaml et al., 1985). Travel agents add value to the tourism industry in several ways. They are geographically close to the tourist and assist the customer by doing much of the searching on their behalf. They are also able to cater to the individual requirements of each tourist and can customize a holiday to suit each client. As the intermediary closest to the customer, they are in the best position to build relationships with customers (Wynne et al., 2001).

Previous research suggests that personal sources are preferred because they are more reliable than impersonal information sources (Murray, 1991). The tourism activity is a high-risk situation with a strong social component. Within this context, personal information sources might play a major role in clarifying problematic issues, while providing feedback to service customers.

Travel agents have played and will continue to play an important role as information sources (Connolly and Olsen, 2001). Indeed, since the early work of Nolan (1976), travel agents have been considered as a source of information examined in several tourism studies. For example, Shoemaker (1984) observed that travel agents were consulted about routes, accommodation and activities at the destination. Travel agents were also shown to be a useful source of information for older travelers (Gitelson and Crompton, 1983; Shoemaker, 1984) and the most used source for tourism both at the individual and group level (Snepenger, 1987). Although there are many pleasure tourists that do their own searching, they tend to habitually use travel agents to do their bookings. Tourists still exhibit a preference for booking through travel agents and appreciate human interaction and personal advice (Ader et al., 2000; Morrison and King, 2002).

The Internet

Nowadays, the internet is assumed to be an important channel for services marketing. The Internet has changed different aspects of our lives, at the private, social, cultural and economic levels. It deals with the essence of human society: communication between people. It allows us to link with others who share similar interests, values and beliefs.

It gives opportunities to share ideas, knowledge and opinions in a broader context (Liu 2006). It is a new way for consumers to interact with firms and other consumers (Alba et al. 1997; Hoffman and Novak 1996).

Consumers have increasingly obtained information access to electronic marketplaces and use this information in a sophisticated way to select their services (Parasuraman and Zinkhan, 2002). Indeed, the Internet was pointed out as being responsible for a revolution in the services sector. Its potential allows service firms to enlarge their market worldwide (Lovelock et al., 1999) providing firms with an unprecedented ability to communicate directly and effectively with potential customers. The Internet allows people to reach many other people in a one-to-many process like mass media, but in a more personalized way (Phelps et al. 2004). This is due to, among other things, the cost-effectiveness of the Internet and the convenience for customers. Increasing digitalization will make it progressively easier to alter particular aspects of a service and quickly observe how customers respond (Wyner, 2000).

In the tourism sector, the Internet has become an important source of information to consumers who are more and more demanding, and who become each day more familiarized with this emergent world of information. Tourism has historically been an early adopter of new technology (Bloch, 1996; Wynne et al., 2001). As in other service sectors, technological developments are altering the nature of the processes in the tourism sector (see: Connel and Reynolds, 1999). With the relatively widespread adoption of the Internet, tourism businesses of all sizes might expand and conquer new customers. The key to the tourist's decision is the existence of relevant information. With the Internet such information might be available and in a better way (Buhalis, 1998). This type of information will naturally help tourists to plan complex tourist activities, such as the planning of long trips (Bieger et al., 2000).

Methodology

The research setting was in a European country (Portugal) in a tourism service, more specifically, in the hotel services sector. In recent years, this country has increased its tourism market exponentially (Miles, 1995). There are high expectations for the future, given that Portugal is now one of the leading countries in terms of conditions and potentialities in the tourism services market, especially for European tourists (Murphy and Murphy, 2002).

We developed a scale to capture the importance that tourists give to information sources in their trip planning. In an early stage, we used previously established scales (Furse et al., 1984; Raitz and Dakhil, 1989) to develop our survey instrument. The initial scales were then translated into Portuguese and adjusted to tourism services users' reality. These scales were then discussed with people capable of understanding the nature of the concept being measured. All the items were assessed through a seven-point Likert scale (ranging from '1 – not important at all' to '7 – extremely important'). The questionnaire was initially developed in Portuguese and then translated into English, French, Spanish and German. After revisions, we used a pre-test sample of 30 tourism students in order to test the reliability of the scales (through Cronbach's alpha). The pre-test results were used to refine the questionnaire further. In order to avoid translation errors, the questionnaires were back-translated into Portuguese.

The final data collection was done between December of 2002 and September of 2003. During this time there were some events that attracted many tourists to Portugal, such as the World Handball Championship and the European Football Championship. Tourists were randomly selected in 19 hotels willing to participate in the study. The questionnaires were given at the hotel reception, together with a presentation letter explaining the objective of this study. The tourists filled the questionnaires at the moment they left the hotel. This allowed us to ensure that the data were not biased and that tourists had significant knowledge about the topic being researched. A final sample of 350 questionnaires was obtained.

Tourists from many countries participated in the survey. Over 60% of the respondents were Portuguese tourists. The rest of the sample was mostly composed of European tourists from Spain (11%), Germany (10%), France (5%) and the United Kingdom (5%). Respondents less represented in the sample, include tourists from Australia, Austria, Belgium, Bulgaria, Brazil, Denmark, Greenland, Iceland, Ireland, Israel, Italy, the Netherlands, Sweden, Qatar and the USA. Most tourists were single (19%) or married with children (60%). More than 40% of the respondents had university education and almost 40% had completed their high school education. Respondents also indicated how often they took holidays per year. The great majority indicated once (45%) or twice (37%) per year.

Data Analysis

In order to assess the validity of the measures, the items were subjected to a confirmatory factor analysis (CFA), using full-information maximum likelihood (FIML) estimation procedures in LISREL 8.3 (Jöreskog and Sörbom, 1993). In this model, each item is restricted to load on its pre-specified factor, with the five first-order factors allowed to correlate freely. After CFA purification, the initial list of 15 items was maintained. A full listing of the 15 final items after CFA purification and their scale reliabilities is included in Appendix A.

The chi-square for this model is significant (X^2=528.61, 80df, p<.00). Since the chi-square statistic is sensitive to sample size, we also assessed additional fit indices: Normed Fit Index (NFI), Comparative Fit Index (CFI), the Incremental Fit Index (IFI), and the Tucker-Lewis Fit Index (TLI). The NFI, CFI, IFI and TLI of this model are .90, .92, .92, and .89, respectively. Appendix A provides an overview of the standardized estimates and t-values of each item on its intended construct. As shown in the Appendix, all five constructs present the desirable levels of composite reliability (Bagozzi, 1980). Convergent validity is evidenced by the large and significant standardized loadings of each item on its intended construct (average loading size was .87). Discriminant validity among the constructs is stringently assessed using the Fornell and Larcker (1981) test; all possible pairs of constructs passed this test.

Conclusion

Understanding consumer behavior is essential in decoding all the activities used to develop, communicate and sell services. On the other hand, it is necessary to understand the motives regarding why some services are preferred or rejected by consumers. With this understanding, it will be possible to influence consumers' decisions by developing appropriate strategies (Seabra et al., 2007).

In this chapter we develop a scale that measures the importance of information sources to the selection of tourism services. Typically research investigates external information sources from a different perspective (mostly in terms of the number of sources used and the amount of information search per source). However, by focusing our research on assessing the importance of specific information sources to service selection this approach presents important implications from both a theoretical and practitioner perspective (Brucks, 1985; Fodness and Murray, 1999; Murray, 1991).

Consumer behavior in services is much more complex than in goods, due to their intrinsic characteristics: intangibility, inseparability of production and consumption, heterogeneity, and perishability (Zeithaml et al., 1985). Tourist consumer behavior is particularly complex. The acquisition process has a strong emotional component and the purchasing is often the culmination of a long process of planning, choice, evaluation and assessment of alternatives by a large number of people. The tourist services intangibility creates uncertainty and perceived risk in the consumer's mind (Hugstad et al., 1987; Zeithaml 1981). So, before buying a tourist service, consumers acquire a large quantity of information and anticipate the consumption (Seabra et al., 2007).

This is an area of particular importance to managers, since information search occurs in the pre-purchase stage, influencing most consumer decisions (Murray 1991). The selection of a strategy for a particular service depends on the information sources they use. It is expected that through the INFOSOURCE scale, tourism firms might have as a basis a framework to develop and implement strategies that might bring value to their services. The INFOSOURCE dimensions might provide some guidance on how to better pursue an information-oriented business strategy. By identifying what sources are really valuable to the final consumer; it becomes possible to make choices regarding which sources to include, guiding managers toward customers' expectations.

The INFOSOURCE scale can also be used for competing purposes. The scale might be used to anticipate what customers value and, hence, help service firms to react faster to information changes than competitors. Finally, the scale developed here can be an important basis for the segmentation of a tourist market, because if we identify the means through which the services and the products are communicated to the consumers, we can influence them (see: Furse *et al.*, 1984).

From a theoretical perspective, to our knowledge, a measurement scale to assess information sources has never been operationalized in a services marketing context. Although we cannot claim to have definitively captured the dimensions of information sources, we believe that we come closer to capturing these overall evaluations by extracting the underlying commonality among dimensions. Towards this fact, we consider that the INFOSOURCE scale presented here contributes to both the tourism and the service marketing literatures. In sum, at a time when marketing researchers are challenged to provide research with practical implications, it is believed that this theoretical framework may be used as a basis to pursue service-oriented business strategies while taking into consideration the sources that customers select.

Limitations and Directions for Future Research

A research instrument was developed in this chapter. Instead of treating INFOSOURCE as a unidimensional construct, various measurement units for each of the five constructs were presented. INFOSOURCE is presented as a model with five first-order constructs: Information from mass media (SOURCE1), institutional brochures (SOURCE2), commercial brochures (SOURCE3), travel agents (SOURCE4) and the Internet (SOURCE5).

There are some limitations of the research to be considered. The first limitation is that the final instrument (i.e. the questionnaire) may have created common method variance that could have inflated construct relationships. This could be particularly threatening if the respondents were aware of the conceptual framework of interest. However, they were not told the specific purpose of the study, and all of the construct items were separated and mixed so that no respondent would be able to detect which items were affecting which factors. Additionally, if common method bias exists, a CFA containing all constructs should produce a single method factor (Podsakoff and Organ, 1986). The goodness-of-fit indices of this CFA (NFI=.45; CFI=.46, IFI=.46, TLI=.37) indicate a poor fit, which suggests that biasing from common method variance is unlikely. Hence, the biasing possibilities of common method variance were, it is considered, minimized.

Second, while the reported research investigates sources for a specific service (tourism), care should be taken in extending the study beyond this specific research set. For example, some studies that have tested the SERVQUAL scale in pure service settings (Carman, 1990), banking (Spreng and Singh, 1993), and different types of retail stores (Finn and Lamb, 1991), suggests that the SERVQUAL scale should be modified to different research settings. Hence, although the fit indices suggest a good fit of the model to the data, future research is encouraged to test our instrument across different services settings. To do so, we encourage researchers to add new items and factors applicable to the research setting. Continued refinement of the INFOSOURCE scale proposed and supported in this study is certainly possible based on further qualitative research.

Third, the research context involved tourists in Portugal in 2002-03, which may limit the generalizability of the results to some degree. The INFOSOURCE scale should also be applied to other types of service users across different countries. To establish its generalizability, multiple samples in other market contexts are also suggested.

Finally, further research is required when analysing the antecedents and consequences of INFOSOURCE. Thus, investigating how the information sources construct is associated with other variables, such as type of tourists, credibility of the information sources and services performance is suggested.

References

Ader J, LaFleur R, Falcone M. 2000. Internet Research. Available from: http:// www.bearstearns.com accessed on 10 April 2004.

Alba J, Lynch J, Weitz B, Janiszewski C, Lutz R, Sawyer A. 1997. Interactive home shopping: consumer, retailer, and manufacturer incentives to participate in electronic marketplaces. *Journal of Marketing* **61** (3): 38-53.

Bagozzi RP. 1980. *Causal Models in Marketing*. John Wiley: New York.

Beatty SE, Smith SM. 1987. External search effort: An investigation across several product categories. *Journal of Consumer Research* **14** (1): 83-95.

Bettman JR, Park CW. 1980. Effects of prior knowledge and experience and phase of the choice processes: A protocol analysis. *Journal of Consumer Research* **7** (3): 234-248.

Bieger T, Laesser C, Gallen S. 2000. Segmenting travel situations on the basis of motivation and information-collection by the traveller. *Revue de Tourisme* **2** (3): 54-64.

Bloch M. 1996. Letter to travel agents. Available from: http://haas.berkley.edu/-citm, accessed 11 April 2004.

Brucks M. 1985. The effects of product class knowledge on information search behaviour. *Journal of Consumer Research* **12** (1): 1-16.

Buhalis D. 1998. Strategic use of information technologies in the tourism industry. *Tourism Management* **19** (5): 409-421.

Carman JM. 1990. Consumer perceptions of service quality: An assessment of the SERVQUAL dimensions. *Journal of Retailing* **66** (Spr): 33-55.

Connolly DJ, Olsen MD. 2001. An environmental assessment of how technology is reshaping the hospitality industry. *Tourism and Hospitality Research* **3** (1): 73-93.

Cronbach LJ. 1951. Coefficient alpha and the internal structure of tests. *Psychometrika* **16** (3): 297-334.

Dodd TH, Pinkleton BE, Gustafson AW. 1996. External information sources of product enthusiasts: Differences between variety seekers, variety neutrals, and variety avoiders. *Psychology and Marketing* **13** (3): 291-304.

Finn DW, Lamb CW. 1991. An evaluation of the SERVQUAL scales in a retailing setting. In *Advances in Consumer Research*, Holman R, Solomon, MR (eds.). Association for Consumer Research: Provo. UT.

Fodness D, Murray B. 1999. A model of tourist information search behaviour. *Journal of Travel Research* **37** (3): 220-230.

Fornell C, Larcker D. 1981. Evaluating structural equation models with unobservable variables and measurement error. *Journal of Marketing Research* **18** (Feb): 39-50.

Furse DH, Punj GN, Stewart DW. 1981. A typology of individual search strategies among purchasers of new automobiles. *Journal of Consumer Research* **10** (4): 417-431.

Gitelson RJ, Crompton JL. 1983. The planning horizons and sources of information used by pleasure vacationers. *Journal of Travel Research* **21** (1): 2-7.

Hodgson P. 1993. Tour operator brochure design research revisited. *Journal of Travel Research* **32** (1): 50-51.

Hoffman DL, and Novak TP. 1996. Marketing in hypermedia computer-mediated environments: Conceptual foundations. *Journal of Marketing* **60** (2): 50-68.

Hugstad P, Taylor JW, Bruce GD. 1987. The effects of social class and perceived risk on consumer information search. *Journal of Services Marketing* **1** (1): 47-52.

Jöreskog KG, Sörbom D. 1993. *LISREL 8: Structural Equation Modeling with the SIMPLIS Command Language*. Lawrence Erlbaum Associates: Hillsdale, NJ.

Liu Y. 2006. World of mouth for movies: its dynamics and impact on box office revenue. *Journal of Marketing* **70** (July): 74-89.

Lovelock C, Vandermerwe S, Lewis B. 1999. *Services Marketing: A European Perspective*. Prentice-Hall: Englewood Cliffs, NJ.

Midgley DF. 1983. Patterns of interpersonal information seeking for the purchase of a symbolic product. *Journal of Marketing Research* **20** (1): 74-83.

Miles P. 1995. Portugal: Tourism goes upscale. *Europe* April (345): 31-32.

Morrison AJ, King BEM. 2002. Small tourism businesses and e-commerce: Victorian tourism online. *Tourism and Hospitality Research* **4** (2): 104-115.

Moutinho L. 1987. Consumer behaviour in tourism. *European Journal of Marketing* **21** (10): 5-44.

Moutinho L. 2000. Consumer behaviour. In *Strategic Management in Tourism*, Moutinho L (ed.). CABI Publishing: New York.

Murphy M, Murphy L. 2002. See you in three month's - An extended stay is one of the best ways to visit Europe, Here's how to start. *Wall Street Journal* Jun (24): p.R.6.

Murray KB. 1991. A test of services marketing theory: Consumer information acquisition activities. *Journal of Marketing* **55** (1): 10-25.

Nolan D. 1976. Tourist's use and evaluation of travel information. *Journal of Travel Research* **14** (2): 6-8.

Parasuraman A, Zinkhan GM. 2002. Marketing to and serving customers through the internet: An overview and research agenda. *Journal of the Academy of Marketing Science* **30** (4): 286-295.

Phelps JE, Lewis R, Mobilio L, Perry D, Raman N. 2004. Viral marketing or electronic word-of-mouth advertising: examining consumer responses and motivations to pass along email. *Journal of Advertising Research* **44** (4): 333-348.

Podsakoff PM, Organ DW. 1986. Self-reports in organizational research: Problems and perspectives. *Journal of Management* **12** (4): 531-544.

Raitz K, Dakhil M. 1989. A note about information sources for preferred recreational environments. *Journal of Travel Research* **27** (4): 45-50.

Seabra C, Abrantes JL, Lages L. 2007. The impact of using non-media information sources on the future use of mass media information sources: The mediating role of expectations fulfillment. *Tourism Management* **28** (3): 1541-1554.

Shoemaker S. 1984. Marketing to older travellers. *Cornell Quarterly* **25** (2): 84-91.

Snepenger DJ. 1987. Segmenting the vacation market by novelty-seeking role. *Journal of Travel Research* **26** (2): 8-14.

Snepenger D, Meged K, Snelling WK. 1990. Information search strategies by destination-naive tourists. *Journal of Travel Research* **29** (1): 13-16.

Spreng RA, Singh AK. 1983 An empirical assessment of the SERVQUAL scale and the relationship between service quality and satisfaction. In *Enhancing Knowledge Development in Marketing*, Cravens DW, Dickson P (eds). American Marketing Association: Chicago.

Srinivasan N, Ratchford BT. 1991. An empirical test of a model of external search for automobiles. *Journal of Consumer Research* **18** (2): 233-242.

Wyner G. 2000. Learn and earn through testing on the Internet. *Marketing Research* **12** (3): 37-38.

Wynne C, Berthon P, Pitt L, Ewing M, Napoli J. 2001. The impact of the Internet on the distribution value chain: The case of the South African tourism industry. *International Marketing Review* **18** (4): 420-431.

Zeithaml VA. 1981. How consumer evaluation processes differ between goods and services. In *Marketing of Services*, Donnelly JH and George WR (eds). American Marketing Association: Chicago.

Zeithaml VA, Parasuraman A, Berry LL. 1985. Problems and strategies in services marketing. *Journal of Marketing* **49** (2): 33-46.

Appendix

Table 3. 1: The INFOSOURCE scale – Constructs, scale items and reliabilities

Constructs, Scale Items and Reliabilities	Standardized coefficients	T-values
INFSRC1- Information from mass media (α=.89; $\rho_{vc(n)}$=.73; ρ=.89)		
V1 Importance of mass media information to route selection	.86	19.59
V2 Importance of mass media information to accommodation selection	.91	21.69
V3 Importance of mass media information to activities selection	.80	17.63
INFSRC2- Information from institutional brochures (α=.79; $\rho_{vc(n)}$=.62; ρ=.82)		
V4 Importance of institutional brochures to route selection	.88	20.31
V5 Importance of institutional brochures to accommodation selection	.88	20.38
V6 Importance of institutional brochures to activities selection	.55	10.73
INFSRC3- Information from commercial brochures (α=.91; $\rho_{vc(n)}$=.76; ρ=.90)		
V7 Importance of commercial brochures to route selection	.78	17.25
V8 Importance of commercial brochures to accommodation selection	.88	20.79
V9 Importance of commercial brochures to activities selection	.94	23.17
INFSRC4- Information from travel agents (α=.95; $\rho_{vc(n)}$=.86; ρ=.95)		
V10 Importance of travel agents to route selection	.86	19.96
V11 Importance of travel agents to accommodation selection	.98	25.03
V12 Importance of travel agents to activities selection	.94	23.54
INFSRC5- Information from the Internet (α=.93; $\rho_{vc(n)}$=.81; ρ=.93)		
V13 Importance of the Internet to route selection	.81	18.12
V14 Importance of the Internet to accommodation selection	.95	23.34
V15 Importance of the Internet to activities selection	.94	22.96

Notes:

α = Internal reliability (Cronbach, 1951);

$\rho_{vc(n)}$ = Variance extracted (Fornell and Larcker, 1981);

ρ = Composite reliability (Bagozzi, 1980)

All scales are anchored by '1 – Not important at all' and ' 7 – Extremely important'.

4 European Tourist Destinations in Internet Search Engines: a Comparison

Estrella Díaz, David Martín-Consuegra, Águeda Esteban, Juan José Blázquez,
University of Castilla-La Mancha

Introduction

Nowadays, tourism is one of the most developed economic sectors due to the extensive use of the Internet for commercial purposes and to the high rate of companies that make use of websites. The tourist sector has used a wide variety of information strategies to reach potential tourists in e-commerce, such as websites, online directory providers, and search engines (Goodman, 2000; Gretzel et al., 2000; So and Morrison, 2003). The boom of the Internet, specially search engines, has changed the media tourist companies use for the distribution of tourist information and also the way in which potential tourists search for and consume information for their journey (Beldona, 2005; Burns, 2006; Gretzel et al., 2006). Using the Internet for information search is profitable not only for tourists, but also for tourist organizations (Palmer and McCole 2000), and it has transformed the concepts of communication and interaction for many tourist firms (Buhalis, 2003).

In this sense, tourist companies require a better knowledge of how tourists use the Internet in order to improve their marketing efforts, reduce costs and provide an up-to-date tool for interactive communication. Buhalis (2000) has suggested that the use of the Internet allows tourist destinations to improve their competitiveness because it increases their visibility and reduces advertising costs. Most tourist organizations therefore concur that accessibility and visibility have become fundamental requirements for tourist companies willing to market their products online (Wöber, 2006; Xiang et al., 2008). The complex nature of the World Wide Web because it provides a great quantity of easily accessible information, however, does not facilitate the visibility and accessibility of tourist companies offering their products to potential or actual customers who want to plan their travel online. But this does not mean that the role played by tourist companies in the connection between destinations and potential tourists is minor (Fogg 1999, 2003; Gretzel, 2004, Gretzel and Fesenmaier, 2007; Kim and Fesenmaier, 2007; Murphy et al., 2003; Xiang and Fesenmaier, 2006). The use of the Internet as a communication medium is quite effective for consumer persuasion, because online marketing efforts may have a strong influence on the choice of destination (Zach et al., 2007).

Once the influence of the Internet on the tourist sector has been considered, the main objective of this research is to analyse the presence or representation of 50 European tourist destinations in four search engines: Google, Yahoo, Microsoft and Ask, with the main aim of testing tourist destination visibility. For this purpose, the analysis of tourism includes both an analysis of the presence of tourism in each destination as well as of the presence of the concept of tourism divided into nine categories. This analysis should provide the factors of destination visibility in each search engine.

This chapter is divided into four sections. The first one deals with the main theoretical concepts of the topic observed here. The second one includes the methodology, and the third presents the analysis and major results of this study. Finally, the fourth section outlines the most important conclusions, limitations and recommendations provided by this study.

The Competitiveness of Tourist Destinations and the Internet

In the research literature, tourism has been described as a system with four main components: destination, marketing, demand and journey (Mill and Morrison, 2002). Tourist destination can be defined as an adaptive system that presents an offer appealing for tourists. This system consists of a number of interrelations among different human, natural and economic environments (Farrell and Twining-Ward, 2004; McKercher, 1999). Destinations are the most difficult entities to manage and market, due firstly to the complexity of their relationships with local agents, the government, companies and the natural environment, second, to the unique needs of each destination and third, to their geographical, environmental and socio-cultural particularities (Buhalis, 2000; Feng et al., 2003; Sautter and Leisen, 1999). Nevertheless, marketing may contribute significantly to improve the perception and awareness of the benefits of destinations (Nielsen et al., 2000).

The competition among destinations in the sector is increasing steadily. The competitiveness of a given destination depends on its ability to provide a rich tourist offer, an attractive infrastructure and a human appeal that attracts visitors, businessmen and citizens. The key to destination success is therefore an effective organization and a local innovation system that on the one hand renovates both destination resources and demand factors continuously and on the other improves the conditions of location and the effective use of marketing (Paskaleva-Shapira, 2007).

Therefore, one given destination may keep its competitiveness, but it also has to be flexible enough to take advantage of the new opportunities available in the external environment. One of the opportunities that should attract the attention of marketing directors is information technologies in general and the Internet in particular. The Internet may be applied to all the components of destinations, and it may easily become an important commercial channel. For business organizations in charge of destination marketing, satisfying tourist demand and maintaining competitiveness in the long-term is imperative and may unavoidably require the use of new technologies and integrated online marketing communication strategies (Gretzel et al., 2000; Hoffman and Novak, 1996; Wang and Fesenmaier, 2006). Online technologies, particularly the World Wide Web, have allowed tourist destinations to promote and sell their tourist products and services more effectively.

In this sense, for tourist companies, the Internet is an essential means of attracting and motivating future visitors by generating pleasant destination images and offering added-value in their products and services. From the point of view of tourist enterprises, to be indexed in a search engine and visible as search result provides an advantage to promote and sell their website as well as the destination (Xiang and Fesenmaier, 2006).

The Influence of Search Engines on Online Tourist Travel Planning and on the Presence of Tourism

Travel planning and information search consists often of a multi-state process: potential tourists have to search for a destination, plan the journey and the route (Gretzel et al., 2006; Jeng and Fesenmaier, 2002; Pearce, 2005). Although there are several sources of online information available for tourists, it is quite obvious that many potential tourists begin their online search using a search engine (Nielsen, 2000, 2004; Pan and Fesenmaier, 2006; Sigala, 2004). In general, a search engine consists of two main components: an offline component that collects websites and constructs an internal representative image (index) and an online component that allows users to search, order and classify documents in order to select the most relevant of them (Henzinger, 2007). The interaction between the potential tourist and the engine can be described as a selection process which concludes when the tourist selects one of the websites related to the specific destination. Kim and Fesenmaier (2008) suggest that the use of search engines has a significant effect on first impression formation, and consequently on the overall evaluation of the website of the tourist firm. The main components of this structure include the tourist, the search engine and online space for tourist information provided by the different tourist organizations (Pan and Fesenmaier, 2006).

As described above, the information search carried out with an online search engine is a cognitive process with different stages. Tourists planning their journey online often begin their plans using search engines (Google, Yahoo, etc.) to find and choose useful information sources (Pan and Fesenmaier, 2006; Wöber, 2006; Xiang et al., 2008). Once the search engine has been selected, the tourist poses a question and launches a search, the results of which correspond to the question posed by the tourist (Hwang et al., 2006; Levene, 2006). So, the search engine delivers and retains a set of results which coincide with the word entered and presents them in a predefined visual format (Yu and Meng, 2003). Search engines facilitate this process because they provide a pre-index of the tourist information space and present the websites to travellers. Particularly, the classification of a search result according to relevance has been considered the most important factor in the traveller's information search behaviour (Pan and Fesenmaier, 2006; Widyantoro and Yen, 2002; Xiang and Fesenmaier, 2006). It has been demonstrated that the position of a search result in the classification determines the revision and evaluation of information by the searcher (Pan et al., 2007). The final step in the process of online information search is the decision to use one specific website. The final decision of the potential tourist is therefore determined by the interaction between traveller and returned website(s) (Pan and Fesenmaier, 2006).

Due to the size of the Internet and to the variable quality of websites, the way in which search engines index and represent the world online has raised numerous issues. However, the main challenge of search engines is to provide exhaustive results and an effective classification of them (Henzinger, 2007). Users' questions tend to be short and most users do not pay attention to results beyond the third page, so it is critical for search engines to provide the most relevant results in the most effective way (Henzinger, 2007; Spink and Jasen, 2004). Consequently, although search engines are capable of returning millions of search results related to a specific question, only a relatively small number of them are presented to the user. The visibility of tourism therefore depends mainly on the classification and position of results, and is small in relation to the number of pages indexed in search engines (Pan et al., 2007; Xiang and Fesenmaier, 2005). Wöber (2006) proved that many tourist companies appeared in a low position in the classification of travel search results. This makes it difficult for online travellers to have access to individual tourism operators through these engines. In another study, Xiang et al., 2008 demonstrated that tourism search results in Google are controlled by a small number of tourist firms, which contributes to the low visibility of many tourist companies.

Due to the fact that search engines provide access to online information of tourist companies or tourist destinations, the main objective of this research is to analyse in what way a number of tourist destinations are presented or represented online in search engines. This analysis will therefore try to answer the following questions:

♦   Which is the general visibility ratio of the tourist sector in each of the search engines and for each of the destinations analysed in this study? Are there any differences among search engines?

♦   Which is the presence of specific tourist information available in each search engine and for each of the destinations analysed here? Are there any differences among search engines?

Methodology

The first step taken in this research was to establish a selection of the main European tourist destinations. The final sample of tourist destinations consists of 50 items. The research proceeds then with the following steps: the identification of the questions entered in the search engine, the results of each search and the choice of search engines used in the different searches. Finally, the final step deals with the analysis of the procedure used here to achieve the planned objectives.

The process of data collection had three steps. First, 150 representative cities from all over the world were selected as important tourist destinations globally. The criterion for selection was the number of visitors each destination received as it appeared on the classification of the 150 most visited cities provided by *Euromonitor International* in 2007. Second, 50 European cities were selected from this list of most visited destinations, according to the number of visitors (see Table 4.1). Finally, the 50 European destinations were divided into two groups depending on whether these cities were the capital of the country. The group of cities which were capitals contained 21 items, whereas the other group consisted of 29 cities which were not country capitals.

The layout of this research permitted the determination of whether the online presence of capital cities was different from that of non-capitals. The first step was the identification of a series of pre-defined words which could be used as keywords in the search engine in order to assess the presence of each of the cities as tourist destination. The selection of these keywords was carried out according to the classification frameworks often used in previous research literature (Smith, 1988; Wöber, 2006; Woodside and Dubelaar, 2002; Xiang et al., 2008; Xiang and Fesenmaier, 2006) and included words frequently used in the websites of several organizations related to tourist destinations. The main aim of this strategy was to make sure that the study was considering valid contents (DeVellis, 1991). Ten keywords related to tourism and tourist destinations were located in a search engine and finally selected for this study: 'tourism', 'accommodation', 'activities', 'areas', 'attractions', 'events', 'information', 'restaurants', 'shopping' and 'places.' These words represent possible questions posed by tourists when looking for information about tourist activities in a particular destination, from the most general approach, such as 'tourism' to the more specific tourism categories.

Table 4.1: European Tourist Destinations According to Number of Visitors

Destination	000 tourist arrivals	Destination	000 tourist arrivals
1.London	15,640	26. Nice	1,227
2.Paris	9,700	27. Stockholm	1,003
3. Rome	6,033	28. Tallinn	1,001
4. Barcelona	4,695	29. Krakow	992
5. Dublin	4,469	30. Manchester	912
6. Istanbul	3,994	31. Salzburg	874
7. Madrid	3,921	32. Helsinki	842
8. Amsterdam	3,901	33. Birmingham	779
9. Prague	3,702	34. Glasgow	741
10. Moscow	3,695	35. Hamburg	739
11. Vienna	3,339	36. Lyon	715
12. Saint Petersburg	3,200	37. Bruges	641
13. Venice	2,927	38. Antwerp	636
14. Warsaw	2,925	39. Liverpool	625
15. Benidorm	2,457	40. Valencia	611
16. Berlin	2,309	41. Granada	606
17. Budapest	2,043	42. Geneva	577
18. Munich	1,925	43. Innsbruck	536
19. Milan	1,902	44. Oslo	522
20. Florence	1,715	45. Bratislava	455
21. Lisbon	1,715	46. Oxford	449
22. Copenhagen	1,375	47. Gothenburg	422
23. Zurich	1,369	48. Luxembourg	406
24. Edinburgh	1,338	49. Bristol	403
25. Seville	1,234	50. Reykjavik	371

The second phase entailed the description of a series of search results obtained by an online search engine. Once the keywords have been entered, two of the characteristics of the search results obtained are necessary to evaluate the presence of a tourist category in a given tourist destination. The first characteristic is the total number of websites listed, that is, the total number of results provided by the search engine in response to a search question. The second characteristic is the total number of web pages accessible to the user, one question has elicited.

The final step of this research was to consider which four search engines were the most representative, in order to determine the presence or representation of tourism in each destination. Four engines were considered the most representative by European users: Google, Yahoo, Microsoft and Ask (Lewandowski, 2008; Sullivan, 2007). For this specific search, we used the international website of each of these engines. Google is arguably the dominant search engine in the European market, with 80% market share in the major European countries (Lewandowski, 2008). The other search engines were selected according to the number of websites they could list. In this sense, while Yahoo and Microsoft could list 1000 websites for each search, Ask could only supply 200. Search engine popularity was also considered in the final selection. According to Search Engine Watch, a website containing information about search engine companies, the four major international search engines are Google, Yahoo, Microsoft and Ask (Sullivan, 2007).

The presence of tourism in each destination as provided by each of the four search engines was measured in two steps. First of all, the presence of tourism in general was measured for each group (capital and non-capital cities). In order to do that, the name of the city and the term 'tourism' were entered together as search keywords in the four search engines used here. Search results were noted as follows: the total number of indexed websites and the number of results found by the engine. These elements were used to calculate the visibility ratio for each question, dividing the number of results found by the total number of websites indexed in the search engine (Xiang et al., 2008).

Second, the procedure continued with an analysis of the presence of tourism in terms of tourist categories for each city group. All 50 tourist destinations were used as search keywords and the search was launched in each engine, using alternatively the name of the city together with each of the nine tourist categories described here ('accommodation', 'activities', 'areas', 'attractions', 'events', 'information', 'restaurants', 'shopping' and 'places'). This procedure generated nine questions per destination and per search engine. The results were noted like in the previous step, i.e., the total number of websites and the number of results found were considered. The data for this study were collected during December 2008.

Results

The main aim of this research is to analyse the presence of tourism in each of the tourist destinations selected, considering also if using one search engine or another yields different results. The analysis included 50 European tourist destinations selected according to number of visitors. Table 4.1 displays the classification of destinations used here, where London gets the higher number of tourist arrivals (15,640,000), followed by Paris (9,700,000) and Rome (6,033,000). The gap tourist arrivals for London and the rest of the destinations is quite significant.

The total number of searches carried out for the first group was 200, that is, 4 searches launched per destination. Table 4.2 shows the results of the group of European tourist destinations that are the country's capital city. The capitals are classified according to the total number of websites indexed in each of the search engines. A total of 84 searches were launched.

As Table 2 shows, the capital cities that generated the highest number of indexed websites by Google are Stockholm (4,890,000 indexed websites), London (4,540,000) and Paris (3,640,000). This means that the most frequently visited cities have the highest number of indexed websites. If one considers Yahoo, the capitals with greater number of indexed websites is also London (72,200,000 indexed websites), Paris (42,200,000) and, contrarily to what happens in Google, Rome (21,500,000). The Microsoft search engines also places London as the tourist destination with the biggest number of indexed websites (11,500,000), followed by Paris (7,820,000), although the third on this list is Luxembourg (7,330,000). Finally, Ask provides results similar to Yahoo's, with London in the first position (10,600,000), followed by Paris (2,064,000) and Rome (1,104,000) as the capitals with the greatest number of websites located by the search engine. If we compare the four search engines, Yahoo stands out as the engine that provides the greatest number of websites for each question, while Google is the engine that finds the smallest number of websites.

However, not all websites are visible to users. If just the websites actually presented websites, that is, websites actually located and marked by the search engine, are con-

Table 4.2: Representation of tourism in European destinations (capital cities) in Google, Yahoo, Microsoft and Ask.

GOOGLE				YAHOO			
Capitals	Total indexed (000)	Results presented	Visibility ratio (%)	Capitals	Total indexed (000)	Results presented	Visibility ratio (%)
Stockholm	4,890	489	0.010	London	72,200	1000	0.001
London	4,540	713	0.016	Paris	42,200	1000	0.002
Paris	3,640	679	0.019	Rome	21,500	1000	0.004
Rome	3,120	657	0.021	Luxembourg	18,100	1000	0.005
Moscow	2,750	547	0.020	Madrid	16,200	1000	0.006
Lisbon	1,780	474	0.027	Berlin	16,200	1000	0.006
Oslo	1,660	527	0.032	Dublin	15,700	1000	0.006
Helsinki	1,580	622	0.039	Amsterdam	14,000	1000	0.007
Copenhagen	1,450	491	0.034	Moscow	11,100	1000	0.009
Warsaw	1,220	508	0.042	Vienna	9,530	1000	0.010
Bratislava	788	656	0.083	Prague	8,830	1000	0.011
Dublin	436	409	0.093	Budapest	6,930	1000	0.014
Berlin	416	611	0.147	Lisbon	5,870	1000	0.017
Amsterdam	408	571	0.140	Stockholm	5,410	1000	0.018
Luxembourg	402	587	0.146	Copenhagen	4,360	1000	0.023
Madrid	339	580	0.171	Warsaw	4,270	1000	0.023
Vienna	292	505	0.173	Oslo	4,220	1000	0.024
Prague	267	464	0.174	Helsinki	3,790	1000	0.026
Budapest	264	491	0.186	Tallinn	1,900	1000	0.053
Reykjavik	229	464	0.203	Bratislava	1,850	1000	0.054
Tallinn	201	200	0.099	Reykjavik	1,250	1000	0.080

MICROSOFT				ASK			
Capitals	Total indexed (000)	Results presented	Visibility ratio (%)	Capitals	Total Indexed (000)	Results Presented	Visibility Ratio (%)
London	11,500	1000	0.009	London	10..600	200	0.002
Paris	7,820	1000	0.013	Paris	2,064	200	0.010
Luxembourg	7,330	1000	0.014	Rome	1,104	200	0.018
Rome	5,990	1000	0.017	Berlin	951	198	0.021
Amsterdam	4,980	1000	0.020	Dublin	655	200	0.030
Berlin	4,970	1000	0.020	Prague	593,1	200	0.034
Madrid	4,170	1000	0.024	Madrid	583,6	200	0.034
Dublin	3,390	1000	0.029	Moscow	473,2	199	0.042
Vienna	2,960	1000	0.034	Vienna	409,9	199	0.048
Prague	2,570	1000	0.039	Amsterdam	386,1	200	0.052
Moscow	2,410	1000	0.041	Luxembourg	348,9	200	0.057
Budapest	1,900	1000	0.053	Budapest	283	198	0.070
Stockholm	1,270	1000	0.079	Stockholm	222,4	200	0.090
Lisbon	1,220	1000	0.082	Lisbon	215,7	200	0.093
Copenhagen	1,120	1000	0.089	Copenhagen	186,7	200	0.107
Oslo	713	1000	0.140	Warsaw	174,3	200	0.115
Warsaw	685	1000	0.146	Oslo	156,1	198	0.127
Helsinki	640	1000	0.156	Tallinn	149	199	0.133
Bratislava	368	1000	0.272	Helsinki	130	200	0.154
Tallinn	314	1000	0.318	Bratislava	63,9	199	0.311
Reykjavik	302	1000	0.331	Reykjavik	41	198	0.483

Table 4.3: Representation of tourism in European destinations (non-capital cities) in Google, Yahoo, Microsoft and Ask

GOOGLE				YAHOO			
Other tourist destinations	Total indexed (000)	Results presented	Visibility ratio (%)	Other tourist destinations	Total indexed (000)	Results presented	Visibility ratio (%)
Barcelona	3,120	516	0,016	Nice	37,300	1000	0,003
Birmingham	2,800	402	0,014	Barcelona	17,000	1000	0,006
Florence	2,280	513	0,022	Manchester	16,200	1000	0,006
St Petersburg	1,500	543	0,036	Birmingham	12,500	1000	0,008
Gothenburg	1,150	562	0,049	Oxford	12,300	1000	0,008
Venice	1,050	685	0,065	Bristol	11,400	1000	0,009
Seville	756	471	0,062	Edinburgh	11,000	1000	0,009
Salzburg	750	449	0,060	Venice	9,660	1000	0,010
Krakow	738	511	0,069	Florence	9,560	1000	0,010
Nice	428	633	0,148	Glasgow	9,310	1000	0,011
Manchester	392	432	0,110	Liverpool	8,930	1000	0,011
Antwerp	379	463	0,122	Milan	8,510	1000	0,012
Oxford	362	407	0,112	Munich	8,160	1000	0,012
Benidorm	351	499	0,142	Geneva	8,000	1000	0,0125
Istanbul	349	511	0,146	Valencia	7,830	1000	0,013
Bristol	320	458	0,143	Istanbul	7,460	1000	0,013
Milan	318	496	0,156	St Petersburg	6,730	1000	0,015
Edinburgh	292	407	0,139	Granada	5,680	1000	0,018
Liverpool	287	419	0,146	Hamburg	5,260	1000	0,019
Geneva	284	520	0,183	Zurich	4,950	1000	0,020
Glasgow	271	422	0,156	Lyon	4,850	1000	0,021
Zurich	270	430	0,159	Seville	3,390	1000	0,029
Bruges	270	502	0,186	Benidorm	2,340	1000	0,043
Hamburg	264	514	0,195	Krakow	2,340	1000	0,043
Valencia	239	479	0,200	Salzburg	2,340	1000	0,043
Munich	236	493	0,209	Antwerp	1,370	1000	0,073
Lyon	177	533	0,301	Innsbruck	1,120	1000	0,089
Granada	161	536	0,333	Gothenburg	1,010	1000	0,099
Innsbruck	67,4	475	0,705	Bruges	955	1000	0,105

MICROSOFT				ASK			
Other tourist destinations	Total indexed (000)	Results presented	Visibility ratio (%)	Other tourist destinations	Total indexed (000)	Results presented	Visibility Ratio (%)
Nice	5,640	1000	0,018	Nice	3,118	200	0,006
Barcelona	4,730	1000	0,021	Manchester	985,1	199	0,020
Manchester	4,090	1000	0,024	Granada	943	199	0,021
St Petersburg	3,670	1000	0,027	Bristol	710,3	200	0,028
Oxford	3,270	1000	0,030	Oxford	708	198	0,028
Florence	2,940	1000	0,034	Glasgow	696,6	199	0,028
Bristol	2,850	1000	0,035	Birmingham	651,8	200	0,031
Geneva	2,830	1000	0,035	Barcelona	581	199	0,034
Birmingham	2,810	1000	0,035	Venice	557,1	200	0,036
Hamburg	2,540	1000	0,039	Liverpool	534	200	0,037
Venice	2,490	1000	0,040	Edinburgh	528,1	200	0,038
Edinburgh	2,360	1000	0,042	Milan	459	200	0,043
Glasgow	1,900	1000	0,053	Florence	441,3	200	0,045
Milan	1,820	1000	0,055	Munich	427	199	0,047
Istanbul	1,730	1000	0,058	Geneva	418,1	200	0,048
Liverpool	1,420	1000	0,070	Hamburg	405,9	200	0,049
Munich	1,310	1000	0,076	Istanbul	285,1	199	0,070
Zurich	1,180	1000	0,085	Lyon	245,7	200	0,081
Lyon	1,100	1000	0,091	St Petersburg	222	200	0,090
Valencia	809	1000	0,124	Valencia	216,5	200	0,092
Salzburg	691	1000	0,145	Zurich	182,3	200	0,110
Granada	551	1000	0,181	Seville	131,4	198	0,151
Krakow	470	1000	0,212	Salzburg	94	200	0,213
Seville	365	1000	0,274	Antwerp	83,3	197	0,236
Gothenburg	209	1000	0,478	Krakow	66,6	200	0,300
Antwerp	207	1000	0,483	Innsbruck	43,3	197	0,455
Innsbruck	188	1000	0,532	Gothenburg	43	199	0,463
Bruges	180	1000	0,556	Bruges	39,3	198	0,504
Benidorm	107	1000	0,935	Benidorm	38,6	200	0,518

sidered, the list of capitals would include first, London (713 presented websites), then Paris (679) and finally Rome (657) in Google. In Yahoo and Microsoft, the number of presented websites remains constant at about 1000 visible and accessible websites, and the classification of capitals is the same as in the case of indexed websites. Similarly, the number of visible websites found by the Ask search engine is more or less constant and oscillates between 197 and 200, although it never goes beyond 200. If we consider the number of results retrieved by each search engine, Yahoo and Microsoft are the engines that present more websites, while Ask displays the worst figures.

Nevertheless, if we considered the visibility ratio, the capitals that occupy the first place in Google change significantly. Reykjavik (0.203%), Budapest (0.186%) and Prague (0.174%) stand out as the capitals with greater tourism visibility. The cities that display the lowest visibility ratio are those capitals with the higher number of indexed websites, that is, Stockholm (0.010%), London (0.016%) and Paris (0.019%). In fact, if we considered that search engines users rarely go beyond the first three result pages (30 results), the real visibility ratio would be much lower. In Yahoo, the greatest visibility ratios are for Reykjavik (0.080%), Bratislava (0.054%) and Tallinn (0.053%), while London (0.001%), Paris (0.002%) and Rome (0.004%) have the lowest ratios. In the case of the Microsoft search engine, the capitals with higher visibility ratios are Reykjavik (0.331%), Tallinn (0.318%) and Bratislava (0.272%); London (0.009%), Paris (0.013%) and Luxembourg (0.014%) obtain the lowest results. Finally, the capitals with higher visibility ratio in the Ask search engine include Reykjavik (0.483%), Bratislava (0.311%) and Helsinki (0.154%). Alternatively, London (0.002%), Paris (0.010%) and Rome (0.018%) have the lowest ratios. Considering these results, it is logical to conclude that in those cities with the higher number of indexed websites tourism is less visible, and vice versa. In all search engines, except for Google, the capitals with the lowest number of indexed websites are less visible for tourism. If we compare the four search engines, Ask and Microsoft provide higher visibility ratios, while Yahoo obtains the lowest because it the engine that indexes more websites. In Table 4.2, countries shaded pale grey are those with highest visibility rations, while those with the lowest ratios are shaded darker grey.

Table 4.3 displays the number of websites indexed, the total of websites presented and the visibility ratio for each of the tourist destinations that are not capitals. The diverse destinations are ordered according to the number of websites indexed by each search engine. As in the previous group, the search was launched using the name of the destination together with the word 'tourism.' A total of 116 searches were carried out.

If we consider the total number of websites found by each search engine, Google displayed the higher number for Barcelona (3,120,000 indexed websites), followed by Birmingham (2,800,000) and Florence (2,280,000). Contrarily, the lowest number of indexed websites corresponds to Innsbruck (67,400 indexed websites), Granada (161,000) and Lyon (177,000). Yahoo indexed more tourist websites for Nice (37,300,000 indexed websites), Barcelona (17,000,000) and Manchester (16,200,000), while Bruges (955,000 indexed websites), Gothenburg (1,010,000) and Innsbruck (1,120,000) yielded the worst results. As for the Microsoft search engine, the greatest number of indexed websites is quite similar to the results found by Yahoo, that is, Nice (5,640,000 indexed websites), Barcelona (4,730,000) and Manchester (4,090,000) as the cities that yielded better results, in opposition to Benidorm (107,000 indexed websites), Bruges (180,000) and Innsbruck (188,000), with the lowest number of indexed websites. Finally, Ask places Nice (3,118,000 indexed websites), Manchester (985,100) and Granada

(943,000) as the destinations with the highest number of indexed websites, in contrast with Benidorm (38,600 indexed websites), Bruges (39,300) and Gothenburg (43,000). In this case, Yahoo is the search engine indexing more websites, whereas Google and Ask yield the worst results.

However, if only the results presented are taken into account, the Google search engine retrieved the greatest number of results for Venice (685 results), Nice (633) and Gothenburg (562). In contrast, Birmingham (402 results), Edinburgh (407) and Oxford (407) were the destinations that appeared less often. In the case of Yahoo and Microsoft, the total number of presented websites does not vary and is a constant number of 1000; as a consequence, the classification of results according to presented results is the same as the classification according to indexed websites. Something similar happens with the Ask search engine, because results presented oscillate between 197-200 and there are no relevant differences with the classification according to indexed websites. The comparison between the four search engines reveals that Yahoo and Microsoft present the greater number of results, whereas Ask displays the lowest figure of presented websites.

Finally, it is necessary to consider the visibility rate of the websites of non-capital tourist destinations presented by each search engine. First, Innsbruck (0.705%), Granada (0.333%) and Lyon (0.301%) stand out as the cities with the highest visibility rate in Google, whereas Birmingham (0.014%), Barcelona (0.016%) and Florence (0.022%) displays the lowest visibility ratios. In Yahoo, the destinations with highest visibility ratios are Bruges (0.105%), Gothenburg (0.099%) and Innsbruck (0.089%); contrarily, Nice (0.003%), Barcelona (0.006%) and Manchester (0.006%) are the destinations with the lowest visibility ratios. The results of the Microsoft search engine place Benidorm (0.935%), Bruges (0.536%) and Innsbruck (0.532%) as the cities with the highest visibility ratios, and the destinations with the lowest visibility ratios coincide with those presented by Yahoo: Nice (0.018%), Barcelona (0.021%) and Manchester (0.024%). Finally, the destinations with better visibility ratios in the Ask search engine are Benidorm (0.518%), Bruges (0.504%) and Gothenburg (0.463%), which contrast deeply with ratio results obtained by Nice (0.006%), Manchester (0.020%) and Granada (0.021%). If we analyse the results of the four search engines, Ask and Microsoft offer the highest visibility ratios again, while Yahoo's ratio is the lowest. In Table 4.4, destinations with high visibility ratios are shaded in pale grey and those with low ratios are shaded in darker grey.

The following step in our study was to analyse the presence or representation of the tourist destinations in the search engines selected, paying attention to a variety of tourist categories. That is, each destination will provide nine questions for each search engine. If we multiply this by the 50 destinations considered here and the 4 search engines, it means that a total of 1800 questions will be used.

In order to make result presentation clearer, results have been displayed in four different tables. Table 4.4 focuses on European capitals with the highest presence of tourist categories in the four search engines. The visibility ratio of each tourist category has also been considered, as well as the differences between search engines. Out of the total sample of 21 European capitals, Reykjavik, Tallinn, Bratislava and Helsinki stand out as the cities with the lowest number of indexed websites. However, if we consider the capitals with the highest presence of tourist categories, the results provided by the four search engines hardly differ.

Table 4.5 shows the cities with lowest presence of tourist categories or lowest visibility

Table 4.4: Highest presence of tourist categories for European capitals in Google, Yahoo, Microsoft and Ask

Other tourist destinations	GOOGLE			YAHOO		
	Total indexed (000)	Results presented	Visibility ratio (%)	Total indexed (000)	Results presented	Visibility ratio (%)
Accommodation	231 Copenhagen	482	0,209	2,620 Reykjavik	1000	0,038
Activities	635 Reykjavik	419	0,066	3,350 Tallinn	1000	0,030
Areas	546 Reyk javik	513	0,094	2,180 Reykjavik	1000	0,046
Attractions	140 Helsinki	362	0,258	1,750 Reykjavik	1000	0,057
Events	465 Budapest	585	0,126	5,890 Reykjavik	1000	0,017
Information	461 Prague	615	0,133	12,900 Reykjavik	1000	0,008
Restaurants	490 Luxembourg	568	0,116	2,540 Tallinn	1000	0,039
Shopping	440 Vienna	535	0,121	3,570 Bratislava	1000	0,028
Places	1,340 Tallinn	502	0,037	2,760 Bratislava	1000	0,036

Other tourist destinations	MICROSOFT			ASK		
	Total indexed (,000)	Results presented	Visibility ratio (%)	Total Indexed (000)	Results presented	Visibility Ratio (%)
Accommodation	307 Reykjavik	1000	0.326	75.2 Reykjavik	200	0.266
Activities	612 Reykjavik	1000	0.163	96.3 Reykjavik	199	0.207
Areas	1,260 Reykjavik	1000	0.079	65.9 Tallinn	200	0.303
Attractions	210 Bratislava	1000	0.476	33.1 Bratislava	200	0.604
Events	1,110 Reykjavik	1000	0.090	186 Reykjavik	200	0.107
Information	1,910 Reykjavik	1000	0.052	263 Reykjavik	200	0.076
Restaurants	395 Bratislava	1000	0.253	111.5 Helsinki	200	0.179
Shopping	753	1000	0.133 Bratislava	51.1	200	0.391 Bratislava
Places	1,240 Reykjavik	1000	0.081	78.8 Tallinn	200	0.254

Table 4.5: Lowest presence of tourist categories for European capitals in Google, Yahoo, Microsoft and Ask

Other tourist destinations	GOOGLE			YAHOO		
	Total indexed (,000)	Results presented	Visibility ratio (%)	Total indexed (,000)	Results presented	Visibility ratio (%)
Accommodation	1,870 Stockholm	483	0,026	116,000 London	1000	0,0008
Activities	44,500 London	522	0,001	187,000 London	1000	0,0005
Areas	21,100 Madrid	494	0,002	215,000 London	1000	0,0004
Attractions	784 Warsaw	536	0,068	85,500 London	1000	0,001
Events	27,600 London	514	0,002	569,000 London	1000	0,0002
Information	227,000 Paris	560	0,0002	906,000 London	1000	0,0001
Restaurants	610 Dublin	302	0,005	246,000 London	1000	0,0004
Shopping	16,500 Paris	443	0,003	616,000 London	1000	0,0002
Places	31,400 Paris	507	0,002	213,000 London	1000	0,0005

Other tourist destinations	MICROSOFT			ASK		
	Total indexed (000)	Results presented	Visibility ratio (%)	Total Indexed (000)	Results presented	Visibility Ratio (%)
Accommodation	24,700 London	1000	0.004	6,470 London	199	0,003
Activities	48,600 London	1000	0.002	30,200 London	200	0,0007
Areas	123,000 London	1000	0.0008	34,700 London	200	0.0006
Attractions	11,700 London	1000	0.008	5,050 London	196	0.004
Events	190,000 London	1000	0.0005	64,100 London	195	0.0003
Information	267,000 London	1000	0.0004	90,600 London	199	0.0002
Restaurants	27,300 London	1000	0.004	14,500 London	199	0.001
Shopping	54,000 London	1000	0.002	25,400 London	200	0.0008
Places	41,900 London	1000	0.002	21,000 London	200	0.0009

Table 4.6: Highest presence of tourist categories for European non-capitals in Google, Yahoo, Microsoft and Ask

Other tourist destinations	GOOGLE			YAHOO		
	Total indexed (000)	Results presented	Visibility ratio (%)	Total indexed (000)	Results presented	Visibility ratio (%)
Accommodation	95,9 Benidorm	375	0,391	1,410 Gothenburg	1000	0,071
Activities	367 Benidorm	406	0,111	22,700 Venice	1000	0.004
Areas	363 Bruges	514	0,141	1,620 Bruges	1000	0,062
Attractions	50,4 Benidorm	339	0,673	1,650 Gothenburg	1000	0,061
Events	399 Geneva	518	0,130	1,880 Benidorm	1000	0,053
Information	421 Glasgow	518	0,123	8,290 Benidorm	1000	0,012
Restaurants	505 Bristol	534	0,106	3,390 Gothenburg	1000	0,029
Shopping	347 Granada	509	0,147	4,410 Antwerp	1000	0,023
Places	439 Benidorm	400	0,091	1,880 Benidorm	1000	0,053

Other tourist destinations	MICROSOFT			ASK		
	Total indexed (,000)	Results presented	Visibility ratio (%)	Total Indexed (,000)	Results presented	Visibility Ratio (%)
Accommodation	212 Gothenburg	1000	0,472	49,8 Bruges	200	0,402
Activities	344 Benidorm	1000	0,291	49,7 Benidorm	200	0,402
Areas	775 Benidorm	1000	0,129	542,3 Lyon	200	0.037
Attractions	153 Benidorm	1000	0,653	25,5 Gothenburg	200	0,784
Events	386 Benidorm	1000	0,259	39,2 Benidorm	200	0,510
Information	939 Benidorm	1000	0,106	154 Benidorm	200	0,130
Restaurants	426 Gothenburg	1000	0,235	91,3 Gothenburg	200	0,219
Shopping	253 Benidorm	1000	0,395	69,1 Benidorm	200	0,289
Places	544 Benidorm	1000	0,184	58,4 Benidorm	200	0,342

Table 4.7: Lowest presence of tourist categories for European non-capitals in Google, Yahoo, Microsoft and Ask

Other tourist destinations	GOOGLE			YAHOO		
	Total indexed (000)	Results presented	Visibility ratio (%)	Total indexed (000)	Results presented	Visibility ratio (%)
Accommodation	34,000 St.Petersburg	587	0.002	84,600 Nice	1000	0.001
Activities	21,300 Manchester	397	0.002	133,000 Nice	1000	0.0007
Areas	23,300 Oxford	508	0.002	165,000 Nice	1000	0.0006
Attractions	2,070 Bristol	425	0.020	101,000 Nice	1000	0.0010
Events	108,000 Nice	594	0.0005	527,000 Nice	1000	0.0002
Information	295,000 Nice	643	0.0002	891,000 Nice	1000	0.0001
Restaurants	8,580 St Petersburg	420	0.005	244,000 Nice	1000	0.0004
Shopping	9,240 St Petersburg	412	0.004	648,000 Nice	1000	0.0001
Places	40,700 St Petersburg	638	0.001	290,000 Nice	1000	0.0003

Other tourist destinations	MICROSOFT			ASK		
	Total indexed (000)	Results presented	Visibility ratio (%)	Total Indexed (000)	Results presented	Visibility Ratio (%)
Accommodation	8,350 Nice	1000	0.012	4,910 St petersburg	200	0.004
Activities	33,300 Nice	1000	0.003	5,309 Nice	200	0.004
Areas	46,100 Nice	1000	0.002	7,949 Nice	200	0.002
Attractions	5,790 Nice	1000	0.017	2,812 Nice	200	0.007
Events	130,000 Nice	1000	0.0008	13,200 Nice	200	0.001
Information	4,850 Antwerp	1000	0.021	22,200 Nice	200	0.0009
Restaurants	17,900 Nice	1000	0.005	10,500 Nice	200	0.002
Shopping	74,100 Nice	1000	0.001	10,880 Nice	200	0.002
Places	52,100 Nice	1000	0.002	13,810 Nice	200	0.001

ratio in each search engine. London is the city with the lowest presence of tourist categories, followed by other important European capitals like Paris, Madrid and Dublin. In contrast to Table 4.4, the capitals with lowest tourist presence in online search engines are those with the highest number of indexed websites. It is also relevant that the capitals with lowest presence in search engines are exactly those that receive the greatest number of visitors. In this case, Yahoo, Microsoft and Ask coincide that the capital with lowest presence of tourist categories is London. Contrarily, Google provides more options when considering the capital with lowest tourist presence.

Tables 4.6 and 4.7 deal with the results of the presence of tourist categories in non-capital cities. On the one hand, Table 4.6 shows that tourist destinations with the lowest presence of tourist categories are cities like Benidorm, Gothenburg and Bruges. As it happened with capital cities, the destinations for which the search engines had found the smallest number of websites have the highest visibility ratio. Considering the results from the four search engines, it is also relevant that there are no significant differences in the destinations with the highest presence of tourism.

On the other hand, Table 4.7 shows that the lowest presence of tourist categories corresponds to Nice, particularly if we consider the results obtained in Yahoo, Microsoft and Ask. In the Google search engine, however, Saint Petersburg is the destination with lowest presence of tourist categories (see Table 4.7). Following the established pattern, the destinations with the biggest number of indexed websites corresponds to the lowest visibility ratio.

A careful observation of results shows that the number of indexed websites varies for each tourist category and for each search engine. Yahoo is the engine that retrieves more websites independently of destination or tourist category. In contrast, Google and Ask are the engines indexing less websites. If we consider the total number of indexed websites in relation to tourist category, it is significant that 'information,' 'events' and 'places' yield the greatest number of indexed websites, although there are relevant variations for each destination and search engine.

Conclusions

The main objective of this study was to analyse the presence or representation of tourism and of tourist categories in 50 European tourist destinations using four Internet search engines: Google, Yahoo, Microsoft and Ask. With this aim, this research has used previous theoretical studies dealing with similar research topics. The results obtain here allow us to reach several conclusions and recommendations that may be useful for tourist and destination organizations.

The quantity of online information available is growing steeply because hundreds of websites are added or updated every day, including websites with tourist content. It is therefore necessary to design tools for quicker and more effective information search, as well as strategies for better indexing capacity, improved information organization and useful (relevant and updated) information discrimination in all search fields, including tourism. Keywords are essential in making information search more precise. It is significant that some tourist categories yield higher numbers of indexed websites than others. 'Information,' 'events' and 'places,' for instance, have retrieved more websites in this study.

When specific keywords are used for online search, the search engines retrieve hundreds of websites containing them; however, only the most relevant and better designed websites, according to the search engine criteria, will be visible in the engine. It is therefore logical to assume that good-quality website design improves visibility. And visibility is the key to success for tourist companies, as the Internet has shown since it was created. The results obtained in this study indicate that, although search engines index a huge number of websites with tourist content, the actual visibility and accessibility of websites created by tourist organizations related to the different destinations is quite low. The low visibility of tourist websites in search engines reveals that there are few opportunities for actual interaction between online tourists and tourist businesses. Furthermore, there are no significant differences between destinations that are country capitals and those that are not.

The analysis of the possible differences between search engines was also a significant aim of this research. From the results obtained here, we can conclude that there are no important differences between Google, Microsoft and Ask. However, Yahoo retrieved a significantly higher number of indexed websites, as a consequence of which it provides lower visibility ratios.

There are however some limitations, both conceptual and methodological, to this research. From the theoretical point of view, other keywords could have been used to search for the presence of tourism in online search engines. From a methodological perspective, the sample and the nature of destinations could have been different. This study has considered only 50 European destinations, and it has focused on the tourist sector exclusively. Expanding the range of this study to other sectors and to the international (not entirely European) context could have provided a more comprehensive view of the online presence of tourism and of tourist organizations globally. Research design may also have a limiting effect, because the study does not consider the evolution of the number of indexed websites. We propose a dynamic study to provide information about the chronological evolution of the data used here.

This study has significant implications and offers important recommendations for tourist organizations in the field of new technological advances applied to the tourist industry and of new marketing strategies for tourist destinations.

Tourist organizations should make sure they are present in a significant number of search engines, because a high percentage of tourists use search engines and websites to make their buying decision. Potential tourists search for information mainly through online search engines. Tourist businesses should therefore design strategies to make sure that users will visualize their services in the search engine. In this sense, a new marketing discipline has recently developed: Search Engine Marketing (SEM). It can be defined as the set of marketing methods that will increase website visibility in online search engines. The success of SEM depends, among other things, on the keyword the user enters in the search engine. Some measures can be taken to facilitate information search by the search engine and to increase website visibility for the potential tourist that expects to solve his or her travel needs.

Organizations may use three main methods to improve website visibility: search engine optimization, advertising in the search engine, or payment for indexation. On the one hand, search engine optimization implies using methods that improve website classification when the user enters keywords in the search engine. This means an effective website structure and adequate website content as well as a variety of hyperlinks to other websites. On the other, search engine advertising refers to acquisition of key visualization positions in the search engines (although not necessary indexation). Finally, payment for indexation implies that the tourist website will be included in the group of websites indexed by the search engine. The first of these three methods in generally considered to be the most effective, for research literature has demonstrated that search engines pay less attention to commercial content than to main lists. Besides, payment does not guarantee better classification.

Results also suggest important limitations in search engine technology, because search engines are unable to facilitate access to a great number of tourist businesses and organizations. The development of new tools to improve marketing objective fulfilment and destination promotion by organizations is necessary (Kim and Fesenmaier, 2008; Wang and Fesenmaier, 2006). In this sense, some systems developed to recommend destinations have become increasingly popular in the tourist sector, because they make suggestions to travellers without specifically asking what they want (Fesenmaier et al., 2006; Gretzel et al., 2004, 2006; Gretzel and Fesenmaier, 2006). Besides, new techniques like Geo-tagging, Web 2.0 and Hotmap will allow better information retrieval, organization and presentation by search engines, therefore improving tourist services.

Finally, further research could focus on a content analysis of the destination websites in order to decide which web design is more efficient. There are three basic dimensions in website design: interactivity and communication, usability (netsurfing simplicity) inside the website and its content. In this line, an efficient web design provides a fluent interaction and communication with their target audiences. In addition, it would be necessary to include other languages to obtain a more rigorous analysis.

In this sense, future investigations could explore qualitative elements in order to obtain which elements differentiate a destination from other tourist destinations. Lastly, it would be advisable to identify which entities have access to destination names, analysing in each search engine and each one word introduced.

References

Beldona S. 2005. Cohort analysis of online travel information search behaviour. *Journal of Travel Research* **44** (2): 135-142.

Bremmer C. 2007. Top 150 city destinations: London leads the way. Euromonitor International. Available at: http://www.euromonitor.com/Top_150_City_Destinations _London _Leads_the_Way.

Buhalis D. 2000. Marketing the competitive destination of the future. *Tourism Management* **21** (1): 97-116.

Buhalis D. 2003. *E-tourism: Information Technology for Strategic Tourism Management*. Prentice Hall: Englewood Cliffs, NJ.

Burns E. 2006. Web design key for online shoppers. Available at: www.clickz,com/stats/ sectors/demographics/print.php/3587781.

DeVellis R. 1991. *Scale Development: Theory and Applications*. Sage: Newbury Park, CA.

Farrell B, Twining-Ward L. 2004. Reconceptualizing tourism. *Annals of Tourism Research* **31** (2): 274-295.

Feng R, Morrison A, Ismail J. 2003. East versus west: a comparison of online destination marketing in China and the USA. *Journal of Vacation Marketing* **10** (1): 43-56.

Fesenmaier D, Wöber K, Werthner H. 2006. Introduction: recommendation systems in tourism. In *Destination Recommendation Systems: Behavioural Foundations and Ap-*

plications, D. Fesenmaier D, Wöber K, Werthner H (eds). CABI: Wallingford..

Fogg B. 1999. Persuasive technologies. *Communications of the ACM* **42** (5): 27-29.

Fogg B. 2003. *Persuasive Technology: Using Computers to Change What We Think and Do*. Morgan Kaufmann Publishers: San Francisco.

Goodman J. 2000. Strategies for driving traffic to your site. *Interactive Marketing* **2** (2):138-147.

Gretzel U. 2004. Consumer responses to preference elicitation processes in destination recommendation systems. Doctoral dissertation: University of Illinois, Urbana-Champaign.

Gretzel U, Fesenmaier D. 2006/07. Persuasion in recommender systems. *International Journal of e-Commerce* **11** (2): 81-100.

Gretzel U, Yuan Y, Fesenmaier D. 2000. Preparing for the new economy: advertising strategies and change in destination marketing organizations. *Journal of Travel Research* **39** (2):146-156.

Gretzel U, Mitsche Hwang Y, Fesenmaier D. 2004. Tell me who you are and I will tell you where to go: use of travel personalities in destination recommendation systems. *Information Technology and Tourism*. **7** (1): 3-12.

Gretzel U, Mitsche Hwang Y, Fesenmaier D. 2006. A behavioural framework for destination recommendation systems design. In *Destination Recommendation Systems: Behavioural Foundations and Applications*, Fesenmaier D, Wöber K, Werthner H (eds). CABI: Wallingford.

Henzinger M. 2007. Search technologies for the Internet. *Science* **317** (5837): 468-471.

Hoffman D, Novak P. 1996. Marketing in hypermedia computer-mediated environments: Conceptual foundations. *Journal of Marketing* **60**: 50-68.

Hwang Y, Gretzel U, Xiang Z, Fesenmaier D. 2006. Information search of travel decisions. In Destination *Recommendation Systems: Behavioural Foundations and Applications*, D. Fesenmaier D, Werthner H, Wöber K (eds). CABI: Wallingford; 3-16.

Jeng J, Fesenmaier D. 2002. Conceptualizing the travel decision-making hierarchy: A review of recent developments. *Tourism Analysis* **7** (1)15-32.

Kim H, Fesenmaier D. 2008. Persuasive design of destination websites: an analysis of first impression. *Journal of Travel Research* **47** (1): 3-13.

Kim H, Fesenmaier D. 2007. Persuasive design of tourism websites in the United States. Proceedings of the Annual Conference of the Travel and Tourism Research Association. Travel and Tourism Research Association, Ljubljana, Slovenia, July.

Levene M. 2006. *An Introduction to Search Engines and Web Navigation*. Addison-Wesley: Reading, MA.

Lewandowski D. 2008. The retrieval effectiveness of web search engines: considering results descriptions. *Journal of Documentation* **64** (6): 915-937.

McKercher B. 1999. A chaos approach to tourism. *Tourism Management* **20** (4): 425-434.

Mill R, Morrison A. 2002. *The Tourism System: An Introductory Text*. Prentice Hall: Englewood Cliffs, NJ.

Murphy P, Long J, Hollerana T, Esterly E. 2003. Persuasion online or on paper: a new take on an old issue. *Learning and Instruction* **13** (5): 511-532.

Nielsen J. 2000. *Designing Web Usability: The Practice of Simplicity*. New Riders: Indianapolis, IN.

Nielsen J. 2004. When search engines become answer engines. Available at: http:/www. useit.com/alertbox/20040816.html.

Nielsen M, Murnion P, Mather L. 2000. Destination marketing: Market segmentation and targeting in a competitive environment. In *Tourism Destination Marketing-Gaining the Competitive Edge*, Flanagan S, Ruddy J (eds). Tourism Research Centre, Dublin Institute of Technology: Dublin; 75-86.

Palmer A, McCole P. 2000. The role of electronic commerce in creating virtual tourism destination marketing organizations. *International Journal of Contemporary Hospitality Management* **12** (3): 198-204.

Pan B, Fesenmaier D. 2006. Online information search. Vacation planning process. *Annals of Tourism Research* **33** (3): 809-832.

Pan B, Hembrooke H, Joachims T, Lorigo L, Gay G, Granka L. 2007. In Google we trust: Users' decisions on rank, position and relevancy. *Journal of Computer-Mediated Communication* **12** (3): 801-823.

Paskaleva-Shapira K. 2007. New paradigms in city tourism management: redefining destination promotion. *Journal of Travel Research* **46** (1): 108-114.

Pearce P. 2005. Tourist behaviour: themes and conceptual schemes. In *Aspects of Tourism*, Cooper C, Hall C, Timothy D (eds). Channel View Publications: Clevedon.

Sautter E, Leisen B. 1999. Managing stakeholders: A tourism planning model. *Annals of Tourism Research* **26** (2): 312-328.

Sigala M. 2004. Reviewing the profile and behaviour of Internet users: Research directions and opportunities in tourism and hospitality. *Journal of Travel and Tourism Research* **17** (2/3): 93-102.

Smith S. 1988. Defining tourism. A supply-side view. *Annals of Tourism Research* **15** (2): 179-190.

So S, Morrison A. 2003. Destination marketing organizations´ web site users and non-users: A comparison of actual visits and revisit intentions. *Information Technology and Tourism* **6** (2): 129-139.

Spink A, Jasen B. 2004. *Web Search: Public Searching of the Web*. Kluwer: New York.

Sullivan D. 2007. Major search engines and directories. Search Engine Watch. Available at: http://searchenginewatch.com/showPage. html?page = 2156221.

Wang Y, Fesenmaier D. 2006. Identifying the success of web-based marketing strategy: An investigation of convention and visitors bureaus in the United States. *Journal of Travel Research* **44** (3):239-249.

Widyantoro D, Yen J. 2002. A fuzzy ontology-based abstract search engine and its user studies. Proceedings of the International Conference on Fuzzy Systems, Melbourne, Australia, December.

Wöber, K. 2006. Domain specific search engines. In *Destination Recommendation Systems: Behavioral Foundations and Applications*, Fesenmaier D, Wöber K, Werthner H (eds). CABI: Wallingford.

Woodside A, Dubelaar C. 2002. A general theory of tourism consumption systems: A conceptual framework and an empirical exploration. *Journal of Travel Research* **41** (2): 120-132.

Xiang Z, Fesenmaier D. 2005. An analysis of two search engine interface metaphors for trip planning. *Information Technology and Tourism* 7 (2):103-117.

Xiang Z, Fesenmaier D. 2006. Assessing the initial step in the persuasion process: Meta tags on destination marketing websites. *Information Technology and Tourism* 8 (2): 91-104.

Xiang Z, Wöber K, Fesenmaier D. 2008. Representation of the online tourism domain in search engines. *Journal of Travel Research* 47 (2): 137-150.

Yu C, Meng W. 2003. Web search technology. In *The Internet Encyclopedia*, Bidgoli H (ed). John Wiley and Sons: Hoboken, NJ.

Zach F, Xiang Z, Fesenmaier D. 2007. An assessment of innovation in web marketing: Investigating American convention and visitors bureaus. Proceedings of the ENTER Conference, Ljubljana, Slovenia, December.

5 Rejuvenating Touristic Consumption:
From a Cognitive Approach to a Symbolic Intent of Modelisation

Vivien R. Moinat, Faculty of Business and Economics, University of Lausanne;
Pablo L. de Diesbach, Lausanne Hospitality Research Lab, Ecole Hôtelière de Lausanne

Introduction

How can one explain that the number of visitors at Antarctica has more than doubled in less than 10 years and today reaches 34,000 per year? How can one explain that an online community on Facebook collects more than 7,600 people sharing their pictures and memories about Stonehenge and that the site in Wiltshire gathers more than 30,000[1] people each year for the summer solstice? How can one explain the success of touristic communities proposed by tour operators (monlookea.fr[2] or Nomadsphère[3])? What about the development of travel agencies specialized in gender travel (Femmes du Monde) or in scientific excursion (Escursia, Aventuresvolcans)? Finally how can one explain the behavior of tourists that are ready to cross the world to learn how to make a kite (Asia Tour Operator), collect data on an community of primates in Africa (Saïga) or to learn how to spin wool in Auvergne (Essorr)?

In other words, new forms of consumption have appeared such as eco-volunteering, scientific tourism, adventure tourism, spiritual or religious tourism, green or fair tourism, tourism for women, etc.. that are far removed from the traditional holidays at the beach or in the mountains. Explaining these forms or these practices with the existing models of consumption might be difficult. Therefore, a new theoretical framework is suggested based on contributions in general marketing. This chapter has to be considered only as a first step in identifying a new construct; it does not aim at trying to operationalize it, or at investigating to what extent observations support it. Further research is needed to address these aspects of this approach.

Model 1: The Cognitive Approach

This approach considers the tourist as an *homo oeconomicus*, as his or her decision making and purchase processes are posited as rational, based on a clear understanding of their needs, based on utility, at all stages of consumption. This has been the mainstream approach for research in tourism marketing from the start of research in this

---

1   http://news.bbc.co.uk/2/hi/uk_news/england/wiltshire/7465235.stm

2   Created by Look Voyages, this community gathers more than 10,000 members, allowing them to share pictures, videos and memories of their last holiday in a Look resort.

3   Created by Accor, for the segment of Nomads, this community gathers more than 43,000 members sharing tips for 300 towns around the world.

field and it is still widely used nowadays. In our modeling review we will observe that scholars constantly posit effects in a sequence of the following type:

Input (I) > Satisfaction with the destination (S) > Future behavioural intentions as output (F)

In most (but not all) cases, Input accounts for Destination Image. It is composed by the evaluation of its physical or objective attributes (hotel, food, shopping, security, accessibility, natural or historic attractions, information centres, etc.). The image (I) of the touristic product influences the satisfaction (S) of the consumer, which in turn helps to predict future behavioral intentions (F).

Figure 5.1: The cognitive approach

This sequence 'I – S – F' appears, among others, in the contributions of Reisinger and Turner (1999), Bigné et al. (2001), Woodside and Dubelaar (2002) and more recently in the work of Chen and Tsai (2007) or Chi Gengqing and Qu (2008). The classical sequence may also be slightly modified (Alampay, 2003), where the sequence appears to be : S – I – F (instead of I-S-F).

In all those articles the relationships between Image, Satisfaction and Future Intentions are usually, although not always strongly, supported. This general ISF sequence (Inputs–Satisfaction–Future Intentions) is a common milestone of the modelling by all those authors. It allows them to express their positing purchase and consumption as cognitive processes.

Model 2: The Emotional Approach

The second approach is called the emotional approach and arose in the 1980s when scholars realized that the previous approach did not account for a number of phenomena (drivers and benefits) in touristic consumption. What differentiates this field of research from the previous one is the fact that emotions[4] or affect are recognized to play a role during consumption and not only cognitive and rational choice. Consumption process is still very often represented by the aforementioned ISF sequence but what is new in this approach, is that the first step of the sequence, the Input (usually the Image), is now split-up into different components, one cognitive or rational and one affective or emotional, as illustrated on the Figure 5.2.

Hereafter follow several examples of this emotional approach: Baloglu and Uysal (1996) seem to be the precursors in such an avenue by integrating these non physical attributes, splitting up the first step of the sequence into *pull* and *push* factors of motivation. Later,

---

4   Emotion and affect are complex and controversial concepts. Definitions vary, sometimes even contradict each other. We will stick to the following definition of Midgley and Diesbach (2007) (2008) basically inspired from Bagozzi (1999): 'an emotion can be considered as a multidimensional construct describing an individual reaction, more or less conscious, to the perception of or exposition to a given situation, encapsulating several behavioural, physical, psychological components, the main dimensions of which are their content, intensity, polarity. They may generate physiological, attitudinal and behavioural reactions. Conversely they may be driven by physiological, attitudinal and behavioural reactions'.

Figure 5.2: The emotional approach

Yoon and Uysal (2005) integrated these *push* and *pull* factors into the above-mentioned sequence, using them to explain the satisfaction, which in turn explains again consumer intentions. Beerli and Martin (2004), and Lee et al. (2007) have also taken into account emotions as drivers of satisfaction. For Hong (2003) and Bigné et al. (2008), the subjective part is expressed by the notion of *pleasure* and *arousal* which both help to predict satisfaction. The latter itself predicts intentions of behavior such as loyalty or willingness to pay more. In some cases, the authors (Lin, 2006) have gone so far as simply eliminating the functional, physical or objective attributes and merely measuring satisfaction and loyalty by evaluating the emotional experience as perceived by the consumer. In conclusion, this second, called emotional, approach is well represented in tourism marketing. What is common to all those authors is the acknowledgment of emotions, feelings, etc. as potential drivers of satisfaction.

Model 3: The Symbolic Approach

The third approach might be called the symbolic approach. Symbols and symbolical consumption are most used but, in our opinion, often with a lack of conceptual definition, in an emerging literature since the 1980s. Originally, the concept came from the Greek word '*sumballein*' which means to throw together, to join, or to put in contact[5] or from '*sumbolon*' for an object cut into two pieces, which served as an identification sign when people joining them could then reassemble the two pieces in one (*Petit Robert de la Langue Française*). Both etymologies converge in that a symbol is always something that projects us towards something that is absent. That 'absent' is clearly understood by the message receiver, thanks to a common cultural background and set of references. If there is no such common background, the symbol is most likely to be non-understandable. That is and it is key: a symbolical communication differs in the extent to which it will be understood to varying extents, with varying levels of depths by receivers, precisely thanks to the depth of the common references and cultural backgrounds between the sender and the receiver. This can be clearly seen in, for example, the analysis of the meaning of a medieval miniature, a Renaissance political or religious painting, as well as a modern Peugeot TV ad (Diesbach, 2006).

We define 'symbol' as 'something that refers to, appeal to a concept or value or idea that makes sense for the subject (here, the consumer), thanks to a common cultural background and shared values with the message sender. Symbolic consumption refers to consumption patterns which values the symbolic dimension of an object' (from conceptualizations by Belk, 1988; Belk, 1989; Kotler and Levy, 1969; Levy, 1999).

The main argument of this chapter is to say that the approach of consumption has received renewed attention by marketers due to the influence of the symbolic and postmodern approach in general marketing, but that this approach has been poorly adapted in tourism marketing. There is therefore a gap in the tourism literature. However, based on what has been written in general marketing and on the embryonic development of

---

5   *Dictionnaire Historique de la Langue Française*

this approach in tourism, it is possible to develop an entirely new branch by using this new approach of consumption in tourism marketing. We define the symbolic approach as follows: some forms of consumption exist based on symbolic relationships. Namely, there are relationships, which generate symbolic value for (some) consumers. 'Symbolic/ expressive value is concerned with the extent to which customers attach or associate psychological meanings to a product. Some products (luxury goods, for example) appeal to consumer's self-concepts and self-worth – that is, they make us feel good about ourselves' (Brock Smith and Colgate, 2007). We suggest that there exist three relationships that are ways to create this symbolic value:

- *The relationship to the place* refers to the relationship one can have with the destination and its inherent attributes;

- *The relationship to the community* refers to the will of connecting oneself with the record of sharing valuable moments, thoughts, experiences, with some group of importance or reference;

  - *The relationship to practices* encapsulates not exactly the activities of a tourist but rather the way or the manner these activities are done. The focus is put not on what they consume but on how they consume it.

At the core of our theoretical framework is the consumer, who is posited to have a self that he or she can project or extend on something. This seminal notion of 'extended self' has been widely discussed among others by Belk (1988, 1989) and more recently by Mittal (2006) and Zukin and Maguire (2004). Consumers are what they consume and consume what they are (Belk, 1988). From their point of view, 'research on consumption should focus on both the production and reception of products, resulting in the production of consumers' (Zukin and Maguire 2004: 192) meaning that the way consumers consume, by forming and expressing their self, allows them to build an added value. We argue that these ways of producing value can be, for tourism, classified into three, namely by a particular relationship to the place, to the community or to the practices of consumption. Therefore from this starting point (the consumer), three dimensions are drawn (place, community, practices) as posited in Figure 5.3.

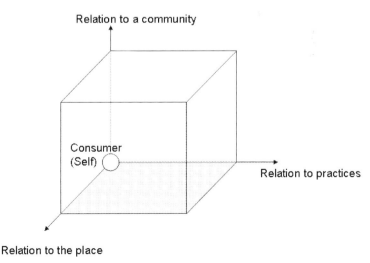

Figure 5.3: The symbolic approach

These dimensions measure the extent to which the consumer is related to the mentioned construct. By the projection or extension of self on these three dimensions, the consumer is able to create symbolic value during the consumption. We are going to present in the following section, how the value creation process can be conceptualized through these three dimensions, as presented in the above commented cube.

Relation to the Place

The first dimension, the relation to the place, is the one (among the three) that has received most attention in tourism marketing. It could be defined as the relation of self to the 'where' of the consumption, the location. What is important here is not what you consume but where you are consuming it. By associating his or her self with specific attributes of the destination/place, the consumer creates symbolic value. For example, newlyweds would decide to travel for their honeymoon to Venice because this place is strongly associated with romantic attributes. Pilgrims will decide to go to Lourdes, Mecca, or Jerusalem, as those destinations are associated with spiritual attributes. The destination choice makes sense for consumers because it allows the enhancement of the value of their touristic consumption, by projecting their self or identity on or associating it with the place. Therefore, we consider relationship to the place as a first symbolic way for consumer to create value. In tourism marketing, the concept of 'relation to the place' is not common. However, it has been often approached by similar concepts such as the 'place attachment'[6] (Gross and Brown, 2006, 2008; Hong, 2003; Moore and Graefe, 1994; Prohansky et al., 1983) and the concept of 'destination-self-congruity'[7] (Beerli et al., 2007; Kastenholz, 2004; Sirgy and Su, 2000) which is probably the one that better illustrates our first dimension.

In summary, the literature in marketing tourism has already acknowledged, through these concepts of 'place attachment' and 'destination-self-congruity', this first dimension, namely the relation to the destination, and its importance for modelling touristic consumption. This dimension is not totally new and has already been used to explain consumption. What is new is to explicitly recognize its importance for creating value for the touristic consumer. Therefore it can be used not only to describe traditional forms of consumption as has been done in the mentioned literature, but also in order to explain new forms of consumption – which is what we are looking at.

Relation to the Community

The second way we believe consumers symbolically create value during the consumption of touristic products can be conceptualized as the 'Relation to the community'. To the authors' knowledge, this dimension has rarely been discussed in tourism.

What defines this dimension is not the 'where' of consumption, but the 'with who' of the consumption. What becomes important is no longer the product but its linking value (Cova, 1997). In general marketing, Cova and Cova (2001) posit that in new forms of consumption, the added value for the consumer comes from the linking capabilities of the product: 'The goods and services which are valued are mainly those which, through their linking value, permit and support social interaction of the communal type' (Cova,

---

6   Formal definition is given by Bricker and Kerstetter (2000: 234): 'Through personal attachments to places, people acquire a sense of belonging and purpose that gives meaning to their lives'.

7   Defined as the degree of 'agreement between the self-concept of tourists and their mental representation of the proposed destinations'.

1997: 307). The topic has been also widely discussed with the works on brand communities (Schouten and McAlexander, 1995; Muniz Jr and O'Guinn, 2001; McAlexander et al., 2002; Cova and Pace, 2006), on tribes[8] (Cova, 2006; Maffesoli, 1988), 'neo-tribal constellation' (Cova and Carrère, 2002), or on 'sub-culture of consumption', defined as 'a distinctive subgroup that self-select on the basis of a shared commitment to a particular product, class, brand or consumption activity' (Schouten and McAlexander 1995: 43). The notion of community has been criticized by Wittel (2001), as it supposes stability, coherence, embeddedness, and belonging. Thus he prefers the notion of 'network sociality'. The authors are aware that 'community' might be an ambiguous term, as it supposes a strong link amongst consumers (which is not the case in tribes or subcultures). In case of tourism marketing, we believe that both notions (community or tribes/subculture) are relevant and this will have to be demonstrated in future publications. From now, we will use the term 'community' as a generic term, encapsulating all these different notions.

In tourism marketing, only a few examples of this concept can be found in the literature. For example, Cova and Cova (2001) shortly present the snowboarders tribe. However, in this case, the consumption form is more related with a sport community or with a brand community (Salomon) than with a real touristic product. Worth mentioning is the article by Pritchard et al. (2002) about Manchester's gay village. They investigate how belonging to a gendered community may have an impact on leisure. But once again, this article has not stated how a relationship with a community may create added value for tourist consumers. One possibly excellent case study would be the brand community set up by Look Voyages, called 'Monlookea'. In this online community, people gathered around a brand that is a touristic product. The form of the community is not directly dependent of the destination, because there are many communities, each of them for a different holidays' village. This online community allows their members to exchange their memories, pictures, video or tips of their last touristic experience they had in a Look Villages.

Relation to the Practices

The third dimension is the relationships between the self of the consumer and the practices of consumption. There exists in tourism marketing an important literature on what tourists consume or on what type they are.[9] However it is rarer to find contributions on how they consume. We suggest that practices or forms of consumption might also be a source of value creation. Therefore, our third and last dimension is the relationship between the self and the consumption practices. In general marketing, the first concept to approach practices of consumption is the one of rituals (McCracken, 1986; Schouten, 1991). The second way to approach those practices is the typology developed by Douglas Holt (1995), to classify to consumption practices and how they were related with the self of the consumer.

In tourism marketing, only a few contributions have made a first step towards acknowledging the importance of 'how' tourists consume. First, in his article describing his experiential trip to Tikidad, R. Ladwein (2002) highlights different touristic behaviors

---

8   For a review of these different new forms of consumption, (Sitz and Amine, 2004) or (Merle, 2004)

9   For example, several typologies have been made showing of what types tourists were 'City, Historical, Active, Alone, and Tour Groups' (Fairhurst et al., 2007), and the impact on the amount of time or money (for an example, see Rosenbaum and Spears, 2006) they spent during their stay.

in a defined space (around the pool). The focus on the behavior becomes central to understand the experiential consumption. The concept of rituals is used in order to illustrate the behavior in a spatialized way. Second, Bouchet et al. (2004) point out a change in the touristic behaviors in the context of winter sport. In order to explain it, they relate the behavior of some consumers with their fundamental expectations. In other words, they recognize the relationship with oneself and the way to consume. Last, during their immersion in the *hypermonde* of Las Vegas, Badot et al. (2006) also recognized the importance of studying the consumption practices, what they call 'les modes d'appropriation de l'expérience de consommation'.

Others authors have also approached specific themes such as hedonism (Arnould and Price, 1993), eroticism (Andrews et al., 2007), wilderness (Curtin, 2005), or lifestyle (Edensor, 2007) that might impact on the way consumers consume or even be consider as consumption practices. However, and even though they show high relevance, those themes have not been explicitly recognized yet as ways to create symbolic value, and it will be extremely valuable to clarify the conceptual link between such mentioned themes (eroticism, etc.) and the creation of symbolical value.

In conclusion, the novelty of the symbolic approach lies not in its three dimensions, but in their use as a basis to represent how symbolic value can be created for tourists during consumption.

Discussion

In this section, two points will be discussed, namely (1) the destination-specific set of values and (2) the complementarity of the three approaches.

Value sets

(1) We propose to characterize each new touristic consumption form by a specific set of values, one for each dimension. We could evaluate each dimension on a percent scale (100% representing a form where the dimension is absolutely present; oppositely, 0% would mean that this dimension is not important at all during the consumption). To illustrate the point above, the example of Ibiza and its well known night-clubbing opportunities will be used. This theme has made this location an important tourism destination. A young European man will choose to travel there, because the place is known to be one the best one in Europe to partying, dancing and having some fun. The following specific set of values (90%, 70%, 60%) could be attributed to this destination:

◆   The relationship with the destination will be extremely important (let say 90%).

◆   The relationship with the community will be very important as well, because our young man is expecting to meet other boys and girls there who will share his pastime of dancing, partying and have fun (let's say 70%).

◆   The practices of consumption will be also important, as clubbers have usually a well defined way of behaving (even if it is implicit), such as doing an *after*, or sleeping all day long on the beach, etc. (let's say 60%).

In short, we suggest defining new forms of consumption by a set of values, expressing the extent to what each dimension is present. In fact, it is precisely in this combination capability that resides the strength of our model. It allows an infinite number of forms of consumption and for each one of them, a way to understand it. Forms of touristic consumption could be represented anyway in our 3D space, by its coordinates, not only on the edge of the cube but also inside it.

Complementarity

(2) To conclude with the general discussion, we want to emphasize the complementarity of the three approaches. As it has been shown and as it is recapitulated in Table 5.1, they do not answer the same research question, they do not consider the same drivers of consumption nor the same outputs. They even do not look at the same forms of tourism. In short, they do not share the same focus on consumption. Therefore, it is crucial to understand that these approaches do not have to be compared to each other. None of them has a bigger value or should be chosen at the end. We have not argued in this contribution that the two first approaches, the cognitive one and the emotional one, should be abandoned, as they are relevant to explain the majority of touristic consumption forms. We only suggest that the symbolic approach has not received enough attention until now in tourism marketing, and that adding this symbolic approach might deepen our understanding of consumption in tourism.

Conclusion

The authors are aware that the present contribution has several limitations. First of all, the aforementioned articles do not represent an exhaustive view of what has been written on tourism marketing. Some contributions may not be classifiable in our framework of three approaches. We are also conscious that the symbolic intent of modelization still remains very conceptual and that an important work of operationalization remains to be done. For instance, we yet cannot propose measurement scales adapted to the symbolic framework; scales for the three dimensions (relationships to the place, community and practices) have to be built and hypotheses have to be formulated. In short, this chapter is only a first theoretical step and empirical research is planned to confirm or disconfirm the validity of the proposed model.

The present chapter contributes to the marketing literature in two ways: first, it allows a better understanding of the current knowledge in tourism marketing. To the best of our knowledge, no contribution has ever proposed an integrative framework of tourism marketing research until now that allows understanding the different approaches, the focus of each, and why they are complementary. Second, by proposing an original theoretical framework for the symbolic consumption, it proposes a helpful platform to build future research in this field. The present contribution gives not only definitions or concepts that were missing in tourism marketing but moreover links them together in order to create an integrative framework. It allows a deeper understanding of how the customer and his or her self, place, community, practices and value creation are related to each other. We believe such framework and future measurement scales that we will develop, will be highly relevant in marketing cities or provinces towards potential inhabitants or companies, that is in city marketing and place branding. The resolution of this conceptual lack was necessary before any empirical research in tourism. Following the adage cited by Tournois (2004), we assume that 'if you can't define it you can measure it and if you can measure it you can't improve it'. Thus, this article has to be considered as a first necessary step before further empirical contributions, using symbolic consumption in tourism.

1. Does the proposed symbolic model fit well with touristic forms of consumption? What are the differences with the same concepts but used in general marketing? In other words, what are the specificities of tourism products and how do they influence the relevance and the internal validity of the model?

2. How to define new forms of touristic consumption (such as eco-volunteering, scientific tourism, adventure tourism, spiritual or religious tourism, green or fair tourism, gendered tourism) that the third approach is supposed to explain? What do they have in common? What part (10%, 20 % or more?) of the overall touristic consumption do they represent? And what is more important, what are their actual growth rate? In other words, what is concealed behind is the question of the external validity of the model.

3. Our three dimensions are expected to predict symbolic/expressive value which in turn should predict three key posited outcomes (willingness to pay, willingness to visit the destination, intention to recommend). This predictive validity assessment would be an excellent track for confirming the relevance of our constructs.

4. Consumers have multiple roles in life, they certainly have a multifaceted self (Belk, 1988) or multiple self (Solomon, 2007). In tourism, this instability of the self and its potential impact on symbolic value creation remain unclear. The authors are aware of such important issue and would recommend its investigation as another research avenue.

5. Finally, we have proposed to use this third symbolic approach in order to explain the success of new consumption forms. But what would be of great interest, is also to look at the failures of new forms consumption, which certainly exist but are not well known. Does the symbolic approach also give useful elements to understand those cases of failure?

It will be possible to answer to those questions and also to validate the interest and relevance of this third approach only by doing empirical research. Therefore, the authors are preparing themselves for this but also make a plea to anyone interested for further empirical work. It will be possible, only after having tested the model, to formulate direct practical implications. As a take-home message, we hope to have at least raised interest if not convinced readers, about the importance, for tourism marketing, of taking into account not only functional and emotional drivers, but also symbolic elements and creation of value.

References

Alampay RBA. 2003. Visitors to Guam: Modeling Satisfaction, Quality and Intention, dissertation, Michigan State University.

Badot O, Lemoine JF, Carrier C, Graillot L, Roux D, Corrion N, Lohr Y, Hazebroucq JM, Raugel I. 2006. De l'expérience en 'hyperréalité' à l'expérience en 'hypermonde': élucubrations suite à une Odyssée ethnomarketing et introspective à Las Vegas.

Bagozzi RP, Gospinath M. 1999. The role of emotions in marketing. *Journal of Academy of Marketing Science* **27** (2): 184-206.

Baloglu S, Uysal M. 1996. Market segments of push and pull motivations: a canonical correlation approach. *International Journal of Contemporary Hospitality Management* **8** (3): 32-38.

Beerli A, Martin JD. 2004. Factors influencing destination image. *Annals of Tourism Research* **31** (3): 657-681.

Beerli A, Meneses GD, Gil SM. 2007. Self-congruity and destination choice. *Annals of Tourism Research* **34** (3): 571-587.

Belk RW. 1988. Possession and the extended self. *Journal of Consumer Research* **15** (September): 139-168.

Belk RW. 1989. Extended self and extending paradigmatic perspective. *Journal of Consumer Research* **16** (1): 129-133.

Bigne EJ, Mattila A.S, Andreu L. 2008. The impact of experiential consumption cognitions and emotions on behavioural intentions. *Journal of Services Marketing* **22** (4): 303-315.

Bigne EJ, Sanchez IM, Sanchez J. 2001. Tourism image, evaluation variables and after purchase behaviour: inter-relationship. *Tourism Management* **22** (6): 607-616.

Bouchet P, Lebrun AM, Auvergne S. 2004. Sport tourism consumer experiences: A comprehensive model. *Journal of Sport Tourism* **9** (2): 127-140.

Bricker KS, Kerstetter DL. 2000. Level of specialization and place attachment: An exploratory study of whitewater recreationists. *Leisure Sciences* **22**: 233-257.

Brock Smith J, Colgate M. 2007. Customer value creation: a practical framework. *Journal of Marketing Theory and Practice* **15** (1): 7-23.

Chen CF, Tsai D. 2007. How do destination image and evaluative factors affect behavioral intentions? *Tourism Management* **28**: 1115-1122.

Chi Gengqing C, Qu H. 2008. Examining the structural relationships of destination image, tourist satisfaction and destination loyalty: An integrated approach. *Tourism Management* **29**: 624-636.

Cova B. 1997. Community and consumption. *European Journal of Marketing* **31**(3/4): 297-316.

Cova B, Cova V. 2001. Tribal aspects of postmodern consumption research: The case of French in-line roller skates. *Journal of Consumer Behavior* **1** (1): 67-76.

Cova B, Pace S. 2006. Brand community of convenience products: new forms of customer empowerment – the case 'my Nutella The Community'. *European Journal of Marketing* **40** (9/10): 1087-1105.

Diesbach P, Midgley D. 2007. Embodied virtual agents: An affective and attitudinal approach of the effects on man–machine stickiness. In *A Product/Service Discovery Engineering Psychology and Cognitive Ergonomics*. Springer: Berlin.

Diesbach P, Midgley D. 2008. *Embodied Agents on Commercial Websites: Modeling Their Effects through an Affective Persuasion Route Persuasive Technology*. Springer. Berlin.

Gross MJ, Brown G. 2006. Tourism experiences in a lifestyle destination setting: The roles of involvement and place attachment. *Journal of Business Research* **59** (6): 696-700.

Gross MJ, Brown G. 2008. An empirical structural model of tourists and places: Progressing involvement and place attachment into tourism. *Tourism Management* **29** (6) : 1141-1151

Holt DB. 1995. How consumers consume: A typology of consumption practices. *Journal of Consumer Research* **22**: 1-16.

Hong KW. 2003. The Role of Involvement in an Integrated Satisfaction Model: The Case of Special Event Tourism, Pennsylvania State University.

Kastenholz E. 2004. Assessment and role of destination-self-congruity. *Annals of Tourism Research* **31**(3): 719-723.

Kotler P, Levy S. 1969. Broadening the concept of marketing. *Journal of Marketing* **33**. 10-15

Ladwein R. 2002. Voyage à Tikidad: De l'accès à l'expérience de consommation. *Décisions Marketing* **28**: 53-63.

Levy S. 1999. *Brands, Consumers, Symbols and Research*. Sage: New York.

Lin KM. 2006. An examination of the relationship between experiential marketing strategy and guests' leisure behavior in Taiwan Hot-spings Hotel. Daphne, United States Sports Academy.

Maffesoli M. 1988. *Le temps de tribus: déclin de l'individualisme dans les sociétés postmodernes*. Méridiens: Klincksieck.

McAlexander JH, Schouten JW, Koenig HF. 2002. Building brand community. *Journal of Marketing* **66** (January): 38-54.

McCracken G. 1986. Culture and Consumption: A theoretical account of the structure and movement of the cultural meaning of consumer goods. *Journal of Consumer Research* **13** (June): 71-84.

Mittal B. 2006. I, me, and mine – how products become consumers' extended selves. *Journal of Consumer Behavior* **5**: 550-562.

Moore RL, Graefe AR. 1994. Attachments to recreation settings: The case of rail-trail users. *Leisure Sciences* **16**: 17-31.

Muniz Jr AM, O'Guinn TC. 2001. Brand community. *Journal of Consumer Research* **27** (4): 412-432.

Pritchard A, Morgan N, Sedgley D. 2002. In search of lesbian space? The experience of Manchester's gay village. *Leisure Studies* **21** (105-123).

Prohansky HM, Fabian AK, Kaminoff R. 1983. Place-identity: Physical world socialization of the self. *Journal of Environmental Psychology* **3**: 57-83.

Reisinger Y, Turner L. 1999. Structural equation modeling with Lisrel: application in tourism. *Tourism Management* **20**(1): 74-88.

Schouten JW. 1991. Selves in Transition: Symbolic consumption in personal rites of passage and identity reconstruction. *Journal of Consumer Research* **17**: 412-425.

Schouten JW, McAlexander JH. 1995. Subcultures of consumption: an ethnography of the new bikers. *Journal of Consumer Research* **22**: 43-61.

Sirgy M, Su H. 2000. Destination image, self-congruity and travel behavior: Toward an integrated model. *Journal of Travel Research* **38**: 340-352.

Solomon M, Bamossy G, Askegaard S. 2007. *Consumer Behavior* 2nd edn.. Financial Times: Prentice Hall.

Wittel A. 2001. Towards a network sociality. *Theory Culture Society*. **18** (6) : 51-76

Woodside A, Dubelaar C. 2002. A general theory of tourism consumption systems: A conceptual framework and an empirical exploration. *Journal of Travel Research* **41** (2): 120-132.

Yoon Y, Uysal M. 2005. An examination of the effects of motivation and satisfaction on destination loyalty: a structural model. *Tourism Management* **26**: 45-56.

Zukin S, Maguire J.S. 2004. Consumers and consumption. *Annual Review of Sociology* **30**: 173-197.

	Classical Approach	Emotional Approach	Symbolic Approach
General Paradigm	Homo oeconomicus Consumption = process of value destruction in order to satisfy a need	Homo ludens Consumption = process of value creation through the stimulation of senses, emotions, feelings	Homo faber Consumption = experience of value creation through the mobilization of symbolic components such as the projection/continuation of the self on a place, a community or on a particular way to consume
Focus	Consumer's behavior, process of consumption	Consumer's behavior, process of consumption	Cultures of consumption, practices of consumption
Key words	Functional, tangible, objective, physical benefits	Emotions, affect	Symbolic, relational
Inputs/Drivers	Physical attributes	Physical and emotional attributes	Relations to the place, relations to the community, relations to practices
Outputs	Satisfaction, attitude, future behavioral intentions (revisit, recommend)	Satisfaction, attitude, future behavioral intentions (revisit, recommend) and creation of emotional value	Creation of symbolic value
Objectives	Explain and predict in a rational and cognitive way, the drivers and outputs of consumption in tourism	Explain and predict in a rational, cognitive and emotional and subjective way, the drivers and outputs of consumption in tourism	Explain new forms or behaviors of consumption with the notion of value created by the consumption of symbolic elements (relations to the place, relations to the community, relations to practices)
Forms of touristic consumption explained	Traditional forms of touristic consumption such as familial holidays at the beach or in the mountains	Traditional forms of touristic consumption such as familial holidays at the beach or in the mountains	New forms of touristic consumption such as eco-volunteering, scientific tourism, adventure tourism, spiritual or religious tourism, green or fair tourism, gendered tourism
References in tourism marketing	Reisinger and Turner (1999); Bigné et al. (2001); Chen and Tsai (2007); Chi Gengqing and Qu (2008; Alampay (2003); Yoon and Uysal (2005); Matzler et al. (2006); Silvestre and Santos (2008); Kaplanidou and Vogt (2006); Woodside and Dubelaar (2002)	Baloglu and Uysal (1996); Yoon and Uysal (2005); Beerli and Martin (2004); Bigné et al. (2008); Hong (2003); Lin (2006); Lee (2007)	Fyall (2003); Bricker and Kerstetter (2000); Gross and Brown (2006,2008); Hosany et al. (1996); Sirgu and Su (2000); Kastenholz (2004); Beerli, Meneses, Gil (2007); Andrieu et al. (2004); Ladwein (2002); Bouchet et al. (2004); Badot (2006); Pritchard et al. (2002)

Table 5.1: Comparison of the three approaches to understanding touristic consumption

6 The Role of Emotions in Consumer Decision Making for Budget City Breaks

Diana Ene, Nottingham University; **Peter Schofield**, University of Salford

Introduction

In the quest to better understand consumer decision making (CDM), a number of models featuring motivation, supply, demand, value, price, quality, cues, information and emotions have been developed (Andreason, 1965; Engel et al., 1986; Howard-Sheth, 1969; Solomon, 1996). Applications in a tourism context (Cooper et al., 1998; *inter alia* Gilbert, 1991; Middleton and Clark, 2001) have attempted to provide a general framework which has tended to assume a vacation scenario and its attendant criteria such as high levels of risk and insecurity, which may not be relevant in all tourism product markets such as short breaks. Moreover, many tourism models have arguably underplayed the complexity of tourist decisions with respect to consumer emotions and attitudes to products, having emphasized the cognitive dimension at the expense of affective aspects and their interrelationship in consumer decisions.

The short break market has been neglected from the perspective of CDM research despite its economic importance for many destinations. It is generally assumed that short break decision making is characterized by lower risk, lower involvement and a more limited information search than decisions relating to vacations, but there is no empirical evidence to support this view. Most studies of the short break phenomenon have focused on tourist motivations, behaviour patterns and destination characteristics (Bloy, 2000; Dune et al., 2006; Jang and Cai, 2002). This study responds to this challenge by examining CDM in the budget city break market and in acknowledgement of the complexity of the CDM process, the research takes an integrated approach to the problem by adapting and extending Hansen's (2005) conceptual CDM framework. This chapter, part of a larger study of CDM in a short break context, has three specific objectives.

1. To identify the significant dimensions of CDM in the budget city break context.

2. To analyse the role of emotions in budget city break decision making.

3. To determine the relative predictive ability of cognitive and affective dimensions in relation to consumer satisfaction with, and behavioural intention towards, budget city breaks.

Literature Review

A number of tourism CDM models, based on general frameworks presented in the consumer behaviour and marketing literature have been hitherto used to conceptualise tourist decision-making. Wahab et al.'s (1976) 'linear model of the tourism decision-making process' acknowledges the familiar sequence of cognitive stages in consumer decisions but arguably places insufficient emphasis on the influence of variables such as price or quality. Schmoll's (1977) model of the travel decision process includes both internal and external variables but excludes a feed-back loop and there is no input to attitude and values (Cooper et al., 1998). By comparison, Mathieson and Wall's (1982) model of the travel buying behaviour features the general stages within the decision making process, the key variables at each stage and the importance of destination image together with the influence of 'trip features' such as party size. Some of the weaknesses of these models were addressed by Gilbert's (1991) CDM framework by examining further the interaction between the influencing variables. Middleton and Clark's (2001) 'stimulus-response' model also addresses the complexity of CDM by examining internal and external influences on consumer behaviour within an input–output structure.

In comparison to staged CDM frameworks, Hansen's (2005) hybrid model, which has hitherto not been applied to tourism, incorporates value, cue utilization, information search and emotional perspectives on CDM. It features linkages between five key constructs: price, quality, involvement, emotions and attitude (derived from these different perspectives), which are investigated in relation to 'purchase intention' (Figure 6.1). Hansen's (2005) framework was developed from his study of Danish students' consumption of consumer goods.

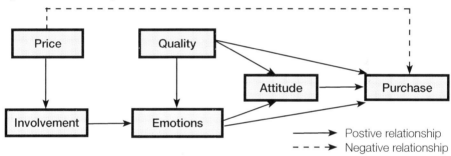

Figure 6.1: Hansen's (2005) Integrated CDM Framework.

The value, cue utilization, information search and emotional perspectives featured in the model are all derived from the pertinent literature. Zeithaml (1988) among others argue that consumers are value driven, that is, decisions are made on the basis of the perceived utility of a product. Value has been conceptualized as low price, particular features that the consumer is looking for, quality that matches a certain price and an expression of consumer monetary sacrifice (Chang and Wildt, 1994; Dodds, 1995; Hansen, 2001; Jacoby and Olson, 1977; Zeithaml, 1988). Involvement is therefore seen as being a critical variable in consumer decisions (Blackwell et al., 2006; Celsi and Olson, 1988) in that the consumer's level of involvement will influence the likelihood of searching and processing information, evaluating product attributes and the decision heuristic employed.

According to cue utilization theory (Richardson et al., 1994; Steenkamp, 1989), consumers may use one or more indicators of the quality or performance of a product, such as price or brand, to reduce the risk from not knowing the quality of a product. Among all the available cues, the buyer is tempted to use the cues that hold a high predictive value and confidence value. When evaluating alternatives, the consumer often considers both intrinsic and extrinsic cues such as brand, store name, price, level of advertising, packaging and country of origin, in combination, to increase the reliability of an appropriate choice. Among all cues, price appears to guide the consumer's decision process when other cues are not available (Dodds, 1991; Hansen, 2005; Peterson and Jolibert, 1995; Richardson et al., 1994).

From the information processing perspective (Blackwell et al., 2006), consumers develop beliefs and attitudes through a cognitive process of ongoing interaction with environmental stimuli through a process of compensatory or non-compensatory decision-making. From this perspective, the consumer is facing a problem-solving situation and is employing their rational capacity reason to reach the best decision (Kassarjian, 1981). Emphasis is therefore placed on awareness, involvement and rules.

By comparison, the emotional perspective acknowledges the significant role of affect, in general, and emotions, in particular, in the decision making process (Bagozzi et al., 1999). Whilst few purchases are entirely emotional, emotions play a part in every purchase decision (MacKay, 1999). Both positive and negative emotions have been found to influence consumer behaviour (Han et al., 2007) not least because of their impact on information processing in relation to encoding and retrieval of information, use of different strategies to process information, evaluations and judgments, and creative thinking (Bagozzi et al., 1999). Various studies (Schwarz and Clore, 1983, 1988; Wyer and Carlston, 1979) demonstrated that emotions can be the basis of the evaluation process because feelings are sources of information to the consumer (Frijda 1986; Schwarz, 1990). Recent research in this area has shown that cognition and affect are used simultaneously in the so-called 'metacognition' process in which consumers use 'affect-as-information' when they consider that their emotions offer important information for the evaluation of alternatives (Avnet and Pham, 2005).

Involvement is concerned with the consumer's level of interest, emotional dedication and time allocated to the searching of a product or service. It is also related to the processes of attention and comprehension (Celsi and Olson, 1988). This means that the degree of involvement influences directly the breadth and/or depth of the decision making process. A high involved consumer would spend more time looking, evaluating and using the relevant information, using compensatory or phased models of decision making. On the other hand, a low involved consumer's information processing would be superficial, the decision being the result of non-compensatory models using conjunctive, disjunctive, elimination by aspect and lexicographic rules and frequency heuristics (Mowen and Minor, 2001).

Quality has been conceptualized from a number of different perspectives (Dodds, 1995; Hansen, 2001; Peterson and Jolibert, 1995). Steenkamp (1990: 312) links perceived quality to emotions in describing it as 'any evaluative judgment such as favorable disposition, liking, or affect'. His 'quality perception process' outlines its complexity and the need to consider a number of variables including intrinsic and extrinsic quality cues, experience quality and credence quality measures. Similarly, the literature outlines various notions of price as an indicator of quality including objective price, perceived non-monetary price, fair price and reference price (Bolton et al., 2003; Chang and Wildt, 1994; Winer, 1986).

In the price–quality–value relationship, price is considered to be a key variable (Monroe and Chapman, 1987; Zeithaml, 1988). According to Jacoby and Olson (1977), consumers first form a perception of price, which ultimately contributes to the formation of perceived quality. Reference price is used as a signal which helps the consumer understand a 'product's perceptive value' (Lin et al., 2006: 240) in a situation of 'information asymmetry' (Kirmani and Rao, 2000). Price should also be examined in relation to a consumer's income. The link between price and perceived value is described by the value for money concept, which indicates that both consumers and providers interrelate the benefits of a product/service to its price (Huber et al., 2001).

The concept of attitude has been variously defined, for example as evaluative judgment or as an affective evaluation created by the cognitive system (Bagozzi et al., 1999). The complexity of attitude at the conceptual level is also related to the relationship between attitude, objects and behaviour, that is, consumers can have attitudes towards physical and social objects and/or towards their own behaviour or actions (Peter and Olson, 2008: 132). The latter relates to buyer's future behavioural intentions expressed as willingness to recommend and repurchase or revisit in the case of tourism products.

The various perspectives differ with respect to risk reduction strategies, the degree of cognitive and affective activity and the degree of trade-offs and evaluations and it is possible that consumers use two or more decision-making strategies simultaneously (Bettman et al., 1998; Hansen, 2005). Consequently, CDM models should incorporate multiple perspectives and recognize the interaction between perceived value, involvement, cognitive and affective dimensions, and both attitudinal and behavioural outcomes. Hansen's (2005) framework was therefore used to model CDM in the budget short city break market because it integrates various perspectives on consumer decision making to accommodate consumers' employment of multiple modes of decision making. The original model has been extended by incorporating two new variables: 'repurchase' and recommendation', which adds a conative dimension to the extant cognitive and affective dimensions (Figure 6.2). Additionally, the original outcome variable, 'buying intention', has been replaced by 'actual purchase' to approximate the CDM process for budget short breaks more closely.

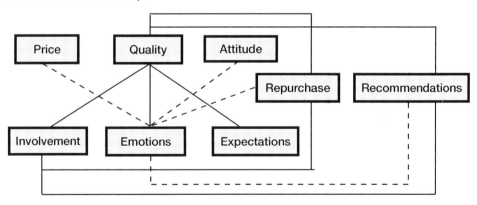

Figure 6.2: Integrated CDM Framework for short city breaks

METHODOLOGY

A mixed-method approach was used, consisting of front-end qualitative exploratory research, using semi-structured interviews, to explore the dimensions of short break CDM and refine the scales used in the e-questionnaire survey. The interviews confirmed both the validity of Hansen's framework in the short break context and that subjects could recall sufficient detail about their most recent short break to provide meaningful responses to questionnaire items.

A number of pre-validated scales were included in the questionnaire: Mittal's (1989) involvement scale; Izard's (1977) emotions scale; and Hansen's (2005) price, quality and attitude scales. The wording of certain scale items was adjusted from the original format on the basis of feedback from a protocol analysis and piloting of the instrument prior to the survey. Additional response sets were added to measure subjects' satisfaction with a recent short break in terms of 'how appealing/pleasing' it was together with a measure of their expectations. Behavioural intention was also measured in terms of the likelihood of recommending and revisiting the destination and similar destinations. Additional scale items also measured subjects' perceptions of their recent break's price and quality relative to previous breaks.

E-mails were then sent to 10,000 students and staff at the University of Salford inviting them to complete the survey; 155 useable questionnaires were obtained. The sample is considered to be relevant to the study because of its focus on budget breaks. It consists of 42.6% males, 36.1% in the 18-24 age group and 50.3% in the 25-34 group. UK residents made up 47.7% of the sample with 52.3% coming from overseas (18.7% from Europe). Of the respondents, 34% had a discretionary income below £200 a month with 15.6% in the over £500 category and 65.2% were single.

Results

The Dimensions of Short City Break Decision Making

An exploratory factor analysis using principal components (PCA) as the method of extraction was used to identify dimensions of consumer decisions for budget city breaks. Oblique rotation was used because small correlations were found between some of the extracted factors (Pedhazur and Schmelkin, 1991). The minimum coefficient for factor items to be included in the final scale was .40, as recommended by Stevens (1992) for the sample size. Thirty-five variables were removed prior to the final analysis because they had loadings of .4 or higher on two or more factors. The Kaiser–Meyer–Olkin (KMO) measure of sampling adequacy (.82) was 'meritorious' (Kaiser 1981) and Bartlett's tests of sphericity reached statistical significance (p <.001), supporting the factorability of the correlation matrix. All factors with eigenvalues greater than or equal to 1.0 were retained.

A five-factor solution explained 67.07% of the variance in the data before rotation. Factor 1 (α = .82) consists of three items relating to 'insecurity/anxiety" and accounts for 32.06% of the variance in the data. Factor 2 (α = .87) loads on five items which seem to indicate 'interest/enjoyment'; this accounts for 16.17% of the variance in the data. Factor 3 (α = .60) loads on two variables relating to 'quality' and accounts for 6.91% of the variance. Factor 4 (α = .51) loads on two items indicating a combination of price and involvement and was labelled as such; it explains 6.70% of the variance and is the least reliable dimension as indicated by its low alpha score. Its complexity compared with the other dimensions may reflect a link between value, conceptualized as low price (inter alia Jacoby and Olson, 1977; Zeithaml, 1988) and the importance of the decision. Factor 5 (α = .88) loads on five variables indicative of 'guilt'; it explains only 5.23% of the variance in the data. The results show that there are three emotion dimensions, one quality dimension and a composite dimension that combines price and involvement.

Independent samples t-tests and one-way analysis of variance (ANOVA) were employed to identify the influence of socio-economic variables (gender; marital status; income) on factor scores. A significant difference was found between subjects on the 'quality' dimension (Factor 3) on the basis of marital status (F= 4.23; p = .003; eta^2 = .1); engaged, married and divorced subjects registered significantly higher levels of agreement with the variables loading on this factor compared with single subjects. There was also a significant difference on the 'insecurity/anxiety' dimension (Factor 1) on the basis of subjects' income (F= 3.458; p = .010; eta^2 = .09); there were significantly higher levels of agreement with the insecurity/anxiety statements in the lower income groups compared with the higher groups. No significant differences in factor scores were found on the basis of gender.

Table 6.1: Dimensions of consumer decision making for budget city breaks

	1	2	3	4	5	Com
Factor 1: Insecurity/Anxiety						
Feel mad at yourself	.667					.660
Feel you dislike yourself	.656					.735
Feel scared, uneasy like something might harm you	.550					.504
Factor 2: Interest/Enjoyment						
Feel alert, curious, kind of excited about something		.899				.811
Feel glad about something		.858				.760
Feel so interested in what you are doing, caught up in it		.829				.670
Feel like what you are doing/watching is interesting		.781				.630
Feel happy		.691				.532
Factor 3: Quality						
Compared to my other budget short city breaks, the quality of my last break was higher			.852			.715
Compared to the average quality of budget short city breaks, the quality of my break was higher			.791			.682
Factor 4: Price/Involvement						
Compared to the average market price, the price of my last budget short city break was lower				.819		.673
I think that the purchase of this product was an important decision				.743		.667
Factor 5: Guilt						
Feel you did something wrong					.886	.782
Feel regret, sorry about something you did					.866	.810
Feel like you ought to be blamed for something					.759	.709
Feel embarrassed when anybody sees you make a mistake					.677	.659
Feel like people always look at you when something goes wrong					.604	.615
Eigenvalue	7.05	3.56	1.52	1.48	1.15	
Variance (%)	32.06	16.17	6.91	6.70	5.23	
Cumulative variance (%)	32.06	48.23	55.13	61.84	67.07	
Cronbach's alpha	.82	.87	.60	.51	.88	
Number of Items (Total = 16)	3	5	2	2	5	

N.B. only loadings above .4 are displayed.

Impact of Emotions and the Prediction of Satisfaction and Behavioural Intention

Least squares regression analysis was used to determine the predictive ability of the dimensions with respect to the four outcome variables in the model: overall satisfaction (defined as 'attitude' towards the purchased product in Hansen's framework); intention to recommend the product (city) to others; intention to repurchase the same product (return to the city) and intention to purchase a similar product. In each case, the regression model achieved satisfactory levels of goodness of fit in predicting consumer satisfaction and future behavioural intention and Durbin–Watson statistics (1.66–2.16) indicate that the assumption of independent errors is tenable. The VIF values (1.000–1.006), and both the tolerance statistics (all above .9), and predictor variable loadings on different dimensions in each of the four regression models indicate the absence of multicollinearity in the data. A forward stepwise procedure was used in three cases because there were two or more statistically significant predictors. In the case of predicting subjects' intention to repurchase the same city break product where there was one significant predictor, a forced entry method was used (Field, 2000). In all models, the confidence intervals indicate that the estimates are likely to be representative of 95% of other samples.

The multiple R value (.34) of the independent variables on the dependent variable (Table 6.2) shows that consumer satisfaction is significantly influenced by 'price/involvement' (Factor 4) and 'interest/enjoyment' (Factor 2), although the R^2 value shows that only 11% of the variability in satisfaction is accounted for by the two dimensions. It is notable that 'price/involvement' and 'interest/enjoyment' make similar contributions: as these factors increase by one unit, satisfaction increases by .29 and .25 units, respectively if the effects of the other predictor variables remain constant.

Table 6.2: Regression - level of satisfaction with budget city breaks on the dimensions

Dimensions	B	SE B	Std Beta	T	Sig.	Tolerance	VIF
Price/involvement (Factor 4)	.290	.097	.249	2.994	.003	.978	1.001
Interest/enjoyment (Factor 2)	.250	.096	.218	2.617	.010	.998	1.002

Multiple R = .337; R^2 = .114; Adjusted R^2 = .100; SE = 1.09474; F = 8.22; p<.001

It is interesting that consumer intention to recommend the city break to others is significantly influenced by two different dimensions: 'quality' (Factor 3) and 'insecurity/anxiety' (Factor 1). The R^2 value (Table 6.3) suggests that the two dimensions account for just over 15% of the variability in consumer intention to recommend the city break product. 'Quality' is more influential (beta = .44) than 'insecurity/anxiety' (beta = .23) and has a positive effect compared with the negative influence of 'insecurity/anxiety' i.e consumer intention to recommend the short break product increases by .44 units for each unit increase in quality and decreases by .23 units for each unit increase in 'insecurity/anxiety'. It is interesting that the 'insecurity/anxiety' emotion dimension is only a significant predictor of consumer intention to recommend the product to others and does not have a significant influence on the other outcome variables.

Table 6.3: Regression – intention to recommend the city break on the dimensions

Dimensions	B	SE B	Std Beta	T	Sig.	Tolerance	VIF
Quality (Factor 3)	.443	.100	.369	4.493	<.001	.985	1.015
Insecurity/anxiety (Factor 1)	-.226	.098	-.189	-2.300	.018	.985	1.015

Multiple R = .394; R^2 = .155; Adjusted R^2 = .142; SE = 1.11705; F = 11.656; p<.001

Only 'interest/enjoyment' (Factor 2) makes a significant contribution to consumer intention to repurchase the *same* city break (Table 4). The R^2 value shows that just under 17% of the variability in the repurchase of the city break is accounted for by this emotion dimension. Moreover, it makes a higher contribution (beta = .61) than any other dimension to any of the other outcome variables. As 'interest/enjoyment' increase by one unit, the probability of repurchase increases by .61 units if the effects of the other predictor variables remain constant. It is interesting that this dimension was also a significant predictor of consumer satisfaction.

Table 6.4: Regression – intention to repurchase the same product on the dimensions

Dimensions	B	SE B	Std Beta	T	Sig.	Tolerance	VIF
Interest/enjoyment (Factor 2)	.609	.120	.411	5.079	<.001	1.000	1.000

Multiple R = .411; R^2 = .169; Adjusted R^2 = .162; SE = 1.36348; F = 25.73; p<.001

There are three significant predictors of consumer intention to repurchase a similar city break product: 'interest/enjoyment' (Factor 2), 'quality' (Factor 3) and 'price/involvement' (Factor 4). The details are given in Table 6.5. The R^2 value shows that just under 16% of the variability in the outcome variable is influenced by these dimensions. 'Interest/enjoyment' makes the largest contribution to the model (beta = .43), with 'quality' and 'price/involvement' making similar contributions (beta = .27 and .26, respectively). The influence of the 'interest/enjoyment' dimension on intention to purchase similar breaks, intention to repurchase the same product and on consumer satisfaction is notable.

Table 6.5: Regression – intention to purchase a similar product on the dimensions

Dimensions	B	SE B	Std Beta	T	Sig.	Tolerance	VIF
Interest /enjoyment (Factor 2)	.427	.126	.280	3.375	.001	.994	1.006
Quality (Factor 3)	.267	.126	.175	2.115	.036	.994	1.006
Price/involvement (Factor 4)	.264	.128	.171	2.067	.041	.998	1.002

Multiple R = .388; R^2 = .151; Adjusted R^2 = .130; SE = 1.42657; F = 7.345; p<.001

Discussion

The PCA produced three emotion dimensions ('insecurity/anxiety'; 'interest/enjoyment'; 'guilt') and two cognitive dimensions ('quality'; price/involvement'). Whilst quality is defined as a cognitive dimension, perceived quality has been linked to emotions by Steenkamp (1990) in that it involves an evaluative judgement such as favourable disposition, liking, or affect. This result indicates that both cognitive and affective dimensions underpin consumer decision making for budget city breaks. Moreover, apart from two exceptions, there were no significant differences in factor scores on the basis of socio-demographic variables.

The results from the regression of the four outcome variables on the five dimensions show that both cognitive and emotion dimensions significantly influence consumer satisfaction with these products and their intention to both recommend budget city breaks to others and to purchase similar city breaks. By comparison, cognitive dimensions were not found to significantly influence the repurchase of the same city break, whereas the 'interest/enjoyment' emotion dimension was significant in this respect. This finding supports Bagozzi et al.'s (1999) research which highlighted the importance of emotions in the decision-making process. Clearly, emotions have a significant influence on all four outcomes in relation to budget short city breaks, which also supports Mackay's (1999) argument that emotions play a part in every purchase decision. This result indicates that emotion is either the basis of the evaluation process (Frijda, 1986; Schwarz, 1990) or that cognitive and affective dimensions are simultaneously influencing the decision with the possibility that consumers are using 'affect-as-information' that is, emotions are considered to offer important information for the evaluation of alternatives (Avnet and Pham, 2005). The combination of price and involvement variables in the case of Factor 4 lends some support to the notion of simultaneous influence as does the combined effect of cognitive and emotion dimensions on consumer satisfaction, intention to recommend the city break to others and intention to purchase similar products, with cognitive dimensions having significantly more influence than emotion dimensions on consumer satisfaction and intention to recommend whereas emotion was significantly more influential in the case of intention to purchase a similar product.

Overall, the 'interest/enjoyment', 'price/involvement' and 'quality' dimensions have the most significant influence on the outcome variables. It is notable that the 'interest/ enjoyment' emotion dimension is a significant predictor of three outcome variables. Furthermore, its impact on consumer intention to purchase similar city breaks and particularly on their intention to the repurchase the same city break is relatively high when compared both with its influence on consumer satisfaction with the product and with the influence of other dimensions on the outcome variables, with the exception of 'quality' on intention to recommend the city break to others. Whilst the 'interest/enjoyment' dimension is clearly important in the budget city break CDM process, it is interesting that it does not make a significant contribution to consumer intention to recommend the product to others. The predictive significance of the 'quality' dimension in relation to intention to recommend the product may indicate that quality represents a more universally recognized standard or 'safer' benchmark to use as a basis for recommending a product than the more personal interest/enjoyment factor, as part of a risk reduction strategy. Moreover, the significant role of quality in consumer intention to repurchase a similar product suggests that this dimension is playing a similar role in this context. The significance of the 'insecurity/anxiety' dimension in combination with quality in relation to this behavioural outcome supports this argument. These emotions are likely to influence information processing, use of different strategies to process information and overall evaluation and judgment (Bagozzi et al., 1999). The significance of both positive and negative emotions in the context of intention to recommend a city break to others also supports the findings of Han et al. (2007) albeit in a different context.

The significance of the 'price/involvement' dimension in relation to consumer satisfaction reinforces the high importance ratings which were given to the involvement variables by subjects. This is interesting in that decision making for sh ort breaks is normally characterized as a low involvement activity. The link between the price and involvement variables seems to indicate the significance of value in addition to the importance of the decision itself. This is likely to impact on searching and processing information, evaluating product attributes and influencing the decision heuristic employed. 'Price/involvement' is also significant in relation to intention to purchase a similar product. The importance of this dimension supports Celsi and Olson's (1988) and Blackwell et al.'s (2006) contention that involvement is a critical variable in consumer decisions and this appears to be the case in the context of this particular product market. It is therefore possible that consumers spend more time looking, evaluating and using the relevant information than is generally thought to be the case. Not surprisingly, this dimension was not found to be significant with respect to either intention to recommend the city break to others or intention to repurchase the same product.

It is interesting to compare the outcomes from the four regression models in terms of the mix of predictive dimensions to further understand the nature of the decisions involved. The emergence of 'interest/enjoyment' as the only significant predictor of consumer intention to repurchase the same product is understandable given that the consumer has already experienced the product and the decision as to whether or not they repurchase becomes less complex compared with that relating to the other behavioural outcomes. The fact that the decision appears to be based on an emotional response to the consumer's previous experience with the product and that no cognitive dimension has a significant influence, may also have important implications for marketing short break products to repeat visitors. By comparison, consumer satisfaction is influenced by 'interest/enjoyment' but also by 'price/involvement' indicating that perceived value and the investment of time and effort have combined with 'interest/enjoyment' as influential elements. Similarly, consumer intention to purchase a similar product is also a more complex decision and not surprisingly, three dimensions, including both cognitive and emotive elements, have a significant influence on the outcome. As discussed earlier, consumer intention to recommend the product to others is also complex because of the difficulty of considering the needs and/or wants of others and the risk of dissatisfaction as a possible outcome of the recommendation. The complexity is also reflected in both the significance of the 'quality' and 'insecurity/anxiety' dimensions and their opposing effects. Overall, the pattern indicates that the number of significant dimensions increases with the increasing complexity of the decision and that repurchase of the same product involves a significant emotional dimension to the decision whereas more complex decisions involve both affective and cognitive dimensions.

It should also be noted that the 'guilt' dimension did not significantly influence any of the behavioural outcomes. Moreover, a large number of emotion variables including those relating to 'arrogance, irritability' and 'surprise' were excluded from the factor analysis because they loaded onto two or more dimensions. This highlights the complexity of emotion within the decision-making process for budget short city breaks.

Conclusion

Whilst the body of empirical research on tourism CDM continues to grow, the short break market has been hitherto neglected despite its importance for many tourism destinations. This study makes a contribution to the literature by examining CDM in the budget short city break market based on actual budget city break purchases rather than being a survey of intention. Moreover, in acknowledgement of the complexity of the CDM process, it employed an integrated approach to the problem by adapting and extending Hansen's (2005) CDM framework rather than using one of the staged CDM models which have hitherto been employed in the tourism literature. Overall, the findings highlight the complexity of decision making in this product market and indicate that the extended version of the composite model is a viable framework to structure the analysis of the CDM process for budget city breaks.

The study identified five significant dimensions of CDM in the budget city break market: three emotion dimensions and two cognitive dimensions. This demonstrates that both cognitive and affective dimensions underpin consumer decision making in this context. More specifically, both cognitive and emotion dimensions significantly influence consumer satisfaction with budget short city breaks and their intention to both recommend these products to others and to purchase similar city breaks. Intention to repurchase the same budget city break was significantly influenced only by an emotion dimension: 'interest/enjoyment'. Given that emotion significantly influenced all four behavioural outcomes, the research demonstrates the significant role played by emotion in CDM for budget city breaks. This is an important finding and lends some support to the emotional perspective on CDM, although it is possible that consumers use two or more decision making strategies simultaneously. Moreover, despite some evidence that cognitive and affective dimensions are simultaneously influencing consumer decisions, the results are inconclusive on this point and it is possible that emotion is the basis of the evaluation process. The fact that emotion is the only significant predictor of consumer intention to repurchase the same city break whereas cognitive dimensions are added as decision complexity increases supports this view.

Overall, the 'interest/enjoyment', 'price/involvement' and 'quality' dimensions were found to have the most significant influence on the outcome variables. 'Interest/enjoyment' was a significant predictor of consumer satisfaction and intention to both repurchase the same product and to purchase similar products, with a significantly higher impact on behavioural intention than on satisfaction. However, it did not influence consumer intention to recommend short city breaks to others; the only emotion to significant influence intention to recommend the product was 'insecurity/anxiety', which had a negative impact. The significance of the 'price/involvement' dimension in the context CDM for short breaks is also an important finding because CDM for short breaks is normally characterized as a low involvement activity. The result indicates that involvement is a critical variable in CDM even in this product market. Moreover, the link between price and involvement indicates the importance to the consumer of both value and the decision itself. The significance of the 'quality' dimension in relation to intention to both recommend the product to others and purchase similar products, but particularly in the case of the former, suggests that this dimension is being used as a risk reduction strategy. The significance of 'quality', despite the low-price dimension of budget city breaks, is supported by the emerging patterns (Dunne et. al., 2006) that indicate tourists are taking longer city breaks and willing to trade more conventional vacations for 2-3 short holidays. Another important finding is the relationship between the number of dimensions and the complexity of the decision; i.e. the results indicate that the number of significant dimensions increases with the increasing complexity of the decision and that more complex decisions involve both affective and cognitive dimensions.

The study has produced some important findings, but the limitations of the research should be noted. First, a relatively small student sample was used because of the exploratory nature of the research and whilst the sample is arguably relevant given the focus of the study on CDM in a budget city break context, nevertheless future studies of CDM in this product market should use a larger sample which is more representative of the market for budget city breaks. Second, whilst the conceptual model appears to be appropriate as a framework to structure the analysis of CDM in the budget city break market, this is its first application in a tourism context and further studies of consumer decision making in the short break market should employ the framework to further assess its validity and applicability in this product market and in relation to tourist decision making generally. Third, given the existing construct's limited ability to explain the variance in the model's outcome variables, perhaps additional dimensions such as 'risk' should be incorporated into the conceptual framework and tested empirically.

References

Andreason AR. 1965. *Attitudes and Consumer Behaviour: A Decision Model in New Research in Marketing.* Institute of Business and Economic Research: Preston.

Avnet T, Pham MT. 2005. Should I trust my feelings or not? The metacognition of affect as information in judgment. In *Emergent Moderators of Affective Response in Consumer Behavior,* Wyer RS. *Advances in Consumer Research* **32**: 38-41

Bagozzi RP, Gopinath M, Nyer PU. 1999. The role of emotions in marketing. *Journal of the Academy of Marketing* Science **27** (2): 184–206.

Bettman JR, Luce MF, Payne JW. 1998. Constructive consumer choice processes. *Journal of Consumer Research* **25**: 187-217.

Blackwell RD, Miniard PW, Engel JF. 2006. *Consumer Behaviour.* 10th edn. Thomson South Western

Bloy D. 2000. An assessment of tourist motivations within a multiple holiday taking context. In *Motivations, Behaviour and Tourist Types–Reflections on International Tourism,* Robinson ML, Long P, Evans N, Sharpley R, Swarbrooke J (eds). Business Education Publishers: Sunderland; 27-44.

Bolton LE, Warlop L, Alba J. 2003. Consumer perceptions of price (Un)Fairness. *Journal of Consumer Research* **29**: 474- 491.

Celsi RL, Olson, JC. 1988. The role of involvement in attention and comprehension processes. *Journal of Consumer Research* **15**: 210-224.

Chang T, Wildt A. 1994. Price, product information and purchase intention: An empirical study. *Journal of Academy of Marketing Science* **22** (1): 16-27.

Cooper C, Fletcher J, Gilbert D, Wanhill S. 1998. *Tourism: Principles and Practices 2nd edn.* Longman: New York.

Dibb S, Simkin L, Pride WM., Ferrell OC. 2006. *Marketing: Concepts and Strategies* 5th European edn. Houghton Mifflin: Boston, MA.

Dodds WB. 1991. In search of value: How price and store name information influence buyers' product perceptions. *Journal of Consumer Marketing* **28**: 307–319.

Dodds WB. 1995. Market cues affect on consumers' product evaluations. *Journal of Marketing Theory & Practice* **3**: 50–63.

Dunne G, Buckley J, Flanagan S. 2006. Understanding the characteristics and behaviour of the international city break visitor–the Dublin experience. Paper presented at the Cutting Edge Research in Tourism–New Directions, Challenges, and Applications, Conference, 6-9 June, University of Surrey.

Engel JF, Blackwell RD, Miniard P. 1986. *Consumer Behavior.* Dryden Press: New York.

Field A. 2000. *Discovering Statistics Using SPSS for Windows.* Sage: London.

Frijda NH. 1986 *The Emotions.* Cambridge University Press: Cambridge.

Gilbert DC. 1991. An examination of the consumer decision process related to tourism. In *Progress in Tourism and Recreation and Hospitality Management vol.3*, Cooper C (ed). Belhaven Press: London.

Han S, Lerner JS, Keltner D. 2007. Feelings and consumer decision making: The appraisal–tendency framework. *Journal of Consumer Psychology* **17**(3): 158-168.

Hansen T. 2001. Quality in the marketplace: A theoretical and empirical investigation. *European Management Journal* **19** (2): 203–211.

Hansen T. 2005. Perspectives on consumer decision making: An integrative approach. *Journal of Consumer Behaviour* **4** (6): 420-437.

Howard JA, Sheth JN. 1969. *The Theory of Buyer Behavior*. John Wiley and Sons: New York.

Hoyer WD, MacInnis DJ. 2007. *Consumer Behaviorl*. 4th edn. Houghton Mifflin: Boston, MA.

Huber F, Herrmann A, Morgan RE. 2001. Gaining competitive advantage through customer value oriented management. *Journal of Consumer Marketing* **18** (1): 41- 53.

Izard CE. 1977. *Human Emotions*. Plenum Press: New York.

Jacoby J, Olson JC. 1977. Consumer response to price: An attitudinal, information processing perspective. In *Moving Ahead with Attitude Research*, Wind Y, Greenberg M (eds). American Marketing Association: Chicago; 73-86.

Jang S, Cai LA. 2002. Travel motivations and destination choice: a study of British outbound market. *Journal of Travel and Tourism Marketing* **13** (3): 111-133.

Kaiser HF. 1981. A revised measure of sampling adequacy for factor-analytic data matrices. *Educational and Psychological Measurement* **41** (2): 379-381.

Kassarjian HH. 1981. Low involvement: A second look. In *Advances in Consumer Research* 8 (1), Monroe K. (ed.). Association for Consumer Research: Ann Arbor, MI 31–33.

Kirmani A, Rao AR. 2000. No pain, no gain: A critical review of the literature on signaling unobservable product quality. *Journal of Marketing* **64** (2): 66-79.

Lin C, Chuang S, Kung C. 2006. The presence of reference price: How value can appear convergent to buyers and sellers. *Advances in Consumer Research* **33**: 237-241.

MacKay H. 1999. *Turning Point: Australians Choosing Their Future*. Macmillan: Sidney.

Mathieson A, Wall G. 1982. *Tourism: Economic, Physical and Social Impacts*. Longman: New York.

Middleton VT, Clark J. 2001. *Marketing for Travel and Tourism* 3rd edn. Butterwoth-Heinemann: Oxford.

Mittal B. 1989. Measuring purchase-decision involvement. *Psychology & Marketing* **6**: 147–162.

Monroe KB, Chapman JD. 1987. Framing effects of buyers' subjective product evaluations. In *Advances in Consumer Research*, Wallendorf M, Anderson P (eds). Association for Consumer Research: Provo, UT; 193-197.

Mowen JC, Minor MS. 2001. *Consumer Behavior: A Framework*. Prentice Hall: Upper Saddle River.

Pedhazur, E and Schmelkin, L. 1991. *Measurement, Design and Analysis*. Erlbaum: Hillsdale, NJ.

Peter JP, Olson JC. 2008. *Consumer Behavior and Marketing Strategy*. McGraw-Hill: Singapore.

Peterson RA, Jolibert AJP. 1995. A meta-analysis of country-of-origin effects. *Journal of International Business Studies* 26: 883–900.

Richardson PS, Dick AS, Jain AK. 1994. Extrinsic and intrinsic cue effects on perceptions of store brand quality. *Journal of Marketing* 58: 28-36.

Schmoll GA. 1977. *Tourism Promotion*. Tourism International Press: London.

Schwarz N. 1990. Feelings as information: Informational and motivational functions of affective states. In *Handbook of Motivation and Cognition: Foundations of Social Behavior*, Higgins ET, Sorrentino RM (eds).Guilford Press: New York; 527-561.

Schwarz N, Clore GL. 1983. Mood, misattribution, and judgments of well-being: Informative and directive functions of affective states. *Journal of Personality and Social Psychology* **45:** 513–523.

Schwarz N, Clore GL. 1988. How do I feel about it? The informative function of affective states. In *Affect, Cognition and Social Behavior: New Evidence and Integrative Attempts*, Fiedler K, Forgas J (eds). C.J. Hogrefe: Toronto; 44-62.

Solomon MR. 1996. *Consumer Behaviour*. 3rd edn Prentice Hall: Englewood Cliffs, NJ.

Steenkamp JEM. 1989. *Product Quality: An investigation Into the Concept and How It Is Perceived by Consumers*. Books International: Van Gorcum, Herndou.

Steenkamp JEM. 1990. Conceptual model of the quality perception process. *Journal of Business Research* **21**: 309-333.

Stevens JP. 1992. *Applied Multivariate Statistics for Social Sciences*. 2nd edn. Erlbaum: Hillsdale, NJ.

Wahab S, Crompton, LJ, Rothfield LM. 1976. *Tourism Marketing*. Tourism International Press: London.

Winer RS. 1986. A reference price model of brand choice for frequently purchased products. *Journal of Consumer Research* **13**: 250-256.

Wyer RS, Carlston DE. 1979. *Social Cognition, Inference, and Attribution*. Lawrence Erlbaum Associates: Philadelphia.

Zeithaml VA. 1988. Consumer perceptions of price, quality and value: A means–end model   and synthesis of evidence. *Journal of Marketing* **52**: 2–22.

7 Tourist Decision Strategies in a Multi-Level Perspective

Alain Decrop, Louvain School of Management; **Metin Kozak**, Mugla University

Introduction

Imagine you were to choose a destination for your summer family holiday. Your choice is likely to be influenced by a substantial number of factors, including who you are as a vacationer (i.e. personal factors such as your knowledge/experience of those three destinations), with whom you are going to make your decision (i.e., social factors such as group membership or accountability to relevant others) and what the characteristics of the decision situation are (i.e. task and context factors such as available time and money). The goals vacationers pursue is another major factor influencing the decision making (DM) process. For example, you may be driven by the goal of preserving family ties while holidaying. For achieving those goals, a broad range of decision strategies, also referred to as decision rules or heuristics, may be used. For example, you will incorporate children's expectations in choosing the vacation destination. Such decision strategies are the focus of this chapter.

As widely pointed out in the consumer behavior literature, choosing and buying products involves decisions and thereby a DM process. Pre-purchase evaluation of alternatives is a major step in such a DM process, which involves consumers' use of decision criteria, strategies/rules and goals (Beach and Mitchell, 1987). Consumers dealing with such complex decisions as travel and vacation choices plan their decisions (Bettman, 1979; Park and Lutz, 1982), i.e. they select from among alternatives of a specific course of action in anticipation of particular needs or problems. Plans are more formally defined as 'those specific procedures or actions taken to achieve a goal' (Miller et al., 1960 in Bettman, 1979: 47). When planning, consumers need to evaluate product alternatives. Therefore, they use decision strategies/rules to make a selection among a set of considered alternatives. Such strategies express the relationship between consumers' contextual and personal situation and the choice they make (Van Middelkoop et al., 2003). Vermeir et al. (2002: 709) underline the major role of decision strategies in consumer DM: 'another important factor of the DMP is the use of decision rules [strategies]. Each consumer uses certain decision rules to base their decisions on'. Despite the growing amount of published research in that field, few studies have explored the factors impacting the use of decision heuristics in evaluating products. This is even more true as far as travel and vacation products are concerned.

A few authors have proposed general models and frameworks in order to understand travel and vacation DM (for reviews, see Decrop, 2006; Sirakaya and Woodside, 2005). Decrop (2006) makes a distinction between micro-economic, cognitive and interpretive models. Micro-economic models use traditional demand theory in order to explain tourism behavior. A rational vacationer is depicted who tries to maximize the utility of his or her choices under the constraint of their budget. Cognitive models focus on the mental processes that are involved in DM. Most of those models lean heavily on classical buyer behavior theory and postulate a (bounded) rational and hierarchical tourist DM. In contrast with both micro-economic and cognitive models, interpretive frameworks are not concerned with how vacationers should but on how they actually make decisions. The personal, social and cultural context of DM is taken into account to present a more naturalistic view of the consumer.

In addition to such general models and frameworks, many studies have focused on particular aspects of the decision and evaluation process, such as motivation (Fodness, 1994; Gnoth, 1997), information search (Fodness and Murray, 1997; Mäser and Weier-mair, 1998), or family DM (Nichols and Snepenger, 1988; van Raaij, 1986). However, the travel and tourism literature remains largely silent about a more focused investigation of decision strategies, such as acknowledged by Van Middelkoop et al. (2003: 76): 'although it has been suggested by several authors that travelers use heuristics, or choice rules, to set priorities for their choice decisions, operational rule-based models of tourist and recreation behavior are rare.' Moreover, most of the time vacation DM processes are examined from a horizontal perspective for individuals (rather than DM units) and specific decisions (rather than generic and modal decisions). This study tries to fill this twofold gap to some extent by (1) exploring which decision strategies are used the most when making vacation choices, and (2) investigating how such strategies vary across both product (generic, modal, specific) and social (single, couple, family, friendship groups) layers from a multilevel decision making (MLDM) perspective. Before going into the presentation of research hypotheses, ideas of decision strategies and of MLDM are first discussed.

Decision Strategies

A decision strategy is like a 'rule of thumb' a consumer applies when making a choice. More technically it may be defined as 'the sequence of mental and effector [actions on the decision environment] operations used to transform an initial state of knowledge into a final goal state of knowledge where the decision maker views the particular decision as solved' (Payne et al., 1993: 9). There is substantial evidence of a strong relationship between decision goals and decision strategies. Based on the decision goal, the decision maker evaluates the costs and benefits of all these strategies and selects the strategy that represents the best accuracy–effort trade-off. This way of using decision strategies is referred to as the top-down method. But people sometimes adjust their strategies depending upon the changing task, which is an example of a bottom-up method of using decision strategies.

The consumer and tourist behavior literature presents decision strategies from different perspectives (for a review, see for example, Arnould et al., 2004). We here introduce a distinction among six different types of strategies: micro-economic rules, cognitive strategies, simplistic rules, emotion-based strategies, constraint-based heuristics, and opportunistic strategies. 'Micro-economic models' follow the classical utilitarian approach in which consumers attempt to maximize the utility of their choices under some constraints. Such a maximizing rule is in line with the presentation of (bounded) rational decision makers and expected utility theory (March and Simon, 1958; Simon, 1955). The basic idea behind expected utility theory is that consumers make choices in order to maximize a utility function, subject to the constraints of time, income, information, and technology. For example, Elisabeth considers distance and cost of living to be the prevailing criteria in her destination choice. She looks into brochures to find as many alternatives as possible and then compares them systematically in order to find the destination that offers the best distance/cost ratio. An alternative to the maximizing is the satisficing strategy, which assumes that consumers will try to make acceptable rather than optimal decisions and implies that consumers set cutoff points on some important attributes for them and then only retain alternatives that meet those cutoff values when making their decisions. Satisficing strategies are characterized by partial or abbreviated search behavior and a high level of adaptiveness (Bettman et al., 1998). In this case, Elisabeth does not look as intensively into brochures and just decides to choose the first destination that passes acceptable cutoffs on distance and cost of living.

'Cognitive strategies' describe consumers as combining pieces of information about alternatives and attributes to reach a decision. They emphasize beliefs rather than utilities, emotions and behaviors. Consumers are assumed to make their decisions in a more or less systematic way by using alternative and/or attribute processing, and compensatory and/or non-compensatory rules. Bettman et al. (1998) propose four major dimensions to characterize cognitive decision strategies, that is, the total amount of information processed, the selectivity in information processing, whether processing is made alternative by alternative or attribute by attribute, and whether the strategy is compensatory or noncompensatory. The usual cognitive decision strategies listed by Bettman et al are weighted adding, lexicographic, satisficing, elimination-by-aspects, equal weight, majority of confirming dimensions, frequency of good and/or bad features, and the componential context model. However, those rules will not be examined in this chapter for methodological reasons (see below).

Consumers are more likely to choose 'simple decision strategies' or rules either out of habit in routine decisions or to simplify the decision process when they need to save time, energy and/or money. Simple strategies are used in complex situations in which there are a large number of alternatives and attributes or a high intercorrelation among attributes, for example, between seaside and climate which complement each other for a summer vacation (Gregan-Paxton and John, 1997; Hammond et al., 2001; Swait and Adamowics, 2001). For example, following a 'brand loyalty strategy', the same alternative may always be chosen by consumers whose DMP is driven by routine and habit, due to a strong preference for a particular product/brand or because a high level of risk aversion. Many vacationers are loyal to a destination or even to a particular hotel where they are going each year; they do not use complex decision strategies but just decide to live the same experience as before. The 'brand familiarity strategy' consists in choosing well established and well known products/brands as a mere exposure effect or because reputation is used as a cue for inferring quality. Inexperienced consumers are more likely to select familiar products/brands to reassure themselves; they pay utmost attention to external factors such as packaging, appearance etc. For example, a French vacationer going to Egypt for the first time may prefer to stay in a hotel chain s/he knows like Mercure or Novotel rather than choosing local brands s/he is not familiar with. Alternatively, in 'price-related strategies', consumers' final decisions are directed by sudden cuts in product prices resulting from sale promotions or coupons. For example, a vacationer could choose the cheapest travel package available or buy a last-minute offer.

Sometimes, tourists make their decisions in a more affective and emotional way than suggested by the cognitive and simplistic strategies. The 'avoiding regret strategy' (or avoiding dissonance) consists in making a decision consumers are least likely to regret. It is most likely to be used when more than one alternative is attractive and the decision is important. Bettman et al. (1998) have shown that minimizing the experience of negative emotion may be a major goal when making choices. Therefore, some consumers will prefer to make a 'safe' choice (i.e. a choice they are not likely to regret) rather than an optimal choice. The 'FLAG strategy' is another emotion-based strategy presented in extant literature. It suggests that the decision maker may sometimes have a 'gut feeling' about the right choice; s/he feels that the decision 'fits like a glove' (FLAG). Embodied DM refers to strategies based on a hoslitic perception and comprehension of a gestalt scenario. Woodside et al. (2006) have explained how the FLAG model and ecological systems theory are relevant and useful to account for leisure and tourism choices.

The discussion of decision strategies should be completed by a short description of adaptive strategies which include constraint-based and opportunistic strategies. In 'constraint-based strategies', the decision is ruled by elements external to the decision item itself, like constraints, motives, or other decision criteria (Decrop and Snelders, 2005). Three types of constraints can be considered as a barrier on decisions (McGuiggan, 2004): intrapersonal (attitudes, values, socio-demographics), interpersonal (group of friends, family structure) and structural (finance, time, climate, access problems). Some vacationers are weighted down by contextual inhibitors such as limited financial resources or the intervention of situational variables (e.g. house moving, health problems). Others are constrained by interpersonal differences or/and conflicts that arise within the DM unit. As a consequence, evaluation strategies are not elaborated; vacationers just take the only decision that is possible according to the constraint(s).

Next, consumers may be characterized by 'opportunistic decision strategies' when they lack well-defined decision criteria and are open to many alternatives (Decrop, 2006). They do not use any well-defined strategy in making their vacation decisions. Decisions are not very planned, nor reasoned but result from opportunities or special occasions. This may be an advertised commercial offer, or propositions or invitations by family and friends. Vacation choices are made haphazardly during discussions, meetings, walks, or phone calls. Both constraint-based and opportunistic strategies may be paralleled with the ideas of constructive choice processes (Bettman et al', 1998) and of 'garbage can' decision process (Cohen et al., 1972) in which almost any vacation solution can be associated with any problem, provided they are evoked at the same time. Decision strategies are developed as long as they are needed and are connected with the problem structure.

Multilevel Decision Making

Most of the time, DM models are presented horizontally in a sequence of steps consumers follow, from 'need recognition' to 'purchase' through 'information search' and 'evaluation of alternatives' (Engel and Blackwell, 1982; Howard and Sheth, 1969). A funnel-like procedure is proposed in which choices are narrowed down through cognitive, affective, and behavioral stages (Payne et al., 1993; Shafir et al., 1997). Recently, the authors (2006) have suggested to investigate consumers' DM processes more thoroughly, adding a vertical and a transversal perspective to the horizontal dimension (Figure 7.1).

On the one hand, the vertical perspective consists in looking at how plans and decisions are made at multiple product levels. The authors' (2006) MLDM model includes three product levels: generic, modal, and specific. The *generic decision* level involves trade-offs between non-comparable alternatives (Johnson, 1984, 1986), for example, going on holiday or buying new furniture. In contrast, 'specific decisions' entail comparable alternatives because these are represented by the same attributes. For example, the consumer may have to choose between three hotels described by attributes such as location, price, and comfort level. The level of 'modal decisions' lies somewhere in between since some decision items are considered in any product alternative (e.g. destination, accommodation, and transportation need to be chosen in both a summer and a winter holiday) while other items are peculiar to only one alternative and then are non-comparable with the other ones (e.g. the ski equipment for a winter sport holiday). On the other hand, the transversal perspective is related to how plans and decisions are made socially. Indeed many buying and consumption decisions are not purely individual

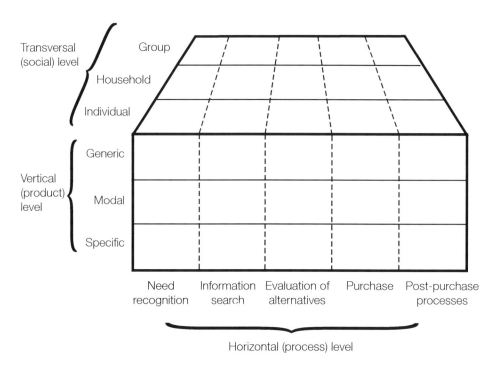

Figure 7.1: Decision levels in tourist decision making

but involve multiple decision makers, for example, within a household. The household itself may participate to a DM process of a still larger group entity, e.g., a party of travelers.

Both vertical and transversal perspectives offer a more realistic approach of the DM process than when only the horizontal level is considered. Moreover, the authors' (2006) MLDM framework is useful to compare micro-aspects related to the different steps in consumers' DM process (e.g. motives, decision goals and strategies, extensiveness of information search) and macro aspects which do pertain to the overall ongoing DM process (e.g. timing and sequencing of decisions, level of decision involvement/complexity, fantasy and daydreaming). A few authors have suggested that the context of choice has a major impact on the decision goals and strategies that are used (see Payne et al., 1992, 1993 for a review). For example, group membership is a moderator of the type of strategies used when evaluating product alternatives. The MLDM framework will be used in this chapter in order to examine which goals are set at different vertical and transversal levels.

Methodology

In order to examine differences between decision strategies in a vertical perspective, three versions of a similar questionnaire have been developed: the first one for the generic level, the second one for modal decisions and the third one for the specific level of the MLDM framework. Each version started with a scenario presenting a decision task asking respondents to choose among three product alternatives, each being described by three attributes. The list of alternatives varied according to the decision level. However, the same attributes (i.e. brand, price and quality) were chosen in order to make data comparable from one version to the other (see Table 7.1). In the generic-decision version, respondents had to choose one among three non-comparable alternatives, i.e. home furniture, a personal computer or summer vacations. In the modal-level version, they were expected to choose among three vacation types, i.e. one week summer holiday, one week winter skiing, or two city-trips of three and four days. In the specific-decision version, respondents had to make a choice among a set of three comparable hotel alternatives. In each version, respondents were asked to mention their preferred product at the end of the choice process.

Table 7.1: Description of the three choice alternatives presented to respondents in each scenario

	Generic Level			Modal Level			Specific Level		
Brand	Furniture (IKEA)	Computer (Packard Bell)	Vacation in France	Package tour (Neckerman)	Package tour (Thomas Cook)	Package Tour (Jet Air)	One night at Ibis hotel	One night at Novotel	One night at Mercure
Price (€)	1,500	1,250	1,750	500	800	650	59	109	89
Quality	Fair	Good	Very Good	Fair	Good	Very Good	Fair	Very Good	Good

After the decision task, respondents were asked to answer a list of 25 structured propositions (see column 2 in Table 7.2) designed to measure the strategies they pursued in their DM process. Those propositions were produced on the basis of a brainstorming session with actual consumers and of the specific literature on decision strategies discussed earlier. Each item was measured on a five-point Likert scale, anchored from 1 (totally disagree) to 5 (totally agree). Of course, as we wanted to measure differences in decision strategies as to the transversal (social) level, we also included a question about the structure of household (i.e. with whom respondents usually make the choice of the decision task). Four types of DM units were distinguished: singles, couples, families, and groups of friends/relatives. The questionnaire included an additional part to obtain information about respondents' socio-demographic profile (i.e. age, gender, education, number of people living in the household, and profession). Finally, questions about respondents' involvement with the product category were included as well. Sirakaya and Woods ide (2005) indeed suggest that the level of involvement influences the decision rules used to arrive at a final choice. The three versions of the questionnaire were pre-tested on 20 respondents.

In July 2006, 450 Belgian subjects were recruited to participate in the survey (150 for each version). Quota sampling was used in order to make the sample representative of the population as to three major criteria, i.e. age, education and household structure. Subjects were approached by three trained interviewers; they were first provided with the relevant information about the scope of the survey, its procedures and the estimated length of time to complete the survey. In total, 408 respondents participated in the survey (136 for each product level). A range of statistical techniques were employed to analyse the data and test the research hypotheses with assistance of the SPSS software. A principal–axis component analysis was performed on the 25 items concerning decision strategies, leaving us with 23 items as two questions appeared to have been misunderstood. The resulting factor solution was then used as the dependent variable in ANOVA and correlation analyses in order to test whether or not significant differences appeared in decision strategies as to vertical (product) and transversal (social) levels, as well as to the socio-demographics described above.

Results

There is no major difference between respondents of the three questionnaires/levels in terms of their socio-demographic characteristics. Demographic characteristics reveal a slight preponderance of females (52%). Each of the five age categories is almost equally represented in the sample (between 17–22%). Subjects are predominantly singles (38%), followed by traditional families (26%), couples (24%), and 'alternative' families (12%; including single-parent and recomposed families) with an average of 2.23 persons per household. As to educational background, 47% of respondents hold a primary or lower secondary school degree, 31% a higher secondary school diploma while 15% graduated from college and 7% from university. In terms of occupation, four major groups prevail in the sample: professional/senior management level (26%), worker (22%), housewife (14%), and education/medical services (11%).

When considering the distribution of product choices for each vertical sub-level, one may see at the generic level that subjects were more likely to first choose a furniture by Ikea (41%), and then a computer by Dell (33%) and a vacation in France (26%). In the modal-level questionnaire, the majority of respondents chose a summer vacation (61%), followed by a weekend trip (26%) and winter sports vacation (13%). Finally, at the specific decision level, the proposed hotel brands rank in the following order: Ibis, Novotel, and Mercure.

Types of Decision Strategies

Looking at decision strategies (23 items) following Kaiser rule of eigenvalues ≥ 1, a six-factor solution was generated after VARIMAX rotation, accounting for 53.19% of the total explained variance (Table 7.2). The first factor (deal-proneness) refers to consumers' want to benefit from good deals as price is low, an item is on sale, or a gift is offered. The second factor includes decision strategies based on product knowledge and experience. The third factor (maximizing) is composed of items relating to consumers' wish to make the best decision as possible. The fourth and fifth factors refer to affective- and social- based strategies respectively. In the former, decisions are directed by emotions, moods and desires while in the latter they are influenced by relevant others (partner, family and friends). Finally, the sixth factor includes three items that express consumers' adaptation to their situation (time, product availability) when making choices.

Variables Impacting the use of Decision Strategies

As to the comparative analysis of decision strategies across product levels (Table 7.3), F tests show a significant difference between the three levels for four of the six decision strategies. Post-hoc Tukey tests further show that the generic level implies a higher use of deal proneness, experience-based, maximizing and affective strategies than the modal level; and a greater use of experience-based rules than at the level of specific decisions. We also see that the affective strategy is used to a larger extent at the specific level than for modal decisions.

When considering comparisons in a social perspective, significant differences appear for four out the six strategies (Table 7.4). Singles appear to use a deal-proneness strategy to a larger extent than couples, and to be more sensitive to experience. Moreover, singles are by far less likely than the three other DM units to base their choices on social aspects. This result is confirmed by the significant positive correlation between the number of people in the household and the use of social heuristics ($=0.36$, $p<0.01$, $n=407$). Friendship groups are also remarkable in that they are the least likely to base their decisions on experience or to try to maximize them.

Table 7.2: Factor solution for decision strategies (VARIMAX rotation; N=408)

Factor Label	Items	Cronbach	Nb. items	Eigenvalue	Total variance explained	
					(%)	Cum. (%)
1. Deal-proneness strategy	I'll take the product on promotion/sale I'll try to make the best deal as possible I'll choose the cheapest product, nothing else matters I'll choose the product for which a gift is provided My decision relies on the availability of money	0.70	5	2.30	9.99	9.99
2. Experience-based strategy	I'll choose the same product as the last time I'll choose the product I know I'll choose the product for which I have the strongest experience I'll choose a product which partly meets my expectations	0.67	4	2.24	9.75	19.74
3. Maximizing strategy	I'll choose the product that completely fulfils my needs I'll make my choice based on the most important characteristic to me I'll choose the product with the highest value on all characteristics I'll combine different characteristics in order to make the best decision as possible	0.64	4	2.18	9.46	29.20
4. Affective strategy	I'll decide according to my current mood Since I don't like to make plans in advance, I'll choose in the last minute I'll let myself guided by my emotions and desires I'll take a decision just because I have to take it	0.65	4	2.17	9.45	38.65
5. Social strategy	I'm depending on my partner or my family to make that choice I'll adapt my final choice to others' needs and wants in my household I'll ask my parents' or friends' advice before making such a decision	0.61	3	1.77	7.68	46.33
6. Situational strategy	I'll adapt my final choice according to the situation I'll adapt my final choice to the product's availability My decision depends on the time I have available to take it	0.52	3	1.58	6.86	53.19

Looking at the other socio-demographic variables, we see that for gender, significant differences appear only for Factors 4 ($F=6.39$, df=1, $p=0.01$) and 5 ($F=8.51$, $df=1$, $p<0.01$). Males are likely to use affective strategies to a larger extent than females whereas females use social strategies more extensively than males. Age is significantly correlated with all decision strategies but one (situational strategy). However, Pearson correlation coefficients are small, ranging from $|0.10|$ to $|0.21|$. Table 7.5 shows that the use of experience-based and maximizing

Table 7.3: Comparison of decision strategies across product levels

	Generic level	Modal level	Specific level	F	p-value
Deal-proneness strategy	3.56[a]	3.32[b]	3.39[ab]	3.18	.04
Experience-based strategy	3.69[a]	3.35[b]	3.41[b]	5.61	.00
Maximizing strategy	4.26[a]	4.06[b]	4.17[ab]	3.06	.04
Affective strategy	2.98[a]	2.53[b]	2.88[a]	7.61	.00
Social strategy	NS	NS	NS	0.17	.84
Situational strategy	NS	NS	NS	1.42	.24
N	136	136	136		

Different letters indicate significant pairwise differences following post-hoc Tukey tests.

Table 7.4: Comparison of decision strategies across social levels

	Singles	Couples	Families	Friendship groups	F	p-value
Deal-proneness strategy	3.57[a]	3.29[b]	3.50[ab]	3.38[ab]	3.17	0.02
Experience-based strategy	3.70[a]	3.37[b]	3.59[ab]	2.82[c]	9.80	0.00
Maximizing strategy	4.19[ab]	4.22[a]	4.11[ab]	3.86[b]	2.74	0.04
Affective strategy	NS	NS	NS	NS	0.74	0.53
Social strategy	2.15[a]	3.56[b]	3.62[b]	3.12[b]	58.82	0.00
Situational strategy	NS	NS	NS	NS	1.95	0.12
N	137	166	75	28		

Different letters indicate significant pairwise differences following post-hoc Tukey tests.

Table 7.5: Pearson correlations between decision strategies and age

	ρ	p-value	n
Deal-proneness strategy	-0.11	0.04	397
Experience-based strategy	0.21	0.00	388
Maximizing strategy	0.10	0.04	394
Affective strategy	-0.10	0.05	403
Social strategy	-0.19	0.00	393
Situational strategy	-0.02	0.64	398

Table 7.6: Comparison of decision strategies across educational level

	Primary/lower secondary	Higher secondary	College	University	F	p-value
Deal-proneness strategy	3.62[a]	3.35[b]	3.17[b]	3.09[b]	7.90	.00
Experience-based strategy	3.67[a]	3.43[ab]	3.21[b]	3.09[b]	7.10	.00
Maximizing strategy	NS	NS	NS	NS	1.47	.22
Affective strategy	NS	NS	NS	NS	2.61	.05
Social strategy	NS	NS	NS	NS	1.42	.24
Situational strategy	NS	NS	NS	NS	0.17	.91
N	192	127	59	30		

Different letters indicate significant pairwize differences following post-hoc Tukey tests.

Table 7.7: Pearson correlations between decision strategies and product involvement

	ρ	p-value	n
Deal-proneness strategy	0.09	0.08	388
Experience-based strategy	0.27	0.00	379
Maximizing strategy	0.22	0.00	385
Affective strategy	-0.06	0.27	395
Social strategy	0.14	0.01	385
Situational strategy	0.10	0.04	389

strategies increases with age, which sounds quite logical as being older means more experience and more rational choices. In contrast, the reference to deal-proneness, affective- and social strategies decreases with age. As far as educational level is concerned (Table 7.6), lower educated people are more sensitive to good deals when making their tourism decisions and use an experience-based strategy to a larger extent than higher educated respondents. Finally, results show that the higher product involvement is, the higher the usage of experience-based, maximizing, social- and situational strategies will be (Table 7.7).

Conclusion

This study had two objectives. First, to explore which decision strategies are used the most when making tourism choices, and second, to investigate how such decision strategies vary across both product and social layers in consumers' DM processes.

As to the first objective, results show that consumers may use a variety of rules when making decisions. We generated a typology of six decision strategies for tourism products which may be paralleled with the strategies presented in the general DM literature. Deal proneness and experience strategies may be considered as involving simple rules related to price and brand-familiarity such as described earlier in the chapter. Authors such as Decrop (2006) and Sirakaya and Woodside (2005) have shown that financial opportunities and routine could be major drivers of tourism decisions. Maximization is in line with the idea of bounded rational consumers who try to maximize the utility of their tourism choices. The affective-based factor relates to emotional strategies which suggest that the decision to travel is not always rational and planned but may result from emotions and moods in a much unconscious way (Woodside et al., 2006). Finally, social- and situation-based strategies are in line with Bettman et al.'s (1998) idea of constructive choice process and Payne et al.'s (1993) concept of adaptive DM. Consumers often have to adapt their choices and to use a decision strategy that takes situation (problem characteristics) and social context into account.

As to the second objective, results show that the use of decision strategies strongly varies according to the product and the social level which is considered for the evaluation process. Overall, it appears that decision strategies are used to a larger extent when making generic decisions than for making modal choices. Such a result may be explained by that decision complexity increases in proportion as alternatives share less common attributes/dimensions (d'Estaintot and Vidaillet, 2005; Payne et al., 1992). As to social levels, findings point out a major difference between singles and the other DMU types. Singles are the most sensitive to good deals and experience when making choices; in contrast, they refer to social-based strategies to a lesser extent than the other types, which sounds logical as they are to decide alone. Results also show that friendship groups are less likely to use experience-based strategies, suggesting that as informal DM units they share less tourism experiences than more formal DM units (Decrop et al., 2004). When considering other socio-demographic variables, age and involvement appear to have a significant impact on the use of decision strategies, which is in line with other papers (e.g. Syrakaya and Woodside, 2005).

This study's findings have both theoretical and managerial implications. From a theoretical perspective, this chapter offers one of the rare efforts to generate a typology of decision strategies which is empirically based. Such a typology indicates that a range of decision strategies relating to a plurality of DM paradigms (from bounded rationality to adaptativity) may be relevant when considering how tourism choices are made. Moreover, significant differences among product and social levels respectively have been highlighted with regard to consumers' reference to decision strategies. This suggests that referring to a MLDM framework may be useful in examining micro- and macro-aspects of consumers' DM processes.

This study's findings are also useful from a practical perspective as it conveys tourism managers information about how their customers may reach their final decision. More specifically, the six strategies depicted hereabove could be used for segmentation purposes. For example, an experience-based strategy is more likely to be used by male, older and less educated consumers who are not part of a friendship group and show a stronger level of product involvement. Tourism managers' marketing mix should also be adapted according to the product domain and the type of DMU as decision strategies may differ according to both vertical and transversal dimensions. Marketers operating in each product level should explore the decision strategies of their segments and develop appropriate programs to better satisfy them.

This chapter entails a few limitations that temper the results presented so far. First, this study is based on a scenario approach, which rests on hypothetical rather than real choices. Other methods such as experiments or laddering (Reynolds and Gutman, 2001) could be used in order to further explore consumers' decision strategies. Second, this study has been limited to the consideration of choice alternatives at each product level independently (three different questionnaires were administered on three independent subsamples). Such a design was necessary to make systematic comparisons among levels; however, it reduces the understanding of the complexity of many choice processes in which generic, modal, and specific decisions are contemplated simultaneously.

References

Arnould E, Price L, Zinkhan, G. 2004. *Consumers*. 2nd edn, Irwin: New York.

Beach LR, Mitchell TR. 1987. Image theory: Principles, goals, and plans in decision making. *Acta Psychologica* **66**: 201-220.

Bettman JR. 1979. *An Information Processing Theory of Consumer Choice*. Addison-Wesley: Reading, MA.

Bettman JR, Luce MF, Payne JW. 1998. Constructive consumer choice processes. *Journal of Consumer Research* **25**: 187-217.

Cohen MD, March JG, Olsen J. 1972. A garbage can model of organizational choice. *Administrative Science Quarterly* **17**: 1-24.

d'Estaintot V, Vidaillet B. 2005. Le décideur en action: comportements et processus psychologiques. In *La décision: une approche pluridisciplinaire des processus de choix*, Vidaillet B, d'Estaintot V, Abecassis P (eds). De Boeck: Brussels; 43-74.

Decrop A. 2006. *Vacation Decision Making*. CABI: Wallingford.

Decrop A, Snelders D. 2005. A grounded typology of vacation decision making. *Tourism Management* **26**: 121-132.

Decrop A, Pecheux C, Bauvin G. 2004. Let's make a trip together: An exploration into decision making within groups of friends. *Advances in Consumer Research* **31**: 291-297.

Engel J, Blackwell R. 1982. *Consumer Behavior*. 4th edn. Dryden Press: Hinsdale .

Fodness D. 1994. Measuring tourist motivation. *Annals of Tourism Research* **21**: 555-581.

Fodness D, Murray B. 1997. Tourist information search, *Annals of Tourism Research* **24**: 503-523.

Gnoth J. 1997. Tourism motivation and expectation formation, *Annals of Tourism Research* **24**: 283-304.

Gregan-Paxton J, John DR. 1997. Consumer learning by analogy: a model of internal knowledge transfer. *Journal of Consumer Research* **24** (3): 266-284.

Hammond JS, Keeney RL, Raiffa H. 1999. *Smart Choices. A Practical Guide to Making Better Decisions*. Harvard Business School Press: Boston, MA.

Howard JA, Sheth JN. 1969. *The Theory of Buyer Behavior*. John Wiley: New York

Johnson MD. 1984. Consumer choice strategies for comparing noncomparable alternatives. *Journal of Consumer Research* 11: 741-753.

Johnson MD. 1986. Modeling choice strategies for noncomparable alternatives. *Marketing Science* 5: 37-54.

March JG, Simon HA. 1958. *Organizations*. John Wiley: New York.

Mäser B, Weiermair K. 1998. Travel decision-making: from the vantage point of perceived risk and information preferences. *Journal of Travel and Tourism Marketing* 7: 107-121.

McGuiggan RL. 2004. A model of vacation choice: an integration of personality and vacation choice with leisure constraints theory. In *Consumer Psychology of Tourism, Hospitality and Leisure Vol. 3I*, Crouch GI, Purdue RR, Timmermans HJP, Uysal M (eds). CABI: Wallingford; 169 -180.

Nichols CM, Snepenger DJ. 1988. Family decision-making and tourism behavior and attitudes. *Journal of Travel Research* 26 (Spring): 2-6.

Park CW, Lutz RJ. 1982. Decision plans and consumer choice dynamics. *Journal of Marketing Research* 19: 108-115.

Payne JW, Bettman JR, Johnson EJ. 1992. Behavioral decision research: a constructive processing perspective. *Annual Review of Psychology* 43: 87-131.

Payne JW, Bettman JR, Johnson EJ. 1993. *The Adaptive Decision Maker*. Cambridge University Press: Cambridge.

Reynolds TJ, Gutman J. 2001. Laddering theory, method, analysis, and interpretation. In *Understanding Consumer Decision Making: The Means-end Approach to Marketing and Advertising Strategy*, Reynolds TJ, Olson JC. (eds), Lawrence Erlbaum Associates: NJ; 25-62.

Shafir E, Simonson I, Tversky A. 1997. Reason-based choice. In *Research on Judgment and Decision Making: Currents, Connections and Controversies*, Goldstein WM, Hogarth RM (eds). Cambridge University Press: Cambridge; 69-94.

Simon HA. 1955. A behavioral model of rational choice. *Quaterly Journal of Economics* 69: 99-118.

Sirakaya E, Woodside AG. 2005. Building and testing theories of decision making by travellers. *Tourism Management* 26 (6): 815-832.

Swait J, Adamowics W. 2001. The influence of task complexity on consumer choice: A latent model of decision strategy switching. *Journal of Consumer Research* 28: 135-148.

van Middelkoop M, Borgers A, Timmermans H. 2003. Inducing heuristic principles of tourist choice of travel mode: A rule-based approach. *Journal of Travel Research* 42: 75-83.

van Raaij WF. 1986. Consumer research on tourism: Mental and behavioral constructs. *Annals of Tourism Research* 13: 1-9.

Vermeir I, Van Kenhove P, Hendrickx H. 2002. The influence of needs for closure on consumer's choice behavior. *Journal of Economic Psychology* 23: 703-717.

Woodside AG, Caldwell M, Spurr R. 2006. Advancing ecological systems theory in lifestyle, leisure, and travel research. *Journal of Travel Research* 44 (3): 259–272.

8 Push Motivations for Tourism Mountain Destinations

Carla Silva, Polytechnic Institute of Viseu; José Luís Abrantes, Universidade Nova de Lisboa; Carmen Lages, ISCTE Business School – Lisbon,

Introduction

Tourism is a social phenomenon of contemporary society (Urry, 2002) that intends to improve people's lives (Furchtgott and Furchtgott, 1999). Tourism has become an important element in a process of social change in which human systems, values and communities are being integrated towards global social and economic systems (Saarinen, 2004). Motivation for tourism is considered crucial for understanding society behaviour because tourism expresses significant social behaviours through which contemporary society can be understood (Cohen, 1993; MacCannell, 1989).

Until recently, tourism had been characterized as a mass phenomenon by the standardization, homogenization and inflexibility of the product. This type of tourism treats tourists as a homogenous group, ignoring their specific and unique demands (Wang, 2000). The consequences of tourism massification and the active life style of contemporary societies are leading to the saturation of traditional tourism destinations (Davidson, 1992). Likewise, in consequence of society values change, new tourist motivations emerge. These values represent new learned beliefs about novel preferred ways of being (Schwartz, 1994), such as a demand for nature-based, educative, culturally and environmentally sustainable places (Blamey and Braithwaite, 1997). Within the context of tourism, it has been noted that the values tourists hold can affect their choice of destination (Muller, 1991), namely alternative tourism proposals such as mountain destinations.

The current context of globalization and the fast social changes call for a reassessment of the questions as to why people travel and why they choose a particular tourism destination (Harrill and Potts, 2002), particularly when considering alternative destinations such as mountain places. Mountain tourism presents itself as an alternative type of tourism through which people intent to satisfy new social desires of challenge experiences associated with nature, learning and status enhancement. Tourists that search for this new kind of tourism seek for both natural and social environment consistent with the life style of local communities (Smith and Eadington, 1995).

Mountain tourism has become one of the most attractive tourism types (McCool, 2002) as demonstrated by the fact that mountain tourism constitutes 20% of the global tourism (Mountain Agenda, 1999). Mountains represent 24% of the earth's land surface (Kapos, Rhind et al., 2000) in which 12% of the global population lives (Huddleston et al., 2003). Also, 14% of the earth population is estimated to live around mountains regions (Meybeck et al., 2001). Beyond tourism areas, mountains are also important as sources of water, as centers of biodiversity and recreation (Messerli and Ives, 1997).

Motivations are an important issue in tourist behaviour because they are the starting points of the travel decision and destination choice processes (Crompton and McKay, 1997). Past research establishes that individuals are guided by socio-psychological motivations variables into making travel decisions (Sirakaya and Woodside, 2005) and that tourism motivations vary from one type of destination to another (Andreu et al., 2005).

Motivation is a vital concept in understanding consumer behavior and the society to which the consumer belongs (Schott, 2004). However, despite wide academic interest in the topic of tourism motivation, it remains understudied from the conceptual and empirical perspectives (Fodness, 1994), particularly in operationalizing motivations and consequently assessing motivations' differences among destinations (Kozac, 2002). Besides, until very recently, tourism research concerned with mountain places were mainly limited to physical, ecological and environmental perspectives (Smethurst, 2000). A tourism perspective on mountain tourism within the motivations context is therefore revealing essential information when considering the reasons that move tourists to travel to a new and specific type of destination.

Therefore the purpose of this chapter is to develop a scale designed to measure push motivations for selection of tourism mountain destinations. In the mountain tourism push motivation (MTPM) scale, individual motivations are related to push factors: needs, desires and personal goals. It allows a better match between tourist motivations and destination characteristics and resources, contributing for an enhanced understanding of tourism motivations, decision-making process and consumer behaviour. Thus, this scale contributes to social science knowledge in order to explain the reasons that move tourists to travel to mountain destinations as well as to consumer behaviour in the context of tourism.

The Mountain Tourism Push Motivation Scale

This study intends to develop a tourist motivations measurement model – the MTPM scale – that assesses the importance of push factors in the decision to travel to mountain tourism destinations. It includes three dimensions adapted from Baloglu and McCleary (1999) tourism motivation model: adventure/excitement, social/knowledge and prestige that affect travel behaviour to tourism mountain destinations.

Adventure/Excitement

Adventure/excitement motivations in tourism are associated with deliberate risk, danger and entertainment seeking (Gyimóthy and Mykletun, 2004).

One of the most attractive tourism characteristics is the ability to provide different and intensive experiences in which the tourist's standard social structures and conventions are eliminated. Accordingly, tourism is an experimental phenomenon (Botterill and Crompton, 1996; Frochot and Morrison, 2000) where experiences are sought in relation to feelings of motivation (den Breejen, 2007).

Some adventure attractions appear to offer that kind of experiences, with excitement and spontaneity, which may be missing from the tourist's daily life (Beedie, 2005). A travel adventure, like any other adventure experience, is normally described as an exciting experience, out of routine life, that cannot be completely planned and which results in some degree of uncertainty (Arnould and Price, 1993).

Tourists who seek for adventure would like to meet uncommon and exotic destinations to acquire new experiences, enjoy the unique environment, and/or test their skills (Tran and Ralston, 2006). They intend to be personally tested in some way, namely experimenting dangerous and or adventurous sport activities (Gyimóthy and Mykletun, 2004). However, some tourists seek this kind of experience not for the actual risk but for the perceived risk in testing their personal limits, which causes pleasure sensations. Risk causes fear and fear causes excitement. Nevertheless, risk sensations in tourism occur always in a controlled context. Adventure/excitement expresses many travellers' inner desires, such as the desire to do exciting things, be entertained, and to undertake adventure sports activities (Baloglu and McCleary, 1999; Gitelson and Kersketter, 1990). Mountain tourism is an ideal kind of tourism to answer to such sorts of push motivations. Mountains represent escape locations which offer excitement, stimulation and adventure (Beedie and Hudson, 2003) that can be an antithesis of routine role behaviour in the institutional domain (Lyng, 1990) and have a positive social evaluation.

Social/Knowledge

Social/knowledge motivations are related with the internal tourist desires for social interaction, socialization, learning, and knowledge (Ray and Ryder, 2003). In contemporary societies, tourism is part of the socialization process (Kelly, 1987) through which people intend to learn more about different persons and places, outside their routine life (Uysal and Hagan, 1993). Tourism is not only an escape from the workday life but an escape to a social space which allows socialization and learning (Wearing and Wearing, 1996). In our time, many tourists seek the novelty and the unknown of each place (Lee and Crompton, 1992). However, those motivations are not new in tourism. The Grand Tour in the 18th century, as one of the greatest events and social interaction in tourism history (Boyer, 2000), had already highlighted social-cultural and learning motivations as major travel reasons (Towner, 1985).

Social/knowledge motivations are one of the most acknowledged categories of travel motivations (Jang et al., 2002). Tourism is a social phenomenon that allows people to develop social interaction, to satisfy social acceptance, approval and integration needs. Tourists do not wish to feel isolated and holidays represent an important social forum for them. Tourism is a form of intercultural meeting and interaction (Ward, Bochner and Furnham, 2001). Tourism activities offer learning opportunities through meeting new and different people and provide tourists an opportunity to develop relationships (Hsu et al., 2007).

Tourists seek a new social experience with new activities, new options of social encounters, knowledge, and learning (Urry, 1996). Tourists contact with different social environments where they can have a social experience of learning (Formica and Uysal, 1996). Thus, social/knowledge push motivations include meeting different people (Ray and Ryder, 2003), developing friendship relationships (Kim and Lee, 2002), and experiencing different cultures and ways of life (Baloglu and McCleary, 1999).

Social and learning experience desired by tourists will be more intense when the perceived differences among places are more significant. Tourists seek the authenticity of the places (MacCannell, 1989) and mountains have specificities that allocate tourists to experience social activities and ways of life very different from their own routine lives, to acquire knowledge and authentic social relations (McColl, 2002).

Prestige

Prestige is related with status enhancement, social recognition, ego, and personal development of the tourist's needs (Goeldner et al., 2000). Generally, people seek the approval of others and will avoid activities that lead to disapproval (Hsu et al., 2007). Being a tourist is a sign of status in contemporary society; if people do not travel, they might lose status and social approval (Urry, 2002). Prestige is an intangible motivational force that pushes an individual to travel (Turnbull and Uysal, 1995), and it is not the only motivation to travel, but is the most popular reason to do so (Zhang and Lam, 1999).

Tourism prestige motivations express two main desires. First, the desire to go to places where tourist friends have not yet been; second, the desire to tell friends about the trip that has been made (Baloglu and McCleary, 1999). These push motivations can be temporarily acquired by travel experiences (Cohen and Taylor, 1976) through tourism, holidays and leisure activities that are universes of social and cultural practices where life styles are created and status competition is established (Bourdieu, 1979).

Prestige promotes popularity and is a personal indicator of success. Tourists are motivated by a desire to impress other persons by choosing prestigious tourist products (Mason, 1981) that represent a social distinction. Some tourism products have prestige value because they confer status to consumers who own or use them. A few tourism destinations are fashionable and unusual, and their selection by tourists allows them to create a high-status impression (Ryan, 1991).

Mountains are an example of prestigious tourism places. They have the potential to attract tourists' attention with their unique natural and historical contexts, their fame, and size. To know and to conquer them is a point of social distinction despite that occurring in a context of control within which a tourism mountain is located (Beedie and Hudson, 2003).

Methodology

The study took place in a European country (Portugal), in a tourism mountain destination. Portugal is one of the five EU countries where mountain areas comprise more than 50% of the territory (Dax, 2004). Portugal was the 16th most visited country in the world in 2004 holding 1.5% of the world travel market (Business Europe, 2005) as estimated by the Economist Intelligence Unit based on international arrivals. In Portugal, tourism plays a significant role in economic development accounting for about 7% of GDP and for 8% of total employment.

This chapter presented a conceptual model of tourism motivation to travel to mountain tourism destinations. From the literature review, it is accepted that motivation is multidimensional. Tourists seek to satisfy not one single need but a number of distinct needs simultaneously (Baloglu and Uysal, 1996). First, a review of literature was conducted to develop a list of motivations items which are generally used to measure push tourism motivations. The push motivational variables are derived from an initial set of 25 items. A seven-point Likert-type scale was used as the response format for the motivation variables, with assigned values ranging from 1, 'Not important at all' to 7, 'Extremely important'. A pre-test sample of 35 tourists was used in order to refine the questionnaire and to test the reliability of the scales through Cronbach's alpha (Cronbach, 1951).

The final data collection was made between October 2003 and April 2004. This period of the year corresponds to the high season of tourism mountain destinations. The questionnaire was personally administered to each individual during the stay at the mountain tourist site. All questionnaires were answered anonymously. Finally, 400 valid responses were obtained, representing a sampling error of 4.9%.

Among the tourists, 53.7% were female and 46.3% were male. The majority of respondents, 71%, were residents of urban areas. About 30% were aged between 18 and 25 years old, 42% were 26 to 35 years old, and 19% were 36 to 45 years old. The remainder were 46 or older. Single people made up 47% of the respondents, 13% were married without children and 36% were married with children. Almost half, 47%, of the respondents had university education and 27.5% had completed their high school education.

Data Analysis

In order to assess the validity of the measures, the items were subjected to a confirmatory factor analysis (CFA), using full-information maximum likelihood (FIML) estimation procedures in LISREL 8.54 (Jöreskog and Sörbom, 1993). In this model, each item is restricted to load on its pre-specified factor, with the three first-order factors allowed to correlate freely. After CFA purification, the initial list of 8 items was maintained. A full listing of the 8 final items after CFA purification and their scale reliabilities are included in Table 8.1.

Table 8.1: The MTPM Scale – Constructs, scale items and reliabilities

Adventure/Excitement [a]	$\alpha=0.84$; $\rho_{vc(n)}=0.63$; $\rho=0.79$
V1 – Doing exciting things V2 – Doing adventure sport activities V3 - Having fun, being entertained	
Social/Knowledge [b]	$\alpha=0.79$; $\rho_{vc(n)}=0.56$; $\rho=0.79$
V4 - Meeting interesting people V5 - Developing friendship relationships V6 - Experiencing different cultures and ways of life	
Prestige [c]	$\alpha=0.77$; $\rho_{vc(n)}=0.63$; $\rho=0.77$
V7 - Going places where my friends have not been V8 - Telling my friends about the trip	

$\alpha=$ Internal reliability (Cronbach, 1951) $\rho_{vc(n)}$ = Variance extracted (Fornell and Larcker, 1981); $\rho_{=}$ Composite reliability (Bagozzi, 1980).
[a] adapted from: Baloglu and McCleary, 1999; Gitelson and Kersketter, 1990.
[b] adapted from: Baloglu and McCleary, 1999; Kim and Lee, 2002; Ray and Ryder, 2003.
[c] adapted from: Baloglu and McCleary, 1999.

The chi-square for this model is significant ($\chi^2=31.49$, 17df, p<0.00). Since the chi-square statistic is sensitive to sample size, we also assessed additional fit indices: Normed Fit Index (NFI), Comparative Fit Index (CFI), the Incremental Fit Index (IFI), and the Tucker–Lewis Fit Index (TLI). The NFI, CFI, IFI, and TLI of this model are 0.99 for all. Table 8.1 provides an overview of all those items. As shown in this table, all three constructs present the desirable levels of composite reliability (Bagozzi, 1980).

Convergent validity is evidenced by the large and significant standardized loadings of each item on its intended construct (average loading size was 0.77). Discriminant validity among the constructs is stringently assessed using the Fornell and Larcker (1981)

test; all possible pairs of constructs (see Table 8.1) passed this test. Evidence of discriminant validity is revealed by the fact that all of the constructs, intercorrelations are significantly different from 1, and the share variance among any constructs is less than the average variance explained in the items by the construct (Fornell and Larcker, 1981; Mackenzie et al., 1999).

Conclusion

A scale was developed to measure push motivation factors driving the choice of tourism mountain destinations. The MTPM scale is a multidimensional model that reflects contemporary society changes through three tourism motivational factors: adventure/excitement, social/knowledge, and prestige, which are grouped in a second order 'push' factor.

The main theoretical implication of this study is that adventure/excitement, social/ knowledge and prestige are among the most important motivational push factors in travel decisions such as tourism mountain destination choice.

People engage in tourism for different reasons. A review of literature reveals the existence of a set of factors that are related with tourism image formation (Beerli and Martin, 2004) and motivation is one of them (Mayo and Jarvis, 1981). Motivation is accepted as the central concept in understanding tourist behaviour particularly in travel and destination choice process. The main managerial implication of this study is that tourism destination managers should give attention to tourist's motivations in order to appeal to tourists' internal desires and needs by providing a range of activities, attractions and services in order to fulfil tourists' socio-psychological needs. When specifically considering tourism mountain destinations, management could provide exciting, adventurous, sportive and entertainment activities to fulfil tourists' excitement/adventure motivations. For satisfying tourists' social/knowledge motivations, tourism mountain destination managers could create opportunities for tourists to experience different ways of life, promoting the contact with local people and culture. In order to fulfil tourists' prestige motivations, it is important to promote the mountains destinations' identity and authenticity.

Furthermore, the MTPM scale can assist mountain destination areas managers in their marketing strategy definition. Effective tourism marketing is impossible without an understanding of consumers' motivations. The MTPM scale can help determine the most successful push motivational factors for tourism product bundles and aid the implementation of effective market segmentation strategies and positioning. The tourism destinations should promote their own differentiating and unique features.

Understanding the implications of push motivational factors can be an advantage for researchers and marketers of tourism destination areas (Uysal and Hagan, 1993) as it allows better understanding of the tourists' behaviour and the society to which they belong as well as developing better marketing mixes.

The present study can also be a useful tool for governmental and official tourism institutions that regulate tourism activity. Whole national economies can be greatly dependent on tourists' needs, which make tourism a highly social activity (Saarinen, 2004). This scale, being an instrument for measuring tourists' needs, can help assess the investments in tourism in mountain areas supported by public funds, can help create mechanisms to match tourists' needs adequately to destination potentialities and to define national and international competitive strategies for each tourism mountain destination.

Finally, the MTPM scale might contribute to tourism and social science literature in understanding the tourist's decision-making process, tourism behaviour and new social forms of tourism consumption.

Limitations and Directions for Future Research

There are still some limitations to be considered. The first limitation is that the final instrument (i.e. the questionnaire) may have created common method variance that could have inflated construct relationships. This could be particularly threatening if the respondents were aware of the conceptual framework of interest. However, they were not told the specific purpose of the study, and the entire construct items were separated and mixed so that no respondent would be able to detect which items were related to which factors. Additionally, if common method bias existed, a CFA containing all constructs would produce a single method factor (Podsakoff and Organ, 1986).

Also, further research is required as to identifying the antecedents and consequents of tourism destination planning. Thus we suggest there is a need to investigate how the tourist motivation construct is associated with other variables, such as tourists' socio-demographic characteristics, information sources, past experience, expectations, and type of residence area (urban vs rural).

Although the focus of this research is in a European country, the multifaceted approach can be applied to other mountain tourism destinations that have experienced social and cultural changes. Comparative studies among mountain places could lead to a new perceptive of mountain tourism motivations.

Finally, and in order to estimate the future evolution and potential of tourism, greater explanatory and forecasting power of consumer tourist behavior is desirable. It is suggested that empirical research in motivation should have a solid theoretical base linked with sociology in order to develop sociology of tourism literature and more deeply analyse the relationship between social value changes and tourism behavior. For that, researchers must consider the fundamental changes that have been taking place in the society.

References

Andreu L, Kozac M, Avci N, Cifter, N. 2005. Market segmentation by motivations to travel: British tourists visiting Turkey. *Journal of Tourism and Travel Marketing* **19** (1): 1-14.

Arnould EJ, Price LL. 1993. River magic: Extraordinary experiences and the extended service encounter. *Journal of Consumer Research* **20** (1): 24-45.

Bagozzi RP. 1980. *Casual Models in Marketing*. John Wiley: New York.

Baloglu S, Brinberg D. 1997. Affective images of tourism destinations. *Journal of Travel Research* **35** (4): 11-15.

Baloglu S, McCleary KW. 1999. A model of destination image formation. *Annals of Tourism Research* **26** (4): 868-897.

Baloglu S, Uysal M. 1996. Market segments of push and pull motivations: A canonical correlation approach. *International Journal of Contemporary Hospitality Management* **8** (3): 32-38.

Beedie P. 2005. The adventure of urban tourism. *Journal of Travel and Tourism Marketing* **8** (3): 37-48.

Beedie P, Hudson S. 2003. Emergence of mountain-based adventure tourism, *Annals of Tourism Research* **30** (3): 625-643.

Beerli A, Martin JD. 2004. Tourists' characteristics and the perceived image of tourist destinations: A quantitative analysis – A case study of Lanzarote, Spain. *Tourism Management* **25** (5): 623-626.

Blamey RK, Braithwaite VA. 1997. A social values segmentation of the potential ecotourism market. *Journal of Sustainable Tourism* **5** (1): 29-45.

Botterill TD, Crompton JL. 1996. Two case studies exploring the nature of the tourist's experience. *Journal of Leisure Research* **28** (1): 57-82.

Bourdieu P. 1979. *La distinction. Critique sociale du jugement*. Paris : Les Editions de Minuit.

Boyer M. 2000. *Histoire de l'invention du tourisme, XVI-XIX siécles*. Paris : Editions de l'aube.

Business Europe. 2005. Industry forecast: Looking to the future. *Business Europe* **45** (7): 6.

Churchill GA. 1979. A paradigm for developing better measures of marketing constructs. *Journal of Marketing Research* **16** (1): 64-73.

Cohen E. 1993. Sociology of tourism, In *Encyclopedia of hospitality & tourism*. Khan M, Olsen M, Van T (eds). New York: Van Nostrand Reinhold. 613-618.

Cohen S, Taylor L. 1976. *Escape Attempts: The Theory and Practice of Resistance to Everyday Life*. London: Allen Lane.

Crompton JL, McKay SL. 1997. Motives of visitors attending festival events. *Annals of Tourism Research* **24** (2): 425-439.

Cronbach LJ. 1951. Coefficient alpha and the internal structure of tests. *Psychometrika* **16** (3): 297-334.

Davidson R. 1992. *Tourism in Europe*. London: Pitman with Techniplus.

Dax T. 2004. The impact of EU policies on mountain development in Austria. In *Regional Studies Association – International Conference Europe at the Margins: EU Regional Policy, Peripherality and Rurality*. France: Angers.

den Breejen L. 2007. The experiences of long distance walking: A case study of the West Highland Way in Scotland. *Tourism Management* **28** (6): 1417-1427.

Fodness D. 1994. Measuring tourist motivation. *Annals of Tourism Research* **21** (3): 555-581.

Formica S, Uysal M. 1996. The revitalisation of Italy as a tourist destination. *Tourism Management* **17** (5): 323-331.

Fornell C, Larcker D. 1981. Evaluating structural equation models with unobservable variables and measurement error. *Journal of Marketing Research* **18** (3): 39-50.

Frochot I, Morrison AM. 2000. Benefit segmentation: A review of its application to travel and tourism research. *Journal of Travel and Tourism Marketing* **9** (4): 21-46.

Furchtgott E, Furchtgott M. 1999. *Aging and Human Motivation*. New York: Kluwer Academic/Plenum Publishers.

Gitelson RJ, Kerstetter DL. 1990. The relationship between sociodemographic variables, benefits and subsequent vacation behavior: A case study. *Journal of Travel Research* **28** (3): 24-29.

Goeldner CR, Ritchie, JR, McIntosh, RW. 2000. *Tourism, Principles, Practices and Philosophies* 8th edn. New York: Wiley.

Gyimóthy S, Mykletun RJ. 2004. Play in adventure tourism: The case of Arctic trekking. *Annals of Tourism Research* **31** (4): 855-878.

Harrill R, Potts T. 2002. Social psychological theories of tourism motivation: Exploration, debate and transition. *Tourism Analysis* **7** (2): 105-114.

Hsu CHC, Cai LA, Wong KKF. 2007. A model of senior tourism motivations – Anecdotes from Beijing and Shanghai. *Tourism Management* **28** (5): 1262-1273.

Huddleston B, Ataman E, Fè d'Ostiani L. 2003. *Towards a GIS-based Analysis of Mountain Environments and Populations*. Rome: FAO.

Jang S, Morrison AM, O'Leary JT. 2002. Benefit segmentation of Japanese pleasure travelers to the USA and Canada: Selecting target markets based on the profitability and risk of individual market segments. *Tourism Management* **23** (4): 367-278.

Jöreskog KG, Sörbom D. 1993. *LISREL 8: Structural Equation Modelling with the SIMPLIS Command Language*. Hillsdale, NJ: Lawrence Erlbaum Associates.

Kapos V, Rhind J, Edwards M, Price MF, Ravilious C. 2000. Developing a map of the world's mountain forests. In *Forests in Sustainable Mountain Development: A State-of-Knowledge Report for 2000*. Price MF, Butt N (eds) Wallingford: CAB International. 4-9.

Kelly JR. 1987. *Freedom to be – A New Sociology of Leisure*. New York: MacMillan

Kim S, Lee C. 2002. Push and pull relationships. *Annals of Tourism Research* **29** (1): 257-260.

Kozac M. 2002. Comparative analysis of tourist motivations by nationality and destinations. *Tourism Management* **23** (3): 221-232.

Lee TH, Crompton JL. 1992. Measuring novelty seeking in tourism. *Annals of Tourism Research* **19** (4): 732-751.

Lyng S. 1990. Edgework: A social psychological analysis of voluntary risk taking. *American Journal of Sociology* **95** (4): 851-886.

MacCannell D. 1989. *The Tourist: A New Theory of the Leisure Class* 2nd edn. London: Macmillan.

MacKenzie SB, Podsakoff PM, Rich GA. 1999. Transformational and transactional leadership and salesperson performance. *Journal Academy Marketing Science* **29** (2): 115–134.

Mayo EJ, Jarvis LP. 1981. *The psychology of leisure travel*. Boston: CBI.

McCool SF. 2002. Mountains and tourism: Meeting the challenges of sustainability in a messy world. In *Conference Proceedings of Celebrating Mountains: An International Year of Mountain Conference*. Jindabyne, Australia.

Messerli B, Ives JD. 1997. *Mountains of the World: A Global Priority*. New York: Parthenon Publishing Group.

Meybeck M, Creen P, Vorosmarty CJ. 2001. A new typology for mountains and other relief classes: An application to global continental water resource and population distribution. *Mountain Research and Development* **21** (3): 34-45.

Mountain Agenda 1999. *Mountains of the World – Tourism and Sustainable Mountain Development*. Berne, Switzerland.

Muller TE. 1991. Using personal values to define segments in an international tourism market. *International Marketing Review* **8**: 57-70.

Podsakoff PM, Organ DW. 1986. Self-reports in organizational research: problems and perspectives. *Journal of Management* **12** (4): 531-544.

Ray NM, Ryder ME. 2003. 'Ebilities' tourism: An exploratory discussion of the travel needs and motivations of the mobility-disabled. *Tourism Management* **24** (1): 57-72.

Ryan C. 1991. *Recreational Tourism: A Social Science Perspective*. London: Routledge.

Saarinen J. 2004. Destination in change: The transformation process of tourist destinations. *Tourism Studies* **4** (2): 161-179.

Schott C. 2004. Young holidaymakers: Solely faithful to hedonism? In *Proceedings of the New Zealand Tourism and Hospitality Research Conference*, Smith KA, Schott C (eds Wellington, Victoria University of Wellington) 364-376.

Schwartz S. 1994. Are there universal aspects in the structure and contents of human values? *Journal of Social Issues* **50** (4): 19-45.

Sirakaya E, Woodside AG. 2005. Building and testing theories of decision making by travellers. *Tourism Management* **26** (6): 815-832.

Smethurst D. 2000. Mountain geography. *Geographical Review* **90** (1): 35-56.

Smith VL, Eadington WR. 1995. *Tourism alternatives: Potentials and problems in the development of tourism*. Wiley: Chichester.

Steenkamp JE, Van Trijp HC. 1991. The use of LISREL in validating marketing constructs. *International Journal of Research in Marketing* **8** (4): 283-299.

Towner J. 1985. The Grand Tour: A key phase in the history of tourism. *Annals of Tourism Research* **12** (3): 297-333.

Tran X, Ralston L. 2006. The influence of culture and needs on travel preferences: A comparison between American and Chinese travellers. In *Conference Proceedings of Annual TTRA Conference*, Dublin, Ireland.

Turnbull DR, Uysal M. 1995. An exploratory study of German visitors to the Caribbean: Push and pull motivations. *Journal of Travel and Tourism Marketing* **4** (2): 85-92.

Urry J. 1996. Tourism, culture and social inequality. In *The Sociology of Tourism. Theoretical and Empirical Investigations* Apostolopoulos Y (ed) London: Routledge; 115-133.

Urry J. 2002. *The Tourist Gaze* 2nd edn. London: Sage.

Uysal M, Hagan R. 1993. Motivation of pleasure travel and tourism. In *Encyclopedia of hospitality and Tourism*, Khan M, Olsen M, Van T (eds), New York: Van Nostrand Reinhold. 798-810.

Wang N. 2000. *Tourism and Modernity: A Sociological Analysis*. Oxford: Pergamon Press.

Ward C, Bochner S, Furnham A. 2001. *The Psychology of Culture Shock* 2nd edn. Routledge.

Wearing B, Wearing S. 1996. Refocusing the tourist experience: The flâneur and the chorister. *Leisure Studies* **15**: 229-243.

Zhang H, Lam T. 1999. An analysis of Mainland Chinese visitors' motivations to visit Hong Kong. *Tourism Management* **20** (5): 587-594.

9 Perceived Authenticity of Cultural Heritage Sites: Towards an Integrative Conceptual Model

Tomaz Kolar and Vesna Zabkar, University of Ljubljana

Introduction

The quest for authentic experiences has long been considered one of the key drives in tourism (Cohen, 1988; MacCannell, 1973; Naoi, 2004). Authenticity is accordingly crucially important for tourism, especially heritage tourism (Apostolakis, 2003; Tourism Trends for Europe, 2006; Yeoman et al., 2007). It is helpful for understanding tourist motivation and behavior as well as strategic and tactical implications concerning tourist destination management.

However, an overview of the literature shows that despite its clear importance, authenticity is an insufficiently explored and problematic concept, which hinders its practical application (Wang, 1999). In terms of the nature and implications of this concept, various approaches and authors not only provide different, but often contradictory views. These are particularly noticeable when sociological and business/marketing views are compared. Such disputes largely go beyond the notion of variations in nuances and conceptualizations, rising to the level of 'ideological oppositions', since commoditization and marketing in tourism are often conceived as destructive forces and a direct antithesis of what is called authentic (for more on this issue, see Olsen, 2002; Reisinger and Steiner, 2006; Shepherd, 2002; Waitt, 2000). In addition, authenticity seems a highly controversial construct in itself. The fragmentation of the authenticity construct is reflected in the various definitions, interpretations and conceptualizations (e.g. Cohen 1988; Hughes, 1995; Olsen, 2002; Peterson, 2005). It is thus no surprise that Reisinger and Steiner (2006) conclude that the different views on (object) authenticity are conflicting and irreconcilable. Because of its problematic nature scholars should abandon the concept altogether. However, Belhassen and Caton (2006) argue that authenticity is indeed alive in the minds of tourists and managers and plays a significant function, so it is up to scholars to study it. What is more, we think that problematic notion(s) and aspects of authenticity should not be avoided but exposed and studied even more thoroughly in order to better understand them. The construct is highly relevant for understanding tourist behavior and important for tourism management, attracts an immense amount of academics' attention, stimulates a lot of endeavors in practice and transcends various disciplines. Its existence and importance therefore simply cannot be put in question, nor abandoned.

Unfortunately, traditional studies of tourism often offer overly critical and dysfunctional approaches to studying contemporary phenomena in tourism (Franklin and Crang, 2001). What is thus needed is a more integrative theoretical examination that would transcend various perspectives on authenticity – from the perspective of the contemporary tourist and manager.

The aim of this chapter is to expose various structural tensions that are involved in conceptualization of authenticity. Furthermore, the managerial relevance and marketing implications of authenticity are discussed, showing that the consumer-based perspective can transcend some 'irreconcilable tensions' involving this concept. What is more, we posit that these tensions and differing conceptualizations in fact represent constitutive aspects (i.e. dimensions) of authenticity construct and should be included in its conceptualization. From managerial perspective they should be approached holistically – as facets of perceived authenticity and not as exclusive types or in/appropriate understandings of it. In order to provide a framework for such an approach, an integrative model of perceived authenticity is proposed that is relevant for examination of perceived authenticity, but also for management of marketing activities that affect its perception at cultural heritage sites.

Structural Tensions of the Authenticity Concept in Tourism

MacCannell (1973) argued that a better understanding of tourist experiences can be accomplished through an examination of various structural tendencies that shape tourists' reality and experiences. As such tendencies, he pointed out the distinctions between the sacred and shallow, modern and primitive, insiders and outsiders, reality and show, tourists and intellectuals. His structural and critical view profoundly influenced subsequent studies and the contemporary conceptualization of authenticity in tourism. Costa and Bamossy (2001) arrived at a similar finding that the concept of authenticity reflects the immense complexity of the interacting phenomena. This interaction involves the purpose of use (e.g. 'primitive' use versus commercial use), a cultural conflict, an identity quest and various dialectical tensions which exist between tradition and change, history and modernity, reality and fiction, and culture and individuality. The proliferation of studies on authenticity in tourism in the past two decades has largely progressed along these structural dimensions. Their oppositional poles are essential for understanding the authenticity concept in its entirety and complexity, and for understanding its problematic nature.

These tensions, interactions and contradictions are however not disputed among various authors and disciplines. Key points of divergence between them seems to be various epistemological assumptions, reliance on various criteria (and sources of authority), the focus (entity, 'unit') of their studies and tourist portrayal at studying authenticity in tourism (see Table 9.1).

One of the basic issues that make the authenticity concept contradictory is the question of whether authenticity is a subjective, socially and individually constructed perception or objectively identifiable property of objects and cultures. According to Reisinger and Steiner (2006) and Wang (1999), classic authors (i.e. objectivist and modernist) argue that there is an evident, objective basis or standard for judging (in)authenticity. However, Cohen (1988) argues that authenticity is a negotiable rather than a primitive concept and that over time cultural developments can attain the status of a so-called 'emergent' authenticity.

Table 9.1: Points and sources of divergence in the conceptualization of authenticity

Point of divergence	Sources (positions) of divergence	
Worldview	Postmodern	Modern

Philosophy
  Ontology
  Epistemology
	Phenomenology, existentialism
	Relativism, constructivism
	Interpretivism
		Realism, utilitarianism
		Objectivism
		Positivism

Discipline	Sociology, anthropology	Economics, marketing
Authority to judge authenticity	Tourist, consumer, laypeople	Intellectuals, scientists
Focus, pertinence (entity)	Authenticity as a phenomenon in the societal context, existential sense, self, individual	Objects, artifacts, cultures, social roles
Tourist portrait	Emotional, hedonist, decision-maker, active, reflexive	Morally inferior, intellectually disabled, harmful, passive

For such a conception of authenticity Wang (1999) used the term constructive (or symbolic) authenticity. Constructive authenticity is relative and refers to the social construction of objects and to beliefs, expectations and their subjective perceptions (Reisinger and Steiner, 2006). Objective and constructive authenticity are still object-oriented and, according to Wang (1999), of limited use in explaining many tourist motivations and experiences. He thus draws a sharp distinction between the authenticity of *objects* and the authenticity of tourists' *experiences* (i.e. existential authenticity) which can be entirely unrelated with each other. For him, existential authenticity is not object-based, but rather activity-based and can be divided into two dimensions: intra-personal (bodily feelings) and interpersonal (self-making).

By conceiving authenticity as constructed, thus as an experience or as a perception, constructivists overcame some tensions based on the assumption that authenticity can be experienced and judged only from the 'outside' – from a historical, cultural distance and with intellectual proficiency. When perceived as such, tourists' experiences can thus be authentic even when they are perfectly aware that the setting has been contrived (Cohen, 1988). Yet this position was unable to resolve a paradoxical finding that inauthentic artifacts or contrived settings can result in authentic experiences. Wang (1999) transcended this paradox through a strict division between the authenticity of objects and of experiences, therefore by 'freeing' the concept of (existential) authenticity from object and place. In this approach he relies on existentialist and phenomenological traditions which conceive authenticity as a given, as a phenomenon per se (Olsen, 2002).

Another divergence in the conceptualization of authenticity is notable between the traditional (modernist) and contemporary (postmodern) paradigms or worldviews. According to Wang (1999) and Bruner (1994), postmodernists do not consider inauthenticity as a problem and largely abandon this construct, especially the authenticity of the original. In this interpretation, postmodern tourists are only concerned with authenticity in a cynical sense – in terms of enjoyment and satisfaction (Reisinger and Steiner, 2006).

The idea that for postmodernists, authenticity has no relevance, that tourists are not interested in it or even reject it entirely might, however, be misleading and problematic. Postmodern society is namely characterized by fragmentation, confusion, emptiness, alienation and by a crisis of morality and identity. Hence, people have become more concerned with identity, meaning and values (Cova, 1999), but also with nostalgia and history (Goulding, 2000). Many authors consequently argue that people in modern and postmodern societies are in fact more interested in authenticity and strive to overcome inauthenticity (Lewis and Bridger, 2000; MacCannel, 1973). The key dilemma here is whether, despite its alleged rejection of authenticity, postmodernism is relevant for conceptualization of authenticity? In our opinion it is, by suggesting that authenticity is not a 'free-floating' concept, an existential phenomenon per se, which implies that tourists' settings and tourists' existence are unrelated realms. In a postmodern manner tourists do not relate and judge settings from an intellectual distance or through sacredness, but rather through emotions and 'mundane experiences'. The postmodern tourist is an experience-oriented, affective-driven, experience-seeking hedonist (Jensen and Lindberg, 2001).

As noted by Goulding (2000), pastiche, parody and mimicry are important features of postmodernist society which produce 'imitation that mocks the original'. The original is thus not as important as the re-creation and interpretation of it, which emphasizes tourists' involvement and participation rather than a distant and passive observation. In this sense, we can propose that the postmodern tourist is still interested in the authenticity of (primarily existential) experiences, while authenticity in terms of an 'original artifact' has become irrelevant.

The boundary between authentic and inauthentic, reality and fiction, genuine and fake has not only become blurred but actively manipulated and, as such, decisive for the postmodern conceptualization of authenticity. One of these tensions is especially problematic yet essential for tourism marketing. This is the heavily discussed opposition between authenticity and commoditization. According to critical sociologists, the commoditization of a local culture destroys its native indigenous character, along with social relations and the original meaning of cultural products (see e.g. Cohen, 1988 for an extensive discussion of this issue). A similar critique is put forward by Waitt (2000), namely that the marketization of history produces a one-sided, partial and contrived version of the truth. Such a critical view is not only characteristic of traditional authors, but is also very much alive today, being called 'landscapes of nostalgia' (Halewood and Hannam, 2001). The central thesis remains the same: the process of commoditization is destructive of and antithetical to authenticity.

What seems especially problematic are the persisting binary distinctions and exclusivist (i.e. either/or) position regarding authentic and inauthentic, object and experience/existence, commodity and culture, but also between tourist, intellectual and host. Such a taxonomy and emphasis on analytical clarity is largely dysfunctional and thus Franklin and Crang (2001) call for a more dynamic, experiential, empirical and 'hybrid' approach to the study of tourism. In a similar manner, Olsen (2002) proposes a more process-oriented and holistic approach that would transcend the binary oppositions and enable an understanding of how authentic experiences are formed, influenced and related to actual tourist behavior. With this purpose in mind, in the next part we discuss the concept of authenticity from the managerial and consumer-based perspective.

Authenticity in Tourism Management and Marketing

As one of the key tourist drivers, the quest for authenticity holds important implications for tourism management and marketing. In this field authenticity is not seen as antithetical to tourism but as a much warranted element of its offer. Yeoman et al. (2005), for instance, convincingly illustrate how authenticity serves as foundation for the promotion of Scotland. Understandably, rather than mutual exclusivity, the practice and theory in this field emphasize the compatibility and convergence of authenticity and marketing, especially in heritage tourism (Apostolakis, 2003). Culture/arts and tourism today enjoy a complementary relationship and are actively encouraged (Hughes, 2002). Certain 'manipulations' (e.g. conservation) that are beneficial for the preservation of historical heritage are in fact necessary, so that tourists can recognize their authenticity (Naoi, 2004). In a similar vein, a commercial presentation often keeps traditional cultures and customs alive since they would otherwise be 'modernized' and lost (Cohen, 1988). Without doubt, tourism brings both beneficial and adverse effects for local economies, residents and the integrity of heritage (see for example, van der Borg et al., 1996). However, the basic meaning and intent of the commoditization of cultural heritage is not the destruction of its authenticity but the exposition of its exchange value (Goulding, 2000). Tensions and conflicts between 'secular' tourism activities and pilgrimage (sacred) aspects of tourism are accordingly more properly conceived and explored in a dialectical rather than an exclusivist manner (Murray and Graham, 1997).

Tourism management and marketing have various influences and an important stake in authenticity for they are involved in its preservation, (re)construction as well as in a (re) definition of its offer. Authenticity is namely acknowledged as something that is socially constructed and the subject of continual change (Costa and Bammosy, 2001; Peterson, 2005). The finding that the objective conception of authenticity 'is now less prevalent in the academic community but still occurs in business circles' (Reisinger and Steiner, 2006: 69) thus sounds obsolete. The constructivist view seems to prevail in both areas, *especially* in the business one. From the managerial standpoint, the dynamic nature of authenticity along with the process of its fabrication and verification (i.e. authentication) is namely particularly important. In line with this Peterson (2005) asserts that authenticity is a claim and that 'authenticity work' can take a number of forms like:

♦   Ethnic/cultural identity (a Chinese cook as a display of the authenticity of food)

♦   Status identity (e.g. 'uncontaminated', native, self-taught artists)

♦   Authentic experiences (e.g. local, undiscovered music clubs)

♦   Self-construction and appearance (e.g. the spontaneous hillbilly look of some country singers), and

♦   Technological mediation (e.g. Internet 'tribes').

To these forms of authenticity, several others can be added, which nevertheless largely overlap. Chronis and Hampton (2008) found that consumer perceptions of authenticity are articulated in five distinct ways, that is as object-related (original artifacts like cannons actually used in the war), factual (historical accuracy), locational (actual places and locations visited), personage (actual protagonists and heroes) and contextual (surrounding milieu). Bruner (1994) discuss four meanings of authenticity that are based on verisimilitude (mimetic credibility), genuineness (historical accuracy – complete and immaculate simulation), originality (of objects and buildings) and authority (duly authorized, certified or legally valid). All these types of authenticity are however not entirely unrelated among themselves what suggests that authenticity is a multidimensional concept of dimensions which are mutually complementary and not exclusive. The final acknowledgment of the authenticity claim is, however, made by tourists. In contemporary tourism, vendors in fact offer and prove authenticity (e.g. with certificates of authenticity issued by authorized institutions) and tourists are its 'receivers' (Chhabra, 2005).

This has resulted in a concept of authenticity which is conceived as an individual experience or perception (Apostolakis, 2003) and applies to cultural tourism as well (Hughes, 2002). The commercial replication of history is authentic when tourists perceive it as such – thus as a faithful and precise reconstruction. Perceived authenticity should be understood as a matter of extent, rather than an either/or issue. Without doubt tourists perceive commercial presentations of history, heritage and culture(s) as (more or less) authentic (Chhabra et al., 2003; Kim and Jamal, 2007; Poria et al., 2003; Waitt, 2000; Waller and Lea, 1999). Even Disneyland, which was built as an entirely artificial amusement park evolved in the eyes of foreign tourists into an authentic American artifact, a symbolic and idealized portrayal of genuine America (Costa and Bamossy, 2001). These findings confirm that tourists do not only conceive of authenticity in terms of the 'absolute originality of an object', but also in terms of the authentic *reproduction* (Bruner, 1994), something which Grayson in Martinec (2004) defines as *iconic* authenticity.

Conceiving authenticity as a multi-meaning, individually-perceived construct raises the question of how it is perceived and which meanings and aspects are important for tourists. McIntosh (2004) found that by an authentic experience of Maori culture tourists understand becoming 'personally involved in the experience', to experience the 'natural context' and 'daily life', but also to experience 'true facts, arts and crafts instead of plastic society'. With heritage museums, Goulding (2000) found three different types of visitors in regard to how they perceive authenticity. The first type, named 'existential' visitors, emphasizes the importance of enjoyment and escape and mainly perceives authenticity through exhibited artifacts. The second type, named 'aesthetical' visitors, perceives history mainly through art, while their central theme is idealized images of history. The third type is 'social' visitors, which emphasizes the importance of learning. They perceive history through social experiences and are especially interested in watching demonstrations and buying in museum shops.

Interestingly, according to tourist surveys, there is an increasingly large proportion of tourists who would like to avoid mass-tourist areas, escape everyday life and get in touch with their true selves (Yeoman et al., 2007). Middleton and Clarke (2004) claim that the cultural tourism and self-actualization in which the 'new consumer' is increasingly interested, represent an alternative to mass, 4S (Sun, Sea, Sand and Sex) tourism and is driven by 4I motives (Intellectual curiosity, Inspiration, Investigation and Involvement). This is well in line with assertions that authenticity represents a central interest of modern Western culture (Grayson and Martinec, 2004) and that the shift in interest 'from abundance to authenticity' is one of the key trends of contemporary consumption (Lewis and Bridger, 2000).

Effective marketing in tourism therefore needs to encompass the consumer-based perspective and focus on the 'new tourist', which is in sharp contrast with the traditional view of the tourist (i.e. passive, shallow, uninterested and condemned to inauthenticity). As shown today, even unserious, leisure tourists are ever more interested in both authenticity and intellectual experiences. Consumption is more and more acknowledged as a process in which 'people attempt to overcome a sense of alienation', and as a 'mode of free expression of the creative subject' (Miller, 2001: 4). The contemporary tourist is thus an amalgam of an intellectual and a consumer. Accordingly, tourism management and marketing needs to adopt the consumer-based perspective when studying the authenticity of tourist experiences. Such a perspective enables a more holistic view of authenticity, along with a more realistic representation of contemporary tourists and more operative implications for tourism marketing. We propose the following:

P: The consumer-based perspective allows for a dynamic and integrative conceptualization of authenticity in which academically and managerially relevant views might be combined.

Following this perspective, we propose an integrative model of perceived authenticity of cultural heritage site (see Figure 9.1).

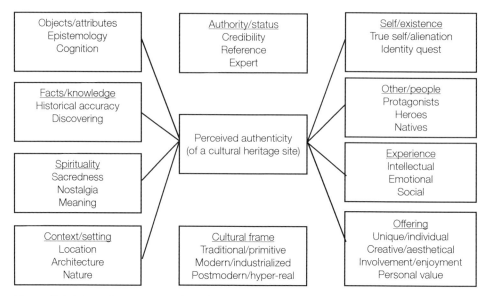

Figure 9.1: Integrative conceptual model of perceived authenticity

Sources: MacCannell, 1973; Costa and Bamossy, 2001; Goulding, 2000; Peterson, 2005; Wang, 1999; Kim and Jamal, 2007; Yeoman et al., 2007; Bruner, 1994; Chronis and Hampton, 2008; Middleton and Clarke, 2004.

The proposed model consists of ten dimensions (facets) that constitute perceived authenticity of a cultural heritage site. It is assumed that tourists form their perception of authenticity of a site through the following ten dimensions and corresponding questions (which might not be stated explicitly):

1. **Objects**: are they original?

2. **Facts**: are they historically accurate?

3. **Authority**: is the authenticity claim credible?

4. **Context**: is this an actual and faithfully preserved environment?

5. **Self**: do I feel in touch with my true self?

6. **People**: are the protagonists actual and/or indigenous?

7. **Spirituality**: do I feel connected with humankind?

8. **Cultural frame**: do I encounter contradiction among primitive, modern and/or post-modern worldviews, lifestyles and values?

9. **Experience**: how pleasant and exceptional are my intellectual, emotional and social experiences during the visit?

10. **Offering**: how aesthetical, unique, involving, inspiring, personal and enjoying are commercial items and services?

Although proposed dimensions represent distinctive concepts, we assume that tourists combine them into holistic perception of authenticity where they combine authority/ status and cultural frame of a cultural heritage site, objects/attributes and experience, context/setting and self/existence, facts/knowledge, spirituality and offering. All these are seen as constitutive aspects of perceived authenticity and should be included in its conceptualization.

Due to the extreme complexity of the perceived authenticity concept, a series of exploratory qualitative analyses are needed to further test conceptual characteristics, explore underlying sources and provide insights into behavioral consequences of perceived authenticity. A search of relevant items of the perceived authenticity scale should be based on literature and expert judges from the field of tourism. Any subjectively perceived construct should follow standard procedures that assure validity and reliability of its measurement (see for example, Churchill, 1999; Clark and Watson, 1995). The first step of such procedure is conceptualization (i.e. defining the nature and domain(s) of a psychological construct or a phenomenon), followed by generation of larger number of questions (pool of items) that measure a construct of interest. Item wording needs careful attention, the content of the pool of items should be 'overinclusive' (Clark and Watson, 1995: 309). The item pool could then be tested on a heterogeneous sample of the target tourist population. Subsequent exploratory factor analysis should reveal high internal reliability consistency in different tourism contexts. Confirmatory factor analysis should be applied to verify the fit of the model. In this respect, the proposed integrative model of perceived authenticity can serve as a framework for operationalization of the construct and development of a measurement instrument. A measurement instrument should enable empirical examination of the perceived authenticity from the tourists' point of view.

Conclusion

Proposed conceptualization might be helpful at overcoming obstacles for practical application of the authenticity concept, which is considered as important and useful, yet problematic (Reisinger and Steiner 2006; Wang, 1999). Operationalization of this highly abstract concept by means of its key dimensions can provide, or at least inspire, various implications for tourism marketers and practitioners. In general, the model might be useful for making marketing strategy of cultural tourism more operative. Its dimensions might be seen as key components of the strategy that needs to be prioritized and managed in order that strategic focus is moved from the mass, '4S' tourism, to the intellectual and spiritual experiences of '4I' tourism (Middleton and Clarke, 2004). For this purpose each dimension might be seen as a complex domain, which requires strategic deliberation about development of competitive advantages. Consider, for instance, the dimension of the cultural frame, which might be of particular interest for marketing of lesser-known destinations. Perceived authenticity is mainly related to experiences of primitive, foreign, distant and lesser-known places. From this standpoint, being unknown, 'primitive' (even undeveloped) and thus in sharp contrast with popular, sophisticated and fashionable destinations, can contribute to perceived authenticity. In this manner, cultural oppositions that represent the core of this dimension might be helpful at turning weaknesses of the destination into its advantages.

More specifically, selected attributes of dimensions can be used as a basis for concretization of promotional claims that are otherwise often limited to an elusive notion of authentic experiences. Each dimension and its attributes represent potential points of differentiation and a basis for competitive positioning of a particular site or destination. As cultural tourism is on the rise and combination of cultural, leisure and entertainment products is advised (see for example, Tourism Trends for Europe, 2006) it might be expected that competition in cultural tourism will increase. This suggests that identifying and promoting potential points of competitive differentiation is ever more important. Promotion is however not the only tactical element for which proposed model dimensions might be of interest. Given that in services marketing there are 7Ps of marketing mix (Product, Promotion, Place, Price, Processes, People, Physical evidence), combining dimensions of proposed model with these 7Ps results in a myriad of possibilities for practical improvements that might enhance perceived authenticity of the site.

Moreover, proposed conceptualization might serve as a promising segmentation base for targeting various tourist segments (e.g. on the basis of importance of particular dimension of authenticity) and can also be useful for development of evaluative measures, needed for examination of tourists' perceptions. Consumer-based perspective posits that perceived authenticity is dependent upon effectiveness of various marketing activities. As such, perceived authenticity might complement other evaluative measures like perceived quality, value and tourist satisfaction and serves as measure of marketing effectiveness. Any serious attempt toward management of perceived authenticity should namely include some assessment of successfulness of these efforts, where each dimension of the proposed model might serve as starting point for development of needed evaluative criteria.

However, the most interesting implications related to the authenticity concept results from further insights into its complex nature. Studying each dimension or aspect of consumer-perceived authenticity in isolation would therefore be too narrow and overly fragmented. Instead, the further integration of the various conceptualizations and contrasting perspectives is warranted. Studying tourists' experiences from the consumer perspective allows such an integration and suggests that the multiplicity of meanings regarding authenticity is an opportunity and not a 'problem' that should be resolved. In this manner, a détente among the various perspectives on authenticity is not only becoming viable but is also particularly warranted.

References

Apostolakis A. 2003. The convergence process in heritage tourism. *Annals of Tourism Research* **30** (4): 795-812.

Belhassen Y, Caton K. 2006. Authenticity matters. *Annals of Tourism Research* **33** (3): 853-856.

Bruner EM. 1994. Abraham Lincoln as authentic reproduction: a critique of postmodernism. *American Anthropologist* **96** (2): 397-415.

Chhabra D. 2005. Defining authenticity and its determinants: Toward an authenticity flow model. *Journal of Travel Research* **44** (1): 64-68.

Chhabra D, Healy R, Sills E. 2003. Staged authenticity and heritage tourism. *Annals of Tourism Research* **30** (3): 702-719.

Chronis A, Hampton RD. 2008. Consuming the authentic Gettysburg: How a tourist landscape becomes an authentic experience. *Journal of Consumer Behaviour* 7 (2): 111-126.

Churchill GA. 1999. *Marketing Research: Methodological Foundations*. Dryden Press: Fort Worth, TX.

Clark LA, Watson D. 1995. Constructing validity: basic issues in objective scale development. *Psychological Assessment*, 7 (3): 309-319.

Cohen E. 1988. Authenticity and commoditization in tourism. *Annals of Tourism Research* 15 (3): 371-386.

Costa JA, Bamossy G. J. 2001. Le Parc Disney: creating an'authentic' American experience. *Advances in Consumer Research* 28: 398-402.

Cova B. 1999. From Marketing to Societing: When the link is more important than the thing. In *Rethinking Marketing: Towards Critical Marketing Accountings*, Douglas T. Brownlie, Robin Wensley, Richard Whittington (eds). Sage Publications: London; 64-83.

Franklin A, Crang M. 2001. The trouble with tourism and travel theory. *Tourist Studies* 1 (1): 5-22.

Goulding C. 2000. The commodification of the past, postmodern pastiche, and the search for authentic experiences at contemporary heritage attractions. *European Journal of Marketing* 34 (7): 835-853.

Grayson K, Martinec R. 2004. Consumer perceptions of iconicity and indexicality and their influence on assessments of authentic market offerings. *Journal of Consumer Research* 31 (2): 296-312.

Halewood C, Hannam K. 2001. Viking heritage tourism: authenticity and Commodification. *Annals of Tourism Research* 28 (3): 565-580.

Hughes G. 1995. Authenticity in tourism. *Annals of Tourism Research* 22 (4): 781-803.

Hughes HL. 2002. Culture and tourism: a framework for further analysis. *Managing Leisure* 7 (3): 164-175.

Jensen Ø, Lindberg F. 2001. The consumption of tourist attraction: A modern, postmodern and existential encounter perspective. In: *Interpretive Consumer Research*. Copenhagen Business School Press: Copenhagen.

Kim H, Jamal T. 2007. Touristic quest for existential authenticity. *Annals of Tourism Research*, 34 (1), 181-201.

Lewis D, Bridger D. 2000. *The Soul of the New Consumer: Authenticity-What We Buy and Why in the New Economy*. Nicholas Brealey Publishing: London.

MacCannell D. 1973. Staged authenticity: arrangements of social space in tourist settings. *American Journal of Sociology* 79 (3): 589-603.

McIntosh AJ. 2004. Tourists' appreciation of Maori culture in New Zealand. *Tourism Management* 25 (1): 1-15.

Middleton VTC, Clarke JR. 2004. *Marketing in Travel and Tourism*. Butterworth-Heinemann: Oxford.

Miller D. 2001. *The Dialectics of Shopping*. University Of Chicago Press: Chicago.

Murray M, Graham B. 1997. Exploring the dialectics of route-based tourism: the Camino de Santiago. *Tourism Management* 18 (8): 513-524.

Naoi T. 2004. Visitors' evaluation of a historical district: the roles of authenticity and manipulation. *Tourism and Hospitality Research* 5 (1): 45-63.

Olsen KH. 2002. Authenticity as a concept in tourism research: The social organization of the experience of authenticity. *Tourist Studies* 2 (2): 159–182.

Peterson RA. 2005. In search of authenticity. *Journal of Management Studies* 42 (5): 1083-1098.

Poria Y, Butler R, Airey D. 2003. The core of heritage tourism. *Annals of Tourism Research* **30** (1): 238-254.

Reisinger Y, Steiner C. J. 2006. Reconceptualizing object authenticity. *Annals of Tourism Research* **33** (1): 65-86.

Shepherd R. 2002. Commodification, culture and tourism. *Tourist Studies* **2** (2): 183-201.

Steiner CJ, Reisinger Y. 2006. Understanding existential authenticity. *Annals of Tourism Research* **33** (2): 299-318.

Tourism trends for Europe 2006. European Travel Commission, September 2006. Available at: http://www.etc-corporate.org/resources/uploads/ETC_Tourism_Trends_for_Europe_09-2006_ENG.pdf

van der Borg J, Costa P, Gotti G. 1996. Tourism in European heritage cities. *Annals of Tourism Research* **23** (2): 306-321.

Waitt G. 2000. Consuming heritage-perceived historical authenticity. *Annals of Tourism Research* **27** (4): 835-862.

Waller J, Lea S. E. G. 1999. Seeking the real Spain? Authenticity in motivation. *Annals of Tourism Research* **26** (1): 110-129.

Wang N. 1999. Rethinking authenticity in tourism experience. *Annals of Tourism Research* **26** (2): 349-370.

Yeoman IS, Durie A, McMahon-Beattie U, Palmer A. 2005. Capturing the essence of a brand from its history: The case of Scottish tourism marketing. *Brand Management* **13** (2): 134-147.

Yeoman IS, Brass D, McMahon-Beattie U. 2007. Current issue in tourism: the authentic tourist. *Tourism Management* **28** (4): 1128-1138.

10 Assessing Mainland Chinese Tourists' Satisfaction with Hong Kong using the Tourist Satisfaction Index

Haiyan Song, Hong Kong Polytechnic University; Gang Li, University of Surrey; Robert van der Veean and Jason L. Chen, Hong Kong Polytechnic University

Introduction

Tourist satisfaction has become an increasingly important issue for destination management organizations. A good understanding of the tourist satisfaction level and its dynamic changes benefits not only tourism goods/services providers, but also government regulators and tourism investors. High tourist satisfaction is likely to contribute to enhanced reputation of tourism product providers and of the whole destination, increased consumer loyalty, reduced price elasticities, lower cost of future transactions and improved productivity (Anderson et al., 1994; Swanson and Kelley, 2001).

Tourism is an integrated system that consists of a number of sectors such as accommodation, catering, transportation, visitor attractions, travel intermediaries (tour operators and travel agencies), retailing and tourism-related public agencies (such as police and travel information centres). Correspondingly, tourists' overall satisfaction with a destination is affected by their satisfaction with each individual component involved in their experiences at the destination. Although many tourism businesses have been carrying out tourist satisfaction surveys within their organizations, and government agencies and academic researchers have also launched a number of one-off tourist satisfaction investigations at the destination level, there has not been a continuous evaluation system that facilitates the assessment of tourist satisfaction on a regular basis at both sectoral and destination levels.

This chapter aims to fill in the above gaps by creating a comprehensive tourist satisfaction index (TSI) system, which will provide government agencies that are responsible for tourism related activities, different sectors of the tourism industry and the general public with much needed information for decision-making and planning purposes.

The empirical study will focus on Hong Kong, where tourism has been seen as one of the major economic pillars (Lo, 2005). In particular, mainland China was the largest source market with the total number of visitor arrivals exceeding 15.4 million in 2007 (HKTB, 2008). Therefore, to evaluate the satisfaction levels within this market is of great practical importance for Hong Kong.

Literature Review

Consumer satisfaction has been extensively researched by scholars and practitioners over the last three decades. One of the most often applied consumer satisfaction models is the expectancy–disconfirmation model developed by Oliver (1980). It has four elements: expectation, perceived performance, disconfirmation and satisfaction. Consumers develop expectations of a product or service before purchasing it, and then compare the actual performance of the product/service with their expectations about the product/service. If the performance of the product/service surpasses their expectations, positive disconfirmation is reached, which would then lead to consumers' satisfaction and willingness to purchase, and vice versa. This model has been further refined by introducing additional constructs to the framework. A comprehensive review of the above approaches can be seen in Oh and Parks (1997).

In tourist satisfaction studies the expectancy–disconfirmation framework has been given a great deal of attention and applied in various contexts. Yoon and Uysal (2005) suggest that tourist satisfaction should be studied in multiple dimensions and a model that integrates alternative approaches would be more effective and desirable in assessing tourist satisfaction. Tourism researchers have been interested in measuring both overall tourist satisfaction with a particular destination (e.g. Alegre and Cladera, 2006) and tourist satisfaction at specific service encounter level, such as accommodation (e.g. Hsu et al., 2003), restaurants (e.g. Chadee and Mattsson, 1996), attractions (e.g. Dorfman, 1979), travel agencies (e.g. Leblanc, 1992), package tours (e.g. Pizam and Milman, 1993) and retail shops (e.g. Reisinger and Turner, 2002). Although the tourist satisfaction research has gained increasing popularity at both levels, there are some gaps between them. Most assessments of tourist satisfaction within a particular destination are based on multi-attribute scales covering a variety of service components and facilities. However, these categories do not necessarily refer to a particular sector within the broad tourism industry. Therefore, the research findings would not be able to provide a clear guidance for the destination government to implement the most effective destination management policies or strategies.

Another problem with the previous tourist satisfaction studies is that most of them overlooked the dynamic nature of tourist satisfaction. Moreover, there has not been any assessment system to carry out tourist satisfaction assessment continuously over time. Given the importance of such a continuous tourist satisfaction assessment system for destination management, there is an urgent need to bridge this gap.

The consumer satisfaction assessment has attracted interest in the general marketing studies which led to the development of national and regional consumer satisfaction indexes (CSIs). For example, Chan et al. (2003) developed the Hong Kong CSI to monitor the changes of households' satisfaction with the products and services they purchased over time. However, no attempt has been made to comprehensively and continuously assess consumer satisfaction from a tourism perspective. The CSI framework provides a useful guideline for developing a TSI system. However, the weighting scheme of CPI adopted by Chan et al. (2003) is not applicable for free-of-charge public services. Therefore, a more appropriate weighting scheme other than the CPI needs to be developed in order to compile an overall TSI.

The above literature review suggests that there is a great need for the development of a TSI system in order to assess tourists' overall satisfaction with a destination. Such an assessment system should have a sound theoretical underpinning and is capable of assessing both the sectoral and destination satisfaction levels over time.

Theoretical Framework of the TSI System

This study presents the first attempt to develop a comprehensive index system for evaluating tourist satisfaction. The proposed framework starts with the evaluation of TSI at the sectoral level. At this level, major tourism related sectors could be included, such as accommodation, restaurants, transportation, attractions, travel agents, retail shops and public services (e.g. customs and police). The satisfaction index of each sector is derived separately based on the proposed model. Then the overall TSI for the destination is aggregated based on the sectoral TSIs.

Theoretical Model of Tourist Satisfaction Evaluation

The proposed theoretical model of TSI evaluation (see Figure 10.1) is based on the expectancy-disconfirmation framework which has been applied to general consumer satisfaction evaluations (e.g. Chan et al., 2003) as well as in tourism and travel research (Oh and Parks, 1997).

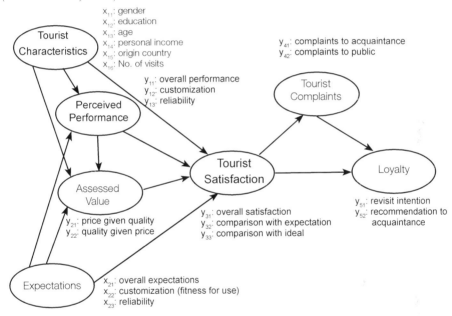

Figure 10.1: The Sectoral Level Tourist Satisfaction Index Model

First of all, expectation and performance are incorporated into the proposed TSI model as important antecedents of tourist satisfaction. Another factor that influences tourists' satisfaction is the assessed value of the encountered tourism-related services in a destination relative to the prices paid (for private goods and services) or time spent (for public services). Adding the value component to the TSI model allows one to distinguish tourists' satisfaction levels when their income and cultural backgrounds are different (Chan et al., 2003; Fornell et al., 1996). Moreover, the aggregation of TSIs based on tourists with different demographic characteristics is also reflected in the TSI model. Tourist complaints and destination loyalty are included as two immediate consequences of tourist satisfaction in the TSI model. Based on the exit-voice theory (Hirschman, 1970), an increase in tourist satisfaction is likely to decrease the incidence of tourist complaints and increase their loyalty towards the destination. To investigate tourists' loyalty to a destination, in particular their intention to revisit, has an important implications for policy-makers in terms of improving the destination competitiveness.

Calculation of the Overall TSI

The overall TSI is calculated based on a confirmatory measurement model. In this model, the overall TSI is formed by their satisfaction towards individual sectors, each measured by the three items as shown in Figure 10.1. The factor loadings indicate the contributions of the sectoral satisfaction to the overall satisfaction and, hence, are adopted as the weights for obtaining the overall TSI. Given the objective weights obtained from a second-order confirmatory factor analysis for destination satisfaction, the calculation of the overall TSI has a strong scientific basis, which in turn guarantees the robustness of overall TSI estimation.

Methodology

A relatively large-scale pilot test was conducted in order to assess the proposed theoretical TSI assessment framework. The target population was set to mainland Chinese tourists visiting Hong Kong. As discussed earlier, this is an important tourist market for Hong Kong and any competitive advancement in this market should be of interest to the government and the tourism industry in Hong Kong. Since the primary purpose of this pilot study is to test the proposed theoretical framework which is directly applicable to any tourism related sectors, only three key tourism related sectors were included in this survey, representing hotels, travel agents and retail shops. Subsequently, only these sectors were included in the computation of the overall TSI, for the purpose of demonstrating the aggregation method. A face-to-face street intercept survey using a self-administered questionnaire was employed. A convenience sampling method was applied. After two days of data collection in November 2008, 279 valid responses were obtained. The details of the sample are presented in Table 10.1.

Table 10.1: Profile of survey respondents

Variable	%	Variable	%
Sex		Education	
Male	51.4	No formal education	.8
Female	48.6	Primary/elementary school	.8
		Secondary/high school	23.5
		College/university	66.8
		Postgraduate	8.1
Age		Number of past visits	
16-25	21.43	0	39.2
26-35	34.92	1	31.5
36-45	20.24	2	9.1
46-55	18.25	3	5.6
56-65	4.37	4	4.3
≥66	0.79	≥5	10.3
Monthly Income (RMB)			
<1,000	3.9		
1001-3000	12.0		
3001-6000	17.2		
6001-7500	18.0		
7500-9000	14.6		
≥9001	4.7		
No regular income	3.9		

Note: all the percentages are calculated based on valid responses.

Unlike many tourist satisfaction studies where direct measurement was employed, tourist satisfaction in this study is measured as a latent variable associated with three indicators: overall satisfaction, confirmation of expectations and comparison with ideal. The tourist characteristics construct is a combination of six commonly used socio-economic indicators: gender, age, education, personal income, origin country (omitted from this pilot study as only one source market was included) and number of past visits. For all the other five constructs, they are all measured by multiple items (see Figure 10.1). The survey questions relating to their indicators use 11-point rating scales from −5 for 'poor' to +5 for 'excellent' indicating a bipolar conceptualization of the dimensions (Schwarz et al., 1991), which is more sensitive to detecting differences (Bandura, 2006). The use of 11-point scales, as well as the use of multiple indicators, can help reduce the negative skewness commonly associated with the distributions of ratings for satisfaction-related indicators (Fornell, 1992; Fornell et al., 1996). The 11-point scales are commonly used in CSI surveys (e.g. Chan et al., 2003).

TSI depicted in Figure 10.1 represents a structural equation model (SEM). A components-based approach known as partial least square is used to estimate the model. A sectoral TSI is first computed using the model-implied weights (ω_{31}, ω_{32} and ω_{33}). For convenience in calculating the indexes, the original scales from −5 to +5 were transformed to a 0 to 10 scale format. The sectoral TSI (Sub-TSI) is then calculated as:

$$\text{Sub-TSI} = \frac{\omega_{31}y_{31} + \omega_{32}y_{32} + \omega_{33}y_{33}}{\omega_{31} + \omega_{32} + \omega_{33}} \times 10$$

(10.1)

That is, tourist satisfaction within a particular tourism sector equals the weighted average of its three satisfaction indicators' mean values (y_{31}, y_{32} and y_{33}) multiplied by a scaling constant 10. Thus each TSI is expressed in a 0-100 scale. The higher the tourists' average scoring on the satisfaction questions, the higher the calculated sectoral TSI.

The overall TSI, as a weighted average of sub-TSIs, is given in Equation (10.2).

$$\text{Overal TSI} = \frac{\sum_{i=1}^{m} g_i \text{Sub-TSI}_i}{\sum_{i=1}^{m} g_i}$$

(10.2)

where g_i s are factor loadings derived from the confirmation measurement model for the overall TSI calculation.

Results

The programme SmartPLS 2.0 M3 (Ringle et al., 2005) was employed to estimate both the inner (structural) and outer (measurement) model. The expectation–maximization algorithm in LISREL-PRELIS was used to replace the missing values with estimates. The reliability analysis was conducted to test the level of internal consistency for the measurements of all the reflective constructs. The indicators of the reflective constructs (*satisfaction, performance, expectations, assessed value*) are reliable because all the standardised indicator loadings for the three sectors are positive and significant (0.72 to 0.95). This means the corresponding error variances were small. In addition, each reflective construct is reliable as shown by the average variances extracted, which are consistently above 70% across the three sectors, higher than the critical value of 50% as recommended by Fornell (1992). This indicates that each reflective dimension and its respective indicators were highly correlated (Chan et al., 2003). The R^2s for the structural equations used to predict satisfaction are quite high for all the three sectors. The structural equations used to predict *performance, assessed value* and *loyalty* also report reasonable explanatory power, except for the *complaints* construct. This result is consistent with that of Chan et al. (2003). The possible reason for the low R^2 of the *complaints* construct might be related to the high level of missing values of its measures.

With regard to the significance of the estimated path coefficients, the majority of the *t*-values are significant (see Figures 10.2-10.4) and support the hypothesised paths (1.96 for alpha level 0.05 and 2.56 for alpha level 0.01). In addition, most of the estimated path coefficients are well above 0.30 or close to it. This indicates that the proposed model has a strong predictive power.

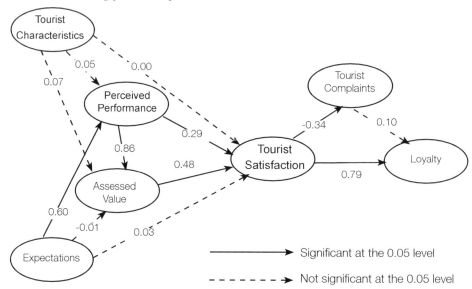

Figure 10.2: The SEM for the Hotel Sector

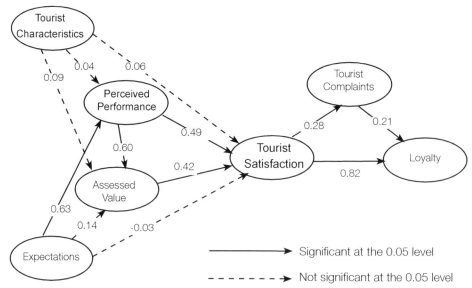

Figure 10.3: The SEM for the Retail Shop Sector

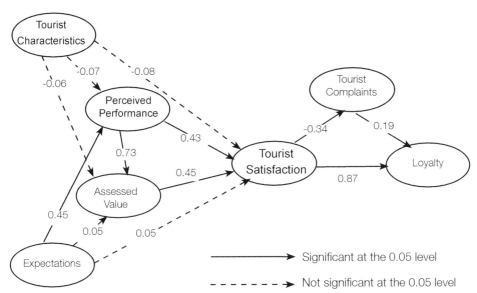

Figure 10.4: The SEM for Travel Agent Sector

Relationships Satisfaction and its Antecedents

The estimated paths from *performance* to *satisfaction* and from *performance* to *assessed value* both appear to be supported, and are in the positive direction across all the sectors. This implies that raising the performance of the hotel, retail shop and travel agent is likely to enhance tourists' satisfaction and assessed value of the received services in these sectors. For instance, a one-point increase in the performance of the hotel increases tourist satisfaction by 0.29 point, and increases perceived value by 0.86 point (see the corresponding path coefficients in Figure 10.2). The same occurrence applies to the relationship between *expectations* and *performance*. This relationship coincides with previous research implying that increasing consumer expectations may raise the product's assessed performance (Johnson et al., 1995). The paths from *expectations* to *assessed value* and from *expectations* to *satisfaction* were not confirmed. Similar findings were reported by other studies which are highlighted by Chan et al. (2003). They note that increasing expectations may have no or weak impact on satisfaction (Johnson et al., 1995; Johnson and Fornell, 1991), or may even yield a decrease in satisfaction (Yi, 1990). The path between *assessed value* and *satisfaction* was in the proposed positive direction and significant among all sectors.

Relationships among Satisfaction and its Consequences

The *complaints* and *loyalty* constructs were proposed as formative and showed consistent sign structures of the estimated indicator weights/loadings across sectors. The structural coefficients from *satisfaction* to *complaints* and from *satisfaction* to *loyalty* are all significant. As expected, the relationship between *satisfaction* and *complaints* carries' a negative sign, while the link between *satisfaction* and *loyalty* is positive. The relationship between *complaints* to *loyalty* was found to be significant, except for the hotel sector, at the 5% significance level. But at a lower level of significance (i.e., 10%), this relationship became significant across all sectors. The structural paths are positive across all sectors.

Tourist Characteristics

Since the *tourist characteristics* construct is a formative construct, the signs of its indicator's weights are not expected to be consistent across sectors. This is also verified in the pilot study. For the travel agent sector, all the weights are negative except for education level. The tourist characteristics dimension had negative effects on the three constructs. As a result, young female tourists with a higher education level which have not frequently visited Hong Kong and with lower monthly income would give lower scores to the evaluation of *performance*, *satisfaction* and *assessed value* of the travel agents. For the retail sector, the signs of all weights were negative, except for education level. The tourist characteristics had positive effects on the three constructs. As a result, younger female tourists with a higher education level, having not frequently visited Hong Kong and with lower monthly income, would give higher scores to the evaluation of *performance*, *satisfaction* and *assessed value* of the retail shops. For the hotel sector, the weights for gender and income level are negative and the others are positive. The tourist characteristics had positive effects on the three constructs. As a result, older female tourists with a higher education level, having frequently visited Hong Kong and with lower monthly income, would give higher scores to the evaluation on *performance*, *satisfaction* and *assessed value* of the hotel sector.

Computed TSIs

Three Sub-TSIs were computed based on Equation (10.1) and the overall TSI was then aggregated based on Equation (10.2). Although the model estimation is complex, the outcome is reasonable simple to interpret as it is set to a 0–100 scale. Among the three sectors included in the pilot study, tourists were most satisfied with the hotel sector (76.84), followed by the sector of retail shops (73.04) and the sector of travel agents (72.69). The overall tourist satisfaction index was calculated as 74.02, with the weights of the component Sub-TSIs being determined by the second-order confirmatory factor analysis using AMOS 4.0. The weights suggest that mainland Chinese tourists' overall satisfaction is influenced most greatly by their satisfaction with the retail shops, followed by their satisfaction with travel agents, and least by their satisfaction with the accommodation.

Conclusion

This chapter presents the results of a pilot study which is a first step of a larger project on developing a tourist satisfaction index to assess Hong Kong's competitiveness as an international tourism destination. The innovative model proposed integrates alternative approaches and captures multiple dimensions of tourist satisfaction. The framework is able to produce tourist satisfaction indexes for individual tourism sectors which combined are used to estimate an overall satisfaction index. The pilot study was conducted to produce tourist satisfaction indexes for three tourism sectors in order to validate the model and the aggregation scheme to assess the overall satisfaction. The results indicate that the framework is capable of assessing both the sectoral and overall satisfaction adequately. The proposed model can be applied to other source markets, other tourism related sectors, and repeatedly over time in order to capture the dynamics of tourist satisfaction. This framework has important practical implications on tourist destination management in the long run. This information is of great importance for decision makers in both public and private sectors to improve the competitiveness of the Hong Kong tourism industries, which will further benefit the economic development and the wellbeing of the local community of Hong Kong.

References

Alegre J, Cladera M. 2006. Repeat Visitation in Mature Sun and Sand Holiday Destinations. *Journal of Travel Research* **44** (3): 288-297.

Anderson EW, Fornell C, Lehmann DR. 1994. Customer satisfaction, market share, and profitability: findings from Sweden. *The Journal of Marketing* **58** (3): 53-66.

Bandura A. 2006. Guide for constructing self-efficacy scales. In *Self-efficacy Beliefs of Adolescents*, F. Pajares F, Urdan T (eds). Greenwich, CT: Information Age Publishing; 307-337.

Chadee DD, Mattsson J. 1996. An empirical assessment of customer satisfaction in tourism. *Service Industries Journal* **16** (3): 305-320.

Chan LK, Hui YV, Lo HP, Tse SK, Tso GK, Wu ML. 2003. Consumer satisfaction index: new practice and findings. *European Journal of Marketing* **37** (5/6): 872-909.

Dorfman PW. 1979. Measurement and meaning of recreation satisfaction: a case study in camping. *Environment and Behavior* **11** (4): 483-510.

Fornell C. 1992. A national customer satisfaction barometer: the Swedish experience. *Journal of Marketing* **56** (1): 6-21.

Fornell C, Johnson MD, Anderson EW, Cha J, Bryant BE. 1996. The American customer satisfaction index: nature, purpose, and findings. *Journal of Marketing* **60** (4): 7-18.

Hirschman AO. 1970. *Exit, Voice, and Loyalty: Responses to Decline in Firms, Organizations, and States.* Harvard University Press: Cambridge, MA.

Hong Kong Tourism Board (HKTB) 2008. *50 Years of Hong Kong Tourism: Hong Kong Tourism Board Annual Report 2007-08.* HKTB: Hong Kong.

Hsu CH, Wong KK, Masuyama Y. 2003. Senior travelers' hotel choice and satisfaction: an investigation based on country of origin. *Review of Business Research* **1** (2): 159-169.

Johnson MD, Anderson EW, Fornell C. 1995. Rational and adaptive performance expectations in a customer satisfaction framework. *Journal of Consumer Research* **21** (4): 28-40.

Johnson MD, Fornell C. 1991. A framework for comparing customer satisfaction across individuals and product categories. *Journal of Economic Psychology* **12** (2): 267-286.

Leblanc G. 1992. Factors affecting customer evaluation of service quality in travel agencies: an investigation of customer perceptions. *Journal of Travel Research* **30** (4): 10-16.

Lo A. (2005). The past, present and future of hospitality and tourism higher education in Hong Kong. *Journal of Teaching in Travel & Tourism* **5** (1/2): 137-166.

Pizam A, Milman A. 1993. Predicting satisfaction among first time visitors to a destination by using the expectancy disconfirmation theory. *International Journal of Hospitality Management* **12** (2): 197-209.

Oh H, Parks SC. 1997. Customer satisfaction and service quality: a critical review of the literature and research implications for the hospitality industry. *Hospitality Research Journal* **20** (3): 35-64.

Oliver RL. 1980. A cognitive model of the antecedents and consequences of satisfaction decisions. *Journal of Marketing Research* **17** (4): 460-469.

Reisinger Y, Turner LW. 2002. The determination of shopping satisfaction of Japanese tourists visiting Hawaii and the Gold Coast compared. *Journal of Travel Research* **41** (2): 167-176.

Ringle CM, Wende S, Will A. 2005. SmartPLS 2.0 M3, www.smartpls.de.

Schwarz N, Knäuper B, Hippler HJ, Noelle-Neumann E, Clark F. 1991. Rating scales: numeric values may change the meaning of scale labels. *Public Opinion Quarterly* **55**: 570-582.

Swanson SR, Kelley SW. 2001. Service recovery attributions and word-of-mouth intentions. *European Journal of Marketing* **35** (1): 194-211.

Yi Y. 1990. A critical review of consumer satisfaction in *Review of Marketing*. 68-123.

Yoon Y, Uysal M. 2005. An examination of the effects of motivation and satisfaction on destination loyalty: a structural model. *Tourism Management* **26** (1): 45-56.

11 Angry or Regretful? The Effect of Dissatisfaction on Tourists' Negative Word of Mouth and Exit

Enrique Bigné Alcañiz, Isabel Sánchez García, Rafael Currás Pérez and Luisa Andreu Simó, Universitat de València

Introduction

Scholars and practitioners have paid special attention to (dis)satisfaction for many decades due to general consensus over its key influence on consumer loyalty/switching behaviour (Bolton, 1998; Lam et al., 2004; Roos, 1999; Zeithaml et al., 1996). In this line, it is widely accepted that one of the main drivers of customers' exit is dissatisfaction experienced after a service failure (Coulter and Ligas, 2000; Roos, 1999), which has led to an increasing interest in service recovery strategies. These strategies encompass all the actions carried out by the provider to reduce or eliminate the negative consequences experienced by a customer after a service failure (Grönroos, 1990; Kelley and Davis, 1994).

Service failures and service recovery attempts are crucial moments of truth for companies (Schoefer and Ennew, 2005; Smith and Bolton, 2002). As Stewart (1998) points out, when a customer has decided to exit it is too late to attempt recovery, which highlights the importance of detecting early signs of dissatisfaction (Hart et al., 1990).

Service failure and service recovery research has a long tradition in marketing (Holloway and Beatty, 2003; Tax et al., 1998). Nevertheless, there are still several issues that deserve investigation (Hoffman et al., 2003; Mattila and Ro, 2008; McCollough et al., 2000). In this regard, even though scholars increasingly accept that post-purchase behaviour is triggered by emotions and not only by cognition (Agarwall and Malhotra, 2005; Bigné and Andreu, 2004; Bigné et al., 2005; Bonifield and Cole, 2007), the mediated or direct effect of some specific emotions on consumer behaviour is still unclear. As Mattila and Ro (2008) point out, 'although prior studies imply that service failures induce negative affects, research on discrete emotions and their influence on behavioural responses is lacking'. Specifically, the existence of a different effect (mediated by dissatisfaction or direct) of some discrete emotions on negative word-of-mouth (NWOM) and exit has received scant attention, and even less in the field of tourism.

Specific emotions with a similar valence, negative in our case, can have different effects on decision making and behaviour (Bonifield and Cole, 2007; Lerner and Keltner, 2001). Hence, it is expected that anger and regret operate in a different manner on dissatisfaction and tourist behaviour and, therefore, show different effects on NWOM and exit.

The main purpose of the present research is to shed light on the influence of anger and regret on NWOM and exit, to find out whether the effect is direct or mediated (through dissatisfaction). As a secondary objective, we aim to compare the influence of dissatisfaction and regret on NWOM and exit in order to detect differences between them. To address these issues we have conducted a survey in the context of restaurants and hotels, focusing on service failure situations.

We proceed in the following fashion. First, we present the theoretical framework and the research hypotheses. Then, the methodology used in the empirical study is detailed. Third, data analysis and the main findings of this study are discussed and, finally, the most outstanding conclusions and implications are presented.

Conceptual Framework and Research Hypotheses

Traditionally, a cognitive approach has dominated consumer behaviour research whereas the affective dimensions of behaviour have been neglected. However, in recent years, scholars have paid increasing attention to the role played by emotions on consumer behaviour (Agarwall and Malhotra, 2005; Bigné and Andreu, 2004; Bigné et al., 2005; Bonifield and Cole, 2007; Mattila and Ro, 2008).

Emotions have been conceptualized either in terms of underlying dimensions or as discrete categories (Bagozzi et al., 1999, 2000). In the former approach, scholars are concerned with the overall valence of emotions and usually distinguish two broad dimensions: negative and positive emotions (Richins, 1997; Russell and Ridgeway, 1983; Watson and Tellegen, 1985). The latter approach, however, focuses on specific emotions such as anger, frustration or regret, aiming to ascertain their idiosyncratic effects on consumer evaluation and subsequent behaviour (Bagozzi et al., 2000; Lerner and Keltner, 2001; Zeelenberg and Pieters, 1999, 2004). In a service failure context, researchers adopting a general valence approach postulate that the overall valence (positive to negative) triggers consumer behaviour (Mattila and Ro, 2008). Nonetheless, several scholars have reasoned that a discrete emotions conceptualization is preferred over the underlying dimensions approach to gain deeper understanding of consumers' behavioural responses to an unsatisfactory experience (Laros and Steenkamp, 2005; Mattila and Ro, 2008; Zeelenberg and Pieters, 2004).

Hence, in this study we focus on discrete emotions, namely anger and regret, analysing their relationships with dissatisfaction, NWOM and exit in a tourist service failure context.

Bagozzi et al. (1999) encourage future research on the relationship between specific emotions: 'How are distinct emotions related to each other? Under what conditions, for example, does frustration lead to dissatisfaction? Shame lead to anger? Or love lead to happiness?' Intending to provide some insight into this topic, we argue that, in the particular case of a service failure, anger could trigger regret. We draw this hypothesis from the theories on basic emotions and from the concept and nature of anger and regret themselves. In this sense, although there is no consensus on whether there are some basic emotions and the rest are built on the basis of them or all the emotions are at the same level (see Solomon, 2002 for a review), several scholars defending the basic emotions approach have considered anger among them (Ekman, 1992; Izard, 1992; Laros and Steenkamp, 2005; Prinze, 2004). Indeed, Solomon (2002) points out that anger 'may in fact be wired into our nervous system more directly and demonstrably' than other emotions. In further support for this idea, anger has been considered as 'one of the most powerful emotions, if we consider its profound impact on social relations as well as effects on the person experiencing this emotion' (Lazarus, 1991). Regret, however, has been conceptualized as an emotion with a cognitive base (Pieters and Zeelenberg, 2007; Zeelenberg and Pieters, 2007) and, to our knowledge, has not been considered as a basic emotion (see Laros and Steenkamp, 2005). Zeelenberg and Pieters (2007) define regret as: 'the emotion that we experience when realizing or imagining that our current situation would have been better, if only we had decided differently. It is a backward looking emotion signaling an unfavorable evaluation of a decision. It is an unpleasant feeling, coupled with a clear sense of selfblame concerning its causes and strong wishes to undo the current situation'.

In many purchase situations, and especially in a tourist service setting, it is difficult for consumers to know what they let pass for not having selected another provider. In such situations, anger could activate regret, leading consumers to imagine what they could have obtained with other alternatives.

So, we reason that anger will be experienced immediately after a service failure and that this feeling could induce consumers to consider that they should have chosen a different alternative and this counterfactual thinking, in turn, leads to regret. For example, imagine a tourist who has selected a hotel because of its views to the sea. He or she is most likely to feel angry if given an inner room. This initial feeling of anger could make the tourist regret the choice. Thus:

H1. In a tourist service failure situation, anger can become an antecedent of regret.

Emotions are associated with specific appraisals (Lerner and Keltner, 2001) and, therefore, emotions with the same valence can show differences on some of the six appraisal dimensions identified by Smith and Ellsworth (1985): certainty, pleasantness, attentional activity, control, anticipated effort, and responsibility. In this sense, anger and regret differ markedly in terms of responsibility and control whereas they share the other four appraisal dimensions (Bagozzi et al., 1999; Lerner and Keltner, 2001). Individuals feel anger when they perceive high other-responsibility for negative events and high other-control over them, since regret involves appraisals of high self-responsibility for and high self-control over negative situations or outcomes (Bagozzi et al., 1999; Bonifield and Cole, 2007; Lerner and Keltner, 2001).

Focusing now on the experiential content approach to emotions, that is, on the components of the emotional experience itself (Bougie, et al., 2003; Roseman et al., 1994), anger and regret also present differences in the five experiential categories proposed by Roseman et al. (1994): feelings, thoughts, action tendencies, actions, and emotivational goals. Regret has been associated with 'having a sinking feeling, thinking about what a mistake one has made and about a lost opportunity, feeling the tendency to kick oneself and to correct one's mistake, actually doing something differently, and wanting to have a second chance and to improve one's performance' (Zeelenberg et al., 1998). However, in the case of anger 'consumers had a feeling like they would explode and that they were overtaken by their emotions. Customers were thinking of violence and of how unfair the situation was. Whereas they felt like letting go and behaving aggressively, they actually complained and said something nasty. Angry customers wanted to get back at the organization and wanted to hurt someone' (Bougie et al., 2003).

Thus, drawn on appraisal theories and experiential content and assuming, as Lerner and Keltner (2001) suggest, that different emotions trigger different changes in cognition and actions, we expect that anger and regret exert different influences upon dissatisfaction and behaviour (Bonifield and Cole, 2007; Wetzer et al., 2007).

Scholars broadly agree that emotions experienced after a service failure will affect overall dis(satisfaction) with the service (Maute and Dubé, 1999; Tsiros, 1998; Westbrook and Oliver, 1991; Zeelenberg and Pieters, 1999). In this line, anger has been shown to be a strong predictor of dissatisfaction (Mano and Oliver, 1993; Oliver, 1997; Smith and Bolton, 2002). Similarly, numerous studies have empirically supported that postpurchase regret has a negative influence on satisfaction (Cooke et al., 2001; Inman et al., 1997; Taylor, 1997). However, Zeelenberg and Pieters (1999) did not find such a significant effect of regret on satisfaction. Based on the previous contributions, it is hypothesized that, in a tourist service failure situation:

H2. Anger will have a positive influence on consumer dissatisfaction.

H3. Regret will have a positive influence on consumer dissatisfaction.

Recent research on emotions has shown that discrete negative emotions following a service failure can affect subsequent behaviour directly over and above dissatisfaction (Laros and Steenkamp, 2005; Mattila and Ro, 2008; Zeelenberg and Pieters, 2004). In line with this approach, the works that have focused on the behavioural consequences of anger have found that anger strongly predicts complaining, NWOM and switching (Bonifield and Cole, 2007; Folkes et al., 1987; Mattila and Ro, 2008; Nyer1997). In the case of regret, Zeelenberg et al. (2001) and Zeelenberg and Pieters (1999, 2004) found that regret was directly related to switching behaviour and to word of mouth, although its influence on this latter behaviour is not consistent among the studies. Therefore we propose that:

H4. Anger has a positive influence on exit.

H5. Anger has a positive influence on NWOM.

H6. Regret has a positive influence on exit.

H7. Regret has a positive influence on NWOM.

Although some researchers have pointed out that the relationship between satisfaction and repurchase intention is more complex than scholars thought (Anderson and Srinivasan, 2003; Mittal and Kamakura, 2001; Patterson, 2004), satisfaction continues to be considered as one of the main precursors of consumer loyalty (Andreassen and Lindestad, 1998; Bolton and Lemon, 1999; Lam et al., 2004; Zeithaml et al., 1996). In this line, numerous researchers have supported that dissatisfaction experienced after a service failure predicts NWOM and switching behaviour (Bougie et al., 2003; Richins, 1987; Singh, 1988). Hence:

H8. Dissatisfaction will have a positive effect on exit.

H9. Dissatisfaction will have a positive effect on NWOM.

The whole set of hypotheses to be tested is depicted in Figure 11.1.

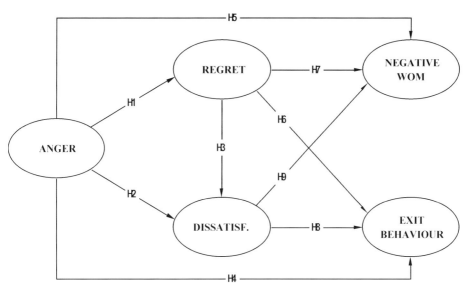

Figure 11.1: Theoretical model

Methodology

To accomplish the research aim a quantitative method was adopted. Furthermore, the approach is causal and the information was collected by means of a structured questionnaire following a recall method. Data were gathered during the month of April 2008 in the province of Valencia (Spain), and the questionnaire was administered personally to the respondents.

The target population comprises individuals over 18 years old who have had an unsatisfactory experience with a hotel or a restaurant in the last year. A one year period was established because hotels are not frequently purchased services. The sample selection was the result of establishing gender and age quotas to ensure that the sample shows the same sociodemographic structure as the target population. The data collection procedure employed in this study was similar to that used by Mangod et al. (1999) and Kaynak and Kara (2002). A total of 55 students were used as interviewers and, in the classroom setting, these students were instructed and trained about how to conduct the data collection process. Each student was asked to interview 12 acquaintances fulfilling the established gender and age quotas. Thus, though students were used to collect the sample, the respondents show the same demographic profile as the target population. One filter question was included at the beginning of the questionaire in order to identify the sample prospects: 'Do you remember having had an unsatisfactory experience with a hotel or restaurant during the last year?'.

We finally obtained a sample size of 660 individuals (308 respondents in the case of hotels and 358 for restaurants). Average age of the respondents is 39 years, gender is almost balanced, with women slightly predominating (47.1% male and 52.9% female), 62.8% had at least secondary studies and 64.8% had an income similar or above the average.

The questionnaire was elaborated on the basis of the literature review, using a retrospective experience method. The recall method approach has been widely use in the context of service failure and emotions (see for example Bougie et al., 2003; Wetzer et al., 2007 or Zeelenberg and Pieters, 1999, 2004, among others). Respondents were asked to think about an unsatisfactory experience with a hotel or restaurant during the last year. Specifically, they were instructed: 'Please describe briefly the unsatisfactory situation that you experienced, trying to remember how you felt and how you responded to the situation', in order to retrieve such experience.

Measures

Since the main purpose of the present work is to analyse relationships among variables and not deepen examination of each of the constructs involved, we focused on global and one-dimensional measures of the variables rather than multidimensional ones. Below we detail the measurement scales selected for each variable.

The scale finally selected for anger is based on Bonifield and Cole (2007) due to the high reliability ($\alpha = 0.90$) and parsimony of their scale. Thus, anger was collected by means of three items in a seven-point Likert scale format:

ANG1 - 'I felt angry about my experience at that hotel/restaurant'.

ANG2 - 'I felt very displeased with the service delivered at that hotel/restaurant'.

ANG3 - 'The more I thought about it, the more hostile I felt towards the hotel/restaurant'.

The scale employed to measure regret is largely based on Tsiros and Mittal (2000) which, in turn, is based on Tsiros (1998) and Oliver (1997). This scale provides good reliability ($\alpha = 0.82$) with a reasonable number of items. Thus, the scale used in the present work contains three items measured through a seven-point Likert scale:

REG1 - 'I felt sorry for choosing that hotel/restaurant'.

REG2 - 'I regretted choosing that hotel/restaurant .

REG3 - 'I should have chosen another hotel/restaurant'.

Dissatisfaction has been conceptualized as global (Hellier et al., 2003) and based on a specific transaction (Oliver, 1993) due to the aim of the study (analyse emotions and behaviours associated with a specific situation, tourist service failure). The measurement scale employed to collect this construct is an adaptation of that employed by Keaveney and Parthasarathy (2001) ($\alpha = 0.75$) and uses a seven-point Likert scale format:

DIS1- 'On the whole, I was dissatisfied with my experience with that service'.

DIS2- 'Overall, my negative experiences outweighed my positive experiences'.

DIS3- 'In general, I was unhappy with the hotel/restaurant'.

The scale employed to measure NWOM is based on Bougie et al. (2003) ($\alpha = 0.69$) and includes three items in a seven-point Likert format:

NWOM1- 'I have said negative things about the hotel/restaurant to other people'.

NWOM2- 'I have discouraged friends and relatives from going to that hotel/restaurant'.

NWOM3- 'I have advised against the hotel/restaurant when someone sought my advice'.

Exit was analysed following Putrevu and Lord (1994) ($\alpha = 0.91$) adapting the items to exit instead of repurchase intentions. Thus, exit was collected by means of three items in a seven-point Likert scale format:

EXIT1- 'After the negative experience, I have not continued to use the services of the hotel/restaurant'.

EXIT2- 'I will probably not use the services of that hotel/restaurant in the future'.

EXIT3- 'I will definitely not return to that hotel/restaurant in the future'.

Reliability and validity assessment

To assess measurement reliability and validity a confirmatory factor analysis (CFA) containing all the constructs in our framework was estimated using EQS 6.1 (Bentler, 2005). The measurement model was tested separately in the two datasets (hotels and restaurants) in order to offer a sounder validity assessment.

In both cases, raw data screening showed evidence of non-normal distribution (Mardia's coefficient normalized estimate for hotels = 34.30; and restaurants = 30.89), so robust statistics (χ^2i − χ>>and t-value) (Satorra and Bentler, 1994) have been provided. The results of the final CFAs confirm that the measurement model provides a good fit to the two datasets on the basis of various fit statistics. CFAs results (see Tables 11.1 and 11.2) provide evidence of reliability, convergent and discriminant validity according to the criteria proposed by Anderson and Gerbing (1988), Bagozzi and Yi (1988), and Fornell and Larcker (1981).

Table 11.1: Reliability and convergent validity of the measurement model

Factor	Item	Convergent validity				Reliability					
		Factor loading (robust t-value)		Loading average		α		CR		AVE	
		(H)otels	(R)estaurants	H	R	H	R	H	R	H	R
ANGER (ANG)	ang1	0.829 (17.63)	0.701 (12.40)								
	ang2	0.832 (20.45)	0.734 (14.09)	.82	.73	.86	.77	.86	.77	.67	.53
	ang3	0.791 (18.75)	0.747 (17.08)								
REGRET (REG)	reg1	0.873 (21.78)	0.819 (20.69)								
	reg2	0.949 (29.61)	0.902 (23.77)	.87	.85	.90	.88	.91	.89	.76	.72
	reg3	0.792 (15.64)	0.826 (17.20)								
DISSATISFACTION (DIS)	dis1	0.729 (13.86)	0.676 (11.96)								
	dis2	0.772 (17.64)	0.681 (15.01)	.79	.73	.83	.78	.84	.78	.63	.55
	dis3	0.880 (19.33)	0.845 (17.35)								
NEGATIVE WORD-OF-MOUTH (NWOM)	nwom1	0.817 (17.93)	0.842 (21.31)								
	nwom3	0.948 (36.76)	0.973 (37.53)	.88	.91	.90	.91	.81	.83	.69	.71
	nwom3	0.846 (21.85)	0.825 (20.95)								
EXIT (EXIT)	exit1	0.673 (9.03)	0.732 (13.80)								
	exit2	0.947 (19.15)	0.955 (29.77)	.81	.84	.88	.92	.77	.82	.63	.69
	exit3	0.932 (16.55)	0.955 (26.67)								

Goodness of fit indexes		NFI	NNFI	CFI	IFI	RMSEA
Hotels	S-B χ^2 (80df)=159.51 (p=0.00)	.944	.962	.971	.971	.057
Restaurants	S-B χ^2 (80df)=148.85 (p=0.00)	.951	.969	.977	.977	.050

Note: α=Cronbach's Alpha; CR=Composite realiability; AVE=Average Variance Extracted; S-B χ2=Satorra-Bentler robust χ2

Table 11.2: Discriminant validity of the measurement model

Hotels dataset

	x	σ	**ANG**	REG	DIS	NWOM	EXIT
ANG	4.90	1.60	.67	.43	.72	.28	.18
REG	4.76	1.76	[.58;.74]	.76	.38	.28	.20
DIS	5.00	1.60	[.77;.92]	[.51;.71]	.63	.34	.14
NWOM	4.57	1.99	[.43;.63]	[.43;.63]	[.48;.68]	.69	.27
EXIT	5.99	1.51	[.31;.55]	[.32;.56]	[.23;.51]	[.42;.62]	**.63**

Restaurants dataset

	x	σ	**ANG**	**REG**	**DIS**	**NWOM**	**EXIT**
ANG	**4.90**	**1.60**	**.67**	.43	.72	.28	.18
REG	4.76	1.76	[.58;.74]	.76	.38	.28	.20
DIS	5.00	1.60	[.77;.92]	[.51;.71]	.63	.34	.14
NWOM	4.57	1.99	[.43;.63]	[.43;.63]	[.48;.68]	.69	.27
EXIT	5.99	1.51	[.31;.55]	[.32;.56]	[.23;.51]	[.42;.62]	**.63**

Note: Diagonal represents Average Variance Extracted; above the diagonal the shared variance (squared correlations) are represented; below the diagonal, the 95% confidence interval for the estimated factors correlations is provided.

Results

Given that the purpose of this research is to analyse the causal relations between emotional and behavioural variables, the proposed set of hypotheses will be tested through structural equation modelling, using the programme EQS 6.1. Since it has been proved that the original measurement scales show good reliability and validity in both datasets (hotels and restaurants), beyond this point we are going to use the complete dataset with a double purpose: obtaining stronger results based on a larger sample and making the process of data analysis more understandable for the reader.

As mentioned in the conceptual framework section, the literature on service failure and emotions has not reached any consensus regarding the relationship between emotions and post-purchase behaviour. Whereas some researchers have found evidence for a direct effect of anger and regret on word-of-mouth and switching (Bonifield and Cole, 2007; Mattila and Ro, 2008; Zeelenberg and Pieters, 1999), others have supported a mediated effect through (dis)satisfaction (Oliver, 1993, 1997; Taylor, 1997). With the aim of clarifying the previous relationships, we are going to proceed in three steps. First, we will test for the direct effects and, so a model that only considers the direct links between anger, regret and dissatisfaction on the one hand and NWOM and exit on the other will be estimated (hypotheses H4 to H9). Second, we will focus attention on indirect relationships (hypotheses H1 to H3, H8 and H9). Finally, we will test a mixed model that reflects the significant relationships obtained in the previous ones.

As Tables 11.3 and 11.4 show, all goodness of fit indicators exceed their corresponding critical values, showing a good global fit. Concerning the direct effects model (model 1 in Table 11.3), results show that only regret and dissatisfaction exert a significant direct impact on post-purchase behaviour. However, contrary to what Bonifield and Cole (2007) and Mattila and Ro (2008) obtained, anger has no direct effect on either NWOM or exit. These findings might be partially explained by the cognitive basis of the considered emotions. In this sense, while it has been widely accepted that satisfaction involves both cognitive and affective components and that regret is an emotion with a strong cognitive base, anger can be considered mainly affective. Hence, we reason that, in a tourist service failure situation, the influence of anger on post-purchase behaviour could operate in a hierarchical fashion, that is, activating some type of cognitive processes first.

The estimation of model 2, focused on the indirect links between anger and regret on post-purchase behaviour through dissatisfaction (Table 11.3), offers additional support for the hierarchical effect of anger on behaviour. It is confirmed that anger is a strong predictor of dissatisfaction and regret, affecting NWOM and exit through them. However, and contrary to expectations (Inman et al., 1997; Taylor, 1997), regret does not have a significant impact on dissatisfaction and, so, a mediated effect is not supported in our research context, in agreement with Zeelenberg and Pieters (1999).

Table 11.3: Structural Equation Modeling: causal relations analysis models 1 and 2

Model 1: direct effects

Hypothesis	Structural relation	Standardized coefficient (β)	Robust t value	Contrast
H4	Anger ⇨ Exit	-.017	-0.17	Rejected
H5	Anger ⇨ NWOM	-.006	-0.05	Rejected
H6	Regret ⇨ Exit	.377	5.72*	Accepted
H7	Regret ⇨ NWOM	.263	4.57*	Accepted
H8	Dissatisfaction ⇨ Exit	.129	1.22	Rejected
H9	Dissatisfaction ⇨ NWOM	..372	3.32*	Accepted

Goodness of fit indexes					
	BBNFI	BBNNFI	CFI	IFI	RMSEA
S-B χ^2 (81)=257.81 (p=0.00)	.955	.959	.969	.969	.058

Model 2: indirect effects

Hypothesis	Structural relation	Standardized coefficient (β)	Robust t value	Contrast
H1	Anger ⇨ Regret	.643	14.97*	Accepted
H2	Anger ⇨ Dissatisfaction	.827	12.41*	Accepted
H3	Regret ⇨ Dissatisfaction	.059	1.07	Rejected
H8	Dissatisfaction ⇨ Exit	.372	6.99*	Accepted
H9	Dissatisfaction ⇨ NWOM	.550	10.90*	Accepted

Goodness of fit indexes					
	BBNFI	BBNNFI	CFI	IFI	RMSEA
S-B χ^2 (85)=317.76 (p=0.00)	.945	.949	.959	.838	.064

* = p< .01

Table 11.4: Structural Equation Modeling: causal relations analysis final model

Hypothesis	Structural relation	Standardized coefficient (β)	Robust t value	Contrast
H1	Anger ⇨ Regret	.643	15.48**	Accepted
H2	Anger ⇨ Dissatisfaction	.850	16.05**	Accepted
H6	Regret ⇨ Exit	.373	6.30**	Accepted
H7	Regret ⇨ NWOM	.262	4.92**	Accepted
H8	Dissatisfaction ⇨ Exit	.115	2.10*	Accepted
H9	Dissatisfaction ⇨ NWOM	.367	6.11**	Accepted

Goodness of fit indexes

S-B χ^2 (84)= 258.18 (p=0.00)	BBNFI	BBNNFI	CFI	IFI	RMSEA
	.955	.961	.969	.969	.056

* = p< .05; ** = p < .01

Taking together the findings obtained in the previous models, we propose and confirm a mixed model that considers an indirect effect of anger on post-purchase behaviour through regret and dissatisfaction, and a direct impact of regret on NWOM and exit (H1, H2, H6 to H9: Table 11.4). The results (Figure 11.2) suggest a dual influence of emotions on post-purchase behaviour in a tourist service failure situation. First, anger only exerts an indirect effect on NWOM and exit whereas regret solely has a direct effect. Second, the standardized coefficients of the antecedents of NWOM and exit show that dissatisfaction is a stronger predictor of NWOM than regret (.367 and .262 respectively) while regret explains exit to a greater extent than dissatisfaction (.373 and .115 respectively). In addition, the total effect of anger on NWOM (.480; p< 0.01) is stronger than its influence on exit (.338; p< 0.01). Hence, as expected, discrete emotions with the same valence operate differently on dissatisfaction and tourist behaviour.

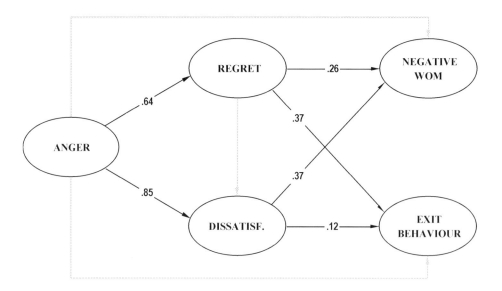

Figure 11.2: Final estimated model

Conclusions

The main purpose of the present research was to gain new insights into the influence of some discrete emotions on tourists' behaviour after a service failure. Drawing on the appraisal and experiential content theories of emotions, we have hypothesized that emotions with the same valence, namely anger and regret, would have different effects on negative word of mouth and exit behaviours.

Results indicate that anger has a very strong positive influence on dissatisfaction, reinforcing the idea that it is a key emotion in dissatisfaction formation, as pointed out by Mano and Oliver (1993), Oliver (1997) and Smith and Bolton (2002). Since dissatisfaction has been proved to significantly increase NWOM and exit behaviours, a mediated impact of anger on post-purchase behaviour through dissatisfaction has been supported. However, in the context of the present study (service failure situations in hotels and restaurants) anger does not have a direct effect on NWOM and exit, contrary to the findings obtained by Bonifield and Cole (2007) and Mattila and Ro (2008). A possible explanation for these apparently inconsistent results stems from the inclusion of dissatisfaction in the analysis. The previous works do not consider explicitly the relationship between anger and dissatisfaction. Thus, when this construct is added, the direct influence of anger on behaviour may not be significant any more because of the mediator role of dissatisfaction.

Findings have also revealed that, in a tourist service failure situation, anger could trigger counterfactual thinking and, as a result, could lead the tourist to regret the choice of one particular service provider rather than another. As far as we are aware, this relationship had not been tested before and, so, future research is encouraged to clarify the nature of this relation and under which conditions it takes place. Since it is confirmed that regret directly affects NWOM and exit, as claimed by Zeelenberg and Pieters (1999, 2004), anger will have an additional indirect impact on post-purchase behaviour through it.

These results suggest that, probably, during a failed tourist service encounter, different discrete emotions appear following a specific sequence or hierarchy, rather than emerging at the same time. Thus, regret and dissatisfaction, which have a stronger cognitive basis, would come out after anger, which can be considered a 'purer' emotion. More research is needed to further confirm or discard this hierarchical effect of emotions on the behaviour that follows service failure, extending also the scope to service recovery.

Concerning the link between regret and dissatisfaction and unlike previous studies (Inman et al., 1997; Taylor, 1997), we have not found a significant relationship. Hence, only a direct impact of regret on post-purchase behaviour has been supported. This could be partially explained because researchers in those studies mainly use experimental designs where, after a choice has been made, participants' knowledge of the non-chosen alternative result is manipulated. In such a context, although initially satisfied, individuals that are aware of better alternatives will regret their choice and this will lead to dissatisfaction. Nevertheless, in a real purchase and consumption setting, and mainly in tourist services, uncertainty about what consumers might have obtained with other providers makes the previous sequence unlikely. In this situation, regret is likely to influence behaviour independently of dissatisfaction or even as a consequence of it.

In further support for the reasoning that discrete emotions with the same valence operate differently on dissatisfaction and tourist post-purchase behaviour, SEM analysis has shown that dissatisfaction and anger are stronger predictors of NWOM whereas regret explains exit behaviour to a greater extent. These findings are consistent with those obtained by Zeelenberg and Pieters (2004) and Mattila and Ro (2008) and could be explained in part by the fact that 'the experience of regret implies that there was a better alternative. Hence, it is likely that customers switch to this alternative provider next time they are in need of the service' (Zeelenberg and Pieters, 2004).

The findings have relevant implications for practitioners in helping them to understand the hierarchical process that links emotions experienced after a service failure and tourists' post-purchase behaviour. Given that anger is an immediate antecedent to dissatisfaction and affects NWOM and exit through both dissatisfaction and regret, trying to detect early signs of anger is a crucial aspect for tourist managers, mainly taking into account that most dissatisfied customers do not complain. There is a great deal of research on the anatomical-physiological language for identifying emotional expressions, associating facial expressions with specific emotions (see Ekman, 1992; Prinze, 2004 and Solomon, 2002 among others). So, providing training to the staff in these 'tangible signs' and encouraging them to observe customers could help the company to anticipate dissatisfaction and respond in time.

It is also important to emphasize that, in service failure situations, tourist managers should aim to reduce post purchase regret in order to discourage customers from switching. Regret could be diminished by trying to increase perceived value of the service through satisfactory service recovery or letting the customer know that the problem is shared by other providers as well in order to avoid counterfactual thinking.

The main limitation of the present study is the use of a retrospective experience method, although this approach has been widely used in a service failure context (see for example Bougie et al., 2003; Wetzer et al., 2007 or Zeelenberg and Pieters, 1999, 2004). Thus, even though respondents are urged to relive the experience, the recalled emotions may differ from the emotions really felt. However, the advantage of this method is the opportunity to collect information on real post-purchase behaviour and not only intentions. This study would benefit from a longitudinal approach, that it is suggested for future research.

Further research is also needed to embrace more emotions (such as disappointment, frustration or guilt), service recovery responses, and other post-purchase behaviours, specifically complaining to the company, complaining to a third part and inertia.

Finally, since consumer involvement has been associated with satisfaction and loyalty (Homburg and Giering, 2001; Ostrom and Iacobucci, 1995), with NWOM proneness (Wagenheim, 2005) and it has been found to act as a moderator of some drivers of switching (Antón et al., 2007), it would be an interesting avenue for future research to analyse the moderating effect of involvement in the relationships between emotions, dissatisfaction and post-purchase behaviour in a tourist service failure context.

References

Agarwall J and Malhotra NK. 2005. An integrated model of attitude and affect: theoretical foundations and an empirical investigation. *Journal of Business Research* **58**: 483-493.

Anderson J and Gerbing D. 1988. The use of pledges to build and sustain commitment in distribution channels: a review and recommended two-step approach. *Psychological Bulletin* **103**: 411-423.

Anderson RE and Srinivasan SS. 2003. E-satisfaction and e-loyalty: a contingency framework. *Psychology and Marketing* **20**: 123-138.

Andreassen TW and Lindestad B. 1998. The effect of corporate image in the formation of customer loyalty. *Journal of Service Research* **1** (1): 82-92.

Antón C, Camarero C and Carrero M. 2007. Analysing firms' failures as determinants of consumer switching intentions. *European Journal of Marketing* **41** (1/2): 135-158.

Bagozzi R and Yi J. 1988. On the evaluation of structural equation models. *Journal of the Academy of Marketing Science* **16** (2): 74-94.

Bagozzi RP, Gopinath M and Nyer PU. 1999. The role of emotions in marketing. *Journal of the Academy of Marketing Science* **27** (2): 184-206.

Bagozzi RP, Baumgartner H, Pieters R and Zeelenberg M. 2000. The role of emotions in goal-directed behavior. In *Why of Consumption: Contemporary Perspectives on Consumer Motives, Goals and Desires*, Ratneshwari S, Mick DG and Huffman C (eds). Routledge: London; 36-58.

Bentler P. 2005. *EQS 6: Structural Equation Program Manual.: Multivariate software.* Encino, CA.

Bigné JE and Andreu L. 2004. Emotions in segmentation. An empirical study. *Annals of Tourism Research* **31** (3): 682-696.

Bigné JE, Andreu L and Gnoth J. 2005. The theme park experience: an analysis of pleasure, arousal and satisfaction. *Tourism Management* **26**: 833-844.

Bolton RN. 1998. A dynamic model of the duration of the customer's relationship with a continuous service provider: the role of satisfaction. *Marketing Science* **59** (April): 45-65.

Bolton RN and Lemon KN. 1999. A dynamic model of customers' usage of services: usage as an antecedent and consequence of satisfaction. *Journal of Marketing Research* **36** (May): 171-186.

Bonifield C and Cole C. 2007. Affective responses to service failure: anger, regret, and retaliatory versus conciliatory responses. *Marketing Letters* **18**: 85-99.

Bougie R, Pieters R and Zeelenberg M. 2003. Angry customers don't come back, they get back: the experience and behavioral implications of anger and dissatisfaction in services. *Journal of the Academy of Marketing Science* **31** (4): 377-393.

Cooke ADJ, Meyvis T and Schwartz A. 2001. Avoiding future regret in purchase-timing decisions. *Journal of Consumer Research* **27** (4): 447-459.

Coulter RA and Liga, M. 2000. The long good-bye: the dissolution of customer–service provider relationships. *Psychology and Marketing* **17** (8): 669-695.

Ekman P. 1992. Are there basic emotions? *Psychological Review* **99** (3): 550-553.

Folkes V, Koletsky S and Graham J. 1987. Research in brief: a field study of causal inferences and consumer reaction: the view from the airport. *Journal of Consumer Research* **13** (4): 534-539.

Fornell C and Larcker D. 1981. Evaluating structural equations models with unobservable variables and measurement error. *Journal of Marketing Research* **18**: 39-50.

Grönroos C. 1990. Relationship marketing approach to the marketing function in service contexts: the marketing and organizational behavior influence. *Journal of Business Research* **20** (1): 3-12.

Hart WL, Heskett JL and Sasse, EW 1990. The profitable art of service recovery. *Harvard Business Review* **68** (July): 148-156.

Hellier P, Geursen G, Carr R and Rickard J. 2003. Customer repurchase intention: a general structural equation model. *European Journal of Marketing* **37** (11/12): 1762-1800.

Hoffman KD, Kelley SW and Chang BC. 2003. A CIT investigation of servicescape failures and associated recovery strategies. *Journal of Service Marketing* **17** (4): 322-340.

Holloway BB and Beatty SE. 2003. Service failure in online retailing. A recovery opportunity. *Journal of Service Research* **6** (1): 92-105.

Homburg C and Giering A. 2001. Personal characteristics as moderators of the relationship between customer satisfaction and loyalty. An empirical analysis. *Psychology and Marketing* **18** (1): 43-66.

Inman JJ, Dyer JS and Jia J. 1997. A generalized utility model of disappointment and regret effects on post-choice valuation. *Marketing Science* **16** (2): 97-111.

Izard C. 1992. Basic emotions, relations among emotions, and emotion–cognition relations. *Psychological Review* **99** (3): 561-565.

Kaynak E and Kara A. 2002. Consumer perceptions of foreign products. An analysis of product-country images and ethnocentrism. *European Journal of Marketing* **36** (7/8): 928-949.

Keaveney SM and Parthasarathy M. 2001. Customer switching behaviour in online services: an exploratory study of the role of selected attitudinal, behavioral and demographic factors. *Journal of the Academy of Marketing Science* **29** (4): 374-390.

Kelley SW and Davis MA. 1994. Antecedents to customer expectations for service recovery. *Journal of the Academy of Marketing Science* **22** (1): 52-61.

Lam SY, Shankar V, Erramilli MK and Murthy B. 2004: Customer value, satisfaction, loyalty and switching costs: an illustration from a business-to-business service context. *Journal of the Academy of Marketing Science* **32** (3): 293-311.

Laros F and Stennkamp JB. 2005. Emotions in consumer behavior: a hierarchical approach, *Journal of Business Research* **58**: 1437-1445.

Lazarus RS. (1991). *Emotion and Adaptation*. Oxford University Press: New York.

Lerner JS and Keltner D. 2001. Fear, anger, and risk. *Journal of Personality & Social Psychology* **81**(1): 146-159.

Mangold WG, Miller F and Brockway GR. 1999. Word-of-mouth communication in the service marketplace. *Journal of Service Research* **13** (1): 73-89.

Mano H and Oliver R. 1993. Assessing the dimensionality and structure of the consumption experience: evaluation, feeling and satisfaction. *Journal of Consumer Research* **20** (December): 451-466.

Mattila A and Ro H. 2008. Discrete negative emotions and customer dissatisfaction responses in a casual restaurant setting. *Journal of Hospitality & Tourism Research* **32** (1): 89-107.

Maute MF and Dubé L. 1999. Patterns of emotional responses and behavioral consequences of dissatisfaction. *Applied Psychology: An International Review* **48**: 349-366.

McCollough MA, Berry LL and Yadav MS. 2000. An empirical investigation of customer satisfaction after service failure and recovery. *Journal of Service Research* **3** (2): 121-137.

Mittal V and Kamakura WA. 2001. Satisfaction, repurchase intent and repurchase behavior: investigating the moderating effect of customer characteristics. *Journal of Marketing Research* **38** (February): 131-142.

Nyer PU. 1997. A study of the relationships between cognitive appraisals and consumption emotions. *Journal of the Academy of Marketing Science* **25** (4): 296–304.

Oliver RL. 1993. Cognitive, affective and attribute based of the satisfaction response. *Journal of Consumer Research* **20**: 418-430.

Oliver RL. 1997. *Satisfaction: a Behavioral Perspective on the Consumer*. McGraw-Hill: New York.

Ostrom A and Iacobucci D. 1995. Consumer trade-offs and the evaluation of services. *Journal of Marketing* **59**: 17-28.

Patterson PG. 2004. A contingency model of behavioural intentions in a services context. *European Journal of Marketing* **38** (9/10): 1304-1315.

Pieters R and Zeelenberg M. 2007. A theory of regret regulation 1.1. *Journal of Consumer Psychology* **17** (1): 29-35.

Prinze J. 2004. Which emotions are basic? In *Emotion, Evolution, and Rationality*, Evand D and Cruse P (eds). Oxford University Press: London; 1-19.

Putrevu S and Lord K. 1994. Comparative and noncomparative advertising: attitudinal effects under cognitive and affective involvement conditions. *Journal of Advertising* **23**: 77-91.

Richins M. 1987. A multivariate analysis of responses to dissatisfaction. *Journal of the Academy of Marketing Science* **15** (3): 24-31.

Richins M. 1997. Measuring emotions in the consumption experience. *Journal of Consumer Research* **24** (2): 127-146.

Roos I. 1999. Switching processes in customer relationships. *Journal of Service Research* **2** (1): 68-85.

Roseman IJ, Wiest C and Swartz TM. 1994. Phenomenology, behaviors, and goals differentiate discrete emotions. *Journal of Personality and Social Psychology* **67** (2): 206-221.

Russell JA and Ridgeway D. 1983. Dimensions underlying children's emotions concepts. *Developmental Psychology* **19**: 795-804.

Satorra A and Bentler P. 1994. Corrections to test statistics and standard errors in covariance structure analysis. In *Latent Variable Analysis: Applications for Developmental Research*, von Eye A and Clogg C (eds). Sage Publications: Thousand Oaks, CA; 399-419.

Schoefer K and Ennew C. 2005. The impact of perceived justice on consumer emotional responses to service complaints experiences. *Journal of Service Marketing* **19** (5): 261-270.

Singh J. 1988. Consumer complaint intentions and behavior: definitional and taxonomical issues. *Journal of Marketing* **52** (January): 93-107.

Smith AK and Bolton RN. 2002. The effect of customers' emotional responses to service failures on their recovery effort evaluations and satisfaction judgements. *Journal of the Academy of Marketing Science* **30** (1): 5-23.

Smith CA, and Ellsworth PC. 1985. Patterns of cognitive appraisal in emotion. *Journal of Personality and Social Psychology* **48** (4): 813-838.

Solomon R. 2002. Back to basics: on the very idea of 'basic emotions'. *Journal for the Theory of Social Behaviour* **32** (2): 115-144.

Stewart K. 1998. An exploration of customer exit in retail banking. *International Journal of Bank Marketing* **16** (1): 6-14.

Tax SS, Brown SW and Chandrashekaran M. 1998. Customer evaluations of service complaints experiences: implications for relationship marketing. *Journal of Marketing* **62** (April): 60-76.

Taylor KA. 1997. A regret theory approach to assessing consumer satisfaction. *Marketing Letters* **8** (2): 229-238.

Tsiros M. 1998. Effect of regret on post-choice valuation: the case of more than two alternatives. *Organizational Behavior and Human Decision Processes* **76** (October): 48-69.

Tsiros M and Mittal V. 2000. Regret: a model of its antecedents and consequences in consumer decision making. *Journal of Consumer Research* **26** (4): 401-417.

Wagenheim F. 2005. Postswitching negative word of mouth. *Journal of Service Research* **8** (1): 67-78.

Watson D and Tellegen A. 1985. Toward a consensual structure of mood. *Psychological Bulletin* **98**: 219-235.

Westbrook RA and Oliver RL. 1991. The dimensionality of consumption emotion patterns and consumer satisfaction. *Journal of Consumer Research*, **18**: 84-91.

Wetzer I, Zeelenberg M and Pieters R. 2007. Consequences of socially sharing emotions: testing the emotion–response congruency hypothesis. *European Journal of Social Psychology* **37** (6): 1310-1324.

Zeelenberg M and Pieters R. 1999. Comparing service delivery to what might have been. Behavioral responses to regret and disappointment. *Journal of Service Research* **2** (1): 86-97.

Zeelenberg M and Pieters R. 2004. Beyond valence in customer dissatisfaction: a review and new findings on behavioral responses to regret and disappointment in failed services. *Journal of Business Research* **57**: 445-455.

Zeelenberg M and Pieters R. 2007. A theory of regret regulation 1.0. *Journal of Consumer Psychology* **17** (1): 3-18.

Zeelenberg M, van Dijk E and Manstead ASR. 1998. Reconsidering the relation between regret and responsibility. *Organizational Behavior and Human Decision Processes* **74** (3): 254-272.

Zeelenberg M, Inman JJ and Pieters R. 2001. What we do when decisions go awry: behavioral consequences of experienced regret. In *Conflict and Decision Making*, Weber E, Baron J and Loomes G (eds). Cambridge University Press: Cambridge; 136-155.

Zeithaml VA, Berry L and Parasuraman A. 1996. The behavioral consequences of service quality. *Journal of Marketing* **60** (April): 31-46.

12 The Concept of Travel Horizon Revisited: Toward More Relevance of Past Travel Experience

Karin Teichmann and Andreas H. Zins, Institute for Tourism and Leisure Studies

Introduction

The fact that prior knowledge is a key issue in consumer decision making has long been recognized in the literature (e.g. Hirschman and Wallendorf, 1982). Whereas some studies conceptualized prior knowledge as a unidimensional construct (Snepenger et al., 1990), others identify past experience, expertise and familiarity as dimensions of prior knowledge (Alba and Hutchinson, 1987; Gursoy and McCleary, 2004b, 2004a; Kerstetter and Cho, 2004). In the tourism context, familiarity has generally been conceptualized as destination-related experiences (i.e. the number of times individuals previously visited a destination) (Baloglu, 2001). Familiarity thus encompasses behavioural aspects. Expertise, however, is cognitively based and represents accumulated skills that enable information acquisition and processing (Alba and Hutchinson, 1987). Due to more sophisticated cognitive structures experts can deal with complex problems more easily than novices can (Kerstetter and Cho, 2004). Past experience refers to an individual's accumulated travel experience with different destinations and activities. Past experience is thus one of the crucial determinants of travellers' decision-making (Snepenger et al., 1990).

More than 10 years ago, Oppermann (1998) stated that studies investigating travel experience and its influence on destination choice as well as studies dealing with travel patterns were almost absent in tourism research. He based his study on Schmidhauser's (1976) conceptualization of travel horizon defined as the maximum achieved distance zone in the past. For instance, if an individual has a high travel horizon this indicates that she or he has travelled far and has been exposed to a different country or culture. Schmidhauser and Oppermann discussed the phenomenon of cumulative travel experience under the headline of travel and destination horizon incorporating the issue of distance: particularly geographic and cultural aspects thereof. The basic premise was that individuals follow an expanding travel/destination horizon in the course of their lives.

Schmidhauser used four categories of travel horizon for Swiss residents: domestic, neighbouring countries, other Europe, and outside Europe. As Oppermann (1998) discussed in his study, these categories are a mixture of geographic and cultural distance factors. In contrast, he distinguished six different destination zones for New Zealand (NZ): same NZ island, respective other NZ island, Australia, Pacific Islands, Europe, and other countries. This categorization of destination zones is, again, to a large degree based on geographical distance. However, it partially accounts for social and cultural distance since Oppermann identified Europe as a separate category due to historical and cultural ties. Different to Schmidhauser's achieved travel horizon during one's lifespan, Oppermann also studied the furthest destination visited on an annual basis.

The concept of travel horizon does not only consider the most distant destination but also how the horizon has been achieved referring to the travel horizon ladder. Oppermann argued that Schmidhauser's travel horizon is unidimensional because it is only possible to ascend but not descend on the horizon ladder. He argued that this individual horizon ladder should be conceived of being bi-directional since many reasons may occur that travellers move down this ladder and choose less distant destinations: either temporarily or for the rest of their lives. Moreover, Oppermann put forward the criticism that the travel horizon one achieves during one's lifespan does not consider personal circumstances such as life cycle which impacts on travel behaviour. It has been shown elsewhere that travel patterns do change depending on an individual's lifespan and/or family career (Oppermann, 1995).

Oppermann (1998) showed that the achieved travel horizon lacks predictive validity since his findings revealed both ascending and descending steps on the travel horizon ladder. Thus, in order to differentiate from Schmidhauser's travel horizon ladder, Oppermann defined and investigated the destination zone ladder where ascending and descending steps are possible. Unfortunately, the sample size went down to 97 respondents who provided information on their destination zone moves during the last 20 years. Based on these data, Oppermann (1998) compared the travel behaviour of the previous 10 years (1985-1994) with the most current destination horizon zone visitation (1995) in order to calculate the probability of a revisit.

In a different study, Oppermann (1995) investigated changing tourism patterns along three time horizons: the last 30 years, across the life cycle, and between successive generations. The findings, however, are more descriptive than predictive. The focus of the study was to explore differences of historical travel behaviour between various age cohorts. Based on these data, no forecasts of future travel demand were made and questions about travel plans were not part of the survey. Thus, the study's diagnostic capability is limited.

Overall, the approach proposed by Oppermann seems appropriate for the description of the evolution of the destination horizons for an entire population or particular cohorts. However, due to the absence of longitudinal studies, the necessary data collection effort is huge in order to meet the requirements of getting trip records year-by-year for different types of trips such as short-break or vacation. In addition to that, reliability suffers the longer the individual recall period is. Oppermann's sample from New Zealand demonstrated clearly that the number of usable cases decreased dramatically if the analysis was to cover a period longer than 10 years back.

To conclude, only a few efforts were taken to investigate people's travel life cycle as well as individuals' travel horizon. Until now, the patterns of past behaviour have not been contrasted to possible future travel patterns. However, with respect to demand forecasting this would be a valuable tool to learn more about changing structures of actual and future destination choice of travellers. Therefore, this chapter explores what role past travel behaviour has on future destination decisions. More specifically, it also explores if demographics or social ties have an influence on future travel plans.

Methodology

In particular, the following research questions will be investigated by this study:

1. What predictive validity does Oppermann's concept of travel horizon have?

2. What predictive validity, in turn, has the concept of prior travel experience along cultural zones?

3. Is the cumulative lifetime travel experience more powerful in determining near-future travel plans compared to the more recent (5 years') travel destinations?

4. Is there a systematic correlation between past and future travel behaviour with the perception of cultural distance of the visited destinations?

5. What impact do other personal characteristics such as social ties into the destination and language proficiency have in destination preference?

This research study used a self-administered questionnaire delivered by hand to each respondent. The data were collected by 35 undergraduate students taking a course on research methods. Each student was instructed to collect data from at least seven subjects. The survey was conducted in December 2008 in Austria. The purposive sampling strategy included quotas for each interviewer: a balanced gender distribution and an equal share of respondents in the age brackets of 20 to 30 and 50 to 60 years were assigned.

The first part of the questionnaire included questions about the subjects' previous travel experience. Concerning previous travel experience, we first used the society clusters according to the GLOBE study (House et al., 2004). The GLOBE study organized 62 countries into ten distinct clusters. These clusters are: *Anglo* including English-speaking countries such as England, Australia, Canada, etc.; *Latin Europe* consisting of the regions influenced by Romanic culture such as Italy, Spain and Portugal; *Nordic Europe* consisting of Scandinavian countries such as Denmark, Finland, and Sweden; *Germanic Europe* including German-speaking societies such as Austria, Germany, and Switzerland; *Eastern Europe* cluster including countries such as Albania, Poland, Russia (based on former Soviet hegemony) but also Greece; *Latin America* consisting of countries such as Argentina, Brazil and Mexico; *Sub-Saharan Africa* such as Namibia, Nigeria, and Zimbabwe; *Middle East* for societies lying in North Africa and West Asia (including Turkey); *Southern Asia* consisting of countries such as India and Thailand as well as Iran; and *Confucian Asia* consisting of countries such as China and Japan. The questionnaire included a list with these ten clusters and examples of countries for each specific cluster. A coloured world map was handed over to the respondents for a better identification of the society clusters. In order to measure how often respondents visited each society cluster the response format ranged from never (= 0) to more than 30 times (= 7) with six answer categories in between representing frequency ranges of five times each.

In order to measure subjective distance and foreignness, one question was included by which respondents were asked to assign values from 0 (for the one society respondents considered themselves belonging to) to a maximum of 10 for the most distant society cluster. Double entries of numbers were possible since it is most likely that people perceive different society clusters as equally close or foreign.

Whereas the first question in the questionnaire measured the frequency of travelling into the ten society clusters during one's lifetime, a similar question was included asking for destinations visited during the past five years (from 2004 to 2008). Respondents had to elicit the destinations (at country level) visited each year during this period for trips that lasted longer than four days. To capture individuals' destination planning horizon, respondents were required to enter those country destinations they plan to visit from 2009 to 2011. Within three years, it is argued, many people shift, postpone or bring forward those destination plans they consider really feasible. Cutting off the planning horizon beyond this threshold should avoid capturing too many unrealistic dreams. No differentiation was recorded whether this plan is binding for a particular year of this period. For each destination mentioned, respondents could indicate with a check mark if this particular trip is motivated by visiting friends and/or relatives. The recent travel history (2004 to 2008) and the destination planning horizon were recoded afterwards into Schmidhauser's travel horizon and the society cluster categories. The final part of the questionnaire comprised questions on demographic characteristics including one question on language capabilities.

Results

The sample consists of 294 questionnaires with the following characteristics: 83% have an Austrian nationality, 4.5% a German, and the remaining participants predominantly a central and eastern European one. 54% of the respondents are female; the two age groups are almost equally represented with 55% younger travellers in the age of 20 to 30 years and 45% older travellers in the age bracket between 50 and 60 years. The gender distribution does not differ across these two groups significantly. The educational level spreads from primary school (1%), apprenticeship (13%), professional secondary school (15%) to high school certificate (38%) and university level (33%). This distribution differs between the two age groups as follows: The share of lower educational levels (apprenticeship and professional education without high school certificate) is three times higher and the share of university graduates is 50% larger compared to the younger age group. Language proficiency coincides with the highest level of education achieved. On average, 2.9 different languages are said to be spoken. For respondents with a primary school level this ratio is 1.3, for the next level it is 1.8, for professional secondary level 2.2 and for the remaining to it is about 3.3. However, younger respondents provide a substantially higher number of languages spoken compared to the older age cohort. German is spoken by all the respondents, 93% checked English as well, 35% agreed with French, 19% with Italian and 16% with Spanish.

The household situation on sample average can be described as following: 18% are living alone, 49% together with a partner, one quarter together with other adult persons; 15% stated that they lived with children below the age of 18 (9% for respondents in the age between 20 to 30 and 22% in the age between 50 to 60), 20% with children beyond this threshold (attributed completely to the older age group under study). 10% shared their households with friends. One third of partner households had children aged 18 and older. In almost every third household of this type, younger children were also present. When comparing the two age cohorts it turns out that the share of single households of younger people (20-30 years) is double the percentage of that of older respondents. Living with friends in one household is not all relevant in older households. In contrast, children aged below 18 are present in 22% of the households of older respondents but only in 9% of the younger ones. Older children are not part of younger households, however they are present in 45% of older ones. Only 28% of the younger respondent group share their household with a partner. This applies in 76% of the older respondent cases.

Before starting to investigate the past and future travel patterns with respect to cultural regions it seems valuable to screen the overall travel activities of the respondents. By summarizing the travel frequencies across all ten world regions a cumulative travel experience can be expressed. In order to make it comparable across different ages this figure was normalized by the time span between the current age and the age of 18. This age limit is assumed to represent the transition time when young people start to take travel decisions independently from their parents. The average travel frequency (considering only trips with at least four overnights) in the sample is 1.9. This compares favourably with the more recent travel history of the past five years which is also 1.9 trips per year. The paired t-test results in a correlation of .42 ($p < .001$). However, the differences among both age groups are tremendous. While respondents in the age bracket of 20 to 30 years – looking back between 2 to 13 years – revealed that they travelled 2.8 times a year in this period, the contrasting age group in the age between 50 to 60 years stated a much lower travel activity of about 1.1 trips per year across a time span of 32 to 43 years.

The more current travel history of the years 2004 to 2008, however, does not show much variation with 1.95 and 1.90 trips respectively. This means that the travel frequency of the younger travellers increased significantly from the early twenties to the late twenties. This is partly due to an overestimation of the records of the lifetime travel experience. This overestimation of travel experience is established as follows: Both measurement approaches – the records on relative frequencies differentiated by ten society clusters and the constructive record on all country destinations visited in each year between 2004 and 2008 – should result in the same amount of past trips. However, differences between responses for both measurement approaches could be found. Interestingly, the overestimation is very large for the age cohort of 20 to 25-year-old respondents for which both measurements should deliver almost congruent figures (3.2 trips for overall recall and 2.0 trips p.a. for the constructive elicitation). This gap is closer for the next age sub-group of 26 to 30-year-old respondents even though the time span underlying both measurements is not identical in this case (2.3 vs. 1.8 trips p.a.). In contrast, the travel activities of the older contrast sub-sample went up from an average of 1.1 trips per year (lifetime travel experience) to 1.9 trips during the more recent five years. If the chosen measurement approach for the lifetime travel frequency is generally in favour of an overestimation (e.g. due to an unclear recall in general or a difficult boundary between dependent and independent trip decision making) then the derived growth in this age cohort would be even more substantial.

Table 12.1 exhibits a comprehensive overview on the travel profile of the sample. The first column demonstrates the lifetime travel frequency into the ten society clusters. Germanic Europe is heading the list with almost 13 trips on average and in total. Domestic trips are counted in this category. The second preferred destination region appears to be Latin Europe (5.7 trips) immediately followed by Eastern Europe (5.2 trips) including for example, Croatia bordering on the Adriatic Coast. The Anglo-American Region has been visited twice on average so far. By comparison, the second column investigates the share of respondents who travelled at least once to the given regions. So, this analysis takes out the volume or frequency of trips undertaken by the individuals. Again, Germanic, Latin and Eastern Europe have been visited at least once by almost every respondent. The Anglo-American cluster follows with 72% coverage among the surveyed travellers. Middle East has been visited by every second respondent. This is certainly related to the fact that Turkey belongs to this society cluster. After inspecting all ten destination clusters it is apparent that there is a decreasing relationship between geographic distance and past visitation, yet some disruptions disturb a concise pattern. Nordic Europe is much closer compared to the Middle East and the Anglo American Region is by far more distant compared to the Middle East and Nordic Europe.

Table 12.1: Past and future destination horizon together with cultural and social relationships

Society Cluster	Lifetime Travel Frequency	Travelled at least once	Lifetime Travel Frequency p.a.	Travel Frequency: 2004 – 2008	Perceived cultural distance*)	Travel intention: 2009 – 2011	Share of VFR Travel intention: 2009 – 2011	Language affinity
Germanic Europe	12.9	98%	1.1	3.2	0.6	0.67	15.9%	100%
Nordic Europe	0.6	35%	0.06	0.2	3.2	0.33	5.3%	2%
Eastern Europe	5.2	92%	0.43	2.1	3.7	0.70	9.1%	15%
Latin Europe	5.7	94%	0.47	2.3	2.9	1.09	9.5%	52%
Anglo American Region	1.9	72%	0.17	0.7	4.1	0.92	15.2%	93%
Latin America	0.3	20%	0.02	0.1	6.0	0.28	3.1%	19%
Sub-Sahara Africa	0.1	9%	0.01	0.04	8.4	0.13	1.9%	0%
Middle East	0.9	52%	0.10	0.6	7.2	0.24	1.5%	1%
South Asia	0.5	19%	0.06	0.2	7.6	0.23	2.3%	1%
Confucian Asia	0.3	15%	0.03	0.2	8.2	0.12	1.6%	3%

Note: *) scale ranges from 0 'closest to my own culture', 10 'most distant perception'.

For an inspection of the more recent travel and destination pattern the fourth column of Table 12.1 should be considered. These figures represent the cumulative number of trips taken during the past five years. On average, the destination regions or clusters show the same ranking compared to the lifetime travel pattern. However, the absolute difference between the clusters shifts from the structure released by the first column. Germanic Europe dropped in importance; the Middle East gained in attractiveness.

Continuing the same regional analysis for the trips planned for the coming three years (2009, 2010 and 2011) an even more substantial shift of travel pattern becomes evident (sixth column of Table 12.1). Latin Europe takes the lead position in the ranking of intended destinations. It is followed by the Anglo American Region and Eastern Europe. Germanic Europe appears only on rank four. The following column seven highlights the fact that travelling to particular destinations is partly motivated by social ties: visiting friends or relatives (VFR). The percentages give the share of trips planned during the following three years which will be taken entirely or partly due to the mentioned social relationships. The highest fraction can be seen for Germanic Europe and in the same amount for the Anglo American Region. Almost 10% of all trips to Eastern and Latin Europe incorporate VFR.

Additional relationships with the society clusters can influence the decisions in favour or against a particular destination region. Column five of Table 1 exhibits the average distance scores as perceived by the respondents. Germanic Europe appears at the bottom of the scale expressing maximum identification with the own culture. Latin Europe

(2.9) comes next followed immediately by Nordic Europe (3.2). Eastern Europe with 3.7 is on third position before the Anglo American Region (4.1). With some larger off-set the list continues with Latin America (6.0). Sub-Sahara Africa is perceived as most distant followed by Confucian Asia. The last column of Table 121.1 expresses language proficiency or affinity. German is spoken by all respondents. English enjoys also a wide coverage with 93%. Some Romanic language capabilities were expressed by about 50% of the sample. Interestingly, cultural distance and language affinity shows some significant correlation. However, this applies only for six out of ten cultural regions (Eastern Europe: -.36; Anglo America Region: -.13; Latin America: -.18; Middle East -.24; South Asia: -.23, Confucian Asia: -.26) and does not mean a very strong link.

The following analysis turns the attention to the two age groups of the study. Table 12.2 delivers the results of the statistical comparison for four indicators. Looking back to the lifetime travel frequency of both sub-samples, it seems that the cumulative travel activities are higher for the older age cohort. Each of the ten society clusters shows a much higher visitation level, not all achieve statistical significance though. In addition, the difference does not allow the conclusion that both age cohorts gathered their destination experience at the same speed. In contrast to this result, the second column gives evidence for the more recent travel behaviour. In this respect, no significant differences appear between younger and older people. The only exception is the Anglo American Region which was visited much more by the younger age group. A similar congruence can be derived when screening column three depicting the travel intentions for the years 2009 to 2011. Again, the Anglo American Region is much more favoured by the younger generation. The Asian destinations are also significantly more attractive for this sub-group. Finally, the perceived cultural distance can be compared across the two age groups. Column four demonstrates that no significant difference can be detected.

Table 12.2: Past and future destination horizon and perceived cultural distance compared by two age groups

Society Cluster	Lifetime Travel Frequency		Travel Frequency: 2004 – 2008		Travel intention: 2009 – 2011		Perceived cultural distance	
	20-30	50-60	20-30	50-60	20-30	50-60	20-30	50-60
Germanic Europe	9.1	18.0*	3.0	3.4	0.6	0.8	0.6	0.5
Nordic Europe	0.5	0.9	0.3	0.2	0.4	0.3	3.2	3.0
Eastern Europe	4.0	6.5*	2.3	1.9	0.7	0.8	3.8	3.6
Latin Europe	3.6	8.1*	2.2	2.4	1.1	1.1	2.9	2.9
Anglo American region	1.5	2.3*	0.9	0.5*)	1.2	0.6*)	3.9	4.2
Latin America	0.2	0.5*	0.1	0.2	0.3	0.3	5.9	6.1
Sub-Sahara Africa	0.0	0.2*	0.0	0.1	0.1	0.1	8.4	8.4
Middle East	0.8	1.1	0.5	0.5	0.2	0.3	7.0	7.4
South Asia	0.4	0.6	0.2	0.2	0.3	0.1*)	7.5	7.7
Confucian Asia	0.2	0.3	0.2	0.1	0.2	0.1*)	8.0	8.4
Cumulative p.a.	2.8	1.1*	1.9	1.9	1.7	1.4*)	-	-

Note: * significant differences at p < 0.5.

After this independent and linear screening of the basic data the analysis turns now to the particular research questions. With the research instrument employed to capture the lifetime travel pattern it is not possible to transform the data into Schmidhauser's travel horizon or Oppermann's destination horizon information. In contrast, the travel history of the immediate preceding five years was recoded in this way. The same transition was exercised for the three years' travel plans. By the means of regression analyses the first research question can be tackled. The past travel horizon is able to predict the future horizon to a rather limited extent: Future Horizon 1 (domestic) to 14%, future Horizon 2 (neighbouring countries) to 16%, future Horizon 3 (rest of Europe) to 13% and future Horizon 4 (rest of the world) to 10%. All four regressions affirm a certain tendency to remain in the horizon travelled in the past because only the past horizon exhibited a significant influence on the same future horizon. Future Horizon 4 behaves slightly differently. In addition to the equivalent past Horizon 4 trips, a reinforcing influence can be attributed to the past Horizon 3 experience. Yet, this function is the weakest in this series ($R^2 = .10$).

Table 12.3: Summary of regressions explaining 3 years' destination planning horizon for society clusters by four different models (R^2- and adj.R^2-coefficients)

Model variants	A			B			C			D		
	Lifetime travel pattern only			Lifetime travel + past 5-years' travel pattern			Perceived cultural distance			A + B + C + social ties + languages		
Planned travel destination 2009 to 2011:	Entire sample	20 – 30 years	50 – 60 years	Entire sample	20 – 30 years	50 – 60 years	Entire sample	20 – 30 years	50 – 60 years	Entire sample	20 – 30 years	50 – 60 years
Germanic Europe	2	2	n.s.	9	6	13	2	2	n.s.	29	26	29
Nordic Europe	n.s.	3	6	6	15	8	n.s.	3	n.s.	17	25	11
Eastern Europe	5	5	12	16	15	24	3	7	n.s.	27	26	38
Latin Europe	4	8	5	10	8	14	3	5	3	20	20	16
Anglo American Reg.	4	6	n.s.	9	11	11	n.s.	4	3	26	29	27
Latin America	3	3	5	5	5	5	n.s.	3	7	18	32	27
Sub-Sahara Africa	5	n.s.	18	7	n.s.	22	4	8	16	22	31	24
Middle East	n.s.	n.s.	n.s.	9	5	12	2	n.s.	n.s.	24	43	24
South Asia	3	n.s.	27	13	12	26	2	5	n.s.	30	29	26
Confucian Asia	16	22	16	29	33	22	12	18	6	48	53	31

Note: regression functions are all significant at a level of at least $p < .05$; n.s. = 'not significant'.

Alternatively, research question 2 challenges the concept of past destination pattern horizon in order to explain the destination planning horizon as differentiated by the ten society clusters. Table 12.3 delivers the appropriate summary statistics for the regressions employed. Model variant A tries to associate the cumulative lifetime travel pattern with the future destination plans. The first column for each model variant depicts the r^2-values for the entire sample. The second and third columns are dedicated to the separate inspection by two age groups. Overall, this much more differentiated analysis – compared to Schmidhauser's four horizons – does not achieve superior results. The Confucian Asia seems to be an exception with an r^2 of 16% on average. All the remaining destination planning horizons cannot be explained sufficiently. Taking the breaks by age into consideration it appears that the destination plans for the older generation can be explained much better through their lifetime travel horizon pattern. South Asia ($r^2 = 27\%$) and Sub-Sahara Africa (18%) show much higher r^2-values.

In order to address the following research question, model variant B incorporates both past destination horizons: the lifetime and the pattern of the past five years. In such a competitive situation it could be seen whether the more recent travel experience or the cumulative lifetime travel pattern or both have an influence for the future destination plans. Block B of Table 12.3 summarizes the regression results. Overall, the predictive power increases compared to model variant A and appears to be slightly better compared to the Four-Horizon structure proposed by Schmidhauser. When analysing the regression functions in detail, it turns out that the lifetime destination horizon pattern is almost completely displaced. For explaining travel plans to Sub-Sahara Africa for the older age group, some long-term elements (Anglo American Region and Confucian Asia) play the dominant role and for explaining future trips into the South Asian zone by the older age group, the lifetime experience to this destination has some major impact.

Before moving into an even more complex analysis of future travel behaviour it should be clarified whether the perceived cultural distance is relevant for the explanation of planned destinations. Model variant C addresses this research question 4. Again, Table 12.3 gives an overview on the overall outcome. The degree of determination is weak and in 30% of the cases, insignificant. It can be observed, that in general the distance perception affects the destination choice negatively. The closer the perception of the society cluster the higher the propensity to visit these destinations. However, some interesting exceptions can be observed. Whereas travel plans for Confucian Asian destinations are negatively influenced by the perceived cultural distance of this region, the cultural distance attributed to South Asia is working in the opposite direction. So, the more foreign South Asia is perceived, the higher is the probability to travel to a Confucian Asian destination. Another example illustrates the explanation for future Sub-Sahara destinations. The younger age group feels more attracted due to a closer cultural distance perception. The opposite mechanism applies for the older age group.

Finally, research question 5 will be answered by regressing the three years' destination planning horizon on all the previous factors together with two personal components: 1. social ties in terms of VFR and 2. language proficiency. In general, the regression models (Table 12.3: model variant D) achieve a much better predictive power. However, it is not true that in all cases visiting friends and relatives contribute most to this explanation. VFR is strongest for Germanic Europe, for Nordic Europe, for Eastern Europe, for Latin Europe (with the exception of the older age group for the latter two), for the Anglo American Region, for Latin America, for Sub-Sahara Africa, for Middle East and Confucian Asia (with the exception of the older age group for the latter two regions).

Conclusion

This study reconsiders the conceptual boundaries and the usefulness of the idea to structure past travel behaviour in a rather simple way. Modelling past trip activities goes far beyond the question of whether a traveller has immediate destination experience or not or if he or she shows a certain level of destination loyalty. Nevertheless, this question is embedded into the broader research domain of prior knowledge and how facets of prior knowledge – such as familiarity, expertise and experience – influence travel decision making. As soon as travel experience is conceived to be more than a simple counter of trips taken within a certain period of time there are already some cognitive elements involved which qualifies for a complex variety of potential conceptualizations.

The difficulty in collecting data on an annual basis for a period longer than ten years motivated the move away from a complete year-by-year record of past trips to a cumulative frequency estimate for each proposed destination horizon. These horizons were redefined using the ten society clusters used in the so-called Globe study (House et al., 2004). These clusters of rather similar cultures enabled us to completely detach the zoning approach as defined by geographic distance. This shift in perspective has the twofold benefit that results of this kind of analysis can be compared for different countries of origin and that the travellers' cultural background is not implicitly tied to the country's dominant culture. The society cluster approach was used in a similar way to record not only the lifetime travel frequency but also the destinations visited during the past five years (2004 to 2008) and the destinations planned to visit during the next three years (2009 to 2011).

Research question 1 addressed the capabilities of Schmidhauser's travel horizon model. Regression and cross tabulation analyses identified a certain destination horizon loyalty in the short run. Only the planned overseas destinations revealed some significantly higher number of recent trips into the third (European) horizon in addition. However, the overall explanatory power ranges between 10% and 16%, a rather low level. The predictive validity of destination horizons along cultural zones was investigated alternatively in research question two. By applying a quasi-experimental design of two age groups (20 – 30 years and 50 – 60 years) the effect of long-term versus short-term travel experience could be evaluated.

In general, the long-term or lifetime travel experience (model variant A) is a very weak predictor for determining the destination planning horizon of the next three years. No differences occur between the two age groups. Extending the approach by the more recent trip records of the past five years, the situation improves. The explanatory power for the ten different destination horizons varies between 5% and 33%. On average, it can be concluded that this approach (model variant B) achieves similar power compared to Schmidhauser's four-horizon model. Nevertheless, this modified destination horizon approach along the ten society clusters allows in part, a more differentiated interpretation. In almost any case, though, the more recent travel history drives the lifetime travel record out of the equation. This applies also for the younger age group for which both time windows are much more overlapping compared to the older age segment. This allows the conclusion that the lifetime travel experience and pattern has no strong predictive power for determining the planned destinations of the near future (research question 3).

Perceived cultural distance was thought to act as a completely alternative approach in explaining destination plans (research question 4). Hence, in a separate attempt (model variant C) the influence of perceived cultural distance on the destination planning horizon was analysed. Yet the results are even inferior to model variant A using lifetime travel experience only. As a consequence, it cannot be uphold that the particular closeness of someone's own culture (with the exception of domestic trips) or the particular perception of strangeness or exoticness acts as strong driver or determinant for destination choices in the future.

In research question 5 it was demonstrated how social and cultural factors linked to the individual traveller may improve the explanatory power. On average, the variance could be explained by 17% to 48%. Differences between the two age groups highlight that the influential factors considered here vary in strength – and sometimes in direction. Social ties (considered here as the motivation to visit friends or relatives) to the investigated destination planning horizons have the strongest impact. Perceived cultural distance together with recent travel experience comes next. Language proficiency is, generally speaking, neither an inhibitor nor a strong facilitator.

The results demonstrate in general that the predictive qualities of the destination horizon concept are rather limited. On a short to medium-term scope the traditional horizon approach more or less reflects the already known phenomenon of destination (region) loyalty. Expanding the concept beyond a dominant geographic calculus however opened the perspective for a more flexible analysis. Future research may identify typical destination horizon patterns in the past to predict future planning horizons in a more thorough way. In addition, this study intentionally kept typical life cycle impacts at a rather low level. However, as results have demonstrated, life stage contingencies together with the macro-economic development represent important factors to account for destination preferences. The limitation of the applied purposive sampling approach should be overcome by testing the concept on a sample of the entire population. Especially when investigating people's travel careers, another direction to follow and to enrich the power of the destination planning horizon, is to take push factors driving the travellers into account.

References

Alba JW and Hutchinson JW. 1987. Dimensions of consumer expertise. *Journal of Consumer Research* **13** (4): 411-454.

Baloglu S. 2001. Image variations of Turkey by familiarity index: informational and experiential dimensions. *Tourism Management* **22**: 127-133.

Gursoy D and McCleary KW. 2004a. An integrative model of tourists' information search behavior. *Annals of Tourism Research* **31** (2): 353-373.

Gursoy D and McCleary KW. 2004b. Travelers' prior knowledge and its impact on their information search behavior. *Journal of Hospitality and Tourism Research* **28** (1): 66-94.

Hirschman EC and Wallendorf M. 1982. Motives underlying marketing information acquisition and knowledge transfer. *Journal of Advertising* **11** (3): 25-31.

House RJ, Hanges, PJ, Javidan, M, Dorfman, PW. and Gupta, V (eds). 2004. *Culture, Leadership, and Organizations: The GLOBE study of 62 Societies.* Thousand Oaks, London, New Dehli: Sage Publications.

Kerstetter D. and Cho, MH. 2004. Prior knowledge, credibility and information search. *Annals of Tourism Research* **31** (4): 961-985.

Oppermann M. 1995. Travel life cycle. *Annals of Tourism Research* **22** (3): 535-552.

Oppermann M. 1998. Travel horizon: a valuable analysis tool? *Tourism Management* **19** (4): 321-329.

Schmidhauser H. 1976. Neue Erkenntnisse über Gesetzmäßigkeiten bei der Wahl des Reiseziels. *Jahrbuch für Fremdenverkehr* **25-26**: 86-102.

Snepenger D, Meged K Snelling M and Worrall K 1990. Information search strategies by destination-naive tourists. *Journal of Travel Research* **29** (1): 13-16.

Part II:

Destination Image, Positioning and Branding

13 Assessing the International Image of an Urban Destination: the Case of Milan

Francesca d'Angella and Manuela de Carlo, IULM University, Milan

Introduction

In today's highly competitive tourism marketplace, destinations have to work hard to build an effective positioning strategy and to differentiate themselves from their competitors. Thus, an appealing image is a fundamental asset for the repositioning process of an urban destination, both in terms of extensive knowledge of tourist behaviour and the development of effective marketing strategies.

From the beginning of the 1970s, several authors and scholars centred their studies on the issues of destination image formation, management and assessment, and the role it plays in the process of destination selection and evaluation made by tourists (Beerli and Martìn, 2004a, b; Pike, 2002). In particular, studies on destination image mainly concentrate on leisure tourism, with a focus on pleasure tourist perceptions and the determinants of leisure destination image. On the contrary, the issue of the formation of business destination image – where travel for attending meetings, exhibitions and incentives play a relevant role – is less explored. However, some authors who contributed to this field (Hankinson, 2005) highlight how theoretical models proposed in studies centred on leisure destinations cannot be applied to business tourism. In fact, the latter presents some distinctive characteristics due to the business-to-business relationships which affect the process of image formation and assessment.

Moreover, in the large variety of contributions on destination image, only a few focus on international urban tourism and, consequently, on the international image of urban business destinations (Bramwell, Rawding, 1996; Calantone et al., 1989; Grabler, 1997; Suh and Gartner, 2004). Thus, in the literature much room has been left for further explorative studies on the determinants of the image of destinations with a business vocation. This chapter aims to contribute to the filling of this gap with an explorative analysis focused on Milan, an urban destination mainly visited by business tourists. The case study is then put in the context of the existing literature on destination image definition and measurement.

Literature Review

Starting from the 1970s, contributions from several authors on the brand and image of tourism destinations have faced numerous issues with significant theoretical and managerial implications. In particular, some authors aim at reinforcing the weak theoretical foundations and the lack of conceptualization which for years characterized empirical research on destination brand and image. These studies assume the image as a dependent variable and aim at defining the concept of tourism destination image and at developing theoretical models to assess it (Alhemoud and Armstrong, 1996; Beerli and Martin, 2004b; Carmichael, 1992; Etchner and Ritchie 1991, 1993; Gallarza et al., 2002; Gartner, 1989; Jenkins, 1999).

A second group of studies consider destination image as an independent variable which affects the individual perceptions and, consequently, some consumer behaviour variables, such as the choice of the destination and the visitor satisfaction (Baloglu and Mc Cleary, 1999; Chen and Hsu, 2000; Chon, 1991; Hunt, 1975; Pearce, 1982; Woodside and Lysonsky, 1989).

Our study, in line with the first group of contributions, aims at reinforcing the knowledge about the determinants of the image formation through an explorative analysis, focusing on an urban business destination. Exploring previous studies about destination image, one of the most recurrent definitions for tourist destination image is that by Crompton (1979: 18), who describes it as 'the sum of beliefs, ideas and impressions that a person has of a destination'.

Some authors (Etchner and Ritchie 1991; Gallarza and Calderon, 2002) categorize image determinants into two groups. The first one refers to the perception of individual attributes, such as the existence of green parks, historical sites and accommodation services. The second one gathers individual imagery, including a mental picture of physical characteristics and atmosphere. Furthermore, every component of destination image includes elements which can be functional/objective (for example entertainment activities, cultural attractions, etc.) or psychological/subjective (for example the perceived quality of services, the reputation, the residents' attitude towards tourists, etc.). According to this perspective, as highlighted by several authors (Baloglu and Brinberg, 1997; Baloglu and McCleary, 1999), the destination image includes two components. The first one is cognitive in nature and concerns the knowledge and convictions about the destination. The second one is emotional in nature and gathers feelings about the destination. In more recent studies, the behavioural element has been added as a third component that summarizes the behaviour that tourists have toward the destination as a result of their knowledge and past experience (Gartner, 1993; Pike and Ryan, 2004; White, 2004).

An interesting synthesis of the numerous studies which tried to identify the determinants of destination's image is proposed by Tasci and Gartner (2007). These two authors point out that 'Despite the ample amount of literature, there still seems to be a gap when it comes to a comprehensive conceptualization of destination image and its intricate relationships. There still seems to be many facets of this complex construct yet to be investigated empirically' (2007: 423). To this respect, our study aims at providing a contribution to fulfil this gap with reference to a specific area of analysis: the international image of a business destination.

In particular our chapter aims at answering the following research questions:

Q1: What are the key destination's attributes which characterize urban destination international image?

Q2: Do these attributes differ according to diverse travel motivations?

Q3: Do these attributes differ according to diverse travel characteristics?

Methodology

In order to answer our research questions we surveyed foreign tourists in Milan through a questionnaire.

The questions are based on the attributes that determine the perceived destination image as proposed in thetourism literature (Beerli and Martin, 2004a, 2004b; Embacher and Buttle, 1989; Etchner and Ritchie, 1991; Walmsley and Jekins, 1993; Walmsley and Young, 1998) as well as specific destination features. In fact, the choice to study an urban destination obliged the authors to formulate the questions giving less relevance to weather and natural environment and more space to the other attributes. In total, 29 variables are used to assess destination image (Table 13.1).

Table 13.1: The items in the questionnaire

#	Item	#	Item
c1_1	Public transport efficiency	c3_7	Special events organization
c1_2	Public transport expensiveness	d3_1	Events communication
c1_3	Taxi availability	d3_2	Easiness of finding tourism information
c1_4	Taxi expensivenes s	d3_3	Clarity of tourism signposting
c1_5	Taxi drivers' friendliness and professionalism	d3_4	The level of English spoken by people
c1_6	Easiness of getting around Milan by car	d3_5	Courtesy to foreign tourists, including those who don't speak Italian
c2_1	Quality of accommodation	e1_1	City cleanliness and tidiness
c2_2	Hotels price/quality ratio	e1_2	Presence of green areas
c2_3	Hotels staff kindness and profes-sionalism	e1_3	Warmness and hospitability
c3_1	Shopping	e1_4	Safety
c3_2	Nightlife	e1_5	Cost of life
c3_3	Quality of music entertainment and performance	e1_6	Traffic
c3_4	Variety of museums and galleries	e1_7	Air pollution
c3_5	Variety of design and architecture heritage	e1_8	Dynamicity of the city
c3_6	Cuisine		

The questionnaire consists of five parts. Sections A and E contain respondents' profiles (such as gender, nationality, job, education, age) and means of transport used to reach Milan. Section B is dedicated to the purpose of the visit. To better evaluate the influence of the motivations on the perceived image, possible travel motivation options include: leisure, business, and meeting. Section C asks tourists their personal opinions about Milan regarding: public and private transport, hospitality, accommodation and entertainment. Section D is centred on heritage and culture and aims at understanding the awareness of Milan's attractions. In section E we ask respondents for their opinions on the personality of the city regarding several intangible attributes.

Respondents are asked to indicate their agreement level for each item, for the sections C, D (partially) and E (partially) on a four-point Likert-type scale, from 'strongly disagree

(= 1)' to 'strongly agree (= 4)'. Researchers decided not to adopt a five or seven-point scale, even if often used in literature, to avoid a sort of 'understatement effect' which make answers concentrate on the average value of the scale.

The sample includes 733 foreign tourists – that means people spending at least one night in the destination – coming to Milan for different purposes. All questionnaires were carried out by face-to-face interviews conducted from 15 December 2007 to 1 February 2008 in leisure and cultural places; airports and train stations; business hotels and fairs and exhibitions. The respondents' profiles are summarized in Table 13.2.

Table 13.2: Respondents' profile

Gender	Frequency	Percent
	(SDEV .49)	
Female	292	39.8
Male	441	60.2
Total	733	100.0
Age	(SDEV .89)	
18-24	102	13.9
25-34	254	34.7
35-49	291	39.7
50 and over	86	11.7
Total	733	100.0
Education	(SDEV .75)	
Secondary school	137	18.7
Bachelor degree	375	51.2
Master or Doctoral degree	198	27.0
Other	23	3.1
Total	733	100.0
Job	(SDEV 2.92)	
Employee	285	38.9
Enterpreneur	106	14.5
Self employed	53	7.2
Retired	10	1.4
Student	75	10.2
Unemployed	4	.5
Director or manager	135	18.4
Manual or crafts worker	12	1.6
Other	53	7.2
Total	733	100.0
Purpose of the journey	(SDEV .74)	
Leisure	230	31.4
Business	324	44.2
Meeting	179	24.4
Total	733	100.0
Means of transport	(SDEV .93)	
Car	48	6.5
Train	67	9.1
Airplane	599	81.7
Other	19	2.6
Total	733	100.0

Length (days)	Frequency	Percent
	(SDEV .81)	
1	88	12.0
2	205	28.0
3-4	236	32.2
5-7	114	15.6
8 and over	80	10.9
DK	10	1.4
Total	733	100.0
Accommodation	(SDEV .64)	
Home	15	2.0
Relatives&friends	62	8.5
Hotel	607	82.8
Residence	18	2.5
B&B	24	3.3
Other	7	1.0
Total	733	100.0
Journey organizer	(SDEV .85)	
Yourself	301	41.1
Company	261	35.6
Travel agency	146	19.9
Other	25	3.4
Total	733	100.0
Visits to Milan	(SDEV .88)	
First	346	47.2
Second	146	19.9
Third or more	241	32.9
Total	733	100.0
Itinerary	(SDEV .83)	
Milan	435	59.3
Milan+surrondings	131	17.9
Milan + tour	167	22.8
Total	733	100.0

Respondents are mainly men (60.2%), with an average age of 35-49 years (39.7%) and 25-34 (34.7%). These tourists have a high level of education – 51.2% have a bachelor degree or a master/doctoral degree (27%). The range of respondents' jobs is quite heterogeneous: 38.9% are employees, 18.4% are directors or managers, 14.5% entrepreneurs, and students 10.2%. The purposes of the travel vary from tourist coming for business (44.2%), the main group, leisure tourists (31.4%) and meeting (conventions, conferences, congresses...) attendance (21.4%). Regardless of motivation, the majority of travellers reached Milan by plane (81.7%), while only a small part reached the destination by train (9.1%) or by car (6.5%).

Tourists usually stayed in Milan 3-4 days (32.2%) or 2 days (28%); 26.7% of respondents stay even longer, while only 12% spent just one night in the city. The accommodation chosen by most of the tourists is the hotel (82.8%), while about 10.5% of respondents stay in a house or with relatives and friends.

Tourists tend to organize their trip themselves (41.1%), even if for business tourists and sometimes even for meetings, the tourists' companies act as travel organizers (35.6%). Travel agencies provide their services only to the remaining 19.9% of tourists. This is also interesting because 47.2% of respondents were visiting Milan for the first time.

Regarding the itinerary of their journey, Milan is the destination of 59.3% of tourists, while 17.9% of those interviewed visited even the surroundings and for the remaining 22.8% Milan is only one leg of the trip.

Data Analysis

The data analysis was conducted in two stages. First, we used a principal component analysis with a varimax orthogonal rotation to investigate the existence of latent variables and to identify groupings of attributes that could be crystallized as dimensions of Milan, and grouped accordingly (Conway and Huffcutt, 2003; Ford et al., 1986). The application of the Kaiser method (Kim and Mueller, 1978) suggested the initial retention of nine factors, collectively explaining 66.9% of the variance. Then we repeated our analysis eliminating those items that either loaded on more than one factor or displayed communality scores lower than 0.50 (Hair et al., 1995) except three variables very close to this threshold. The variables excluded are about the ease of getting around by car in Milan (c1_6), night life (c3_2), safety (e1_4) and dynamicity (e1_8).

In the second part of the analysis, to understand the influence of the purpose of the trip on destination image, we calculated factor scores for each observation by multiplying the ratings by their loadings (Kim and Mueller, 1978). The subsequent aggregation of factor scores by purpose of the trip enabled us to compare, through an ANOVA test, the destination image according to the three main tourism segments: leisure, business and meeting tourists. Besides, with the same methodology and t-test analyses, we investigated similarities and differences in the destination's image according to travel characteristics.

As Jenkins (1999) notes, in studies about destination image, structured methods such as factor analysis, cluster analysis and other multivariate analyses are more common than unstructured ones. In fact, the methodologies used in this research – factor analysis, ANOVA and independent t-tests – are often used in tourism studies to analyse image formation, differences according to different tourism segments (Hankinson, 2005; Kozak, 2002) and destination residents (Long et al., 1990).

Evidence from the Survey

The first part of the empirical analysis provides an answer to the first research question. The results of the analysis indicate nine factors as determinants of Milan's image, explaining the 66.92% of the variance (Table 13.3).

Table 13.3: The variance explained by the nine factors

Compon ent	Extraction Sums of Squared Loadings			Rotation Sums of Squared Loadings		
	Total	% of Variance	Cumulative %	Total	% of Variance	Cumulative %
1	4.215	16.860	16.860	2.189	8.757	8.757
2	2.753	11.012	27.872	2.180	8.719	17.476
3	2.252	9.006	36.878	2.149	8.597	26.074
4	1.598	6.392	43.270	1.894	7.575	33.649
5	1.389	5.554	48.824	1.855	7.420	41.069
6	1.246	4.984	53.808	1.737	6.947	48.016
7	1.205	4.821	58.629	1.736	6.945	54.961
8	1.065	4.259	62.888	1.592	6.369	61.330
9	1.010	4.041	66.929	1.400	5.599	66.929

Extraction Method: Principal Component Analysis.

The Determinants of Milan's Perceived Image

The nine components are related to: destination transports (factors 1 and 6), leisure offer (factor 2), accommodation (factor 3), events (factor 4), city life standards (factors 5 and 8) and city breadth of attractions (factors 7 and 9).

Factor 1 (16.86% of the variance) includes three items: 'availability of taxi, cost of taxis, and professional drivers'. We interpreted this factor as tourists' perception of Milan's *private transport*. For an urban destination, the importance of this element is coherent with the characteristics of its tourism segments, mainly business or leisure with a high expenditure capacity. Moreover, for Milan it also indicates a lack of public transport, which is not comparable, for extension and efficiency, to other European urban destinations, such as London, Vienna, Prague or Paris.

Factor 2 (11.01% of the variance) includes three items – accommodation quality, hotels price/quality ratio and kindness/cordiality of hotel staff – and indicates tourists' perception of the *accommodation* offer. This factor is relevant because accommodation is one of the core services of a destination tourism offer. Furthermore, when the destination offers few welcome services to tourists (information centres, welcome desks, etc.), hotels are considered as substitutes (see item C2_3).

Factor 3 (9% of the variance), indicated in this study as *leisure offer*, includes five items: quality of shopping, music entertainment and performance quality, variety of museums and galleries, variety of design and architecture heritage and good cuisine. This factor is relevant to image formation for different reasons. First, shopping is a component of Milan's tourism offer that is very well communicated and, as demonstrated by previous researches (Coccia, 2007; Di Fraia and Orsucci, 2006) it is one of the main reasons for visiting Milan. The relevance of music is mainly due to the theatre 'Teatro alla Scala', an international icon. Heritage is relevant because Milan is one of the largest Italian heritage cities in terms of number of heritage sites and monuments. Finally, the cuisine is significant because the sample includes only foreign tourists, who mainly associate Milan, as an Italian city, with a good quality of food.

The quality of events (music performances) hosted in Milan, their organization and communication loaded on factor 4 (6.39% of the variance), interpreted as tourists' perception of destination *events*. The importance of events as image makers (Getz, 2008, 1997) or as attributes affecting existing destination image (Bieger et al., 2003; Crompton 1979; Echtner and Ritchie 1993; Fakeye and Crompton 1991; Gartner and Shen 1992; Prentice and Andersen, 2003) is well developed in tourism literature. However, they are not often included in previous studies about destination image determinants.

Factor 5 (5.55% of the variance) includes three items, cost of living, traffic congestion, and air pollution, and it has been interpreted as a measure of *life quality*. The low relevance of this factor is coherent with the motivations of urban tourists; few are influenced by urban life quality and are more interested in the elements of the tourism offer.

Factor 6 (4.98% of the variance) comprises 2 items, public transport efficiency and costs, that means the overall quality of *public transport*. This is consistent with what we stated to explain the first factor (private transport).

Two items (tourism information availability and clearness of signposting) loaded onto factor 7 (4.82% of the variance), which summarizes perceptions of *tourism information availability and clearness*. The poor variance explained by this factor suggests a low level of relevance of tourism information in the destination's image formation. In this case it isn't so important because business tourists don't need to gather information about the location of places and attractions. The same remarks count for leisure tourists coming to Milan for shopping and for groups of tourists, who visit the city with guides.

The eighth factor consists of three variables: cleanliness of the city, the presence of green areas and the atmosphere of the city (warm and hospitable), which express the *city environment*. Comments on life quality are valid also for this factor.

The last factor, '*residents' receptiveness*' includes two variables: the level of English spoken and the courteousness of local people towards foreign tourists, including those who don't speak Italian. Remarks concerning tourism information are valid also for this factor. In particular, all business tourists represent a tourism segment which only slightly interacts with the destination.

Differences in Image Determinants According to Tourism Segments

To give an answer to the second research question, we focused the analysis on three tourism segments: leisure, business and meeting. As shown in Table 13.4, there are statistically significant differences on six factors: private local transport (F1), accommodation (F2), events (F4), life quality (F5), public transport (F6) and tourism communication (F7).

Regarding factor 1, diversities are ascribable to the cost of taxis, which is not usually borne by business people or participants in meetings; in contrast, taxi fares are paid for by leisure tourists. The opposite motivation explains factor 6, which refers to public transport. In fact, segments which give average high ratings on private transport – meeting and business – are those which give lower ranking on the public transport.

Differences in the means related to factor 2, as demonstrated in Table 13.5, are not due to the accommodation chosen when staying in Milan.

Table 13.4: Differences in the perceived destination's image according to purpose of the trip

		N	Mean	Std. Deviation	Sig.
REGR factor 1: private transport	Leisure	226	-.2477767	1.14207630	.000
	Business	320	.0766208	.90893636	
	Meeting	178	.1768477	.90402949	
	Total	724	.0000000	1.00000000	
REGR factor score 2: accommodation	Leisure	226	-.1949643	1.22208586	.002
	Business	320	.0849741	.84877529	
	Meeting	178	.0947765	.90400889	
	Total	724	.0000000	1.00000000	
REGR factor score 3: leisure offer	Leisure	226	.0924168	1.05044384	.127
	Business	320	-.0803158	.91977435	
	Meeting	178	.0270497	1.06493652	
	Total	724	.0000000	1.00000000	
REGR factor score 4: events	Leisure	226	-.1528896	.99676809	.000
	Business	320	-.0250406	.99033193	
	Meeting	178	.2391351	.98269758	
	Total	724	.0000000	1.00000000	
REGR factor score 5: life quality	Leisure	226	-.1808741	1.04218544	.003
	Business	320	.0490666	.94019380	
	Meeting	178	.1414394	1.02209071	
	Total	724	.0000000	1.00000000	
REGR factor score 6: public transports	Leisure	226	.2381501	.90827269	.000
	Business	320	-.1475047	1.05446090	
	Meeting	178	-.0371934	.95865247	
	Total	724	.0000000	1.00000000	
REGR factor score 7: tourism information availability and clearness	Leisure	226	.1711401	.85011841	.000
	Business	320	-.1789665	1.11935504	
	Meeting	178	.1044474	.89533917	
	Total	724	.0000000	1.00000000	
REGR factor score 8: city environment	Leisure	226	.1019444	.89371616	.152
	Business	320	-.0661403	1.04066467	
	Meeting	178	-.0105310	1.04704635	
	Total	724	.0000000	1.00000000	
REGR factor score 9: residents' receptiveness	Leisure	226	-.1291319	.96974845	.056
	Business	320	.0763198	.99164851	
	Meeting	178	.0267499	1.04138503	
	Total	724	.0000000	1.00000000	

Table 13.5: Accommodation chosen by respondents

	Accommodation			
	Leisure	Business	Meeting	Total
Home	3%	2%	1%	2%
Relatives&friends	17%	2%	11%	8%
Hotel 5*	7%	15%	18%	13%
Hotel 4*	45%	62%	50%	54%
Hotel 3*	18%	11%	13%	14%
Hotel <3*	3%	0%	2%	2%
Residence	0%	4%	2%	2%
B&B	6%	2%	2%	3%
Other	2%	1%	1%	1%
Total	100%	100%	100%	100%

Needs expressed by the various tourism segments are different: businessmen and meeting tourists search for accommodation that facilitates their work (internet access, high accessibility, 24h check in/out, etc.), while leisure tourists are interested in a pleasant atmosphere, good connections with the city centre, and a good quality/price ratio.

The diverse judgements assigned to the event factor derive from the different role they play in the travel experience of the three tourist segments. For leisure tourists, indeed, events are a central element of their visit, whereas they are less important, or not relevant at all for the other two targets.

Regarding the life quality (factor 5), the different means are explained by the diverse way the three segments experience the city. For leisure tourists, the interest in heritage, entertainment and events prevails over some elements of the life quality, which on the contrary, influence more meeting and business tourists.

With reference to factor 7, there is a clear difference in the importance ascribed to tourism information by leisure tourists – who walk through the city and visit attractions quite a lot – and the other two targets, and therefore, to the judgement assigned to the two variables included in this component of Milan's image. Thus, the first group has a more positive perception than the other two.

Interestingly, the factors which do not vary among the three tourism segments are leisure (F3), city environment (F8) and city welcome to foreigners (F9).

Regarding the leisure offerings (F3), all tourists experience leisure services and attractions in the same way, regardless of the purpose of their trip and, accordingly, the importance of these services in their visit is lower.

Finally, in reference to the city environment (F8) and the residents' receptiveness (F9), differences between segments are not significant because all tourists directly perceive the same characteristics of the environment and the inhabitants' attitudes toward tourists.

Differences in Image Determinants According to Travel Characteristics

In the last part of our research, we explored through one-way ANOVA and t-tests the existence of significant differences according to diverse trip characteristics in terms of: itinerary, number of visits to the destination and length of the journey.

Regarding the itinerary, we divided tourists into two groups: people who visit only Milan and tourists who consider Milan only one leg of their journey. In the second analysis, we split respondents into 'first visitors' and 'repeat visitors', while in the third case, we identified three groups of tourists according to the length of their stay in Milan: 1-2 days, 3-4 days and 5 or more days.

All the results of these three analyses show no significant difference in the majority of the factors.

The Determinants of an Urban Destination's International Image

Our analyses led to the identification of nine key dimensions of destination's international image, which only partially reflect those identified in previous studies. This is due to the characteristics of the territory analysed – a business-oriented urban destination – where natural and environmental variables are less relevant in tourists' perception.

The first innovative element is the heterogeneity of the variables included in each factor, which gathers both functional elements – objective features and resources of the destination – and psychological elements – subjective perceptions of the destination given by respondents. We deem this result quite relevant because it shows that material and objective elements which compose the set of resources and attractions of the destination are a crucial component of the destination's perceived image.

Moreover, our results indicate that the components which explain the greater part of the variance (43.26%) are elements of the tourism offer: local private transport (F1), accommodation (F2), leisure offer (F3) and events (F4). Nevertheless, they cannot be separated from intangible elements added over time to the set of attractions and resources through management and communication activities carried out at destination level. For example, the factor 'city environment' includes both functional elements (green) and psychological ones (warm and tidy).

The second interesting finding of the analysis points out the differences in the means registered for every single factor according to tourism segments (leisure, business and meeting). On the one hand, these results are in line with Gartner's work (Gartner 2007, 2004) which points out significant differences in the perceptions of international urban tourists according to the purpose of the trip (the two groups analysed are pleasure and business). On the other hand, our results highlight several factors with no significant differences according to the three tourism segments: leisure offer (F3), city environment (F8) and residents' receptiveness (F9).

Third, besides considering objective and subjective elements of the destination's perceived image, our study has tested the relevance of aspects connected to the features of the experience in the destination, only marginally considered in previous studies. In relation to this point, our analysis shows that there are no significant changes in the image determinants according to the length of the experience in the destination, the existence of opinions on the destination based on previous visits and the scope of the journey, which may include only the destination or other places as well.

Conclusion

This chapter focuses on the process of international image formation of a tourist destination. Our results indicate that there are nine components of the international image of Milan, intended as an urban destination: private transport (taxis), accommodation, leisure offer, events, life quality, public transport, tourism communication, city environment and residents' receptiveness. Interestingly, some of these elements are part of the destination resources while others are part of the tourism offer of the destination.

The implications of this study are worthy of note for both destination managers and firms. First of all, results provide destination managers with original insights for the implementation of effective destination marketing strategies. Moreover, as the analyses show significant differences according to the purpose of the travel, it gives insights for both leisure planners and managers who are responsible for the business offer of the city. In terms of implications at firm level, the assessment of the determinants of destination's image allows a deeper understanding of the roles and responsibilities of different kinds of firms. This is useful for the selection of partners for events and permanent cooperation within the urban area.

We are aware of the fact that our study holds some limitations, largely due to the features of our sample. First of all, our results mainly reflects the judgement of European tourists, hence their generalizability to other continents may be questioned. Further research covering tourists coming from different non-European countries is probably needed to test the soundness of our results. In this sense, our study may act as a pilot study to be replicated across different settings, with the aim of developing a more reliable tool for research and practice.

Second, it could be argued that our results may be affected by the composition of our sample, in that men prevail over women and adults over young and older people. Indeed, this sample reflects the characteristics of tourists who nowadays visit Milan. We believe, however, that the issue is worth further exploration. On the contrary, the methodological approach can be generalized and it represents the theoretical contribution of this study on this topic.

References

Alhemoud A, Armstrong E. 1996. Image of tourism attractions in Kuwait. *Journal of Travel Research* **34** (4): 76-80.

Baloglu S, Brinberg D. 1997. Affective images of tourism destinations. *Journal of Travel Research* **35** (4): 11–15.

Baloglu S, McCleary KW. 1999. U.S. international travelers' images of four Mediterranean destinations: A comparison of visitors and nonvisitors. *Journal of Travel Research* **38** (November): 144–152.

Beerli A, Martin J. 2004a. Tourists' characteristics and the perceived image of tourist destinations: a quantitative analysis – a case study of Lanzarote, Spain. *Tourism Management* **25**: 623-636.

Beerli A, Martin J. 2004b. Factors influencing destination image. *Annals of Tourism Research* **31** (3): 657–681.

Bieger T, Laesser C, Johnsen J, Bischof L. 2003. The impact of megaevents on destination images – the case of the annual meeting of the WEF in Davos, *TTRA Annual Conference*.

Bramwell B, Rawding L. 1996. Tourism marketing images of industrial cities. *Annals of Tourism Research* **23**: 201–221.

Calantone RJ, Di Benedetto C, Hakam A, and Bojanic D. 1989. Multiple multinational tourism positioning using correspondence analysis. *Journal of Travel Research* **28** (2): 25–32.

Carmichael B. 1992. Using conjoint modelling to measure tourist image and analyse ski resort choice. In *Choice and Demand in Tourism*, Johnson P and Thomas B (eds). Mansell: London; 93-106.

Chen JS, Hsu CHC. 2000. Measurement of Korean tourists' perceived images of overseas destinations. *Journal of Travel Research* **38** (May): 411–416.

Chon K. 1991. Tourism destination image: Marketing implications. *Tourism Management* **12**: 68–72.

Coccia F. 2007. Il turismo a Milano: una risorsa economica [Tourism in Milan: an economic resource]. *Impresa e Stato* **81**: 42-43.

Conway JM, Huffcutt AI. 2003. A review and evaluation of exploratory factor analysis practices in organizational research. *Organizational Research Methods* **6** (2): 147-158.

Crompton JL. 1979. An assessment of the image of Mexico as a vacation destination and the influence of geographical location upon that image. *Journal of Travel Research* **17** (4): 18-23.

Di Fraia G, Orsucci V. 2006. *Europa vede Milano* [Europe sees Milan], Research project financed by the Chamber of Commerce of Milan.

Echtner C, Brent Ritchie JR. 2003. The meaning and measurement of destination image. *Journal of Tourism Studies* **14** (1): 37-48.

Echtner C, Brent Ritchie JR. 1991. The meaning and measurement of destination image. *Journal of Tourism Studies* **2** (2): 2-12.

Embacher J, Buttle F. 1989. A repertory grid analysis of Austria's image as a summer vacation destination. *Journal of Travel Research* **28** (3): 3–23.

Fakeye PC, Crompton JL. 1991. Image differences between prospective, first time, and repeat visitors to the Lower Rio Grande Valley. *Journal of Travel Research* **30** (3): 10-16.

Ford JK, MacCallum RC, Tait M. 1986. The application of expiratory factor analysis in applied psychology: A critical review and analysis. *Personnel Psychology* **39** (2): 291-314.

Gallarza M, Saura I, Garcia H. 2002. Destination image. Towards a conceptual framework. *Annals of Tourism Research* **29** (1): 56-78.

Gartner W. 1989. Tourism image: Attribute measurement of state tourism products using multidimensional scaling techniques. *Journal of Travel Research* **28** (2): 16-20.

Gartner W. 1993. Image formation process. *Journal of Travel and Tourism Marketing* **2** (3): 191-212.

Gartner WC, Shen J. 1992. The impact of Tiananmen Square on China's tourism image. *Journal of Travel Research* **30** (Spring): 47–52.

Getz D. 1997. *Event management and event tourism* (1st ed.). New York: Cognizant Communications Corp.

Getz D. 2008. Event tourism: Definition, evolution, and research. *Tourism Management* **29**, 403–428.

Grabler K. 1997. Perceptual mapping and positioning of tourist cities. In *International City Tourism-Analysis and Strategy*. J. Mazanec (ed.). London: Cassell.

Hair JF, Black B, Babin B, Anderson RE, Tatham RL. 2005. *Multivariate Data Analysis.* 6th edn. Pearson Prentice Hall.

Hankinson G. 2005. Destination brand images: a business tourism perspective. *Journal of Services Marketing* **19** (1): 24-32.

Hunt JD. 1975. Image as a factor in tourist development. *Journal of Travel Research* **13** (Winter): 1–7.

Jenkins O. 1999. Understanding and measuring tourist destination images. *International Journal of Tourism Research* **1**: 1-15.

Kim J, Mueller CW. 1978. *Factor Analysis. Statistical Methods and Practical Issues*. Sage University Paper: Newbury Park, CA.

Kozak M. 2002. Comparative analysis of tourist motivations by nationality and destinations. *Tourism Management* **23**: 221–232.

Long P, Perdue R, Allen L. 1990. Rural resident tourism perceptions and attitudes by community level of tourism. *Journal of Travel Research* **28** (3): 3-9.

Pearce PL. 1982. Perceived changes in holiday destinations. *Annals of Tourism Research* **9**: 145–164.

Pike S. 2002. Destination image analysis – a review of 142 papers from 1973 to 2000. *Tourism Management* **23**: 541–549.

Pike S, Ryan C. 2004. Destination positioning analysis through a comparison of cognitive, affective, and conative perceptions. *Journal of Travel Research* **42** (4): 333-342.

Prentice R, Andersen V. 2003. Festival as creative destination. *Annals of Tourism Research* **30** (1): 7-30.

Suh Y, Gartner W. 2004. Perceptions in international urban tourism: An analysis of travelers to Seoul, Korea. *Journal of Travel Research* **43** (8): 39-45.

Tasci A, Gartner W. 2007. Destination image and its functional relationships. *Journal of Travel Research* **45** (4): 413–425.

Walmsley DJ, Jenkins JM. 1993. Appraisive images of tourist areas: application of personal constructs. *Australian Geographer* **24** (2): 1-13.

Walmsley DJ, Young M. 1998. Evaluative images and tourism: The use of perceptual constructs to describe the structure of destination images. *Journal of Travel Research* **36** (3): 65–69.

White CJ. 2004. Destination image: To see or not to see? *International Journal of Contemporary Hospitality Management* **16** (5): 309–314.

Woodside A, Lysonski S. 1989. A general model of traveler destination choice. *Journal of Travel Research* **27** (Spring): 8–14.

14 A Study of Non-visitors: Which Image Do They Hold of Destinations Not Visited?

Isabelle Frochot, CEMAGREF and University of Savoie; Luc Mazuel, Armelle Maumelat, Enita Clermont-Ferrand

Introduction

Image has always been a topic of interest among tourism scholars and practitioners as it represents a central element in consumers' selection and consumption processes. If numerous studies have been conducted on current customers, the market of non-consumers remains relatively unexplored. Non-visitors constitute a segment of potential customers holding interesting information on the image shortcomings and therefore on strategic marketing orientations that should be taken. This chapter is concerned with the reasons why a destination might not be chosen. The destination selected for the study was that of Auvergne, in central France, which has suffered image problems for many years. After a literature review, the chapter will describe how a study was conducted (focus groups) with Parisian participants. The novel method used to elicit and understand better the limits of the Auvergne image (i.e. drawing) will be described.

Literature Review

Image has been the object of intense academic interest over the past decade since it is a critical element in the tourist visitation intention (Baloglu and McCleary, 1999; Chon, 1990; Crompton, 1979; Goodrich, 1978; Sirakaya et al., 2001; Um and Crompton, 1990; Woodside and Lysonski, 1989).

Image is a vast and vague concept, which has been defined as 'an attitudinal construct consisting of an individual's mental representation of knowledge (beliefs), feelings and global impressions about an object or destination' (Baloglu and McCeary, 1999: 70). Tourist destination image is therefore constituted not solely of the sum of individual tangible and intangible attributes, it refers also to a more holistic and global feeling about the destination (Crompton, 1979; Echtner and Ritchie, 1991; Gallarza et al., 2002). In other terms the study of image needs to integrate the idea that a tourist destination image cannot be reduced to a set of cumulative attributes, it is also the result of more global feelings, which translate into abstract impressions about a destination. For instance, the atmosphere, the spirit of the destination, its exotic/different dimensions, all contribute to the image formed in tourists' minds. This holistic component has been stressed in Echtner and Ritchie's work (1991), among others, and represent an important part of image analysis.

However, differentiating cultural, national, historical and formal tourist information in a tourist image can be difficult to achieve. For instance, Gunn (1988) has clearly shown that an image is made of several components. First of all a destination holds an organic image, which is the result of a global and ongoing knowledge about that destination. For instance, consumers are exposed to journalistic information, school history/geography teaching programmes, TV, movies, advertisements, friends' stories about their travel, etc. and this ongoing flow of information will contribute to developing an organic image. This dynamic process explains how customers will hold images of destinations even if they have no intention to visit them.

According to Gunn, the organic image evolves into an induced image once customers have become interested in the destination and have collected specific tourist information. The organic image is renown to be the most static image and the hardest one to change.

Image is seen as an attitudinal construct which has both cognitive and affective dimensions. The perceptual/cognitive dimension refers to the knowledge about a destination's attributes while the affective dimension refers to more elusive feelings about the place. The affective side of image is meant to be influenced by the motives expressed for destination selection (Balogly and McCleary, 1999; Gartner, 1993). Both dimensions will influence the image formed by consumers (Baloglu and McCleary, 1999). It is traditionally assumed that cognitive factors precede and influence the affective ones.

MacKay and Fesenmaier (1997) have also shown that affective images are superior when people have a high level of familiarity with a destination. In a study on national parks, these authors have clearly identified that previous visitors to a park displayed an emotional reaction to an advertisement about this site, while non-consumers had a purely cognitive reaction to the advertisement. It has also been shown that familiarization trips for travel agents lead to more efficient sales through better cognitive and emotional comprehension of destinations (Baloglu and Mangaloglu, 2001).

Non-visitors and Tourism

While consumers have been and are the object of intensive academic interest, the study of non-visitors is often wrongly neglected. Non-visitors are in fact a very interesting market to study as they hold in themselves precious knowledge for managers. They can help to understand what triggers there are that could help to communicate better on that destination, identify barriers that stop the destination from being selected and design more efficient marketing campaigns (Selby and Morgan, 1996).

Gnoth (1997) indicates that in situations where a tourist considers a destination for the first time, he/she will often 'depend on drives as motivators in addition to cognitions and pull-factors' (page 89). Drive theory stipulates that non-selective activity is triggered by feelings of deprivation whose strength will depend on the length of the deprivation. The following behaviour will aim at reducing the level of deprivation and thereby creating satisfaction. If the drive is successfully reduced, tourists will remember the behaviour that lead to this successful action and will employ it again, as an acquired habit. Therefore the presence of stimuli that can trigger and suggest promises of rewards/pleasures is an important factor in engaging potential visitors towards choosing the product.

There are of course several contexts that can explain why a destination is not selected. First of all, destinations that are exposed to a risk (terrorism, war or a major natural disaster like a tsunami or a volcanic eruption) will necessarily encounter difficulties in attracting visitors. Although consumers have become more 'accustomed' to the notion of risk when travelling and have shunned destinations in crisis for a shorter time, a major incident will always lead to a sudden fall in bookings. Some destinations might also have a sombre image due to ongoing political instabilities and lack of information. For instance, Stepchenkova and Morrison (2008) have conducted an interesting study on the image of Russia as a tourism destination and shown the difficulties it is encountering in the tourism market due to a bleak and weak image.

A case that is more problematic is that of a destination that has not experienced any considerable crisis, has a reasonable tourism offer but still does not attract visitors. In this situation, which aspects can explain that consumers will still not be attracted to holiday there? This does not necessarily apply to a destination at the beginning of the life cyle, it might simply be part of those destinations that have amenities and positive tourism attractions but that fail to pick up on the tourism market.

Previous studies have tended to show that destinations not chosen are usually destinations that have a limited appeal: rather than having a totally and persistent negative image, it is rather an unclear image that is problematic. Woodside and Lysonski (1989) state that neutral images might come from a lack of awareness of an area as a vacation destination. This neutral or weak image might explain why those destinations might not make their way to the choice set. A study on Franche-Comté (2002), a similar area to Auvergne in eastern France, showed that despite the fairly high awareness of this destination, consumers having not chosen to visit it claimed first and foremost that it was an unknown region to them (they were perfectly aware of the name but had no idea what sort of place it was). Globally, 45% of the people interviewed could not think of any strong asset to the Franche-Comté region and the furthest away they lived from the destination, the stronger this feeling became (57% of inhabitants from the Mediterranean region could not think of any positive point).

Beyond the fuzzy image, it is also the feeling of boredom that dominates the discourse of non-visitors. Non-consumers often express the view that they see a limited diversity in the offering and that they can't envisage what they would do if they took a holiday at the destination. For example in a study on Kansas, Hsu et al. (2003) identified that 'Kansas is boring' was a significant negative predictor and leading determinant of overall image for non-visitors. For destination marketing organizations, such a result needs to be further analysed. Boredom means that customers fail to project themselves as tourists at the destination but the reasons of this failure need to be further analysed. Which aspects do the customers feel are absent from the destination? Is it a global feeling about the destination or an elaboration of some minor elements? Some studies have investigated the differences between visitors and non-visitors to a destination and will be detailed thereafter.

Comparison Between Visitors and Non-visitors

In his model of destination image formation, Gunn (1988) also identified a third step called the complex image: the image that is formed after a trip has been taken at the destination. Several studies have shown that after a holiday, visitors would develop a more varied and positive image of the destination visited (Ahmed, 1991; Baloglu et al., 2001; Bojanic, 1991; Chon, 1990). Seeing the destination 'in the flesh' can also help in bringing a strong positive touch to destinations that might have had a persistent negative image. For instance, a study on South Korea (Kim and Morrison, 2005) showed that the image of that destination changed after visitors attended a World Cup event.

Within the study of the complex image, the few studies that have compared the images held by visitors and non-visitors (or first-timers) bring some very interesting information. For instance, Phelps conducted a study on consumers visiting Spain in 1986 where first-time visitors and customers already accustomed to Majorca were compared. Results showed that first-time visitors had a preconceived vision of Majorca, which was in fact more or less a fusion image of Mediterranean destinations. In that image were present cliché images of Spain (flamenco, corridas, night clubs, large hotels), of Mediterranean countries (olive groves, vineyards, wind mills, almond trees) and images probably directly taken from the brochures and related to the comfort of their stay (hotel, bedrooms, swimming pools, beaches). Visitors who had already been at the destination had a more precise image especially of the local particularities that could be found (distilleries, cheese making facilities, strong wind, soldiers, pine trees and long sandy beaches). Visitors clearly had a neater and more complete vision of the island that did not simply rely on a mix of cliché Mediterranean images than the non-visitors. Similar results were identified by Rezende-Parker *et al.* (2007) in an online study of Brazil image. Their results identified that only previous visitors to Brazil were able to differentiate this country from neighbouring Hispanic countries. Altogether, these studies show that, due to lack of knowledge, non-visitors tend to hold a global vision mixing in geographical and cultural images from neighbouring countries (Brazil is associated to Hispanic culture, Majorca to Mediterranean culture, etc.).

These strong differences identified between the induced image of visitors who choose to holiday at a destination and their complex image after their stay does bring some serious questioning. Indeed, this would imply that consumers who choose to visit a destination have a positive, but obviously incomplete, image of that destination. Despite the information and advertisements conveyed by the destination, tourists only seem to get a complete image once they have visited the destination. This could be linked to the fact that a destination is not solely constituted of different attributes, it is also experienced through different senses. In other words, elements such as different smells (jasmine in Tunisia, spices in India, etc.), air humidity, background noise, general atmosphere, etc. can never fully transpire in an advertisement.

Context of the Study

The study was launched in January 2009 and is part of a vast research project called PSDR: *Pour et Sur le Développement Rural* (For and On Rural Development) funded by the National Research Institute in Agricultural Research (INRA), the national research Institute in Agriculture and Forestry (CEMAGREF) and the Regional Council of Auvergne. Those three institutes act both as partners and as financers. The aim of PSDR initiatives is to encourage applied research projects whereby researchers work hand in hand with local authorities. In this case the project was designed with local tourism authorities (*Comité Régional du Développement Touristique* in Auvergne, also known as CRDTA and SPOT – a regional tourists' statistics authority). Those authorities have conducted extensive studies on consumers and have found out that previous communication campaigns have lead to a restrictive image of Auvergne.

Auvergne is an area at the centre of France, which is both mountainous (up to 1885 meters high) and agricultural (with cattle breeding and cheese production among other activities). Its prominent feature is a chain of old volcanoes, which is known throughout France. This theme has been heavily developed and used in tourism promotional campaigns. To date, the 2007 campaign has retained a lot of the public attention; it was shown in France and extensively in the Paris subway. The central theme of this campaign was based on the notion of open spaces, with pictures of wide green landscapes and mountains (middle-range mountains with volcanic peaks). The landscapes showed did not display many tourists, the dominating theme was rather that of natural and open spaces with some strong notions of wilderness. This campaign, as agreed by the local authorities, has not been totally beneficial to Auvergne as the open space images were rather intimidating (no human beings, no houses, no heritage sites, etc). Since 2008, in order to counterbalance these limits, the CRDTA has launched a new campaign, which has 'humanized' the image portrayed of Auvergne by reintegrating tourists in the pictures. The focus, this time, is on outdoor activities with the clear message that tourists can undertake numerous outdoor activities in those open spaces (walking, bike riding, horse riding, canoeing, hot air ballooning, etc.).

Added to this general tourist communication about Auvergne, another important advertising campaign has been developed by 'Vulcania'. Vulcania is a tourist site that opened in 2002 and is devoted to vulcanology. It is located within the volcanic chain not far from the main town of Auvergne (Clermont-Ferrand). The site offers an 'edutainment' experience with modern technological interpretation equipments all based around the understanding of volcanoes. It is one of the most recent sites of this type opened in France and has received a lot of public attention despite its limited success (visitors complain that it is too educational and lacks entertainment). The Vulcania campaign therefore reinforced the association of volcanoes to Auvergne.

The image of wild open spaces and volcanoes used in the 2007 advertising campaign has been strongly reinforced by another advertising campaign, that of the mineral water Volvic which, both in its national TV advertising campaign and on its bottles, uses the image of a green volcanic mountain chain. The repetitive use of this image over more than a decade and its presence on the bottle means that it has become a dominant feature of Auvergne for most consumers in France and abroad.

Methodology

Researchers decided to conduct the study through focus groups. The 10 participants interviewed were recruited by email, using different email listings to guarantee that they were contacted from independent sources. The participants were screened to only retain those who had not yet visited Auvergne on a main holiday (a rapid questionnaire allowed the researchers to identify among other questions those non-visitors). The use of the questionnaire was necessary to be able to screen the respondents without letting them know that the study would cover the subject of Auvergne. Indeed, participants knowing that the study concerned a specific area they had little knowledge of, could have decided to undertake an information search before participating to the focus groups.

The focus group took place in Paris, at the head office of the Gîtes de France, at the end of a Monday afternoon. Participants were rewarded with books and a USB key. The focus group lasted two hours and was both taped and videoed.

Two other focus groups have been planned at the end of March 2009, then excursionists or short-stay visitors will be investigated in closer markets (Lyon and Clermont-Ferrand) in the summer of 2009. These other focus groups will aim at understanding what are the different image dimensions between non-visitors, occasional visitors and near-by excursionists.

The interview guide was designed in order to elicit the images from non-visitors as freely as possible. First of all participants were requested to draw a coloured image of Auvergne and add a list of words that best represented that destination. The objective of asking people to draw the image right at the beginning was to get participants to give their image as spontaneously as possible before any discussion took place. Visual reproductions are also renown to be more salient when tourists' experience/involvement is low (Day et al., 2002; Fairweather and Swaffield, 2001; Mackay and Fesenmaier, 1997), therefore the use of drawings was appropriate for the market under scrutiny. The use of drawings also aimed at counteracting the recognised limits of structured instruments such as questionnaires which tend to 'force' visitors to respond to ready set characteristics that might not match their feelings (Dann, 1996; Echtner and Ritchie, 1991; Ryan and Cave, 2005).

The indication of words, along with the drawing, was also very interesting in obtaining spontaneous themes/words used to describe the destination. The drawings were then further investigated and corroborated by the following discussion that took place. The researchers could then see which images/notions came spontaneously or only when prompted.

The interview guide was divided into three parts. The first part included questions related to the perceived accessibility of Auvergne (perception of distance and travelling time), climate description, identification of sites and towns and main economic activities of Auvergne.

The second part was dedicated to the perception of holiday experiences, which will not be developed in the present study. The last part was devoted to the possibility of spending a holiday in Auvergne: perceived positioning of the region, typical types of holidays that can be enjoyed in Auvergne, the strong and negative points of the region, perception of local inhabitants, known tourists sites, comparison to other tourism regions, etc.

Data Analysis

During the focus groups, the discussions were taped and content analysed by a team of five researchers who compared their classification strategies.

First the pictures were analysed by the team: objects represented and their shape, colours, season, people represented were all analysed. However, the simplicity of the drawings meant that this analysis was rather straightforward. The words were then transcribed in order to be content analysed. Both the description of the pictures and the list of words indicated are presented in Table 14.1.

The analysis resulted in the identification of 15 themes, which identified more precisely the profile of Auvergne as seen by non-visitors. This portrait was then put against the drawings that had been analysed previously to check whether what the consumers had drawn matched their discourse.

Out of the ten people, seven undertook to do a drawing and for the other two it was rather a schematic graph, one participant provided words only. Eight of the ten people present indicated a list of words characterising Auvergne.

Table 14.1: Spontaneous terms and drawings regarding Auvergne

Individual	1	2	3	4	5	6	7	8	9	10	Total
Terms											
Specific regional or town names		8	2	6	2	3					21
Local rural food	I	I	I	I	I					I	6
Wild spaces	I									I	5
Personalities		2	I	I		I					5
Volcanoes		I	I			I				I	4
Mountains	I								I	I	3
Vulcania					I	I	I				3
Nature	I								I		2
Countryside		I			I						2
Michelin		I				I					2
Ski activities				I	I						2
Old spa resorts		I									1
Tour de France						I					1
Water						I					1
Sunshine									I		1

Individual Drawing

1	Blue sky, round green mountains with snow tops, country house
2	Administrative map of Auvergne,
3	Sun, Volcanoes with smoke, lakes, flowers, pine trees
4	Administrative map of Auvergne with location of towns and regions
5	Volcanoes road, town with cathedral, sun
5	Green and brown volcanoes, road, 'tour de France'
7	Map of France with Auvergne a, cathedral, green mountains, Michelin logo
8	Bottle of wine, green mountains, blue sky, few clouds, sun, different fields colours
9	Green mountains, a lale
10	No drawing

Seven out of the nine drawings portrayed Auvergne as a mountainous region, and most of them with volcanoes. The quality of the drawings does not allow the differentiation between a small mountain and a volcano. Nevertheless, by far the dominating image of Auvergne can be summarised as middle range mountains/volcanoes in a wild environment. Regarding the words mentioned on the drawings, the icons of Auvergne are also constituted of known personalities (Giscard d'Estaing, a previous French president from Auvergne), Michelin (a known tyre factory). Finally the local food (mostly cheeses) is mentioned by four participants. This might be linked to a local dish made with cheese (Aligot) but also to a previous advertising campaign by cheese producers that portrayed Auvergne as a big cheese platter, this campaign is still vivid in participants' memories.

Two participants did not draw Auvergne as a landscape but as an administrative map, the words they used to describe Auvergne were also related to physical sites (towns, mountains' names and/or departments).

Seven out of the nine drawings represented Auvergne in summer, under a bright sunshine and with very green and lush colours. No people were represented in the images, and only once was a house drawn. Surprisingly, one participant drew a wine bottle even though Auvergne can clearly not be described as a famous wine making region.

As an example, two drawings are given underneath and illustrate the types of responses collected.

Text Content Analysis

The purpose of the following questions was to clarify further the portrait of Auvergne in the eyes of non-visitors but also to see to whether or not or to what extent, the verbal information matched the drawings previously produced.

Necessarily, the content of the text brought some interesting information regarding the scope and diversity of the image.

For instance, no human beings were represented in images whether these might be locals or tourists. When asked about local inhabitants, two-thirds of the participants agreed that they had no image of *Auvergnats* (Auvergne inhabitants). For the rest of the group, the only human image that Auvergne elicited was that some French presidents came from that region and that *Auvergnats* had the reputation to be mean and rough (peasants).

Probably the most interesting information came from the perception of the tourism offer in Auvergne. Participants had difficulties seeing images beyond that drawn or expressed of a mountainous/volcanic and wild region. Indeed, the feeling of wilderness went a bit too far: not a single participant knew what could be found behind the main town Clermont-Ferrand. Half of the participants mentioned that if travelling in Auvergne, they would probably need to go back to this town in order to find tourist accommodation. In fact all of the participants gave a pretty sombre image of Auvergne 'behind the mountains'. One even wondered if 'outside Clermont-Ferrand, could I find proper hotel accommodation?'.

Two participants mentioned that Auvergne was a rustic country, this was meant in a negative sense: a region that has been left behind and is stuck in time. In consequence when asked what were the main limiting factors to spending a holiday in Auvergne, participants indicated that it was basically far away from everything and that beyond the volcanoes there was probably not much to do and see. They thought that the landscapes encountered were all similar and that they would probably need to drive a long time to find some activities, lakes would probably be too cold to swim, they might not find shops and restaurants, etc. In fact beyond the mountain front, customers could only see a social and cultural desert. Hardly any cultural sites were really mentioned: only one person referred to the Clermont-Ferrand's cathedral and another one to a farm. However, if the roads were not present in the discussion they were portrayed in three of the drawings. This was either used in reference to the Tour de France or as an important item to the holiday (sightseeing). What is very disappointing for local authorities is the sheer lack of vision of any other assets such as their rich cultural heritage (Roman churches, Bourbon heritage, etc.), events or outdoor activities other than walking.

Somehow the positive sides to Auvergne constitute also its own limits: landscapes, nature, calm, air quality, volcanoes, etc. qualities that are insufficient to consider spending a long holiday there. As a result Auvergne can only be envisaged, potentially, as a short-stay destination.

Finally when asked to describe who would be a typical tourist in Auvergne, the verdict was rather limited: it was either families with young children (for seven people), walkers or spa customers (for four individuals). In fact the notion of health resorts came very much last in the discussion and only when prompted on tourists' sites. This is surprising as Auvergne is renown for its mineral water (Volvic) and spa resorts (Royat, Châtel-Guyon, Vichy, La Bourboule, Le Mont Dore, etc). These resorts have a very unattractive and old fashioned image for the ten non-visitors interviewed, despite the fact that some of them have modernized part of their offer.

Results

The results of the focus groups brought some very interesting information. Their objective was to understand what image was held by non-visitors to Auvergne. The survey achieved this objective but somehow brought different results than those identified in the literature review. The results corroborate existing research which state that destinations not chosen or visited, lack diversity (Hsu et al., 2003; Stepchenkova and Morrison, 2008; Woodside and Lysonski, 1989). Clearly in this case, Auvergne is a destination that is seen as uninspiring by non-visitors who cannot see much diversity in it and what they would do at the destination as tourists.

However, by looking at the pictures drawn by the participants and the contents of the focus groups, another aspect appeared. In the case of Auvergne, the notion of fuzzy image does not totally apply. Indeed, the volcanoes and the mountainous dimension of Auvergne were clearly present in all participants' visions of Auvergne, so it can be said that non-visitors do have a fairly clear (pictorial) and accurate image of the main feature to be found at the destination but this vision dominates the rest. This image has been repeatedly used in tourist promotional campaigns and in Volvic promotional campaign, so much that it is the main image that customers can see. Of course, the fact that non-visitors have a very limited interest in the destination implies that their image is probably more easily contaminated by advertising campaigns they have been exposed to. Therefore, if the Volvic advertising campaign keeps on using the volcano theme, it is probably more useful for tourism authorities to move away from this theme (or use it as a background) and focus on other aspects of their offer.

The results demonstrate the superiority of the organic image in a market of non-consumers. One also has to keep in mind that those individuals do not have a first-hand experience of the destination, therefore their knowledge of it is very much stereotypical and pragmatic (indeed, no comments of an emotional nature were collected in the focus groups). This confirm the vision that individuals that have not visited a destination mostly have a cognitive perception of it (Baloglu and Mangaloglu, 2001; MacKay and Fesenmaier, 1997).

Finally, the results show that there is an ambiguity between the rural and mountainous positioning of Auvergne, it is neither fully one thing nor the other.

No particular contradictions between the text or the drawings could be identified apart from the description of the weather: most drawings portrayed Auvergne under a bright sunshine while the content of the focus groups revealed a much bleaker perception of the weather.

The Advantages and Disadvantages of the Techniques Used

The researchers' main concern was to know if the use of drawing in a focus group provided some interesting results. The focus group conducted showed that the participants had no difficulties undertaking the task, regardless of their drawing skills. Another advantage of the drawing exercise was to 'break the ice', it allowed customers to relax about the interview and get 'in the mood'. While customers were asked to indicate only a few words, some proceeded to write whole sentences and really enjoyed the free time and possibility of expressing themselves.

The pictures produced were very interesting to analyse, they gave a very good return on the clichés and stereotypical images of Auvergne. Then the interviews helped the researchers to investigate whether there was any depth to the images drawn. Would its tourism qualities only come up when mentioned by researchers? How much knowledge had interviewees beyond the clichéd images?

While one of the limits of qualitative research is linked to the potential subjective interpretation of the researchers involved. The team of researchers who worked on this project felt that the drawings produced by the participants were very clear and evocative and the strength of their message was unavoidable and served as a frame all along the analysis.

Conclusion

In conclusion, the present study brought some interesting results regarding the images held by non-visitors. If the literature has identified that individuals do not choose a destination mostly because of a fuzzy image and perceived lack of variety, the present study brings some contrasting results. The notion of potential boredom and lack of diversity at the destination was also a major inhibitor to the consideration of spending a holiday in Auvergne. However, customers did not appear to have a fuzzy image but a rather clear but extremely limited image of the destination. The main feature of Auvergne, i.e. volcanoes and mountains, remain such a dominant feature that it has stopped visitors from being able to perceive any other aspects of the destination.

This would suggest that, in the case of non-visitors, when destinations have a limited image, the organic image can be strongly influenced by repetitive and dominant information (here the national tourism advertising campaign coupled with the Volvic mineral waters campaign). Hence, in the case of a destination that has a limited comparative advantage, the impact of advertising campaigns can be stronger especially if it reinforces commonly identified themes rather than diversifying them. The study also identified areas that need to be strongly developed (the cultural aspects, events, outdoor activities), those elements need to be asserted further in the advertising campaigns.

While other focus groups will be conducted to clarify further the image of Auvergne, researchers are thinking ahead to new ways to identify a destination image shortcomings on larger samples. They are designing online and interactive surveys as a new way to address image studies.

References

Ahmed ZU. 1991. The influence of the components of a state's tourist image on product positioning strategy. *Tourism Management* **12** (4): 331-340.

Baloglu S, McCleary SW. 1999. A path analytic model of visitation intention involving nformation sources, socio-psychological motivations and destination image. *Journal of Travel and Tourism Marketing* **8** (3): 81-90.

Baloglu S, Mangaloglu M. 2001. Tourism destination images of Turkey, Egypt, Greece, and Italy as perceived by US-based tour operators and travel agents. *Tourism Management* **22** (1): 1-9.

Bojanic D. 1991. The use of advertising in managing destination image. *Tourism Management* **12** (4): 352-355.

Chon KS. 1990. The role of destination image in tourism: A review and discussion. *Tourist Review* **2**: 2-9.

Crompton JL. 1979. Motivations for pleasure vacations. *Annals of Tourism Research* **6** (4): 408-424.

Dann G. 1996. Tourists' images of a destination – An alternative analysis. *Journal of travel and Tourism Marketing* **5** (1/2): 41-55.

Day J, Skidmore A, Koller T. 2002. Image selection in destination positioning: a new approach. *Journal of Vacation Marketing* **8** (2): 177-186.

Echtner CM, Prasad P. 2003. The context of third world tourism marketing. *Annals of Tourism Research* **30** (3): 660-682.

Echtner CM, Ritchie JRB 1991. The meaning and measurement of destination image. *Journal of Travel Research* **2** (2): 2-12.

Embacher J, Buttle F. 1989. A repertory grid analysis of Austria's image as a summer vacation destination. *Journal of Travel Research* Winter: 3-7.

Fairweather JR, Swaffield, SR. 2001. Visitor experiences of Kaikoura, New Zealand: an interpretative study using photographs of landscapes and Q Method. *Tourism Management* **22** (3): 219-228.

Fakeye PC, Buttle JL. 1989. Image differences between prospective, first-time and repeat visitors to the Lower Rio Grande Valley. *Journal of Travel Research* **30** (2): 10- 16.

Gallarza MG, Saura IG, Garcıa HC. 2002. Destination image: Towards a conceptual framework. *Annals of Tourism Research* **29** (1): 56-78.

Gartner WC. 1993. Image formation process. *Journal of Travel and Tourism Marketing* **2** (2/3): 191-215.

Gnoth J. 1997. Tourism motivation and expectation formation; *Annals of Tourism Research* **24** (2): 283-304.

Goodrich JN. 1978. The relationship between preferences for and perceptions of vacation destinations: application of a choice model. *Journal of Travel Research* **17** (2): 8-13.

Gunn C. 1988. *Vacationscape: Designing Tourist Regions*. Van Nostrand Reinhold: New York.

Hsu CHC, Wolfe K, Kang SK. 2004. Image assessment for a destination with limited comparative advantages. *Tourism Management* **25** (1): 121-126.

Kim SS, Morrison AM. 2005. Change of images of South Korea among foreign tourists after the 2002 FIFA World Cup. *Tourism Management* **26** (2): 233-247.

Mackay KJ, Fesenmaier DR. 1997. Pictorial element of destination in image formation. *Annals of Tourism Research* **24** (3): 537-565.

Phelps A. 1986 Holiday destination image – the problem of assessment. An example developed in Menorca. *Tourism Management* **7** (3): 168-180.

Rezende-Parker AM, Morrison AM, Ismail A. 2007. Dazed and confused? An exploratory study of the image of Brazil as a travel destination. *Journal of Vacation Marketing* **9** (3): 243-259.

Ryan C, Cave J. 2005. Structuring destination image: a qualitative approach. *Journal of Travel Research* **44** (November): 143-150.

Selby M, Morgan NJ. 1996. Reconstructing place image: A case study of its role in destination market research. *Tourism Management* **17** (4): 287-294.

Sirakaya E, Sonmez SF, Choi HS. 2001. Do destination images really matter? Predicting destination choices of student travellers. *Journal of Vacation Marketing* **7** (2): 125-142.

Stepchenkova S, Morrison A. 2007. Russia's destination image among American pleasure travellers: revisiting Echtner and Ritchie. *Tourism Management* **29**: 548-560.

Um S, Crompton JL. 1992. The roles of perceived inhibitors and facilitators in pleasure travel destination decisions. *Journal of Travel Research* **30** (3): 18-25.

Woodside AG, Lysonski S. 1989. A general model of traveller destinations choice. *Journal of Travel Research* **17** (4): 8-14.

15 Effect of Controllable and Non-controllable Sources of Information on the Image of Turkey

Sara Campo Martínez, Universidad Autónoma de Madrid; **Maria D. Alvarez**, Bogaziçi University

Introduction

The concept of image has been widely researched in the tourism literature, applied to the study of perceptions regarding countries as tourism destinations. Several of these investigations have been concerned with the image of developing countries in particular (Grosspietsch, 2006; Sönmez and Sirakaya, 2002; Tasci et al., 2007), concluding that the perceptions regarding these destinations are generally negative. However, some authors have pointed to the need to distinguish between the image of the country in general, and as a tourism destination. For example, Echtner (2002) determines that there is a difference between how individuals perceive Third World countries as virgin paradises, free from the damage derived from development, but also as insecure, poor and underdeveloped. In relation to Turkey, Öztürkmen (2005) proposes that there is a paradox between the favourable perceptions of this country as an attractive tourism destination due to its natural and historical resources, and its negative image from an economic, political and social perspective. These findings support the need to treat the image of the country and that of the tourism destination as two different constructs.

The literature has also followed this approach, and the image of the country and that of the tourism destination have been investigated as two different concepts, analyzed under different research areas (Nadeau et al., 2008). While the image of the country has mainly been investigated by international marketing researchers, the image of the destination has primarily been the concern of tourism investigators. However, according to the country of origin research (Han, 1990), the image of a country influences the way that its products, including tourism, are perceived. Therefore, these two concepts should be treated as different, although related, and analysed under the same perspective, in order to determine the effect of communication strategies directed at influencing the image of the country on the perceptions regarding the destination, and vice versa.

As a dynamic process, the formation of an image is influenced by sources of information, including those that cannot be controlled by managers, such as movies, printed press or news broadcasted in the mass media (Martin and Eroglu, 1993). The effect of uncontrollable sources of information on the image of a country, in particular, has not been sufficiently investigated (Sönmez and Sirakaya, 2002), and there are no studies that compare the effect of controllable and non-controllable information sources on the image of a country or a destination. Therefore, the aim of the research is to determine the influence of controllable versus non-controllable sources on image, while distinguishing between general country image and destination image. The study is applied in the context of the image of Turkey, as a developing country and a tourism destination, with the objective of analysing the varied effect of the sources of information on the two constructs under scrutiny. This analysis is carried out through an experiment that allows the researchers to separate the perceptions of the individual and establish causal relations.

Theoretical Background

The image of a place has been defined as the 'sum of beliefs and impressions people hold about places', which is formed when the individual simplifies all of the associations and pieces of information that are connected to that location (Kotler and Gertner, 2002). Similarly, destination image has been defined as 'the totality of impressions, beliefs, ideas, expectations and feelings accumulated towards a place over time' (Kim and Richardson, 2003). Both of these definitions coincide in their understanding of image as a dynamic and complex concept, which may include cognitive as well as affective evaluations. Cognitive aspects encompass beliefs and opinions that the individual holds regarding the characteristics and attributes of the object (Baloglu, 1997; Crompton, 1979; Pike and Ryan, 2004), while affective evaluations comprise feelings and emotions (Baloglu and McCleary, 1999a; Beerli et al., 2002; Bigné et al., 2001; Chen and Uysal, 2002; Kim and Richardson, 2003; Moutinho, 1987). In more recent studies authors have also agreed on the need to include a conative component to the concept of image (Choi et al., 2007; Dann, 1996; Gartner, 1989; Gartner, 1993), which represents the behaviour of the individual after the cognitive and affective evaluation (Prebensen, 2007). The dynamic aspect of image implies its modification across time (Chon, 1991; Gartner, 1993; Gartner and Hunt, 1987), due to experience or the receipt of additional information.

The fundamental difference between country image and destination image relates to the fact that the former represents a combination of generic associations that are not tied to a particular context (Mossberg and Kleppe, 2005), while the image of the destination refers to the tourist's perspective, and may indicate a city, region, country or another specific location (Chon, 1991; Echtner and Ritchie, 1993). Therefore, the difference between both concepts is that the concept of country image is more general, while that of destination image is related to the evaluation of a place visited. Although different, both concepts are seemingly related, since the image of a country influences beliefs and opinions regarding its products (Kleppe, 2002), including tourism. Furthermore, the image of a country influences the intention to visit, return and recommend the destination (Nadeau et al., 2008). However, an individual's evaluations regarding a country may differ depending on the context (Alvarez and Korzay, 2008).

Specifically in relation to Turkey, several authors have noted the ambiguity of individual perceptions towards this country. From a political perspective, Turkey has suffered from a relatively negative image, especially as related to human rights and its treatment of minorities, while it enjoys a much more positive image as a tourism paradise with sun, beaches and rich cultural resources (Alvarez and Korzay, 2008; Öztürkmen, 2005). Recent studies have also determined that initially negative perceptions regarding Turkey are transformed into positive evaluations following the tourists' visit to the country (Yarcan and Inelmen, 2006). The visitors' exposure to the country's richness of resources, both natural and cultural, may offer a possible explanation for this finding.

People construct images and representations about places from the information they receive (Avraham, 2000; Sönmez and Sirakaya, 2002). Pioneer studies by Gunn in the

1970s established a dual theory based on images being developed both internally, due to tourism experience and visitation, and externally, through received and processed information (Sönmez and Sirakaya 2002). Similarly, Galí Espelt and Donaire Benito (2005) state that it is necessary to distinguish between the a priori image (mental constructions of the individual that are not connected to a physical place), the in situ image (during the visit, as a contrast between what is expected and what is found), and the image obtained after the visit (through the recollection of the experience). Therefore, the sources of information influence the formation of the image at two different levels. First, they create what is referred to as the organic image, which is formed through external sources of information, such as news, interviews or movies. Second, they may also cause the induced image, which is transmitted through the marketing activities aimed at promoting the place (Kim and Richardson, 2003).

Kim and Richardson (2003), on the basis of previous research (Herbert, 1996; Squire, 1994), state that external and non-controllable sources of information affect the formation of the image of the destination. However, only a few studies empirically investigate this influence. Specifically, Butler (1990, cited in Kim and Richardson, 2003) affirms that the information emitted through movies and news influences the formation of the destination image more strongly than that transmitted through controllable sources, due to it being more credible to the consumer. Among the non-controllable sources of information, it is possible to highlight the mass media who interpret the information they transmit and therefore have a strong influence in the formation of perceptions regarding a place (Hall, 2002). Similarly, other authors (Baloglu and McCleary, 1999b) observe a significant relationship between the type of the information source, and the affective destination image.

Following this literature, the present study aims to determine the influence of the controllable information, transmitted by the government in relation to the attractiveness of the country, and the non-controllable information, broadcasted by the international media. The research seeks to establish the effect of both types of sources on the image of the cognitive and affective image of the country and the tourism destination. Moreover, another objective of the investigation is to establish whether the information provided through different types of sources affect the individual's preference for the destination.

Methodology

The research is based on experimental methodology, following the studies of Kim and Richardson (2003) and Tasci et al. (2007), with the objective of determining the influence of controllable and non-controllable sources of information on the image of Turkey as a country and as a tourism destination. In order to establish causal relations that provide a better comprehension of the perceived image formation process, an experiment is used, as it allows the separate analysis of the perceptual changes (Sönmez and Sirakaya, 2002).

The research subjects were gathered among all tourism students of a Spanish university, with the aim of obtaining a relatively homogeneous sample that allowed the elimination of random sources of error. The students were solicited in class, and were encouraged to participate through the provision of a small academic incentive. Moreover, foreign students present through exchange programmes, as well as those that had visited Turkey before, were eliminated from the sample. The survey included questions on the respondents' level of information regarding Turkey, and their cognitive, affective and conative perceptions about the country and the tourism destination. A total of 198 completed questionnaires were obtained in this phase of the data collection process. This represents approximately 70% of the total number of students registered in the tourism programme of the university where the research was conducted. The remaining 30% corresponds to those students that had visited Turkey beforehand, were not Spanish nationals, or did not attend class on the day that the data were collected.

The second part of the experiment was carried out one and a half months later, in order to ensure minimum recollection. The same subjects were divided into three different groups. While two of the groups were exposed to different stimuli before being required to again complete the questionnaire, the third group was used as a control group and was only asked to answer the survey. In this phase 180 questionnaires were obtained, of which 157 were those corresponding to students that had participated in the first part of the experiment. In both phases, the respondents were identified in the questionnaire, with the aim of matching the answers before and after being exposed to the stimuli.

In order to measure the effect of non-controllable sources of information on the image of the country and that of the destination, a news item that had previously been emitted on Spanish television was used. This piece was selected after reviewing all the main video-based news items on Turkey available on the websites of the main Spanish news companies during the month previous to the research. The news item was selected because of its neutral tone and attempt to objectivity. On the other hand, the influence of controllable sources was determined through a promotional video of the destination, which had already been successfully used in the study of Tasci et al. (2007). This promotional item was produced by the Turkish Ministry of Culture and Tourism and was being used at the time of the research to promote Turkey in foreign television channels, such as CNN. Both of these videos were of similar length, in order to ensure that the subjects were required a similar level of processing effort. While the television news item explained the current political situation of the country and the polarization of the Turkish society in relation to the use of the headscarf at universities, the promotional video showed attractive pictures of Turkey and its tourism resources.

In order to further control the effect that previous experience might have on the perceptions of the respondents, those students that had already visited Turkey were eliminated from the sample. Further control was provided through the inclusion of several questions in the survey aimed at measuring the students' level of knowledge regarding historical, cultural, political and economic aspects of Turkey, together with their level of awareness regarding the country in general and its tourism resources. The descriptive statistics regarding these questions are included in Table 15.1.

Table 15.1: Descriptive statistics on the level of knowledge regarding Turkey

	Mean	Std. Dev.
Level of information on historical aspects [a]	2.78	1.34
Level of information on cultural aspects [a]	3.09	1.30
Level of information on political aspects [a]	2.40	1.26
Level of information on economic aspects [a]	2.36	1.13
Level of information on the country in general [a]	3.19	1.12
Level of information on the touristic attractiveness [a]	3.63	1.32

[a] 1 = Not at all informed; 7 = Totally informed

These results show that the level of knowledge of the respondents is very low for all the different aspects, and especially regarding the political, economic and historical issues.

Recent studies have determined that image is formed by both a cognitive and an affective component (Baloglu and McCleary, 1999b; Lin et al., 2007; Sönmez and Sirakaya, 2002). Moreover, Sönmez and Sirakaya (2002) also confirm that both components are independent and may be treated in an individual fashion, view which is adopted in the present research. In order to measure the cognitive component of country image a 7-point semantic differential scale is applied to the question: 'In general, my opinion about Turkey as a country is (negative – positive)'. For the cognitive component of destination image, the following question is used: 'In general, my opinion about Turkey as a tourism destination is (negative – positive)'. In order to measure the affective components of both country and destination image, again a 7-point semantic differential scale is applied to the questions: 'In general, Turkey as a country awakens in me (negative-positive) emotions' and 'In general, Turkey as a tourism destination awakens in me (negative-positive) emotions'. Following the study of Guodenough et al. (1999), facial expressions ranging from anger ☹ to happiness ☺ are used to better capture these emotions. Finally, a conative component is also included to determine the individual's preference for the destination, in comparison to other competing ones. This is measured through a 7-point Likert type of scale in response to the following statement: 'I would prefer to visit Turkey rather than other similar tourism destinations'.

Results

In order to determine whether the evaluation of Turkey as a country is different from that as a tourism destination, a paired-samples t-test is applied on the pre-stimuli sample ($n = 198$). Table 15.2 shows the results obtained. According to the findings, the evaluation of Turkey as a tourism destination is significantly more positive than that of the country, both in relation to the cognitive and the affective components ($p = 0.000$). In relation to the tourism destination image, the cognitive evaluations are higher than the affective ones, in contrast to the country image, where the opposite is true. The results also show a significant correlation between the country and the destination image ($p = 0.000$). However, it can be argued that both concepts are related although different, as the correlation coefficient is around 0.60 but not close to 1.

Table 15.2: Paired-samples t-test – data collected pre-stimuli exposure (n = 198)

	Mean	Std. Dev.	Means Difference	Correlation
Affective country image [a]	4.55	.864	−.444	.607
Affective destination image [a]	4.99	.887	(p = 0.000)	(p = 0.000)
Cognitive country image [a]	4.51	.785	−.505	.629
Cognitive destination image [a]	5.01	.843	(p = 0.000)	(p = 0.000)

[a]1 = Negative image; 7 = Positive image.

The results during the two phases of the experiment were analysed using a paired-samples t-test. For individual comparisons between the results obtained before and after the administration of the stimuli, only those subjects that participated in both phases were considered ($n = 157$). The findings show that individuals' perceptions on their level of knowledge related to Turkey changes after being exposed to the information provided (Table 15.3). Moreover, the changes in the perception are different depending on the information shown. Specifically, those individuals that were exposed to the promotional video consider themselves to be significantly more informed about Turkey and its tourism attractions. This change is significant at the 0.01 level for the information regarding the country, and at the 0.001 level for the information on its tourism attractions. In contrast, those subjects that were exposed to the television news consider themselves significantly better informed about the country ($p = 0.02$), but not about its tourism attractions. No significant change is observed in the control group, so that the validity of the experiment is thus confirmed.

Table 15.3: Paired-samples t-test – data pre- and post- stimuli exposure (n = 157)

	NEWS STIMULI GROUP A					PROMOTIONAL STIMULI GROUP B					CONTROL GROUP GROUP C				
	Mean pre-	Mean post-	Mean diff.	St. Dev.	p	Mean pre-	Mean post-	Mean diff.	St. Dev.	p	Mean pre-	Mean post-	Mean diff.	St. Dev.	p
Information on the country [a]	3.11	3.41	-.30	.91	.02	3.08	3.36	-.29	1.02	.01	3.27	3.27	.00	.69	1.00
Information on the tourist attractions [a]	3.49	3.60	-.11	1.57	.63	3.56	4.05	-.49	1.25	.001	3.54	3.88	-.33	1.04	.13

[a]1 = Not at all informed; 7 = Totally informed

When the findings regarding the image are analysed, it is concluded that the promotional video has a greater effect on the subjects' evaluations. The positive influence of this stimuli is significant in relation to the affective country image ($p = 0.05$). However, although the subjects' evaluation of the cognitive country and destination image and the affective destination image increase after being exposed to the promotional stimuli, these changes are not significant. In contrast, for those individuals exposed to the television news, the evaluations regarding the country and the destination image decrease slightly, although this decrease is only significant at the 90% confidence level in relation to the cognitive destination image ($p = 0.07$). In relation to the conative preferences, there is a greater intention to choose the tourism destination as opposed to other similar destinations among those subjects that have received the promotional stimuli, while no significant differences are observed among those that have been exposed to the news stimuli or those in the control group.

Table 15.4: Paired-samples t-test – data pre- and post- stimuli exposure (n = 157)

	NEWS STIMULI GROUP A					PROMOTIONAL STIMULI GROUP B					CONTROL GROUP GROUP C				
	Mean pre-	Mean post-	Mean diff.	Std. Dev.	p	Mean pre-	Mean post-	Mean diff.	Std. Dev.	p	Mean pre-	Mean post-	Mean diff.	Std. Dev.	p
Affective country image [a]	4.64	4.57	.064	.791	.583	4.57	4.82	-.250	.790	.005	4.35	4.42	-.077	.560	.490
Cognitive country image [a]	4.55	4.45	.106	.759	.341	4.54	4.66	-.120	.688	.114	4.35	4.46	-.115	.431	.185
Affective destination image [a]	5.04	5.02	.021	.821	.860	5.08	5.12	-.036	.735	.657	4.58	4.62	-.038	.720	.788
Cognitive destination image [a]	5.17	4.94	.234	.890	.078	5.08	5.07	.012	.720	.880	4.50	4.69	-.192	.694	.170
Preference for Turkey versus other similar destinations [b]	4.26	4.32	-.064	1.40	.757	4.08	4.49	-.405	1.39	.009	3.73	3.73	.000	1.62	1.00

[a] = Negative image; 7 = Positive image.   [b]1 = Lowest preference; 7 = Greatest preference.

Table 15.5 summarizes the findings related to the paired samples t-test, comparing the results obtained before and after the exposure to the stimuli in the three groups. These results show a significant difference in the post stimuli evaluations of the affective country image. Those individuals that have been exposed to the promotional video (group B) evaluate the affective country image significantly better than those that were exposed to the news (group A) or were part of the control group (group C). Similarly, there are significant differences between the evaluation of the affective destination image among those that have been exposed to the promotional stimuli and the control group. However, there are no significant differences between the groups in relation to the cognitive image.

Table 15.5: Mean differences between the groups: data post-stimuli exposure (n = 180)

	Mean group A	Mean group B	Mean group C	Mean A-B	Bilateral significance A-B	Mean A-C	Bilateral significance A-C	Mean B -C	Bilateral significance B-C
Affective country image [a]	4.53	4.80	4.49	−.270	.059	.049	.782	.319	.060
Cognitive country image [a]	4.47	4.66	4.54	−.197	.155	−.077	.644	.120	.455
Affective destination image [a]	5.00	5.10	4.74	−.103	.443	.257	.151	.361	.030
Cognitive destination image [a]	4.95	5.05	4.83	−.098	.480	.120	.512	.217	.193
Preference for Turkey versus other similar destinations [b]	4.31	4.46	3.91	−.149	.478	.396	.198	.545	.035

[a] 1 = Negative image; 7 = Positive image.
[b] 1 = Lowest preference; 7 = Greatest preference.

When the differences between the groups are analyzed in relation to the preference towards Turkey in comparison to other similar tourism destinations, the results show that the group that was exposed to the promotional stimuli shows a greater preference, as opposed to the other two groups. This difference is significant between group B and the control group C. Moreover, the group that has been exposed to the news (group A), also exhibits a greater mean preference for Turkey compared to the control group C, but this difference is not significant.

Conclusion

The study examines the difference between the influence of the controllable and the non-controllable sources of information on the image of the country and the tourism destination, through an experiment. As part of the research, the subjects were exposed to two different stimuli, a promotional video or a television news item. The results of this study differ from those of Butler (1990), cited in Kim and Richardson (2003), and those of Martin and Eroglu (1993) regarding the greater influence on the image of the destination of the non-controllable sources of information, as compared to the controllable ones. The current research concludes that controllable promotional sources of information have a stronger impact on the country and destination image.

Specifically, the study points to a greater positive influence of controllable information in the form of audiovisual promotional material, on the image of the country and that of the destination, as opposed to the negative influence of the non-controllable sources. This promotional information positively and significantly influences the affective country image. That is, it affects the feelings and emotions that the consumer has towards Turkey as a country. Moreover, the promotional sources also affect the preference that the individuals have towards the tourism destination, as opposed to other competing places. The changes in the cognitive image as a result of watching the promotional stimuli are positive, although non-significant. Furthermore, the non-controllable sources of information negatively affect the country and destination image, although this influence is weak and non-significant.

These findings confirm that the perceived image is dynamic, and changes according to the type of information received by the individual. This assertion is based on the results from the current research, which establishes a relationship between the information received and the changes in the level of knowledge on the country and its tourism attractions. Those individuals that were exposed to the promotional stimuli consider themselves more knowledgeable, not only about tourism aspects, but also about the country in general. In contrast, those respondents that were exposed to the news item, only claim to be better informed about general issues of the country. Furthermore, the perceptions regarding the level of knowledge about Turkey of those individuals that were part of the control group, and therefore had not received additional information, did not change.

This study provides important implications that can be applied to the management of country destinations, as it confirms the importance of audiovisual material for promotional purposes. Moreover, this medium becomes an important source of information for individuals, as their level of knowledge is increased not only as regards to tourism aspects, but also in relation to other more general country issues. Therefore, the research establishes the use of controllable information sources to positively influence the country image and the individual's intention to visit the destination. Furthermore, the effect of non-controllable information sources, such as television news, is found to be less influential, which is favourable to countries like Turkey that are frequently negatively portrayed in the international media.

From an academic perspective, the study also determines the need to include in future research country image as a different concept to that of destination image. Further investigations are needed to clarify the degree of independence and correlation of these two constructs. Furthermore, studies that determine the effect of various factors on these concepts need to be undertaken for a deeper comprehension of these two images. Another potential area for research includes the use of tourism promotional efforts and previous experience of the tourist as ways to modify the general country image, with potential consequences for the political, economic or international trade arenas.

To conclude, the information received influences in the short term the individual's level of knowledge and perceptions regarding countries, and significantly results on more positive affect and emotions regarding the place. However, in order for the knowledge received to be assimilated, and for it to influence the individual's behaviour, the information received through the stimuli should be retained and stored in the memory (Ajzen and Seyton, 1999). Therefore, it is necessary that future research analyses the influence of various types of information sources on the image of the country and that of the destination from a continuous and long-term perspective.

References

Ajzen I, Seyton J. 1999. Depth of processing, belief, congruence and attitude-behavior correspondence. In *Dual Process Theory in Social Psychology*, Chaiken S, Trope Y (eds). Guilford Press:New York

Alvarez MD, Korzay M. 2008. Influence of politics and media in the perceptions of Turkey as a tourism destination. *Tourism Review* **63** (2): 38-46.

Avraham E. 2000. Cities and their news media images. *Cities* **17** (5): 363-370.

Baloglu S. 1997. The relationship between destination images and sociodemographic and trip characteristics of international travellers. *Journal of Vacation Marketing* **3**: 221-233.

Baloglu S, McCleary K. 1999a. US international pleasure travellers' images of tour Mediterranean destinations: a comparison. *Journal of Travel Research* **38** (2): 44-152.

Baloglu S, McCleary K. 1999b. A model of destination image formation. *Annals of Tourism Research* **26** (4): 868-97.

Beerli A, Diaz G, Pérez P. 2002. The configuration of the university image and its relationship with the satisfaction of students. *Journal of Education Administration* **40** (4/5): 486-505.

Bigné JE, Sánchez MI, Sánchez J. 2001.Tourist image, evaluation variables and after purchase behaviour: Inter-relationship. *Tourism Management* **22**: 607-616.

Butler R. 1990. The influence of the media in shaping international tourist patterns. *Tourism Recreation Research* **15**: 46-53.

Chen JS, Uysal M. 2002. Market positioning analysis: A hybrid approach. *Annals of Tourism Research* **29** (4): 987-1003.

Choi KS, Lehton XY, Morrison AM. 2007. Destination image representation on the web: content analysis of Macau travel related websites. *Tourism Management* **28**: 118-129.

Chon KS. 1991. Tourism destination image modification process: Marketing implications. *Tourism Management* **12** (1): 68-72.

Crompton JL. 1979. An assessment of the image of Mexico as a vacation destination and the influence of geographical location upon the image. *Journal of Travel Research* **14** (4): 18-23.

Dann GMS. 1996. Tourists' images of a destination – An alternative analysis. *Journal of Travel and Tourism Marketing* **5** (1/2): 41-55.

Echtner C. 2002. The content of Third World tourism marketing: A 4A approach. *International Journal of Tourism Research* **4**: 413-434.

Echtner CM and Ritchie, JRB. 1993. The measurement of destinations image: An empirical assessment. *Journal of Travel Research* **31** (4): 3-13.

Echtner CM and Ritchie, JRB. 2003. The meaning and measurement of destination image. *Journal of Tourism Studies* **14** (1): 37-48.

Galí Espelt N, Donaire Benito JA. 2005. The social construction of the image of Girona: A methodological approach. *Tourism Management* **26** (5): 777-785.

Gartner WC. 1989. Tourism image: attribute measurement of state tourism products using multidimensional scaling techniques. *Journal of Travel Research* **28** (2): 16-20.

Gartner WC. 1993. Image formation process. *Journal of Travel and Tourism Marketing* **2** (2/3): 191-215.

Gartner WC, Hunt JD. 1987. An analysis of state image change over a twelve-year period 1971-1983. *Journal of Travel Research* **26** (2): 15-19.

Grosspietsch M. 2006. Perceived and projected images of Rwanda: visitor and international tour operator perspectives. *Tourism Management* 27: 225-234.

Guodenough B, Dongen K, Brouwer N, Abu-Saad HH, Champion GD. 1999. A comparison of the faces pain scale and the facial affective scale for children's estimates of the intensity and unpleasantness of needle pain during blood sampling. *European Journal of Pain* 3: 301-315.

Hall CM. 2002. Travel safety, terrorism and the media: the significance of the issue–attention cycle. *Current Issues in Tourism* 5 (5): 458-466.

Han CM. 1990. Testing the role of country image in consumer choice behaviour. *European Journal of Marketing* 24 (6): 24-40.

Herbert D. 1996. Artistic and literary places in France as tourist attractions. *Tourism Management* 17: 77-85.

Kim H, Richardson SL. 2003. Motion picture impacts on destination images. *Annals of Tourism Research* 30 (1): 216-237.

Kleppe IA. 2002. Country images in marketing strategies: Conceptual issues and an empirical Asian illustration. *Journal of Brand Management* 10 (1): 61-74.

Kotler P, Gertner D. 2002. Country as brand, product and beyond: A place marketing and brand management perspective. *Journal of Brand Management* 9 (4/5): 249-261.

Lin CH, Morais DB, Kerstetter DL, Hou JS. 2007. Examining the role of cognitive and affective image in predicting choice across natural, developed, and theme-park destinations. *Journal of Travel Research* 46 (November): 183-194.

Martin IM, Eroglu S. 1993. Measuring a multi-dimensional construct: Country image. *Journal of Business Research* 28: 191-210.

Mossberg L, Kleppe IA. 2005. Country and destination image – Different or similar image concepts? *Service Industries Journal* 25 (4): 493-503.

Moutinho L. 1987. Consumer behaviour in tourism. *European Journal of Marketing* 21 (10): 5-44.

Nadeu J, Heslop L, O'Reilly N, Luk P. 2008. Destination in a country image context. *Annals of Tourism Research* 35 (1): 84-106.

Öztürkmen A. 2005. Turkish tourism at the door of Europe: perceptions of image in historical and contemporary perspectives. *Middle Eastern Studies* 41 (4): 605-621.

Pike S, Ryan C. 2004. Destination positioning analysis through a comparison of cognitive, affective, and conative perceptions. *Journal of Travel Research* 42 (4): 333-342.

Sönmez S, Sirakaya E. 2002. A distorted destination image? The case of Turkey. *Journal of Travel Research* 41: 185-196.

Squire S. 1994. The cultural values of literary tourism. *Annals of Tourism Research* 21: 103-120.

Tasci ADA, Gartner WC, Cavusgil ST. 2007. Measurement of destination brand bias using a quasi-experimental design. *Tourism Management* 28: 1529-1540.

Yarcan S, Inelmen K. 2006. Perceived image of Turkey by US-citizen cultural tourists. *Anatolia: An International Journal of Tourism and Hospitality Research* 17: 305-312.

16 'We'll All Go Down Together': the Marketing Response of Australia's Outback Destination to Recent Declines in Performance

Dean Carson and Andrew Taylor, Charles Darwin University

Introduction

In 2005, Desert Knowledge Australia released a report into the future of 'outback tourism' which noted that outback destinations had suffered more and were slower than other Australian destinations to recover from recent shocks such as the Asian financial crisis of the later 1990s, the terrorist attacks of 2001 and 2002, and the SARS and bird flu health scares. The *Our Outback* report identified the need for outback destinations to collaborate in a range of ways to counteract individual destination's lack of critical mass and economic resources. Areas recommended for collaboration were the exchange of knowledge, staff training, and lobbying for improvements in funding and infrastructure. Marketing collaboration was specifically omitted from the report because each of Australia's mainland states and the Northern Territory wanted to retain control of brand development for their own outback regions. Between 2005 and 2008, Australian tourism experienced four or five years of solid growth in international visitor numbers and held steady in what was previously a declining domestic market. The global financial crisis beginning in 2008 presents a new challenge (Tourism Research Australia, 2008a).

The aim of this chapter is to review the performance of Australian outback destinations during the 2000s and to investigate whether the state and territory push to emphasise 'points of difference and uniqueness' (Desert Knowledge Australia, 2005) is apparent in the content of their online marketing sites. In doing so, the chapter highlights the tension between retention of iconic tourism image (as might also apply to Europe's Alps, the Caribbean's beaches, Africa's savannahs and so on) and the need to distinguish destinations from one another in the search for competitive advantage.

The Political Geography of Outback Tourism

Images of 'the outback' have played a central role in the marketing of Australia to international and domestic tourists for many years. In 2001, the Bureau of Tourism Research (Barry and Robbins, 2001) identified the outback as a key driver for international tourism, and suggested that those destinations with some claim to host authentic outback experiences were well set up for continuing growth in visitor numbers. Visiting the out-back has also been suggested as a significant aspiration for domestic tourists (Tourism Research Australia, 2008b). According to these reports, changes in consumer travel behaviour is set to benefit destinations which offer 'deep' experiences with authentic representations of nature and culture. The suggested model is a transition from sun and sand 'mass' tourism to 'alternative' tourism which recognises the unique values of a destination and leverages a desire by tourists for achievement and personal fulfilment (Weaver, 2006). The model has, however, received strong criticism for representing little more than wishful thinking and neglecting ongoing evidence of consumer preferences for resort-style holidays (Butler, 1990; Saarinen, 2006). Nevertheless, alternative tour-ism offers a way for more peripheral destinations to identify markets they might attract and experiences they might offer (Skuras et al., 2006).

Australia's outback is home to iconic natural attractions like Uluru (Ayer's Rock) which are truly located 'out back' of the major population centres, but also includes unique wildlife and Indigenous cultures which are readily found in more accessible places. The outback mythology is strong with tourism researchers and practitioners highlighting its competitive advantage based on wildlife and Aboriginal culture (Fuller et al., 2006; Highes et al., 2005; Gorman-Murray et al., 2008; Rodger et al., 2007). Juxtaposed to this view is a fear is that such competitive advantages will lead to such increase in tour-ism demand that it will become more and more difficult to manage the environmental and cultural impacts (Christen, 2006; Higham and Bejder, 2008). Part of the reason put forward for expected continued growth is the ongoing reliance on images of the outback in the marketing initiatives of the national tourism organisation, Tourism Australia. The major coup for Tourism Australia in 2008 was the negotiation of a licence for all Australian tourism operators to use images from the movie *Australia* in their individual product and destination marketing (Tourism Australia, 2009). These images almost ex-clusively feature natural settings associated with the outback.

In short, 'the outback' is represented very strongly to international and domestic visi-tors in spite of most visitors (international and domestic) spending most of their time on leisure trips in Australia's major cities and beach-side resorts (Edwards et al., 2007). Outback destinations are encouraged by the national marketing agency to both collabo-rate to ensure a strong outback image, and to compete to establish their unique claim on the image. For example, Western Australia promotes itself as having 'the real outback' (www.outback-australia-travel-secrets.com) and the Northern Territory is the 'heart of the outback' and also 'Australia's real outback' (en.travelnt.com). But there is no need to travel 'out back' to experience the outback with a theme park and theatre restaurant located on the Gold Coast (outbackspectacular.myfun.com.au) and any number of out-back tours available from Sydney and extending no more than 100 kilometres beyond the metropolitan area to such places as the Blue Mountains.

In Australia, each state and territory government defines official 'tourism regions' which are used as the basis for distribution of government marketing and industry develop-ment funds. There are 85 tourism regions across Australia's five mainland states, two mainland territories, and the island state of Tasmania. Four of Australia's mainland states – Queensland, New South Wales, South Australia, and Western Australia – have their own formally designated regions labelled 'outback'. The Northern Territory has adopted the label 'Australia's Outback' as the consolidated brand for its six travel re-gions. The appropriation of the outback label by so many different destinations suggests its perceived importance but a glance at the map of Australia's official tourism regions, however (Figure 16.1), shows that outback destinations may well be simply those that were 'left over' after the allocation of destinations in the more popular coastal zones was made (Carson, 2008).

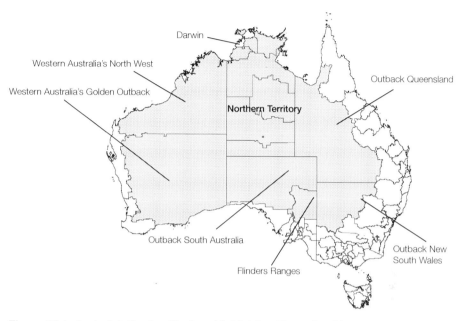

Figure 16.1: Australia's Tourism Regions Highlighting 'the outback'

Three annotations have been made to Figure 16.1 which are important for the interpretation of 'outback tourism' in this research. In South Australia, the 'Flinders Ranges' destination has been highlighted. While the Flinders Ranges and Outback South Australia are two separate regions for statistical purposes, they are marketed and administered under a single Regional Tourism Association (RTA) (www.flindersranges.com.au). In Western Australia, the 'Golden Outback' is commonly connected with the 'North West' in outback itineraries promoted by Tourism Western Australia (Carson, forthcoming). Tourism data for the Northern Territory usually distinguishes between the capital city, Darwin, which nestles on the northern coast and is an urban destination, and the rest of the Northern Territory, which is more representative of outback values (www.tra.australia.com/regional.asp?lang=EN&sub=0167). In total, then, there are six regions which make overt claims on the outback label – Outback Queensland, Outback New South Wales, the Flinders Ranges and Outback South Australia (FROSAT), Western Australia's Golden Outback, Western Australia's North West, and the Northern Territory (excluding Darwin).

Outback destinations are geographically the largest in each of their states and the most sparsely populated areas with none of the six regions analysed in this research having a town with greater than 30,000 people at the 2006 Census and just four towns approaching or exceeding the 20,000 mark. There are no international airports in the outback regions, and only Alice Springs and Broken Hill have domestic airports with regular scheduled flights outside their home state. There is limited rail access, with two lines penetrating Outback Queensland, the Ghan line running from the South Australian capital of Adelaide through FROSAT and the Northern Territory to Darwin, and the India Pacific line from Adelaide through the Golden Outback region to the Western Australian capital of Perth. Consequently, road-based tourism dominates the market with around 80% of all visitors travelling in their own or a hired vehicle (Desert Knowledge Australia, 2005). Coach travel is prominent at some destinations like the Northern Territory where around 40% of international and 20% of domestic visitors in 2007 travelled by coach during at least part of their trip (Tourism NT, 2007).

In addition to being geographically peripheral, the outback regions appear to be economically marginal. Tourism NT (2007) cites 21 external causes for the poor performance of its tourism sector between 1999 and 2007. Just one positive influence is cited – the launch of a new Tourism NT marketing campaign in 2005. The Tourism NT argument is that the Northern Territory is more susceptible to external shocks than more accessible and better resourced destinations. The strength of the outback brand – the images of remoteness, isolation, vastness, 'roughing it' and so on – may also be the key to its weakness (Beeton, 2004). Beeton's argument was that such images give a confused impression about whether what is 'out there' is suitable for a tourist experience. The argument also applies from a supply perspective, with remote, isolated, and peripheral regions less able to attract a critical mass of product and investment to enhance their resilience to shocks (Moscardo, 2005).

There is universal agreement that the key to addressing the barriers to sustained economic development in peripheral areas is a continual process of innovation which emphasises the distinctive characteristics of the area in new initiatives which improve access to markets (Wellstead, 2007). Marketing innovation is just one of the many forms of innovation which regional and remote destinations need to be actively engaged in (Carson and Macbeth, 2005), but it is our focus in this chapter. It is difficult to know how to tell when a region has been innovative (Edquist, 2005), but the essence is that the development path has been more successful than that of other regions with similar starting conditions (Lloyd and Letzer, 2006). In tourism marketing, innovation is likely to be reflected in marketing messages that distinguish one destination from another, apparently similar one, while reinforcing its core values (Fyall and Garrod, 2005). This research analyses the extent to which the six outback tourism destinations in Australia have distinguished themselves in their online marketing, and relates evidence of marketing innovation to evidence of economic performance during the current decade. While positioned in Australia's outback, the research offers insights about the challenges of competitiveness for other destinations linked by their location within areas of iconic imagery.

Methodology

Each year, around 40,000 international visitors are interviewed about their Australian trip in the departure lounges of Australia's international airports. The International Visitor Survey (IVS) includes information about where visitors went and how long they spent in each location. The National Visitor Survey (NVS) interviews 40,000 Australian residents by telephone at their homes each year asking about their most recent trip away from home (for at least one night). Regional statistics derived from these surveys are subject to high standard errors, and as a result limited regional data are available on an annual basis. Regional data include estimates of international visitor numbers and the proportion of international visitors who visited the region for leisure and business purposes. Regional domestic data are more comprehensive and include estimates on the number of visitors, number of nights spent in the region, and the amount of expenditure that can be attributed to visits to each region.

Other data regarding the performance of tourism regions are available from the Survey of Tourist Accommodation (STA) and the Census of Population and Housing both conducted by the Australian Bureau of Statistics. The former provides information about employment in the accommodation and food services industry while the Census data on industry of employment were available from the 2001 and 2006 Census.

These data sets have been accessed for the period 2001 to 2006 except for IVS data which were only available for 2002 to 2006 to calculate the following statistics for each of the six outback tourism regions, and for Australia as a whole:

- Estimated domestic visitors, nights and expenditure per year (NVS)
- Estimated international visitors per year (IVS)
- Number of accommodation establishments (hotels and motels with 15 rooms or more) at June 30 each year (STA)
- Number of rooms in accommodation establishments (hotels and motels with 15 rooms or more) at June 30 each year (STA)
- Mean annual occupancy rate (STA)
- Number of people (aged between 15 and 64 years and available for employment) employed in the accommodation and food services industry (Census)

The percentage change in the number and in market share (relative to the total Australian value) between the first and last years in the relevant series was calculated. Changes in resident population were used as a temper for changes in tourism performance data as the official tourism data did not allow for separation of intra-regional travellers. It is expected that destinations with stronger resident population growth experience stronger tourism population growth through increased visiting friends and relatives trips (which accounts for 40% of the market in Australia) and business tourism (Eccles and Costa, 1996).

Marketing Analysis

A semiotic analysis was made of the content of state tourism organisation managed web sites relating to the outback destinations, including downloadable brochures. Semiotics is a qualitative study of signs and symbols to ascertain how meaning is constructed (Echtner, 1999). It has been applied in a limited fashion to the study of tourism marketing materials to identify how destinations 'see' and present themselves including ascertaining whether similarities can be identified between regions (see, for example, Bramwell and Rawding, 1996; Franklin and Crang, 2001). Semiotics extends traditional techniques such as content analysis, discourse analysis, and deconstruction which are more widely applied to the examinations of language and imagery in promotional materials in tourism (for example, Schellhorn and Perkins, 2004). In this study a modified semiotic process to that which has been outlined by Echtner (1999) was employed as follows:

1. Define and select a closed set of data whose meaning can be analysed independently to any historical context (or what Echtner describes as a synchronitic perspective).

2. Identify and specify the elements of analysis (such as themes or phrases) and break down the data accordingly.Record the frequency of occurrence of elements (or units within these) and record common instances where the elements are combined.

3.   Examine the structured relationship between elements through syntagmatic and paradigmatic structures to identify key combinations of words and images and the ways in which they are linked to form the entire image.

4.   Compare across regions to identify common underlying layers of meaning and significance.

It is important to note that semiotic analysis is a subjective task, and the labels we have used for messages contained in text are our own. What we have provided is analysis of those messages that is consistent within the scope of this study. While different labels may be applied to messages by different researchers, convergence or divergence between regions is relatively independent of the labels provided. And while many additional sites with relevant content are produced by private companies and local tourism associations, the intent was to critique the initiatives of the government sponsored marketing agencies.

Results

Destination Performance

The overall picture of outback tourism between 2001 and 2006 is one of decline (see Table 16.1). While the accommodation statistics reflect strong performance in most destinations (with the possible exceptions of the Northern Territory and FROSAT), visitor numbers (–10%), market share (–9%), and accommodation industry employment (–5%) declined across the outback as a whole. Domestic visitor numbers were down 3 percent and international visitor numbers down nearly 15%. On a market share basis, the domestic market was not as weak (down 2%) since the total domestic market in Australia declined by 1%. However, international market share was down nearly 27% as the total Australian market grew by 16%. Domestic visitor nights (–3%) and domestic visitor expenditure (–10%) were also down, and the market share of expenditure was down over 17%.

The worst performing destinations in the domestic market were Outback New South Wales (–25%) and FROSAT (–11%), while Australia's North West experienced an increase in the domestic market (21%). Domestic nights declined the most in FROSAT (–22%) and the Northern Territory (–18%) and domestic expenditure declined by 18% or more in four of the six regions – the exceptions being Outback New South Wales (–7%) and Australia's North West (an increase of 39%). FROSAT and the Northern Territory both saw declines in international visitor numbers of 34%, but the other four regions had some growth, including a doubling of visitor numbers in Australia's Golden Outback. These results, and the fact that only 5% of all visitors were international visitors, meant that total visitor numbers declined in four of the six regions, with just Outback Queensland (7%) and Australia's North West (4%) experiencing increases.

The accommodation statistics are less clear cut. While employment in the sector declined by 5% (while increasing by 6% nationally), and declined in all regions except Australia's North West (where it remained at around 6% of all employed people), the number of accommodation establishments, the number of rooms, and the average annual occupancy rate all increased. There was a 20% increase in the number of large hotels (15 or more rooms) across the outback, and increases in every region except the Northern Territory, which remained static at 56 establishments. Similarly, there were increases in rooms available (19% across the outback) except in the Northern Territory, where there was a marginal decline (–1%). Mean annual occupancy percentages were up in all regions except FROSAT (–2%).

Table 16.1: Tourism performance indicators, Outback Australia 2001 – 2006

	Australia	Total Out-back	Out-back QLD	Out-back NSW	FROSAT	WA Golden Outback	WA North West	NT (exc. Darwin)
VISITORS								
Change in total visitor numbers (%)	-1.0	-10.3	7.0	-33.7	-2.2	-8.9	3.6	-22.9
Change in total market share (%)	-	-9.4	8.0	-33.0	-1.2	-8.0	4.7	-22.1
Change in domestic visitor numbers (%)	-1.3	-3.3	-2.2	-24.5	-11.2	-0.8	21.4	-5.7
Change in domestic market share (%)	-	-1.9	-0.9	-23.5	-10.0	0.6	23.1	-4.4
Change in international visitor numbers (%)	16.4	-14.7	17.9	0.0	-33.9	120.8	48.8	-34.4
Change in international market share (%)	-	-26.7	1.3	-14.1	-43.2	89.8	27.9	-43.7
Change in domestic visitor nights (%)	-1.3	-2.8	-5.5	1.3	-21.6	-7.3	26.4	-18.1
Change in domestic visitor expenditure (%)	8.9	-9.8	-18.2	-7.0	-20.9	-29.4	38.9	-24.4
ACCOMMODATION								
Change in number employed in accommodation 2001 - 2006 (%)	6.4	-5.0	-11.1	-0.1	-0.6	-8.5	0.4	-16.0
Change in number of accommodation establishments (%)	9.6	20.5	25.0	23.7	18.5	57.1	10.9	0.0
Change in mean annual occupancy rate (%)	12.2	11.6	15.9	4.3	-2.0	7.9	30.6	5.0
Change in rooms capacity (%)	8.4	18.9	20.7	40.8	19.5	45.9	23.5	-1.1

Western Australia's North West experienced growth in all the indicators listed in Table 16.1. Conversely, the Northern Territory and South Australia declined across all visitor indicators and some of the accommodation indicators. Results in other regions were more mixed. The strong performance of Western Australia's North West may owe something to its increase in resident population between 2001 and 2006 (7%). It was the only outback destination to experience resident population growth at or above the national average (7%). Australia's Golden Outback increased its resident population by 1% and the Northern Territory by 6%, while the other regions experienced population declines (6% in Outback Queensland, 2% in FROSAT, and 1% in Outback New South Wales). The failure of the Northern Territory to achieve tourism growth despite having resident population growth is an interesting anomaly, and warrants additional research.

Marketing Analysis

Frequently used phrases included 'epitome of the outback', 'true outback', 'heart of the outback', 'authentic outback', and 'essence of the outback'. Paradigmatically such messages often preceded discourse on the people, communities, or 'characters' of the outback, which themselves were frequently borrowed from historical contexts like the gold rush era in Western Australia, and the emergence of QANTAS from outback Queensland:

> Journey to the 'heart of the Outback' and experience the heritage and cultural history that has shaped the nation.
>
> (Outback Queensland – http://www.outbackholidays.info)

Experientially the chief messages were positioning outback regions as, above all, places for ADVENTURE travel. Adventure is heavily 'sold' by all regions and the word appears on average more than five times within each web page or downloadable brochure. Its framing is inconsistent between regions though with some, like Australia's North West, ascertaining that visiting the region (independent of any activities or attractions) is what constitutes the adventure:

> Australia's North West is ... the place to go for an authentic Aussie outback adventure
>
> Australia's North West, http://www.australiasnorthwest.com

But in most cases, regions market the adventure experience as being obtainable through activities, forms of transport (especially four-wheel driving), and accommodation (or combinations of these):

> You don't need a 4WD to have fun exploring the secrets of the region. But if you do, lock those hubs and lock onto some serious adventure!
>
> FROSAT, http://www.southaustralia.com/FlindersRangesOutback

Tourism WA offers one point of difference insofar as it promotes the 'Aboriginal Outback' as an adventure in its own right:

> For a real outback adventure, let the traditional landowners show you the wonders of this sun-kissed land.
>
> Tourism Western Australia, http://www.westernaustralia.com

Four underlying themes were discerned and found to be common to the marketing language for all regions (in no specific order):

Spirituality and Mysticism

Regions have attempted to depict opportunities for engaging and connecting with the 'spiritual-self' along with spiritual and mystic elements denoted as features of the region. Statements are invariably broad and open to interpretation:

> We invite you to spend 5-6 days with us to truly appreciate the majestic beauty and spirit of Kakadu.
>
> Tourism NT, http://en.travelnt.com/explore/kakadu-arnhem.aspx

In some cases we observed 'cover all' statements in which the syntactic and paradigmatic structure was linked to other elements identified in the results (like adventure) and combined with underlying themes:

> The Flinders Ranges has been named one of Australia's outstanding national landscapes – recognised as an emotionally uplifting destination, where adventure, spirituality and tranquillity co-exist.
>
> FROSAT, http://www.southaustralia.com/FlindersRangesOutbac

Indigenous people and their cultures were firmly interwoven within the spiritual and mystic narratives and featured, to varying degrees, in the materials of all outback regions. As well as emphasising these elements, around half of all regions also spoke of 'strong' Aboriginal culture to promote the authenticity of their Indigenous tourism assets:

> Aboriginal culture is strong in Tennant Creek.
> > Tourism NT, http://en.travelnt.com/explore/tennant-creek.aspx

> Wholly aboriginal owned land, Arnhem Land is known for its strong aboriginal culture.
> > Tourism NT, http://en.travelnt.com/explore/kakadu-arnhem.aspx

Exploration and Discovery

All regions emphasised the opportunity for visitors to 'explore' and 'discover' their destinations:

> It's all waiting to be discovered by you – today's Outback adventurer!
> > Tourism Queensland, http://www.outbackholidays.info

> Explore fascinating European heritage sites via two of Australia's most famous trails.
> > FROSAT, http://www.southaustralia.com/FlindersRangesOutback

Paradigmatic structures within this theme were commonly notated alongside specific places of interest, landscapes, geomorphologic, and historical elements. But in some cases the offer of 'discovering' things about the residents of the region was co-presented:

> Tennant Creek is also known as the Territory's heart of gold; a reference to
> the friendliness of its people and the area's gold mining history.
> > Tourism NT, http://en.travelnt.com/explore/tennant-creek.aspx

Plentitude

Language projecting images of vastness, expansive grandeur, and unbounded spaces filters through in the materials for all regions. This is invariably accompanied by superlative descriptors of landscapes, flora and fauna. From birds to grass, and rocks to stars, regions habitually signal such assets to be so plentiful in supply that they simply cannot be counted:

> Visitors are invariably awestruck by the profound impact of space, the myriad of stars in the night sky.
> > Tourism NSW, http://www.visitoutbacknsw.com.au

> Go camping and see stars which stretch forever…
> > Outback Queensland, http://www.outbackholidays.info

> The Outback is big on first impressions. You'll be struck by its vastness and the deafening silence.
> > FROSAT, http://www.southaustralia.com/FlindersRangesOutback

Exclusiveness

Each region identifies assets which are bigger, older, one of the most important, or the only one of its kind in Australia or the world. Unlike the more generalised structure of much of the outback discourse, dialogue on exclusive elements was largely within paragraphs on specific natural, cultural, and historical assets or attractions:

Visit some of the world's largest open cut mines and watch in wonder as the world's longest trains hurtle past.

Australia's North West, http://www.australiasnorthwest.com

Kakadu National Park, in Australia's Northern Territory, is one of only a handful of world heritage sites listed for both its natural and cultural values.

Tourism NT, http://en.travelnt.com/explore/kakadu-arnhem.aspx

Within this theme diversity within exclusive elements (especially landscapes, flora and fauna) was bought forward to enhance the perception of exclusiveness. And interspersed throughout dialogue on exclusive assets we found many references to 'untouched' elements, also projected in such a way so as to demonstrate regional exclusiveness:

As well as being home to a huge number and wide variety of bird species...

Australia's Golden Outback, http://www.australiasgoldenoutback.com

And on its coast lie some of the world's most beautiful beaches, untouched coral atolls...

Australia's North West, http://www.australiasnorthwest.com

This untouched wilderness is part of the arid core of Australia: home to ancient and dramatic landscapes.

FROSAT, http://www.southaustralia.com/FlindersRangesOutback

A further observation is the high frequency use of the words 'red' (soils, rocks, skies at sunsets, and so on) and 'rugged' (plains, rocks, islands, and so on). The former was observed to be nested with descriptors of flora or fauna (like the 'golden fields' of Outback NSW) while the latter was most often associated with non-specific elements, mainly contained in the same sentence as the word 'adventure', and within paragraphs themed on exploration or discovery.

Regional Points of Difference

Points of difference were difficult to identify with the results indicating a consistent and pervasive thematic discourse. The notable exception was Western Australia's North West region, which, although it does not appear to have adopted substantially different marketing strategies, has three distinguishing features. First, it promotes the idea of the 'coast' as part of the outback – a strategy which is not available to Outback Queensland and Outback New South Wales and is not heavily employed by the other destinations. Second, while the term 'outback' is used throughout the marketing material, it is not used in the name of the destination itself. This puts it more in line with other destinations in Australia who are able to call upon the outback mythology which represents the entire country without having to justify a specific labelling. The third key difference between Western Australia's North West and most other outback regions is the growth in its resident population between 2001 and 2006.

A further variation in approach, although supplied within the same thematic context, was observed from Tourism Queensland. Here, a specific set of activities (fossicking, fishing, outback station stays, and visiting outback pubs) are promoted in the materials in contrast to other regions where the primary objective is to encourage visitors to 'see things'. The language around each activity emphasises the role of (supposedly) friendly, informative and knowledgeable local residents (often found in the pubs) in generating the experience:

> From stories of courage and survival to the odd 'tall tale', the people are the beating heart of Queensland's Outback.
>
> Outback Queensland, http://www.outbackholidays.info/more-information/
> brochure-rack.cfm

Conclusion

Echtner (1999) argues that it is the role of semiotic analysis to uncover the structure of the tourism experience through language (words and images). In this respect differentiation of experiences between outback regions is hard to identify since the fundamental elements are the same in each region. There was no region or subset of regions which stood out as actively differentiating themselves from the standard outback images of adventure, spiritualism, exploration, plentitude, and exclusiveness. The lack of diversity in marketing messages is linked, then, to the relative consistency of performance trends in the 2001 to 2006 period.

The need to justify the use of the outback label is a key underlying theme of the marketing material. Each outback region aggressively positions itself as the 'true', 'real', 'authentic' outback, distinguishable from other outbacks because by its grander space, or bigger assets, or better claims to European (and occasionally Indigenous) history. The message is that it should be a sufficient achievement for visitors to experience this 'true outback'. Exactly how the achievement might play out (apart from the act of seeing things that are bigger or rarer here than elsewhere) is left largely to the interpretant to decide. Surely, then, some level of confusion about which outback is suited to the needs of specific tourists is likely to emerge, and it is not surprising that the performance trends suggest more and more tourists are settling for an 'accessible outback' found at the Gold Coast theme park, the Blue Mountains, or other near-urban rural settings.

Continuing this theme, there is very little in the marketing material about what sort of traveller (apart from the 'adventurous') should visit the outback. And there is little attempt by any of the destinations to claim a different market to their outback colleagues, with the possible exception of Tourism Queensland's activities focus. If there is some foundation in Australia's attempt to convert from anonymous mass tourism to niched alternative tourism, it has not been picked up by outback destinations and this may help explain the poor performance relative to the total Australian industry over the past several years.

Marketing of Australia's outback destinations has largely failed to move beyond the aspirational. It becomes clear in analysing web sites and downloadable brochures that there is 'nothing out there' (and this is even used as a hook in some destinations). Potential visitors may well fear that there will be 'nothing out there', and this fear leads them to question the value of the time and expense required to access outback destinations. If indeed there is 'nothing out there', then it may make more sense for outback destinations to more specifically target markets for whom this is an attractive asset. That sort of market identification is largely absent with the occasional exception of approaches to the four-wheel-drive market. Even then, the four-wheel-drive traveller would be hard pressed to distinguish one destination from another.

All outback regions face similar challenges of access and critical mass. They rely on similar types of natural attractions as the foundation for their tourism industries. They have generally experienced low population growth or even population decline during the 2000s. The exceptions are Western Australia's North West region, where tourism growth has accompanied population growth, and the Northern Territory, where it has not. The loss of employment in accommodation has occurred at the same time that the stock of accommodation has increased across the outback. The research here has not been able to explain this phenomenon, and further research is warranted. It may be that tourist accommodation in the outback (at least among the larger properties) has become more labour efficient and so offers relatively less in the way of employment generation in local communities. It is almost certainly the case that the market has become more concentrated in these larger accommodation establishments given that capacity and occupancy have increased while overall visitor numbers and nights have declined. This does not bode well for product diversification, at least so far as accommodation is concerned.

The marketing analysis provided some additional insights into product innovation in outback tourism. Overall, products appear to be very much restricted to immediate exploitation of the visual appeal of natural attractions and limited interaction with Indigenous culture. Even the more active pursuits such as four-wheel-driving, bicycling, and hiking are essentially about sightseeing. And while they extend the mass coach tourism model into somewhat new markets, there continues to be a lack of variety of such experiences, and the experiences are marketed in much the same way in all destinations.

The 2008 global financial crisis is likely to impact on international and domestic tourism in Australia for at least the next two or three years. On the evidence presented here, there is reason to believe that outback destinations will continue to perform poorly compared with other destinations in Australia. Western Australia's North West has been able to buck that trend in the recent past because of its promotion of its coast and the increasing critical mass engendered by resident population growth. The other destinations, however, need to rethink their approach to marketing along with addressing deficiencies in product diversity and necessary infrastructure. The current failure by state tourism organisations to distinguish outback destinations from one another, while at the same time being unwilling to accept Desert Knowledge Australia's challenge to collaborate on marketing and brand positioning, has not worked. The state and the regional bodies need to either commit to a national outback brand through which all destinations may benefit or lose, or commit to a process of promoting the competitive advantage of individual regions which may position some as winners and some as losers.

It is useful to think about 'the outback' as a collection of destinations which share a fundamental geographic attribute, much in the same way as one might think about Europe's Alps, the Caribbean's beaches, or Africa's savannahs. The simple fact, however, is that tourists have to make decisions about where in these large areas they want to go. A universal outback image is a real benefit to raising awareness of the destination type, but it is insufficient to position specific destinations as competitors for the tourism dollar. In Australia, the outback image is so universal that having the outback label in your destination name or slogan is insufficient to establish competitive advantage. The outback regions instead appear as catch-alls for those parts of states that do not otherwise have an identity, while the outback image is successfully used by other destinations (like the Gold Coast and Blue Mountains) to add to their appeal. Outback regions are large regions which are quite diverse internally, and so perhaps are too large to be effectively marketed as single destinations. If Australia and its States really want the outback to be a major drawcard, and if they really want the 'real' outback regions to experience the benefits, then changes need to be made to the political geography of Australian tourism and how it is reflected in destination marketing. If not, outback destinations are likely to become increasingly *peripheral and* marginal as Australian tourism struggles to adjust to the global financial crisis and whatever woes emerge next.

References

Barry T, Robbins P. 2001. Tourism trends and opportunities: What do they mean for regional Australia? Paper presented at Outlook 2001: Australian Bureau of Agricultural and Resource Economics National Conference. Canberra, Australia. 27 February – 1 March.

Beeton S. 2004. Rural tourism in Australia – has the gaze altered? Tracking rural images through film and tourism promotion. *International Journal of Tourism Research* 6 (3): 125-135.

Bramwell B, Rawding L. 1996. Tourism marketing images of industrial cities. *Annals of Tourism Research* 23 (1): 201-221.

Butler R. 1990. Alternative tourism: Pious hope or Trojan horse? *Journal of Travel Research* 28 (3): 40-45.

Carson D. 2008. (Self drive) tourism futures for desert Australia: changing patterns of visitor flows. Paper presented at the 2008 Desert Knowledge Symposium and Business Showcase. Alice Springs, Australia. 3-6 November.

Carson D, Macbeth J. 2005. Regional tourism systems and the implications of innovative behaviour. In *Regional Tourism Cases: innovation in regional tourism*. Carson D, Macbeth J (eds). Common Ground: Melbourne; 125-129.

Christen K. 2006. Tracking properness: repackaging culture in a remote Australian town. *Cultural Anthropology* 21 (3): 416-446.

Desert Knowledge Australia. 2005. *Our Outback: Partnerships and Pathways to Success in Tourism*. Desert Knowledge Australia: Alice Springs.

Eccles G, Costa J. 1996. Perspectives on tourism development. *International Journal of Contemporary Hospitality Management* 8 (7): 44-51.

Echtner C. (1999). The semiotic paradigm: implications for tourism research. *Tourism Management* 20 (1). 47-57.

Edquist C. 2005. Systems of innovation: perspectives and challenges. In *The Oxford Handbook of Innovation*. Fagerberg J, Mowery DC, Nelson RR (eds). Oxford University Press: Oxford 181-208Edwards D, Griffin T, Hayllar B. 2007. *Development of an Australian Urban Tourism Research Agenda*. Sustainable Tourism Cooperative Research Centre: Gold Coast.

Franklin A, Crang M. 2001. The trouble with tourism and travel theory. *Tourist Studies* 1 (1): 5-22.

Fuller D, Caldicott J, Wilde S. 2006. Ecotourism enterprise and sustainable development in remote Indigenous communities in Australia. *International Journal of Environment, Workplace and Employment* 2 (4): 373-384.

Fyall A, Garrod B. 2005. *Tourism Marketing: A Collaborative Approach*. Channel View Publications: Clevedon.

Gorman-Murray A, Darian-Smith K, Gibson C. 2008. Scaling the rural: reflections on rural cultural studies. *Australian Humanities Review* **45**. Available from: http://www.australianhumanitiesreview.org/archive/Issue-November-2008/gormanmurray.html, accessed 29 December 2008.

Hingham J, Bejder L. 2008. Managing wildlife-based tourism: edging slowly towards sustainability? *Current Issues in Tourism* **11** (1): 75-83.

Hughes M, Newsome D, Macbeth J. 2005. Case study: Visitor perceptions of captive wildlife tourism in a Western Australian natural setting. *Journal of Ecotourism* **4** (2): 73-85.

Lloyd C, Metzer J. 2006. Settler colonization and societies in history: patterns and concepts. XIVth International Economic History Congress. Helsinki, Finland. 21-25 August.

Moscardo G. 2005. Peripheral tourism development: challenges, issues and success factors. *Tourism Recreation Research* **30** (1): 27-44.

Rodger K, Moore S, Newsome D. 2007. Wildlife tours in Australia: Characteristics, the place of science and sustainable futures. *Journal of Sustainable Tourism* **15** (2): 160-179.

Saarinen J. 2006. Traditions of sustainability in tourism studies. *Annals of Tourism Research* **33** (4): 1121-1140.

Schellhorn M, Perkins C. 2004. The stuff of which dreams are made: representations of the South Sea in German-language tourist brochures. *Current Issues in Tourism* **7** (2): 95-133.

Skuras D, Petrou A, Clark G. 2006. Demand for rural tourism: the effects of quality and information. *Agricultural Economics* **35** (2): 183-192.

Tourism Australia. 2009. *Australia the Movie Tool Kit*. Available from: http://www.tourism.australia.com/Marketing.asp?sub=0451&al=3034, accessed 21 January 2009.

Tourism NT. 2007. *Territory Tourism Selected Statistics 2007*. Available from: http://www.tourismnt.com.au/nt/system/galleries/download/NTTC_Research/Territory_Tourism_select-stats_FINAL_2007.pdf , accessed 18 December 2008.

Tourism Research Australia. 2008a. *Forecasts*. Available from: http://www.tra.australia.com/forecasts.asp?sub=0084, accessed 21 January 2009.

Tourism Research Australia (2008b). *Through the Looking Glass: the future of domestic tourism in Australia*. Available from: http://www.tra.australia.com/domestic.asp?sub=0036, accessed 18 December 2008.

Weaver D. 2006. *Sustainable Tourism Theory and Practice*. Butterworth-Heineman: Oxford.

Wellstead A. 2007. The (post) staples economy and the (post) staples state in historical perspective. *Canadian Political Science Review* **1** (1): 8-25.

17 The Prospects and Challenges of Positioning Ghana as a Preferred African-American Tourist Destination

Ishmael Mensah and Eunice Amissah, University of Cape Coast

Introduction

Ghana is one of the most popular tourist destinations in Sub-Saharan Africa, due to its all-year-round attractions including, warm climate, coconut-fringed white sand beaches, historic monuments and a diverse culture. The sector contributed 4.8% to GDP in 2004 and is expected to grow by 5.9% per annum between 2004 and 2014 (WTTC, 2004). The USA is Ghana's second highest tourist generating market outside Africa. Arrivals from the USA almost doubled between 1994 and 2002 (Table 17.1).

Table 17.1: Tourism inflows to Ghana by countries 1994-2002

Country	1994	1996	1998	2000	2002
USA	17896	20108	22950	26317	31834
UK	23490	26395	30126	34546	41787
Germany	13090	14709	16788	19251	23286
France	9804	11016	21573	14418	17440
Netherlands	6568	7380	8423	9659	11684
Canada	3645	4096	4675	5361	6485
Switzerland	2573	2891	3300	3784	4577
Scandinavia	3621	4096	4644	5325	6442
Italy	3294	3702	4225	4845	5860

Source: Ghana Tourist Board; 2004

A segment of the USA market which is of interest to Ghana is the African American market. It is composed of Americans who are of African ancestry or who relate to their history or culture (Magazine Publishers of America, 2004). Blacks in the USA form 13% of the total population (US Census Bureau, March 2002). African American travellers are interested in participating in cultural events, urban nightlife and gambling (Soul of America, 2004). They are particularly interested in learning their shared cultural heritage with Africa. In a 2000 Gallup poll commissioned by the National Summit on Africa,

73% of them indicated that they were interested in learning more about Africa. This is epitomized by a study conducted by Abanga (1999), which revealed that cultural heritage is the most important reason for African Americans visiting Ghana.

Table 17.2 Organisations and stakeholders involved in the promotion of Ghana

Organization	Aims	Promotional Activities
Ministry of Tourism and Modernization of the Capital City (MOTMCC)	Initiate and formulate tourism policies taking into account the needs and aspirations of the Ghanaian people so as to make Ghana a sustainable and international quality destination.	Determine the overall promotional strategy for the country. Develop special projects and events to enhance the image of the country such as the 'Joseph Project' and Emancipation Day celebrations.
Ghana Tourist Board (GTB)	To ensure standards of tourism businesses are of international quality and to enhance the image of the country so as to capture a fair share of the tourism market.	Market tourism locally and internationally; by attending international trade-shows, publications and other public relations and social activities.
Tour Operators' Union of Ghana (TOUGHA)	To contribute to tourism development and ensure high standards in the industry.	Created a comprehensive website to market Ghana's tourist attractions Contribute money towards helping the MOTMCC with its marketing activities. Promote domestic tourism among first-cycle students through essay competitions and organized tours.
Ghana Investment Promotion Centre (GIPC)	To encourage, promote and facilitate investments in all sectors of the economy including tourism	Collect, collate, analyse and disseminate information about investment opportunities and sources of investment capital, and advise on the availability, choice or suitability of partners in joint-venture projects. Provision of incentives such as tax exemptions to investors in tourism under the Ghana Investment Promotion Centre Act, Act 478.

Source: Telephone interview with representatives

It has been suggested that parts of West Africa, including Ghana, are the best destinations for African Americans who want to return to their ancestral homeland (Wyllie, 1990). This is perhaps due to the fact that the majority of slaves sent to the 'new world' (Americas) from Africa were from West Africa in general and Ghana in particular (Curtin, 1969; Perbi, 1995). Since independence, in 1957, Ghana has been one of the countries most often chosen by repatriated Africans from the Diaspora. Dr. Kwame Nkrumah through his policies on Pan-Africanism, welcomed diasporan Africans, including African Americans into Ghana (Lake, 1995). Also, the efforts of Nkrumah in developing Ghana's traditional arts endeared him to some prominent blacks in the Diaspora, prompting people like Maya Angelou, Malcolm X, Richard Wright and W.E.B Dubois to visit the country (Greene, 1998). African Americans continue to visit Ghana both as tourists and to relocate permanently. Of the Diaspora's African population in Ghana as at 1989, 60% was African American (Lake, 1995). Also, in 2003, 27,000 tourists visited Ghana from the Americas, with approximately 10,000 of these African Americans (Bernhadt and Eroglu, 2004).

The Ministry of Tourism and other tourism organizations have recognized the potentials of this market and continue to develop new products to appeal to it. However, it seems the travel and tourism industry has not yet devoted significant levels of marketing efforts to encourage the African American traveller to consider all that Ghana has to offer (Saunders, 2004). A study conducted by Bernhadt and Eroglu in 2004 revealed that African Americans have very little awareness of Ghana, and the little they know is often inaccurate. Though Ghana has been branded with images such as 'the black star of Africa', 'home of pan-africanism', 'proverbial hospitality', and 'Mecca for African Americans', there appears to be no consensus as to which images to project as the various organizations and stakeholders involved in the promotion of the country seem to be doing things independently (Table 17.2).

This chapter therefore looks at the prospects and challenges of positioning Ghana as a preferred tourist destination for African American tourists.

Literature Review

Positioning is a very important element of every organization's marketing strategy since it contributes essentially to the realization of the entire marketing programme for a destination (Heath and Wall, 1992). Though it has been described in different ways such as: managing customers' perceptions of a product, service or place (Arnott, 1993) and how a brand can effectively compete against a specified set of competitors in a particular market (Keller, 2003). There seems to be a consensus that it is a process of establishing a distinctive place for a product or service in the minds of the target market (Echtner and Ritchie 1993; Kotler et al., 1993; Ries and Trout, 2001). According to Aaker and Shansby (1982), positioning is concerned with three issues; segmentation decision, image creation and selection of product features to emphasize.

Positioning has become one of the important aspects of destination marketing and has engaged the minds of tourism researchers (see Chacko, 1997; Ibrahim and Gill, 2005; Pike and Ryan, 2004; Sorma, 2003). Kim et al. (2005) define tourism destination positioning as the process of locating a destination or the attractions of a destination in the minds of potential tourists within its target markets. This will consequently inform how they (the tourists) define such destination in relation to other competing destinations.

Connected to the positioning of a destination in a market segment is the image of the destination (Ryglova and Turcinova, 2004). Image is a set of ideas and impressions that a people have about an object or place (Crompton, 1979; Kotler, 2003). The link between images and positioning is that destination positioning is essentially a process of building and maintaining images for a destination (Sarma, 2003). In view of this, Ibrahim and Gill (2005) recommend that a destination-positioning strategy should be based on the customers' (tourists') image of the tourism product. There have been a number of studies on destination positioning and images (Botha et al., 1999; Chacko, 1997; Etchner and Ritchie, 2003; Power et al., 2005;) but most of these studies have been undertaken in western industrialized countries with very little done on destinations in Sub-Saharan Africa.

Images of destinations are formed on the minds of actual or potential tourists, so to position a destination, such images are either enhanced or recreated. Ryglova and Turcinova (2004) are of the view that the image that people have of a place is a complex variable. It is influenced by both past and present internal and external environment factors. The complexity is also due to the fact that tourist images coincide with images reflecting various other domains of the reality of the world such as geographic, historical, cultural, social, political and economic among others (Levy and Matos, 2002). Destination images also have different dimensions; organic and induced (Fakeye and Crompton, 1991; Gunn, 1972); and cognitive and affective (Baloglu, 1999; Dann, 1996; Pike and Ryan, 2004). Pike and Ryan (2004) add a third dimension, conative, which they describe as the intent or action component of destination images. Tapachai and Waryszak (2000) also introduced the concept of a 'beneficial image' which they defined as what influences the tourist's decision to visit the destination.

Travellers' level of knowledge about a destination culminates in the image of the destination that they perceive. Their level of knowledge about the destination is influenced by their learning, media news stories, their previous travelling experience as well as the geographical and cultural distances between their originating country and the destination. Marketing activities can also be deliberately used to influence peoples' knowledge about a place and hence the place's image (induced image). In spite of this, Pike and Ryan (2004) are of the view that images alone are not enough for understanding the position of a product or service on the mind of the consumer but are also a frame of reference with the competition. Reich (2001) suggests a detailed analysis of all aspects of an organization's internal activities and its competitive marketplace in order to determine its position on the market.

Developing a market position strategy for travel destinations

According to Rigger (1995), the lack of a comprehensive definition is inhibiting both practitioners and academic scholars in developing appropriate means of measuring the operationalization of positioning. Moreover, positioning services is more difficult than positioning physical goods due to the peculiar characteristics of services (Bateson, 1995; Blankson and Kalafatis, 1999). Chacko (1997) also believes that positioning the destination, which is intangible, is a complicated process.

On account of the above difficulties, the literature is replete with a number of prescriptions on how to position a destination accurately. These include the creation of images using the attributes of a destination perceived as important by visitors (Crompton et al., 1992; Witt and Moutinho, 1995); positively reinforcing what already exists on tourists' minds (Botha et al., 1999) and matching benefits provided by a destination with benefits sought by a target market (Crompton et al., 1992; Woodside, 1982). Morgan (1996) with reference to Splashdown Leisure pool, cites a three-pronged strategy for positioning; derivation of the key benefits sought by the customers (tourists), design of the product in accordance with customer preferences, and communication of the product features to the target market through promotional campaigns. According to Chacko (1997) there are two tests of effective positioning. First, the position must be believable in the tourist's mind. Second, the destination must deliver that promise on a consistent basis.

Positioning Ghana: Actions, Prospects and Challenges

There have been attempts by successive governments and private organizations to position Ghana with African Americans through diverse initiatives. During the immediate pre-independence era (1956), and post independence era (1957-66), the Convention Peoples' Party (CPP) government under the leadership of Kwame Nkrumah made Ghana the hub of the pan-African movement. The socialist-inclined government did not however deliberately promote tourism development (Akyeampong, 1996). This none-theless led to a number of African Americans including George Padmore, Maya Angelou and W.E.B Dubois coming to live in Ghana. Some state resources were branded with the 'black star label' proposed by Marcus Garvey; Black Star Line (the state shipping line), Black Stars (the national football team) and Black Star Square (now known as the Independence Square). Also, specific products which afford African Americans the opportunity to visit the 'motherland' have been developed by tour operators. These are tours to slave sites in Ghana, Nigeria, Benin, Senegal and Gambia.

Ghana was a key player in the Transatlantic Slave Trade and is therefore playing an instrumental role in the Slave Route Project proposed by UNESCO. The Slave Route Project provides a common platform for integrating some of Ghana's attractions with other slave route features in other West African countries, so as to promote a common heritage of monuments, sites, manuscripts, archives and documents related to the slave trade among these countries. The Ministry of Tourism has also launched a programme termed 'the Joseph Project' to encourage blacks in the Diaspora to return to their roots. Due to the importance that the government attaches to diasporans in general and Afri-can Americans in particular, the name of the tourism ministry was changed from Min-istry of Tourism and Modernisation of the Capital City to Ministry of Tourism and Diasporan Relations on 28 April 2006.

Events have also been used to position Ghana; notable among them is the Pan African Historic Theatre Festival (PANAFEST) which is used to promote the ideals of Pan-Af-ricanism through theatrical and musical performances. Also, Emancipation Day, which was already being celebrated in the black Diaspora has been adopted and is celebrated annually in Ghana. The African American community also observes 'Juneteenth' and Black History Month.

There have also been efforts by governments to brand the country. According to the American Marketing Association (cited by Kotler, 1997), a brand is 'a name, term, sign, symbol or design or a combination of these intended to identify the goods or services of one seller or group of sellers and to differentiate them from those of competitors'. Branding the country has been through the use of slogans like 'the friendliest people on earth', 'proverbial Ghanaian hospitality', and 'best kept secret in Africa'. Ghana has also been positioned as 'the gateway to West Africa'. Under this strategy, the Ghana Investment Promotion Council (GIPC) and the Ghana Free Zones Board (GFZB) were created to attract investment; there was a symbolic return of the mortal remains of two slave ancestors back to Ghana through the 'door of no return' of the Cape Coast Castle for final interment at Assin Manso, an important slave market; and the expansion of the Kotoka International Airport, to reinforce the gateway position.

Also, in the tourism strategy document for 2003-07, Ghana has been branded as a pre-ferred tourism destination in Africa (MOTMCC, 2003). The government in June 2005 repositioned Ghana as 'a golden experience', based on advice from a team of investment advisors (*Ghanaian Times*, 2005). There has been another slogan which seems to be a convergence between the gateway slogan and the golden experience; 'Ghana, Africa's golden gateway'. In this regard, President J.A Kufuor launched Africa's Golden Gateway Project in Washington aimed at stepping up Ghana's efforts at attracting American in-vestors and tourists (*Daily Graphic*, 31 October 2005). The current slogan is 'a golden experience at the centre of the world'. This is because Ghana is uniquely positioned at the centre of the world geographically. However, a content analysis of the brochures and websites of some major tour operators and other stakeholders in Ghana reveal that there is no uniformity in the images projected (Table 17.3). Images of hospitality, unspoilt attractions, gateway to Africa, and a golden experience have been projected in their brochures and on their websites.

A destination's image must be positioned to match the reality, if the slogan does not mirror what is on the ground; it shrouds the destination's credibility in doubt (Kotler et al., 1993). Also, a brand image must send a singular or unique message that communicates a product or destination's major benefits and positioning (Kotler et al., 2003). This is partly the problem with the positioning of Ghana, the inconsistency between slogans and the situation on the ground as well as no uniformity in slogans used to market the country. Though the African American market offers some prospects to warrant special marketing attention from Ghana, effectively positioning Ghana on the market is fraught with some challenges.

Table 17.3: Slogans, clichés and images for positioning Ghana

Organization	Slogan/cliché	Image(s) Portrayed
Blast Tours	Undiscovered/ discovering Ghana	Undiscovered tourist destination
Citi Travels and Tours ltd.	Home of hospitality	Hospitable people
Connectworld Group	A safe, affordable and friendly destination	Hospitable people/ affordable destination
Discover Ghana Tours	Ghana is an amazingly friendly country With wonderful, unspoilt places to visit	Hospitable people/ Unspoilt attractions
Eco Travel and Tours	The land of smiles	Hospitable people
Ghana Association of Travel and Tour Agencies (GATTA)	Smiles/ friendly and hospitable people	Hospitable people
Ghana Travel and Tours	Golden country that will dazzle you with culture, wildlife, history and landscape	Golden experience/ rich natural and cultural experience
Land Tours	The gateway and heart of Africa	Gateway country to the region/ heart of Africa
Ministry of Tourism and Modernisation of the Capital City (MOTMCC)	A golden experience at the heart of the world	Golden experience/ heart of the world
Tour operators union of Ghana (TOUGHA)	We have a smile for you/ the world's most hospitable people	Hospitable people

Source: websites of organisations and telephone interview with representatives

Prospects

First, the African American market represents a market with growth potentials. It is growing rapidly, is younger and has more buying power than ever before. The population has been increasing by 15.6% since 1990 (Centre for Media Studies, 2003). The estimated annual expenditures of the African American consumer market grew from

US$316.5 billion in 1990 to US$645.9 billion in 2002 and were expected to increase to US$852.8 billion by end 2007 (Wellner, 2003). This increase in purchasing power implies a greater propensity to travel to long-haul destinations like Ghana. This is reinforced by a Gallup poll on the vacation preferences of Americans which revealed that household earnings and the likelihood of taking vacations away from home are strongly related, with 90% of those with good income ($75,000) taking vacations away from home while those at the highest income level travel abroad for their vacations (Jones, 2005). Even within the United States alone, tourism involving African Americans increased by 16% between 2002 and 2004 though the industry itself grew by only 1% (Barbosa, 2004 cited in Santana Pinho, 2008). These prospects are to be translated into travel by African Americans to Africa as they are becoming more aware of the rich cultural and historical heritage of Africa (Saunders, 2004).

Second, Ghana has a wide collection of relics, and landmarks as legacy from the slave trade. Ghana was an active participant in the transatlantic slave trade (Curtin, 1969; Perbi, 1995). This incident saw some 10-12 million Africans being exported from the continent to Europe and the Americas (Perbi, 1995). During the slave trade, a lot of people were sent from the Gold Coast (presentday Ghana) into slavery in the Americas. According to Perbi (1995), from 1620 to 1807, Ghana alone provided about 16% of the total slave output required in the USA. Curtin (1969) on the other hand projects that 14.4% of slave exports from Africa between 1711 and 1810 were from the Gold Coast. Ghana can therefore provide a platform for African Americans to reunite with their kith and kin and to rediscover their roots. Already, a number of African Americans travel within the USA for family reunions (Dickerson, 2006; Vargus, 2002) and this could serve as a catalyst for annual pilgrimages to Ghana.

The Cape Coast and Elmina Castles have been designated World Heritage Sites by UNESCO and out of about 43 forts and castles connected with the slave trade in West Africa, 33 are in Ghana alone. Out of these about 25 are in good condition (GIPC, 2005). A survey undertaken by the Midwest Universities Consortium for International Activities (MUCIA) further revealed that no less than 96 forts and castles were constructed along Ghana's coast (MUCIA, 1995). Also, under the Slave Route Project, a number of slave landmarks, relics and monuments have been identified in Ghana as part of the project launched by UNESCO in September 1994. These monuments are a source of interest to African Americans because these were where their ancestors were held captive before being shipped to the USA. They could therefore serve as strong selling points if well packaged and marketed.

Moreover, Ghana is one of the most peaceful and stable countries in the West-African sub-region. After the 11 September, 2001 terrorist attacks on the USA, security issues have become of prime concern to Americans especially and the whole world in general. Americans have become more cautious about where they travel to. A number of countries in the West African sub-region have remained unstable for some time now, including Liberia, Sierra Leone, Ivory Coast and Togo. Ghana however remains one of the safest havens in a troubled and turbulent sub-region. After embracing multi-party democracy in 1992, five successful elections have been held. This peaceful political atmosphere is a good recipe for travel and tourism which thrives in a peaceful atmosphere. A study by Eilat and Einav (2003) revealed that political risk has a significant impact on tourism demand in both developed and developing countries. Ghana's relatively stable political atmosphere is therefore a good ingredient for tourism development and a positive image for crafting a position on the African American market.

Challenges

Firstly, a lot of concerns have been expressed about the cost of visa acquisition and air transportation to Ghana. Ghana is seen as a relatively expensive destination in terms of cost of travel. African Americans find it cheaper travelling to destinations in the Caribbean such as Jamaica which also offer most of the tourist products in Ghana. Even within Africa, it is cheaper travelling to some destinations like Egypt, South Africa and Kenya. International airlines charge between $1800 and $2000 from USA to Ghana, whereas the same airlines charge about $850 from USA to South Africa, which is a longer distance (Daily Graphic, 6th June, 2005). The difficulty of travel to Ghana is also evident in the difficulty of acquiring visas. The acquisition of visas to Ghana has been described as costly and inconvenient (Barney, 2002).

Second, there seem to be a general lack of understanding of the African American market. A more effective understanding of the African American market is necessary for destination marketers to develop the products and services necessary to effectively serve this growing market (Strom Thurmond Institute, 1998). According to Kotler (1982), 'the key to positioning is to identify the major attributes used by the target market to evaluate and choose among competitive offerings'. However, in Ghana, there is a general lack of understanding of the African American market, in terms of their motivations, tastes and preferences and this is evident in the development and promotion of tourism products targeted at this market as well as the attitudes of Ghanaians towards them. African Americans want the truth of the slave trade to be established, that is why they took exception to the restoration and preservation of the Cape Coast and Elmina castles in the early 1990s. This was under the Historic Preservation Project which involved the stabilization and restoration of the three World Heritage monuments, Cape Coast Castle, Elmina Castle and Fort St Jago (Bruner, 1996; Osei-Tutu, 2003). The fact is there has not been adequate research to obtain insights into the demographics, psychographics, motivations and interests of the African American market.

Also, African Americans want to be seen by Ghanaians as brothers and sisters rather than strangers. However, Ghanaians often refer to them as '*obroni*', a Twi word for whites (Barney, 2002; Bruner, 1996). African Americans in Ghana have also complained about the mistreatment and cold reception meted out to them by Ghanaians (Mensah, 2004; Zachary, 2001). There have also been accusations of name calling and hostilities among Africans and African Americans in the USA (Mwakikagile, 2005). This apparent lack of understanding can be attributed to the fact that Ghanaians and African Americans grew up in different environments, have different cultures and have formed different perceptions about each other.

Finally, another obstacle that needs to be corrected in order to effectively position Ghana on the minds of African Americans is the negative image of Africa among the African American community. Ankomah and Crompton (1990) cite negative images as one of the inhibitors of tourism development in sub-Saharan Africa. Due to centuries of separation and the influence of the western media, Africa is perceived in a negative light by African Americans: poverty, primitive, diseases, famine, HIV/AIDS and the jungle. According to Kromah (2002) western media practitioners present fatalistic and selectively crude images of Africa. The resultant effect is the negative images that Blacks in the Diaspora harbour about the continent and its people. Unfortunately, African countries including Ghana have not done enough to correct these negative images. In Ghana, the Ministry of Tourism is preoccupied with producing a number of products to attract African Americans to the country; PANAFEST, Emancipation Day, Slave Route Project and

Joseph Project among others. However, very little has been done to correct the image of the country. Image is very important in destination marketing because tourists evaluate and purchase place products based on perceptions and images formed on their minds.

Conclusion

In effect, the Ghanaian government is trying to make the country a destination of choice for African Americans; however, these efforts have been restricted to developments of new products and branding. There seem to be no clear understanding of the African American market and there is no consensus yet on what images and slogans to use. Though Ghana's stock of monuments and relics of the transatlantic slave trade as well as its relative stability could draw African Americans, the obstacles that could deter them from coming to the country such as the perceived negative image of Africa and the relatively high cost of travel to Ghana are not being addressed with the urgency they deserve.

Positioning Ghana as a preferred destination for African Americans should be informed by an analysis of the country as a tourist destination, other competing destinations like Nigeria, Senegal, Benin and South Africa as well as the African American market. This will enable the Ghana Tourist Board (GTB) to identify opportunities and challenges to effective positioning. This calls for further research into the motivations, characteristics and psychographics of the African American market, which will form the basis for further analysis of the market.

Ghana currently seems to lack a clear position on the African American market. There is however the need to clearly position the country along the lines of its shared cultural and historical heritage with African Americans, centred on the 'Slave Roots'. This should also reflect the slogans that are used to brand the country. Fortunately, some African Americans already perceive Ghana as a destination of black heritage (Abanga, 1999), and this should be positively reinforced as suggested by Botha et al. (1999), rather than committing other resources towards creating conflicting images like 'Golden experience' and 'Gateway to Africa'. Ghana is endowed with a diversity of historical resources like slave castles, relics, monuments and events more than most of the other countries connected with slavery and these could be harnessed to position the country in the Slave Roots just as Egypt has also capitalized on its pyramids, Pharoahs and other rich historical resources to effectively position itself as 'the cradle of civilisation'.

A major problem with positioning Ghana is the lack of uniformity in images projected by different organizations. Stakeholder consultations on the benefits to emphasize to African Americans in all external communications are very vital to the positioning process. Consultations between the GTB and the various stakeholders will help develop an appropriate positioning statement that will guide the marketing activities of all stakeholders at the destination. This will enable the destination to arrive at a single and relevant image. Such a meeting will also afford the GTB the opportunity to address some of the perceived positioning problems with the supply side of the destination such as the cost of travel to Ghana and the quality of services provided by tourism-related organizations. The GTB and other stakeholders will also agree on the benefits that Ghana offers that should be emphasized to African American travellers.

African Americans like to participate in cultural events, reunite with their kith and kin (family reunions) as well as trace their roots and learn more about the slave trade. Ghana can therefore emphasize benefits like its authentic and colourful festivals and celebrations, the hospitality of its people and the diversity of castles, forts, monuments and other relics connected with the slave trade. These will enable African Americans to reconnect with their ancestors and to embark on a healing process.

Finally, the need to embark on public relations (PR) campaign to address negative perception of the destination cannot be overemphasized. The negative image held about Africa of which Ghana is part, is a major constraint on positioning the country. Ghana is not insulated from the negative perceptions of West Africa as unsafe and insecure (Bernhadt and Eroglu, 2004). The solution to this problem is a deliberate PR campaign geared towards correcting this negative image and erroneous impressions associated with Ghana. The PR outfit could make use of media patronized by African Americans such as 'Ebony' and 'Black Entertainment Television'. The private sector could also support the GTB financially to undertake a common promotional campaign in the USA by setting up a promotional office in a major USA city like Atlanta, Washington or New York which will be tasked with marketing the country.

References

Aaker DA. and Shansby JG. 1982. Positioning your Product. *Business Horizons* May-June: 56-62.

Abanga JK. 1999. Developing an Effective International Marketing Strategy for Ghana's Tourism Industry: a Focus on the African-American Market. Unpublished MPhil thesis, University of Cape Coast.

Akyeampong OA. 1996.Tourism and Regional Development in Sub-Saharan Africa. A Case Study of Ghana's Central Region. PhD. dissertation, University of Stockholm.

Ankomah PK. and Crompton JL. 1990. Unrealized tourism potential; the case of Sub-Saharan Africa. *Tourism Management* March: 11-28.

Arnott, D.C. 1993. Positioning: redefining the concept. *Warwick Business School Research Papers* 8: 24.

Baloglu S. 1999. A path analytic model of visitation intention involving information sources, socio-psychological motivations, and destination image. *Journal of Travel & Tourism Marketing* 8 (3): 81- 90.

Barney S. 2002. *Gateway to West Africa?* (on-line): http//www.blackelectorate.com, retrieved 7 June 2005.

Bateson J. 1995. *Managing Services Marketing*. 3rd edn. London: Dryden Press.

Bernhadt K and Eroglu S. 2004. *Marketing Plan for Ghana's International Tourism*, GSU- TCDI Project, Georgia State University, Atlanta.

Blankson C. and Kalafatis SP. 1999. Issues and challenges in the positioning of service brands. A review, *Journal of Product and Brand Management* 8 (2): 106-118.

Botha C. Crompton J and Kim S. 1999. Developing a revised competitive strategy for Sun/Lost City, South Africa. *Journal of Travel Research* 37 (2): 341-52.

Bruner EM. 1996. Tourism in Ghana: the representation of slavery and the return of the black Diaspora. *American Anthropologist* 98 (2): 290-304.

Centre for Media Studies. 2003. *Reaching African Americans*. San Diego, CA: Ethnic Print Media Group.

Chacko H. 1997. Positioning a destination to gain a competitive edge. *Asia Pacific Journal of Tourism Research* 1 (2): 69-75.

Crompton JL. 1979. An assessment of the image of Mexico as a vacation destination. *Journal of Travel Research* 17: 18-23.

Crompton J, Fakeye P and Lue C. 1992. Positioning: the example of the Lower Rio Grande Valley in the winter long stay destination market. *Journal of Travel Research* **31** (fall): 20-26.

Curtin PD. 1969. *Atlantic Slave Trade – A Census.* University of Wisconsin Press: Madison.

Daily Graphic. 2005. PANAFEST in Danger. 6 June 2005.

Dann GMS. 1996. Tourists' Images of a destination: an alternative analysis. *Journal of Travel and Tourism Marketing* **5** (1/2): 41–55.

Dickerson DJ. 2006. Reunited and it feels so good, African-Americans search for their roots, *Opinion Journal of Wall Street Journal* (on-line): http://www.opinionjournal.com/taste/?id=110009264, retrieved 24 November 2006.

Echtner CM and Brent Ritchie JR. 2003. The meaning and measurement of destination image. *Journal of Tourism Studies* **14** (1): 37-48.

Eilat Y and Einav L. 2003. The determinants of international tourism: A three-dimensional panel data analysis. unpublished working paper.

Fakeye P and Crompton, JL. 1991. Image differences between prospective first-time and repeat visitors to the Lower Rio Grande Valley. *Journal of Travel Research* **30** (2): 10-16.

Ghana Investment Promotion Centre. 2005. *Profile of Ghana.* Available from: http://www.gipc.org.gh/IPA_Information.asp, accessed 5 July 2005.

Ghanaian Times. 2005. *Ghana Promises the World a Golden Experience,* 27 June 2005.

Greene SE. 1998. Developing the arts for development: perspectives on Ghana. *Africa Notes*: February 1998.

Gunn CA. 1972. *Vacationscape: Designing Tourist Regions.* Austin Bureau of Business Research: University of Texas.

Heath E and Wall G. 1992. *Marketing Tourism Destinations, a Strategic Planning Approach.* John Wiley and Sons: New York.

Ibrahim EE and Gill J. 2005. A positioning strategy for a tourist destination based on an analysis of customers' perceptions and satisfaction. *Marketing Intelligence and Planning* **23** (2): 172-188.

Jones JM. 2005. *American Vacation Habits.* The Gallup poll Tuesday briefing. **52** (2) Expanded Academic ASAP, Thomson Gale. Available from: http://www.galegroup.com/itx/infomark, accessed 24 November 2006.

Keller KL. 2003. *Strategic Brand Management: Building, Measuring, and Managing Brand Equity.* 2nd edn. Prentice Hall: Upper Saddle River, NJ.

Kim SS, Guo Y and Agrusa J. 2005. Preference and positioning analyses of overseas destinations by mainland Chinese outbound pleasure tourists. *Journal of Travel Research* **44**: 212-220.

Kotler P. 1982. *Marketing for Nonprofit Organizations.* 2nd edn. Prentice Hall: Englewood Cliffs, NJ.

Kotler P. 1997. *Marketing Management Analysis, Planning, Implementation and Control.* 9th edn. Prentice-Hall: Upper Saddle River, NJ.

Kotler P, Bowen J and Makens J. 2003. *Marketing for Hospitality and Tourism.* 3rd edn. Prentice Hall: Englewood Cliffs, NJ.

Kotler P, Haider DH, and Irving R. 1993. *Marketing Places: Attracting Investment, Industry and Tourism to Cities, States and Nations*. Free Press: New York.

Kromah GV. 2002. Africa in the Western media, cycle of contra-positives and selective perceptions. A paper presented at University of Indiana, Bloomington African Studies Program, Bloomington. 24 April 2004.

Lake O. 1995. Toward a pan-African identity: Diasporas African repatriates in Ghana. *Anthropological Quarterly* **68** (1): 21-36.

Levy B. and Matos R. 2002. Transforming the tourist image of Geneva from a leisure to business destination and its cultural implications. In *City Tourism*, Wober KW (ed.). Springer-Verlag: New York; 241-250.

Magazine Publishers of America. 2004. *African American Market Profile*. New York.

Mensah I. 2004. Marketing Ghana as a Mecca for the African-American tourist. Ghanaweb feature article. Available from: http://www.modernghana.com/news/114445/1/marketingghanaasameccafortheafricanamerica.html.

Midwest Universities Consortium for International Activities. 1995. *Conservation of Slave Monuments and the Development of Cultural Tourism*. The Slave Route Project Conference, Accra, 3–4 April 1995.

Mill CR, Morrison AM. 2002. *The Tourism System*. 4 edn. Kendall/Hunt Publishing: Iowa.

Ministry of Tourism and Modernization of the Capital City. 2003. *Ghana Tourism Strategy 2003-2007*, MOTMCC, Republic of Ghana, Accra.

Morgan M. 1996. *Marketing for Leisure and Tourism*. Prentice Hall: Harlow

Mwakikagile G. 2005. *Relations between Africans and African Americans: Misconceptions, Myths and Realities*. National Academic Press: Grand Rapids, MI.

Osei-Tutu B. 2003. Monuments and the expression of historical reality: African-Americans and Ghana's slave castles on a transnational landscape. Paper presented at the Fifth World Archaeological Congress, Washington, DC, 21-26 June 2003.

Pike S, Ryan C. 2004. Destination positioning analysis through a comparison of cognitive, affective and conative perceptions. *Journal of Travel Research* **42**: 333-342.

Perbi A. 1995. The slave trade and slave routes in Ghana, The Slave Route Project Conference, Accra, 3–4 April 1995.

Power J, Haberlin D, Foley A, Frampton A. 2005. Developing the positioning of the Irish rural tourism product, the role of image and market focus, a paper presented at the Tourism and Hospitality Research in Ireland, Exploring issues conference, University of Ulster, 14-15 June 2005.

Reich AZ. 2001. Determining a firm's linear market position: In search of an effective methodology. *Journal of Hospitality & Tourism Research* **25** (2):159-172.

Ries A and Trout J. 2001. *Positioning: The Battle of Your Mind*. McGraw Hill: New York.

Rigger W. 1995. *Positioning in Theory and Practice: Towards a Research Agenda*, 24th EMAC Conference Proceedings, 1, 16–19 May, ESSEC, France, 991-1009.

Ryglova K. and Turcinkova J. 2004. *Image as an Important Factor of Destination Management*. Working Papers of the Finnish Forest Research Institute 2 July 2005.

Santana Pinho P. 2008. African American roots tourism in Brazil. *Latin American* Perspectives **35** (3): 70-86.

Sarma MK. 2003. Towards positioning a tourist destination, a study of North East India. *ASEAN Journal on Travel and Tourism* **2** (2): 104-117.

Saunders DJ. 2004. *Will Africa Become the Tourism Destination of the Future for African-American Travellers and Investors?* Available from: http://www.africa-ata.org/african_americans.htm. [Accessed on 5 October 2005].

Soul of America. 2004. Black travellers similar to average, yet key differences exist Available at: http:/www.soulofamerica.com/travel/dem_travel.html, retrieved on 24 April 2005.

Strom Thurmond Institute. 1998. *African American Travellers*. Clemson University.

US Census Bureau. 2002. *The Black Population in the United States*. March 2002. Washington DC, issued April 2003.

Tapachai N and Waryszak R. 2000. An examination of the role of beneficial image in tourist destination selection. *Journal of Travel Research* **39** (1): 37–44.

Vargus ID. 2002. More than a picnic: African American family reunions. The Emory Centre for Myth and Ritual in American Life Working Paper No. 21, September 2002. Available at: http:/www.marial.emory.edu/pdfs/vargus022-03.pdf, accessed 15 July, 2006.

Wellner AS. 2003. Black consumers: By the numbers. *American Demographics Forecast* **23**: 1-3.

Witt SF and Moutinho L. 1995. *Tourism Marketing and Management Handbook*. Prentice-Hall: Harlow

Woodside AG. 1982. Positioning a province using traveller research. *Journal of Travel Research* **20** (Winter): 2-6.

World Travel and Tourism Council. 2004. *Ghana Travel and Tourism Forging Ahead*. WTTC: London.

Wyllie RW. 1990. *Ghana Tourism- Prospects and Possibilities*. Akan Torede: Accra.

Zachary P. 2001. Tangled roots: for African-Americans in Ghana, the grass isn't always greener. *Wall Street Journal*, March 14.

18 Sports Tourism and Motorsports – an Exploration

Bruce Braham, Bournemouth University, UK

Introduction

Sport enriches the quality of tourists' experience (Harrison-Hill and Chalip, 2005) and has become a vital component in the marketing mix for many tourist destinations (Getz, 1998; Gibson, 1998c). Such tourism is generated during the event itself whilst also enhancing the destination's image with added exposure through news and advertising media coverage. In many cases the media coverage helps to encourage additional visits throughout the year (Dwyer et al., 2000). Media exposure on television, and through both event and destination advertising, affect dimensions of the destination's image. Research has shown that the event media coverage must have a positive effect on the viewer's image of the destination to have a positive effect on long-term tourist visits (Chalip et al., 2003).

But who is included in the definition of the sport tourist? Discussion surrounds whether just professional sports people should be included and over the position that recreational leisure activities occupy (Hall, 1992). Also, are sport tourists solely the active participants or are they just the spectators? (Glyptis, 1991). In practice a widely accepted definition of sport tourism is that it is 'leisure based travel that takes individuals temporarily outside of their home communities to participate in physical activities, to watch physical activities or to venerate attractions associated with physical activities' (Gibson, 1998c). It is therefore a much more inclusive term than has necessarily always been appreciated.

Sports events are an element of event tourism which was identified as the fastest growing component of the leisure travel market towards the end of the 20th century (Shifflet and Bhatia, 1999). Sports events have therefore become effective in the economic development mix of destinations including both cities and regions (Burgan and Mules, 2001; Chalip and McGuirty, 2004).

It has been said that the fundamental psychological theory of a schema or 'a cognitive representation of expectations about a domain' applies where both the destination itself and the sports event are domains (Chalip and Costa, 2005). The destination's image is a key factor in tourist development (Hunt, 1975) and plays a role in the consumer's choice (Dichter, 1985). The host destination's image, as projected through advertising and the sport event media, has in practice been found to be 'significantly related to intention to visit' (Chalip et al., 2003).

> The increasing demand for accountability requires event organisers and destination marketers to demonstrate that their events add value to the life of the community in which they are held. The more effectively that each event is built in to the marketing strategy and communications mix of the host community, the more value the event can be expected to provide, and the more viable it consequently becomes.
>
> (Chalip et al., 2003)

So powerful are the associations of destinations with events that the latter can overcome the former. For example, the Loire valley town of Le Mans is picturesque in its own right but the 24 Hours of Le Mans motor race has become better known worldwide than the place itself (Pryor and Brodie, 1998). Similarly, despite many other industrial and sporting activities, 'throughout the world, Indianapolis is most recognized as the racing capital of the world and home of the Indianapolis 500' motor race (Klacik and Cook, 2004).

In 2002 the 1.6 million overseas visitors to the UK who either watched a sporting event or participated in amateur sport spent £1.1 billion during their stay, some 9% of the total spending of all overseas visitors to the UK in 2002 of £11.7 billion. The average spend per visit was £674, considerably higher than the average for all overseas visitors to the UK in 2002 of £481. They spent less per day but stayed nearly twice as long as the average overseas visitor to the UK (Visit Britain, 2002)

Motorsport's Heritage

The sophisticated and dynamic harnessing of competing machines on the 21st century race tracks of the world by global brand managers has evolved from the time the internal combustion engine was first invented. The brands represented by the brand managers are there to compete in front of an audience. Research shows that the sponsors of motorsport aim to position and to create a favourable impression of their brand whilst hoping to generate sales through these activities (Grant-Braham, 2009).

The competitive nature of the *homo sapiens* has previously been expressed through athletics, the racing of horses and chariots as well as sail and steam powered competitions prior to the internal combustion engine's discovery. In the future, alternative fuels ranging from solar to hydrogen will continue to provide means of transport and no doubt there will be a demand to make such technologies compete against each other as progress continues. Motorsport will continue to be used as a live laboratory to test the vehicles and their propulsion systems of the future.

Once the internal combustion engine had been created the vehicles into which it was to be implanted, following the capitalist model, needed to be marketed. The early vehicle manufacturers identified a desire to promote their primitive machines as being both reliable and fast.

At an early stage, competitive events were organized specifically to emphasize the elements of reliability and speed of a vehicle within the marketing mix. The media, then in print form, not only reported such events but also used them to promote their circulations, thus becoming some of the sport's first title sponsors. Their readership became on off-site audience for the events whilst large crowds were the curious on-site audience when early competitions took place on public roads.

As vehicles evolved, the manufacturers realized the benefits of association with motorsport. Tyre, oil and fuel suppliers started to use association with competition vehicles as a validation for their products. As media interest in competitive motorsport increased and a wider audience was generated, marketing refined too. The benefits of association became apparent to brands that had no obvious link to motoring. The impact of television coverage and its global reach would bring multinational brands into the sponsorship equation, which is the historical point which has currently been reached.

Various forms of sponsorship have been embedded within motorsport from its earliest days with many of those early participants still represented today. From outside the

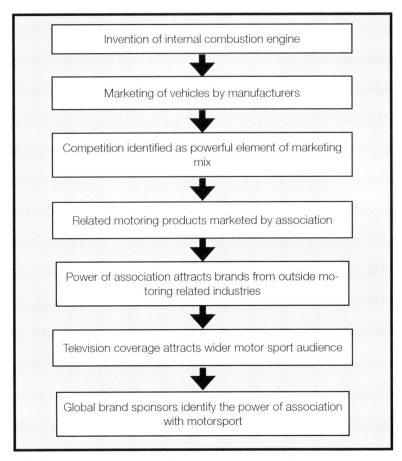

Figure 18.1: The evolution of commercial sponsorship in motorsport

motoring related industries there have always been organisations willing to associate with hallmark events. In motorsport, tourism has been a motivation for those organising motorsport events and such associations are illustrated in Figure 18.2. Tourism has been involved with motorsport for 107 years.

Tourism-related Motorsport Sponsorship

Tourism and motorsport events have been firmly linked since the start of the 20th century (Figure 18.2). However, it is only comparatively recently that the academic interest in the field of sport tourism has developed (Delpy, 1998; Gammon and Robinson, 1997; Gibson, 1998a, 1998b; Standeven and De Knop, 1999).

Studies have in the main concentrated on the economic effects of individual sports on host regions in terms of income generation and tourism potential (Sofield and Sivan, 1994; Turco, 1998). More specifically, reports published by UK Sport outline the importance of sport events in the UK, especially as income generators from tourism expenditure (UK Sport, 1998a, 1998b, 1999). These studies suggest that there are clear economic benefits from the attraction of sport events that have tourism potential. It is also clear that in most sports it is not only the spectators that may be classed as tourists

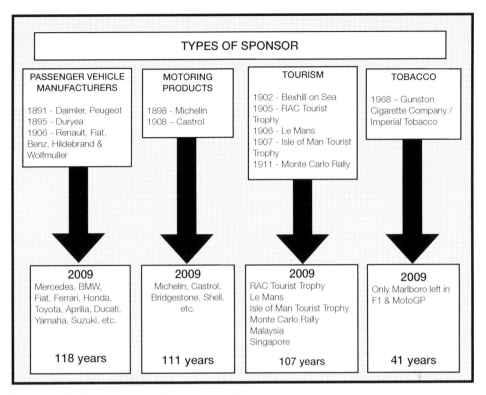

TYPES OF SPONSOR

PASSENGER VEHICLE MANUFACTURERS	MOTORING PRODUCTS	TOURISM	TOBACCO
1891 - Daimler, Peugeot 1895 - Duryea 1906 - Renault, Fiat, Benz, Hildebrand & Wolfmuller	1898 - Michelin 1908 – Castrol	1902 - Bexhill on Sea 1905 - RAC Tourist Trophy 1906 - Le Mans 1907 - Isle of Man Tourist Trophy 1911 - Monte Carlo Rally	1968 – Gunston Cigarette Company / Imperial Tobacco
2009 Mercedes, BMW, Fiat, Ferrari, Honda, Toyota, Aprilia, Ducati, Yamaha, Suzuki, etc. **118 years**	**2009** Michelin, Castrol, Bridgestone, Shell, etc. **111 years**	**2009** RAC Tourist Trophy Le Mans Isle of Man Tourist Trophy Monte Carlo Rally Malaysia Singapore **107 years**	**2009** Only Marlboro left in F1 & MotoGP **41 years**

Figure 18.2: The duration of different types of motorsport sponsorship

but also the competitors. This can be seen to include drivers, support teams, mechanics, marshals and so on. As Gibson suggests, there are three major types of sport tourism: nostalgia sport tourism, active sport tourism and event sport tourism (Gibson, 1998b), and motorsport may be seen as a sport where this model is appropriate.

In practice, as far back as 1902, the 8th Earl De La Warr organised the first automobile racing on British soil, 'as part of a campaign to promote Bexhill-on-Sea as a fashionable new resort'. This is the first identified reference to the concept of motorsport being used as a boost to a local economy thanks to the spectators [tourists] so attracted. The attraction of the sport to those in the media was demonstrated by the entry list which included the Mercedes of Lord Northcliffe (Alfred Harmsworth) the founder of the *Daily Mail* newspaper. Harmsworth was known for using his newspapers to promote inventions such as motorcycles, motor cars and aircraft. In Bexhill-on-Sea, 'the local hotels and boarding houses were packed with the curious who had come to witness the spectacle of motor cars racing at speeds in excess of 50mph when the speed limit of the day was a mere 12mph'. The success of the meeting encouraged the Earl De La Warr to make Bexhill the British venue for motor racing until the Brooklands circuit opened in 1907 (Bexhill-on-Sea, 2005) on part of Lord Northcliffe's estate near Weybridge.

The two longest running events for cars and bikes in the UK have both specifically used the word 'Tourist'. Both competitions, which are still running in 2009, originated in the Isle of Man. The first RAC Tourist Trophy to be held for cars was in 1905 and the even more famous Isle of Man TT (Tourist Trophy) for motorcycles in 1907. The former Tourist Trophy is now the feature race at the Goodwood Revival race meeting which attracted 116,000 spectators in 2007 considerably boosting the West Sussex economy. The Isle of Man TT, meanwhile, is still a major element of the Manx tourism offer. It is today co-ordinated by the Isle of Man's Department of Tourism and Leisure (DTL).

Sponsorship of the 1906 Le Mans GP came partly from the town of Le Mans (FIA, 2004a) which had at an early stage recognized the tourism benefits of an association with such a hallmark event:

> Special trains from all over the continent and many private cars conveyed hordes of enthusiasts to the area. Le Mans was en fete for days before the midweek race. Hotels and inns were booked solid for sixty miles around.

> (F1 Racing, 2006a)

Similarly, the Monte Carlo Rally of 1911 was devised as a rival attraction to Nice carnival in the hope of attracting wealthy car owners who might stay for the winter in a beneficial climate (FIA, 2004b). In northern France, Dieppe had been keen to hold the Grands Prix de l'ACF in 1907, 1908 and 1912. The town of Dieppe 'had bid the ACF quite a few thousand pounds to hold the GP there as they hoped for and got quite a flock of visitors for four or five days'. The town's hotels were full and the casino and cafes well frequented (Darling, 2006). Such events had, and still have, an economic impact on their host cities by generating employment opportunities and fan spending (McDaniel and Mason, 1999).

By 2006 the costs of hosting a F1 event had become so high that governments of host countries were willing to pay in order to advertise their nation for prestige and tourism benefits (F1 Racing, 2006b). Sylt (2007) revealed that street-circuits are excellent for tourism related motorsports events because, 'they focus viewers' eyes on the host city and its monuments, making it an ideal magnet for tourism'. One Australian city that has taken advantage of this is Surfers Paradise, near Brisbane, which has until recently hosted a Champ Car World Series Race which was described as, 'an indelible part of the Gold Coast tourism landscape' (*The Paddock*, 2007b). Another example is the Malaysian Government's support of Singapore, which wanted a F1 race to promote itself as 'Asia's party town' and to 'strengthen its allure and promote its metamorphosis into the gambling capital of South East Asia' (Youson, 2006). Indeed the Malaysian Prime Minister confirmed this when he said that F1, 'has always been a key tool for the government in enhancing the country's image and in the promotion of Malaysia as a leading international tourist destination' (Badawi, 2007). In Singapore, the Tourism Board, Land Transport Authority and the Singapore Sports Council worked closely with the race promoter. The CEO of Singapore's Tourist Board, Lim Neo Chian, budgeted for the race to generate incremental tourism receipts of S$100 million annually (*The Paddock*, 2007a). 'The event will give a strong boost to our tourism sector', he said, 'such as hotel, food and beverage, retail, entertainment and even private wealth management companies benefiting from it.' In leveraging the race there was to be an extensive media campaign covering television, print, new media, outdoor advertising and motorsports-related media which would pitch Singapore as 'The Monaco of the East' (Sport Business International, 2007).

Circuit racing is not alone in using motorsports events to encourage tourism. The Abu Dhabi Tourism Authority has recently become the first 'official destination partner' of the World Rally Championship. The relationship is intended to encourage travellers to visit Abu Dhabi (*The Paddock*, 2007c).

Specific Examples of Motorsport Tourism

UK - British F1 Grand Prix

A 2002 economic impact survey of the British F1 Grand Prix at Silverstone (MIA, 2003) concluded that as a major event it had a substantial tangible impact on the local economy around Silverstone. An estimated expenditure of £34.7 million was attributed to the event as were 1150 UK FTE jobs. UK income, though, was only calculated at £17.2 million. The significant gap between estimates of expenditure and income was suggested to be because a substantial proportion – maybe as much as 50% – of expenditure 'leaks out of the UK economy'. This was explained by the international nature of the event whilst also reflecting the conservative multipliers used in the study, especially at the UK level.

The hypothesis of the British Grand Prix not occurring was addressed and it was felt that, 'much of this expenditure might be expected to be transferred elsewhere within the UK economy, as people spent money on other forms of entertainment and on other items'.

However, the importance of the event in attracting, 'significant numbers of international visitors who would not otherwise visit the UK' was emphasized. The research indicated that the impacts of teams and overseas visitors were estimated to account for around 20% of the overall economic impact – expenditure additional to the UK economy.

The survey showed that 44% of overseas visitors in the sample indicated that they had come to the UK especially to see the F1 Grand Prix with most spending a significant length of time in the UK – the average being 13 nights. As a result, significant levels of expenditure were recorded. Each overseas visitor spent £414 in total in the UK with £131 of that being on-site, £118 off-site and £165 elsewhere in the UK. On-site expenditures were high relative to the sample as a whole as many overseas visitors spent large sums of money on merchandise.

The survey also identified that the British F1 Grand Prix has significant 'additional intangible benefits for the UK'.

USA – Indianapolis

Joie Chitwood, senior vice president business affairs for Indianapolis Motor Speedway (IMS),says that his circuit's three main events (Indianapolis 500, Brickyard 400 and United States Grand Prix) provided US$727 million dollars (annually) to the economy of Indianapolis. Racetracks are special, he said because they draw tourists from all over the country – and the world. 'What racetracks really do', he said, 'is draw people from at least 300 miles away. What motorsports does is it brings people to town, and it's that dollar that comes from outside the community that provides the greatest impact' (IMS, 2004).

Malaysian – F1 Grand Prix

The Malaysian Grand Prix, held at the Sepang circuit for the first time in 1999, was purposely created to make an economic impact on Malaysia. The presence of a world class event has primarily been used to create Malaysian brand awareness by projecting the country internationally. Whilst local technology and skills transfer is aided by the race which provides the opportunity to link intensive research and development through an associated training ground for engineers –from local companies such as Proton and Petronas – the race enables the tourism industry to promote Malaysian tourist spots, hospitality, food and beverage outlets, retail, transportation and entertainment. The race therefore not only plays a role in promoting Malaysia, but it also generates income for the country (Mahathir, 2008).

A research study on the economic impact of the Petronas Malaysian Grand Prix (PMGP) was undertaken by the Faculty of Economics and Administration of Malaya University in 2005 which found that:

♦   Average total expenditure for year 2004 and 2005 is RM285m.

♦   Spending by foreign spectators for each year exceeded RM139m.

♦   Spending by local spectators for each year exceeded RM88m.

♦   Each year the PMGP attracts more than 80,000 spectators.

♦   On average 34% of the PMGP spectators are international spectators.

♦   Each year the PMGP race is watched by 580 million TV viewers and it is broadcast in 184 territories.

(Source: Mahathir, 2008)

In Malaysia each of the eleven F1 teams competing brings between 150 and 200 people, all of whom are defined as potential tourists. The Malaysian government finds that an annual sporting event such as F1 is more beneficial to them in tourist terms than a one-off event such as the Commonwealth Games and to be able to generate as much as RM285m for the country from a single weekend sporting event is regarded as 'phenomenal' (Mahathir, 2008).

The total number of spectators for the Malaysian Grand Prix and the percentage of ticket sales by Continent are shown in Table 18.1. The figures illustrate that whilst the total on-site audience has steadily risen over the years the proportion of overseas spectators – who should be regarded as tourists – has increased too. In 2006 almost exactly half of the on-site audience was from outside Malaysia. The total number of individual 'tourist' spectators on-site would therefore have been 53,278. There is also a strong loyalty for the event as is demonstrated in Table 18.2 where the figures for overseas tourists from outside Malaysia intending to re-visit are impressive.

Table 18.1: Total spectators for Malaysian F1 Grand Prix

	2003	2004	2005	2006	2007
Total Spectators	101,485	84,010	106,422	107,634	115,794
Europe (%)	6.0	11.0	10.0	10.75	9.23
South East Asia (%)	11.3	25.9	16.5	29.5	14.3
Asia (%)	2.3	4.87	5.01	7.22	4.2
Others (South Africa, America, Canada) (%)	1.3	2.64	2.49	2.03	2.07
Malaysia	80.1	55.59	66.0	50.5	70.2
TOTAL (%)	100	100	100	100	100

(Source: Mahathir, 2008)

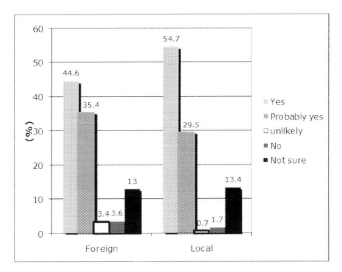

Table 18.2: Percentage distribution of foreign and local spectators by intention to attend future PMGP

Australia – Surfers Paradise

The organizers of the Gold Coast IndyCar race have made the most of their event for tourists by organising subsidiary events to increase the size of their market, the length of the event and the economic and media impacts as recommended in theory by Jago et al (2003). The race is preceded by 'The Indy Carnival' which is a festival lasting a week and which comprises both social and other racing events (Chalip and Costa, 2005). Such an approach addressed the challenge set by previous academic research which suggested that the organizers of sport event tourism should bundle event elements with the host destination's attractions. It was suggested that a mixed bundling strategy should include appropriate event elements that, 'support the subculture of the sport, as well as complementary cultural events' (Chalip and McGuirty, 2004). The illustration used was of the Gold Coast Marathon thereby illustrating that the expertise was already available in the locale to the organizers of the Gold Coast Indy Car race.

The organisers of the 2006 event revealed that that it was then Australia's largest motorsport festival with over 312,000 spectators attending over the four days, slightly less than 2005's record of 316,459. The Queensland event was then bigger than the F1 Grand Prix held in Melbourne, which attracted about 300,000 (Travelmole.com, 2006).

Research confirm the impact of the event, which had been in existence for 16 years, generated in the region of A\$70 million for the Queensland economy, making it the State's most lucrative tourism event. Queensland's Premier, Peter Beattie approved an investment of \$12 million a year into the event (Travelmole.com, 2006).

It is considered that the inclusion of a V8 Supercar round in the event has also been significant in this Queensland success story (Travelmole.com, 2006).

UK – Network Q Rally

An economic impact study of the 1998 Network Q Rally of Great Britain (Lilley and DeFranco, 1999), part of the then World Rally Championship (WRC), yielded £11.1 million for the local economies with £6.7 million or 60% of it from outside the impact area. The businesses that benefited most were those which were part of the tourism industry:

♦ local hotels, motels, and campgrounds – £2.1 million;
♦ local eating and drinking establishments – £3.3 million;
♦ local retail stores – £2.6 million;
♦ local service businesses in transportation – £2.2 million
♦ the special stages and their attendant facilities – £0.9 million.

Many local businesses, such as hotels, eagerly anticipated 100% volume revenues/sales during the November rally week when there would otherwise be a lull in the total number of visitors.

It was estimated that an additional £17 million was stimulated in subsequent tourist spending in the rally area due to the television coverage of the event. The television coverage was seen as, 'a force for converting television viewers into post-Rally tourists to the Wales area' and to encourage tourists to make, 'Wales their destination because they were stimulated by the area scenes and verbal mentions carried on Rally television coverage'.

The overall promotion of the Network Q Rally to tourists was organized to achieve four main aims:

♦ Bringing in outside money
♦ Bringing in new visitors
♦ Enabling cross-promotion of the area for repeat rally visitors and non-rally visitors
♦ Filling hotels

Post-event analysis established that 'Rally television coverage is uniquely valuable to the areas hosting the rally'. The coverage, 'is uniquely suited to making the host areas attractive tourist destination points and World Championship Rally television coverage in particular generates economically significant tourist spending subsequent to the Rally'.

Thus the television coverage of a premier rally event provides the host areas with extensive television coverage of the route areas as tourist destination points. For rural, mountainous and small-town areas of Wales, the rally coverage provides numerous minutes of expensive television promotion that the Wales Tourist Board could not justify as a single buy in the commercial television advertising market.

The research quantified the value of the television coverage as if the Wales Tourist Board had bought that amount of time. Such calculations, which are standard in establishing the cost-effectiveness of motorsport (Grant-Braham, 2009), concluded that the total value to Wales as an ultimate tourist destination of Rally Q television converge was £575,000.

EIRE – Rallye Ireland

Research conducted by the University of Ulster on the 2008 Rally Ireland WRC established that the additional spending generated by the event was worth €48 million (£36 million) to the economy. More than 250,000 spectators attended the cross-border event making it the largest sporting event ever hosted on the island of Ireland.

Of those attending, 7% were from overseas with the average fan mainly being a young adult male who attended with a group of friends. The research also revealed the mean spend per spectator for their trip was €320.78 (RTE, 2008).

USA – North Carolina

In the state of North Carolina in the USA, the motorsport effects on travel and tourism are taken very seriously. Motorsport is an industry that in 2005 generated US$251,898,111 from tourism for North Carolina (Connaughton and Masden, 2006) and the relevant state authorities have drawn up a specific action plan to encourage such spending. The Travel and Tourism Division of North Carolina's Department of Commerce has been recommended to produce a comprehensive motorsports tourism guide whilst also developing a logo and slogan to be branded over time as synonymous with North Carolina motorsports. Each of the state's welcome centres has been asked to provide a kiosk where promotional materials on motorsports tourism opportunities are available. The State's General Assembly was also asked to either make appropriations or to allow for grants to help maintain North Carolina's motorsports museums and also to find funds to support events, provide sanctioning fees and promotional costs for new racing events (UNC, 2004).

Return on Investment

Much has been made of the importance to local and national economies of hallmark motorsport events. Table 18.3 shows the situation where the 2007 F1 was concerned and the investment made by governments and associated organizations. In some case the perceived return on investment from a government viewpoint is very favourable.

Conclusion

Motorsport events have generated sport tourism for more than a hundred years and continue to do so.

The various economic impact studies quoted in this chapter illustrate the importance of tourism to the viability of hallmark motorsport events. The importance of tourism is increasing as some of the events would not take place without government subsidy – largely attracted on the back of the income generated by inward tourism. Certainly in F1, the promotion of events is increasingly being undertaken under the auspices of government finances although a caution over the future of motorsport comes from Saward (2008) who says that public money is hard to find in countries, 'where the public is allowed a voice'.

Many of the tourism benefits of motorsport events discussed in the various economic impact studies have implied that tourists are individuals from overseas. Whilst the figures certainly back the finding that motorsport events do generate impressive overseas tourist numbers this should not obscure the local tourism market. Visitors from within the host country too may travel considerable distances. The work at Indianapolis in the USA talks about bringing money in from 'outside the community' which is important to recognize. Sport tourists in this case are being perceived as people from outside Indianapolis whether in the USA or not. Closer to home, for example, the Network Q Rally was

Table 18.3: Government contributions to and returns on the 2007 Formula 1 Grands Prix (Note: All values are US$.)

Race	Circuit	Government Spending 2007	Type of Government Assistance	Local Economic Impact 2007	Return on Investment (i)	Circuit Owner
Japanese GP	Juji International Speedway	$4m	Local government	$70m	1750% ($17.5m)	93.4% Toyota, 4% Mitsubishi Estate, 2.6% Taisei Corporation
Monaco GP	Circuit de Monaco	$7m	National government	$120m	1714% ($17.1m)	Government (ii) (Public roads)
French GP	Circuit de Nevers de Magny-Cours	$8m	Local government	$100m	1250% ($12.5m)	Government (ii) (Regonal Conseil de la Nievre)
Bahrain GP	Bahrain International Circuit	$45m	National government	$395m	878% ($8.8m)	Government (ii)
Spanish GP	Circuit de Catalunya, Barcelona	$15m	Local government	$125m	833% ($8.3m)	Real Automovil Club de Catalunya
Belgian GP	Spa-Francorchamps	$4m	Local government	$25m	625% ($6.3m)	Walloon regional government (ii)
Turkish GP	Istanbul Park	$30m	National and local government	$150m	500% ($5m)	Formula One Group
Hungarian GP	Hungaroring	$14m	National government	$65m	464% ($4.6m)	66% government (ii), 34% privately owned
Australian GP	Albert Park, Melbourne	$33m	Local government	$125m	379% ($3.8m)	Government (ii) (Public Parkland)
Canadian GP	Circuit Gilles Villeneuve, Montreal	$20m	National and local government	$70m	350% ($3.5m)	Government (ii) (Public parkland)
Chinese GP	Shanghai International Circuit	$40m	National and local government	$120m	313% ($3.1m)	Government (ii)
Malaysian GP	Sepang International Circuit	$40m	National government	$125m	313% ($3.1m)	Malaysia Airport Holdings Bhd (iii)
European GP	Nurburgring	$15m	Local government	$25m	167% ($1.7m)	Government (ii) (90% Rhineland Palatinate, 10% Landkreis Ahrweiler)
United States GP	Indianapolis Motor Speedway	0	None	$100m (iv)	n/a	George family
British GP	Slverstone Grand Prix Circuit	0	None (local government funds some circuit improvements)	$60m (iv)	n/a	British Racing Drivers Club
Italian GP	Autodromo Nazionale do Monza	0	None (local government funds some circuit improvements)	$55m (iv)	n/a	Government (ii) (municipalities of Monza and Milan)
Brazilian GP	Interlagos, Sao Paulo	0	None (local government funds some circuit improvements)	$100m (iv)	n/a	Government (ii)
TOTAL		$275m		$1520m		

(i)   Figures in brackets denote dollars invested in the local area because of the race, per million dollars invested in the race by the government

(ii)   Denotes local and/or national government ownership and races held on public roads or parkland.

(iii) Ownership transferred in August 2007 to Khazan Nasional, the state investment agency

(iv)   Not included in total for the purpose of calculating ROI, since no investment was made by the national government. The total including the local economic impact of Grands Prix where governments make no investment is $1835m.

(Source: (www.formulamoney.com, 2008)

largely held in Wales, a country steeped in rallying tradition. Would the very many sport tourists who came from England be regarded as 'overseas' tourists within the definitions applied within some impact studies?

To encourage the motorsport tourist, whilst also helping them to make the decision to stay longer, it is suggested that the host community organize supplementary events in the form of a festival or a carnival along the successful lines applied by the Queensland event organizers.

In practice the sport tourist has always been the target of the organizers of hallmark motorsport events and in certain parts of motorsport, notably F1, this is increasingly becoming the major justification.

References

Badawi D. 2007. Malaysian PM wants GP future secured. Available from: http://www.autosport.com, accessed 18 January 2007.

Bexhill-on-Sea. 2005. Welcome to Bexhill-on-Sea, Motor Racing History. Available from: http://www.bexhill-on-sea.org/bexhillmotorracing.php, accessed 19 January 2005.

Burgan B, Mules T. 2001. Reconciling cost–benefit and economic impact assessment for event tourism. *Tourism Economics* 7: 321–330.

Chalip L, Costa CA. 2005. Sport event tourism and the destination brand: towards a general theory. *Sport in Society* 8 (2): 218–237.

Chalip L, McGuirty J. 2004. Bundling sport events with the host destination. *Journal of Sport Tourism* 9 (3): 267–282.

Chalip L, Green BC, Hill B. 2003. Effects of sport event media on destination image and intention to visit. *Journal of Sport Management* 17: 214-234.

Connaughton JE, Madsen RA. 2006. The economic impact and occupational analysis of the North Carolina Motorsports Industry for 2005. Available from: http://www.motorsportsnc.org/docs/Updated%20Motorsports%20EI%20Study.pdf, accessed 4 January 2009.

Dalaks V, Madrigal R, Anderson, KL. 2004. 'We are number one!' The phenomenon of basking-in-reflected-glory and its implications for sports marketing. In *Sports Marketing and the Psychology of Marketing Communications*, Kahle LR, Riley C, eds. Lawrence Erlbaum Associates: Mahwah, NJ; 61–99.

Darling G. 2006. In the paddock of pioneers. *Motor Sport* **LXXXII** (1): 70–73.

Delpy L. 1998 An overview of sport tourism: building towards a dimensional framework. *Journal of Vacation Marketing* 4 (1): 23-38.

Dichter E. 1985. What is an image? *Journal of Consumer Choice* 13 (4): 455–472.

Dwyer L, Mellor R, Mistilis N, Mules, T. 2000. A framework for assessing 'tangible' and 'intangible' impacts of events and conventions. *Event Management* 6: 175 –189.

Fairley SD. 2003. In search of relived social experience: group-based nostalgia sport tourism. *Journal of Sport Management* 17 (3): 284–304.

FIA. 2004a. 'Centenary Book' page 31. http://www.fia.com/mediacentre/100_Years/fia_centenary.html# , accessed 18 July 2005.

FIA. 2004b. 'Centenary Book' page 35. http://www.fia.com/mediacentre/100_Years/fia_centenary.html#, accessed 18 July 2005.

F1 Racing. 2006a. *'High Speed Sign Language'* February: 24–25.

F1 Racing. 2006b. *'Expose: Spa out: first of many?'* March: 20–21.

Formulamoney.Com. 2008. The 500 Club. *The Paddock* **3** (8): 34–36.

Gammon S, Robinson T. 1997. Sport and tourism: a conceptual framework. *Journal of Sports Tourism* **4** (3).

Getz D. 1998. Trends, strategies, and issues in sport-event tourism. *Sport Marketing Quarterly* **7** (2): 8–13.

Gibson H. 1998a. Active sport tourism: Who participates? *Leisure Studies* **17**: 155–170.

Gibson H. 1998b. The wide world of sport tourism. *Parks and Recreation* **33** (9): 108–115.

Gibson H. 1998c. Sport tourism: A critical analysis of research. *Sport Management Review* **1** (1).

Glyptis SA. 1991. Sport and tourism. In *Progress in Tourism, Recreation and Hospitality*. Cooper C. (ed.). Wiley: New York; 165-183.

Grant-Braham B. 2009. An investigation into motorsport sponsorship: a comparative analysis of two and four wheeled sponsorship. PhD thesis: Bournemouth University.

Hall CM. 1992. *Hallmark Tourist Events*. Bellhaven Press: London.

Harrison-Hill T, Chalip L. 2005. Marketing sport tourism: Creating synergy between sport and destination. *Sport in Society* **8** (2): 302–320.

Hill B. 2003. Effects of sport event media on destination image and intention to visit. *Journal of Sport Management* **17**: 214–234.

Hunt J. 1975. Image as a factor in tourism development. *Journal of Travel Research* **13** (3): –7.

IMS. 2004. Motorsports workshops highlight speedway's huge economic impact. Indianapolis Motor Speedway. Available from: http://www.indianapolismotorspeedway.com/news/3826/Motorsports_Workshops_Highlight_Speedway's_Huge_Economic_Impact, accessed 24 June 2008.

Jago L, Chalip L, Brown G, Mules T, Ali S. 2003. Building events into destination branding: Insights from experts. *Event Management* **8** (1): 3–14.

Klacik D, Cook T. 2004. *Motorsports Industry in the Indianapolis Region*. Center for Urban Policy and The Environment, Indiana University – Purdue University: Idianapolis.

Lilley III W, DeFranco LJ. 1999. The economic impact of the Network Q Rally of Great Britain – 1998, FIA and MSA. Available from: http://www.tourisminsights.info/ONLINEPUB/SPORT%20AND%20EVENTS/SAET%20PDFS/rallyrep.pdf, accessed 4 January 2009.

Mahathir DM. 2008. Investment in F1 sports – issues, impacts, opportunities. Proceedings of 1st Commonwealth Conference on Sports Tourism 2008, 13th–15th May, Malaysia.

McDaniel SR, Mason DS. 1999. An exploratory study of influences on public opinion towards alcohol and tobacco sponsorship of sporting events. *Journal of Services Marketing* **13** (6): 481–499.

MIA. 2003. The economic impact of the 2002 FIA Foster's British Grand Prix – final report, Motorsport Industry Association, July.

Pryor K, Brodie RJ. 1998. How advertising slogans can prime evaluations of brand extensions: Further Empirical results. *Journal of Product and Brand Management* **7** (6): 497–508.

RTE Sport. 2008. Rally Ireland generates huge economic boost. Available from: http://www.rte.ie/sport/motorsport/2008/0111/rallyireland.html, accessed 24 June 2008.

Saward J. 2008. *Autocourse*. CMG Publishing: Silverstone; 30–35.

Shifflet DK, Bhatia. 1999. Event tourism market emerging, *Hotel and Motel Management* September (6): 26.

Sofield T, Sivan A. 1994. From cultural festival to international sport: the Hong Kong Dragon Boat Races. *Journal of Sports Tourism* **1**(3) 5-22.

Sport Business International. 2007. *Monaco of the East* **130** (12.07): 46.

Standeven J, De Knop P. 1999. *Sport Tourism*. Human Kinetics: Champaign, IL.

Sylt C. 2007. 'Day and night, 24/7', *The Paddock*, June, p.8.

The Paddock. 2007a. 'Singapore starts F1 Preparations', September, p. 34.

The Paddock. 2007b. 'Victoria assesses F1 in Melbourne', December, p. 30.

The Paddock. 2007c. 'Abu Dhabi partners with World Rally', December, p. 32.

Travelmole.com. 2006. 'Indy fulfils tourism impact'. http://www.travelmole.com/stories/1113520.php, accessed 24 June 2008.

Turco DM. 1998. Travelling and turnovers: measuring the economic impacts of a street basketball tournament. *Journal of Sports Tourism* **5** (1).

UK Sport. 1998a. *Major Events: A Blueprint for Success*, UK Sport, London.

UK Sport. 1998b. *A UK Strategy: Major Events*, UK Sport, London.

UK Sport 1999. *Major Events: The Economics*, UK Sport, London.

UNC. 2004. *North Carolina Motorsports Economic Impact and Development Study*. University of North Carolina, Urban Institute: Charlotte.

Van Den Berg L, Braun L, Otgaar AHJ. 2000. *Sports and City Marketing in European Cities*. Euricur: Rotterdam.

Visit Britain. 2002. *Sports Tourism UK*, A survey by VisitBritain included in the International Passenger Survey conducted by the Office for National Statistics. http://www.tourismtrade.org.uk/Images/Sports%20Tourism%202002_tcm12-12496.pdf, accessed 2 January 2009.

Youson M. 2006. 'The shape of things to come', *Red Bulletin*, GP Great Britain, June, pp. 22–27.

19 Marketing and Managing Nation Branding during Prolonged Crisis: the Case of Israel

Eli Avraham, University of Haifa

Introduction

The Middle East generally and Israel specifically draw much attention in the international media. Positive coverage and esteem for Israel's achievements have been accompanied by reports of the wars with its Arab neighbours, violent conflicts, and terror attacks as central components of the country's international media coverage since the 1970s, and even earlier. The result is a problematic public image of Israel, which has impeded tourism, investment, and immigration. Israel's decisions makers, foreign and tourism ministries, Jewish organizations and other players face an extremely difficult challenge regarding the country's problematic media and public image. These players believe that the country's special attractions, diverse culture and history, its centrality to Judaism, Christianity and Islam, and its advanced economy and technology can potentially attain a much better public image and make Israel more attractive. Using the multi-step model for altering a place's image (Avraham & Ketter, 2008a) this chapter analyses strategies that have been applied to restore Israel's positive image. The analysis of Israel's image and its marketing efforts can help us better understand how marketers manage nation branding and marketing during prolonged crises and under constant conflict.

Nation's Image, Branding and Public Diplomacy

A country's image has many components, including location, leadership, kind of regime, economic situation, government stability and more (Kunczik, 1997). Although the design of an image seems highly dynamic, it is actually based on a stereotype. We think of a country in a stereotypical manner, hence these images are so hard to change (Elizur, 1987). Many places internalize the importance of their image, and invest much time and effort to improve it. A nation's media image has to be kept distinct from its public image: the former concerns the country's portrayal in the mass media, the latter its perception in international public opinion (Avraham, 2000). A foremost field of knowledge used by marketers to create countries' positive images is 'place promotion'. This concept has acquired many definitions (see Short et al., 2000), but Nielsen (2001) stresses the difficulty of achieving a positive image, especially regarding an image-related crisis: 'Promoting a destination in normal circumstances is a difficult task, but promoting a destination that faces tourism challenges – whether from negative press, or from infrastructure damage caused by natural disasters or man-made disasters – is an altogether more arduous task' (pp. 207-208).

To improve both their media and their public image, nations apply the tool of public diplomacy, a term with many different definitions. Malon (1985, in Gilboa, 2006: 717) claims that policymakers typically define public diplomacy as 'a direct communication with foreign people, with the aim of affecting their thinking and ultimately, that of their government'; in most cases the goal is to create a favorable image of nation's policies, actions, political and economical system (Gilboa, 2000). According to Hassman (2008), who offers many definitions of public diplomacy, it means expanding the dialogue among the nation's citizens, establishing relationships among the different communities, and understanding each one's culture and needs; these goals are achieved through the press, electronic media, the Internet, and also through promoting cultural, educational and scientific exchange, mounting art exhibitions, and providing information to journalists. Recent years have seen increasing use of 'branding' in place marketing and place image-making. The academic literature contains analyses of many case studies of countries and tourist destinations that have sought to re-brand themselves (e.g., Anholt, 2005; Dinnie, 2008).

Managing a Nation's Image During Crises

When dealing with a nation's image crisis, Parsons (1996, in Ritchie et al., 2003) suggests a method to distinguish three types of crisis: (1) immediate crises, where little or no warning exists, as in the case of the 2004 tsunami in South-East Asia; (2) emerging crises, which develop slowly, and may be stopped or limited, as in the UK foot-and-mouth epidemic; (3) sustained crises, which may last for weeks, months or years. In any of the three types of crisis listed, the media play a significant part in handling the situation. The crisis in the Middle East in general and in Israel specifically belongs to the third kind of crisis. Since the Western powers departed the region in the 1940s, conflicts and wars have characterized it. The result is a problematic image of an unsafe area, dangerous for tourists with every case of violence reported in the media turning into a prolonged tourism crisis in all the surrounding countries. Mansfeld (1994), for example, describes tourism to Israel as rising and falling cycles of numbers of visitors, depending on the particular conflict the country was involved in.

Israel's International Image 1948-2009

Israel public and media image has undergone major changes over the years. After World War II there was generally little international interest in the Middle East. Following Israel's establishment in 1948 the country was perceived as a place for Jewish immigrants who were building the only democratic country in the region, with manifold economic difficulties; its very survival was subject to doubt. Israel was perceived as the David, against the Goliath of the Arab countries, which failed to destroy it (Elizur, 1987). Israel's victory in the 1967 Six Day War moved the power component to the center of Israel's international image; its control of the territories, the next wars with Arab states (1973, 1982, 1991, 2006), and two Palestinian intifadas (1987, 2000 and the Gaza conflict in 2009) have reinforced the centrality of this component in the country's image. The media's tendency to sympathize with the weaker side of a conflict (the Palestinians), the Arab states' intensive exploitation of international organizations, their public relations and their sophisticated promotion of the 'victim image' of the Palestinians have made Israel the Goliath in the conflict (Gilboa, 2006; Navon, 2006; Galloway, 2005). While this general description of Israel's media image holds true around the world, there is a difference between its perception in the American and European media. In America, there tends to be more sympathy for the Israeli side of the ongoing conflict, based in large part upon the close ties and strong common values between the two nations. In Europe, however, there is much more sympathy for the Palestinians (Galloway, 2005; Wolfsfeld, 1997; Gilboa, 2006). For several years Israel has been searching for the right branding. The foreign and tourism ministries lead the branding process with the help of Jewish organizations and donors (Kaufman, 2008).

The Multi-step Model for Altering Place Image

Avraham and Ketter (2008a) offer a holistic multi-step model to restore a place's positive image. The first step consists of preliminary analyses (CAP characteristics) which include examining the crisis and the place where the crisis occurred, and singling out the target audience for whom the place aims to alter its image. That done, place marketers should define the campaign's goals and the timing of the launch of the campaign. Next is the stage of choosing the most suitable marketing strategy – or perhaps a mix of several strategies – as indicated by the preliminary analysis and the campaign objectives and timing. The choice can be among three groups of media strategies: with the focus on the source of the message, on the message itself, and on the target audience (SAM strategies: source, audience and message). Once a media strategy has been chosen, several techniques (e.g., advertising, public relations, promotion) and channels (e.g., TV, radio, press, the Internet) are available for delivering the campaign.

Methodology

The goal of this article is to answer the main research questions:

1. What terminology, slogans, images, and visuals, were used by Israel's marketers in order to combat which of the country's negative image characteristics?

2. What media policies, work routines and relationships with the international media were adopted by Israel's marketers in order to improve the country's media image during the years?

In order to answer these questions we analysed the use of SAM strategies adopted by Israel's marketers to combat its problematic image. The study is based on the careful analysis of dozens of advertisements, news articles, interviews with Israeli officials and marketers published in local and international magazines and newspapers (such as the *New York Times*, *Ha'aretz*, *The Marker*, *Israeli*, *Maxim*, and *Conde Nast Traveller*), on the Internet (YouTube website, *Ynet*, the Israeli tourism and foreign ministries' websites, and the websites of various Jewish organizations) and also in academic articles on Israel's marketing strategies. We used Qualitative Content Analysis to search in these various resources and media for slogans (like: 'Come see for yourself', 'Why I am in Israel now'), texts (like marketers' interviews in the media), and visuals (the models' gender, sexual preferences, religious symbols appearing in the ads) used while promoting Israel.

Qualitative Content Analysis

The qualitative approach is especially useful for studies attempting to explain social interaction in general (Tuchman, 1991). Qualitative methodology makes use of inductive reasoning, generalizing from the social reality to a more comprehensive theory (Denzkin and Lincoln, 1994). This method is based on a thorough understanding of the analysed units and examines the 'common signifying process.' Researchers using this method believe that texts reveal general discourse patterns (Pauly, 1991) through the appearance of motifs, labels, definitions, stereotypes, visuals, slogans and generalizations presented in the ads as exclusively characterizing specific social group, social status or place (van Dijk, 1988).

Results

In the findings section we would like to present three kinds of strategies used to restore Israel's positive image according to the model.

Source-focused Strategies

Many localities believe that news people tend to describe the crisis' events much more negatively than they really are (Avraham, 2000). Aware of the importance of media coverage of the crisis's implications for the audience, the country's decisions makers attempt to influence journalists. Over the years Israel likewise has exerted efforts to sway the patterns of coverage of events. They have also sought alternatives so as to bypass the media to reach the target audience.

Attempting to Influence the Media

Israeli leaders have attempted to influence their county's media image in various ways. The establishment of positive relations with the newspeople was the goal of some Israeli leaders, but at the same time they also tried to prevent them from covering problematic events that might have a negative effect on the country's perception abroad.

Cooperation and Developing Media Relations

Since its establishment as a democratic country with a free press and freedom of expression, Israel has cooperated with the foreign media by conducting press conferences, sending out press releases and responding to journalists and informing them about future events; officials and military commanders have been readily available for interviews. In recent years the army has been willing to allow journalists to cover ever more events and operations, such as clandestine actions against terrorists. Officials believe that international public opinion will understand better the difficulties the army faces in its pursuit of terrorists as a resolute of this unprecedented openness with the media (Navon, 2006; Hassman, 2008).

Putting Pressure on the Media

Beyond the wish to create positive media relations, Israel has exerted some pressure on certain media outlets to adjust Israel's negative coverage. This was done through complaints from the foreign ministry or the Israeli army to media owners against biased coverage and distortion of the events covered (*New York Times*, 1 July 2002). Here it is important to mention the activity of several media-watch organizations that monitor the media, mainly in the USA. These organizations, such as CAMERA and Honest Reporting, are not sponsored by the Israeli government but their activities contribute greatly to the pressure exercised on media outlets whenever Israeli officials feel that coverage is biased and distorted (Gerstenfeld and Green, 2004).

Blocking the Media

Going a step farther than the above, some places choose to block all media access to events that might have a negative affect on the place's image. By preventing the presence of newspeople, decision makers hope that controversial issues will remain uncovered, and hence will not create a negative image. Places where wars or violent conflicts are common, block media access as a matter of course, but in our context this strategy only refers to places where newspeople are denied access as part of a particular deliberate and systematic attempt to obstruct negative media coverage (Wolfsfeld, 1997). Israel chooses this technique rarely, for example, in the first Lebanon war in 1982, during the intifadas and during the GAZA conflict in 2009. The countries' leaders soon realized that such blocking was no longer possible for technological reasons and because the media outlets were able to use local residents (Lebanese and Palestinians) as reporters and photographers instead of professional newspeople.

Alternatives and Substitutes: Replacing the Media

The main idea of the following type of source strategies is the quest for finding alternatives to the traditional media. A nation's decision makers understand that their attempts to develop positive relations with journalists, pressuring the media, and even blocking the media do not always prevent 'bad press'. So by using 'alternative' strategies they aim to bypass the traditional foreign media in order to directly reach the target audience. Israel has done this because in many cases the foreign media have been perceived as hostile and biased. Alternative source have been use of the film industry, strategies 'come see for yourself', using celebrities and the Internet.

Using the Film Industry

One strategy is to support the local film industry with the hope that movies distributed abroad will present Israel in different context other than war, conflict and violence, subjects that are deemed the staple of the traditional media. The new Israeli movies dealt with global, day-to-day subjects, almost without mentioning the Arab-Israeli conflict (During the last several years many Israeli films won international rewards, including: *Broken Wings*, *The Band's Visit*, *Late Marriage*). Israel used these films to improve its image. For example, at the 11th Toronto International Film Festival, the Israeli movie *The Bubble* was shown. The screening was attended by an official Israeli delegation, including representatives of El Al Israel Airlines and of the Israeli culture bureau. The movie was intended to serve as a PR tool to improve Israel's international image and attract visitors (*The Marker*, 2006; Avraham and Ketter, 2008a). The foreign ministry has also recently sponsored Israeli film festivals in China and other countries, and has promoted one at New York's Lincoln Center.

Using Celebrities and Opinion Leaders

Another strategy adopted by many cities and countries is using celebrities and opinion leaders who are willing to deliver the message that a place is safe to visit from their own experience. Here the goal is to contradict the place's negative and unsafe portrait spread by the media coverage. On the main page of Israel's tourism ministry website (2005) there was a video clip of Madonna's visit to Israel, filmed at a press conference with the world-famous pop star. The headline stated, 'I feel very safe and very welcome'. In the clip Madonna tells the audience that the time she felt the most unsafe during her entire visit to Israel was when she encountered some 'very naughty paparazzi' outside her hotel (www.goisrael.com). In this instance Israeli officials used Madonna to counteract the country's common association with violent conflict. The use of a celebrity seems able to help get the opposite message across through reliance on this person's credibility. In addition, Israel has hosted at least 2,000 public opinion leaders yearly, such as academics, clergy, journalists, politicians and community leaders, to show them that the country – its sights and people – are very different from those that appear in its media coverage (Avraham and Ketter, 2008a).

'Come see for Yourself'

Another strategy used by marketers of places that have received 'bad press' is to invite the target audience to 'Come see for yourself' that the place is safe, rather than relying on the negative media reports. By means of this strategy, places can deny their media mediated image as 'dangerous' and assert that in reality they are safe. The marketers believe that if they can convince the target audience to visit the place, these tourists will see that the 'unsafe' stereotypes (usually spread by the media) are false and the place is vibrant, thriving and safe. This strategy, for example, was used by India and the UK after image crises resulting from epidemics (Avraham and Ketter, 2008b). It has also been employed by Israel, seeking to combat its media image as an unsafe destination. In a campaign launched in the 1990s Israel used the slogan 'Come see for yourself,' inviting visitors to see the place with their own eyes. During the second Palestinian uprising, which was launched in 2000, ads for Israel used the slogan 'Why I am in Israel now,' in which visitors explained how they discovered the 'Israel that you do not see in the news' (*Ha'aretz*, December 21, 2000).

The Internet as an Alternative to the Media

Frustration with the tradition media led many place marketers to find alternatives so as to reach the target audience directly; the Internet is known to offer many ways to do this. It provides countries with the opportunity to present themselves as they wish and to gain positive support (Gilboa, 2006). Both the Israeli foreign and tourism ministries run websites and also use the Internet to air clips, ads and videos at video-sharing websites. These means offer the country's perspective on specific events, expand the country's image, or combat its negative perception as a focus for terror attacks, which are seen in the media worldwide (Ynet, 4 April 2008). Israeli officials also recently launched a Myspace page representing the entire country and created a blog (Israeli.org) which offers stories and news about the country culture, arts, fashion, music, and cuisine (Kaufman, 2008).

Message-focused Strategies

The second group of media-strategies focus, rather than scrutinizing the source, is on the message itself. While these strategies vary in emphasis, they share a common denominator in their direct handling of the place's negative image.

Conveying Opposite Messages to the Problematic Image Characteristics

The goal of this strategy is to convey messages that are the opposite of the negative characteristics associated with the country. Since the establishment of Israel its enemies have set out to question its legitimacy – at times using a well-funded campaign, accusing the country of being a Western-style superpower, or an apartheid state that does not wish to compromise (Bard, 2005; Navon, 2006; Gilboa, 2006). In addition, the international media coverage which was focused on the violent conflicts between the Israeli army, Jewish settlers in the West Bank, and the Palestinians has led to the perception of Israel as a country populated only by ultra-Orthodox Jews, dominated by men, and injuring innocent Palestinian children and civilians (Navon, 2006; Kaufman, 2008; Katz, 2008). The result of the activity of Israel's opponents and the media coverage was the total omission of any non-conflictual/political characteristics from the country's image and its perception as a dangerous and menacing place, in which no 'fun' or normal life was to be found. Analysis of dozens of Israeli officials' media interviews and ads (look at:www. youtube.com), reveal that the county's marketers concentrated on combating these elements of Israel's problematic image.

An example is seen in the Israeli foreign ministry's website (www.mfa.gov.il), where many historical surveys and evidence of the connection between the Jews and the Land of Israel are presented, as well as facts and information about Israel among the nations and details of Israel's efforts to cede land for peace. In addition, many videos can be found on numerous video-sharing websites, some distributed by the Israeli army and some by the foreign ministry; they show how the Palestinians use children in pitched battles with the Israeli army, and how the Palestinian Authority promotes terror. The goal of the data is to fight the allegations against Israel and to convey contrasting, positive messages. The goal of the ads produced by the tourism ministry (www.tourism.gov.il) is to fight the negative perception and to show that Israel is a cool, 'fun', lively and dynamic country (Kaufman, 2008).

Multiple Facets, Human Touch and Softening the 'Hard' Image

When a place is involved in a prolonged violent conflict, it acquires a undesirable hard image that has to be softened; the place has to be given a human touch and an association with groups of people perceived as opposite to soldiers wearing helmets and bullet-proof vests, riding in tanks and firing guns. In the last decade, Israel seems to have made extensive use of such a strategy, and many campaign concentrate on children, women, minorities and multiple-facets. Israel's 2006 campaigns featured the famous international model Bar Refaeli. The July 2007 edition of the journal *Maxim* ran an Israeli government-sponsored campaign containing photos of sexy bikini-clad women soldiers who served in the Israeli army. The setting of the campaign, entitled 'Women of the Israel Defense Forces', was Israeli tourist attractions. This initiative was not unique. The tourism ministry contacted lifestyle, tourism and fashion magazines to gain exposure for Israel (Kaufman, 2008). The idea behind these initiatives was to soften the country's hard image.

Last year, two campaigns endeavored to present the human side of the country and its multiple aspects. The 'Shalom' campaign, which presented the slogan 'You'll love Israel from the first Shalom,' displays interesting Israelis and their special connection to the landscape and land (Lerer, 2008). The second campaign, titled 'I am Israeli', presents different Jews who have immigrated to Israel from all over the world, conveying the message that Israel is a multi-cultural country. Using humor is also considered an efficient way to soften a place's hard image. One amusing example was the 'Soccer ad' aired in 2006. It showed young Israelis playing on the beach, but they could not concentrate on the game because of the good-looking men and women strolling on the beach. At the end the narrator states dryly: 'No wonder we didn't make it to the World Cup' (http://www.youtube.com/watch?v=SfDZsM7tqxU).

Expanding the Image

A third form of the message-focused strategy is to expand the place's image. By this strategy, places acknowledge their negative image but try to add new positive components to it. Israel's marketers believed that the media's tendency to concentrate on conflict and violence have gravely constricted the country's image. In response they have aimed to expand the country's image beyond the conflict (Hassman, 2008). Many ads convey the message that Israel is much more than violent encounters; its many achievements in medicine, science, technology, culture and art help people all over the world and contribute globally in many ways. Also, by adopting public diplomacy techniques the foreign ministry sponsors events involving Israeli films, design exhibitions, recitals by musicians, appearances of writers, dancers, and drama. The role of these techniques is the expansion of Israel's image 'beyond the conflict'. Since 2001 the Israel21c (www.

Israel21c.net) non-profit website has assisted the foreign ministry in conducting this strategy, and initiated the 'Israelity' project, which emphasizes 'The face of Israel today' (Katz, 2008).

Branding Opposite to the Stereotypes

By this strategy, marketers promote the opposite of their place's 'well-known' negative image (Coaffee and Rogers, 2008). The idea is to initiate an extreme and overall change in place marketing that will lead to different perception. This is done by branding the place counter to the negative stereotype associated with it. An interesting example is found the German city of Nuremberg, which branded itself as a 'peace and human rights' city in diametrical opposition to its negative image seared into the city by its Nazi past. In the 1990s Israel use such a strategy to brand itself as a 'sea-and-sun' destination, contrary to the image of conflict and violence. Morgan et al. (2002), describes the branding process of Israel in 1993-98 for British visitors. In the branding process Israel was described as a destination for high quality sea-and-sun vacations, offering a Mediterranean atmosphere together with a rich heritage and an exotic touch. Because many places offer vacations with sea, sand and sunshine, the campaign managers wanted to create a unique identity for Israel by emphasizing its multiple strengths. This branding process proved highly successful, yielding a steep rise in incoming tourism from England (Morgan et al., 2002). Branding Israel as 'sea-and-sun' destination was considered then a good idea to thus contradict war and conflict perception.

Ridicule the Stereotype

The idea behind this strategy in advertisements is that the marketers themselves present the negative stereotype of the place, show how ridiculous it is, and thereby nullify it. Concerned with Israel's negative image as an unsafe place, Israel's marketers are using this strategy more and more. For example, an Israeli NGO handed out condoms to American students who were considering coming to Israel for a visit. The condom wrappers were printed in the blue and white colors of the Israeli flag and carried the catchphrase 'Israel – It's still safe to come'. Similarly, in a campaign created by a private consultancy partnership in Israel, the same strategy was used to illustrate how ridiculous Israel's stereotype as unsafe was. In the commercial, a young woman tourist is walking along the Israeli seashore when she suddenly spots a handsome man sitting on the sand. As she continues walking she keeps on looking at him, and collides with a pole. At that point the narrator declares, 'Indeed, Israel can be a dangerous place.' The consumer thereby realizes that the stereotype of Israel is overdone and its potential hazards are no worse than bumping into a wooden post on one of Israel's sunny beaches (Avraham and Ketter, 2008a).

Audience-focused Strategies

The common denominator of the strategies that focus on the audience is the effort by place marketers to improve the place's image by reaching the audience directly. They hint or suggest that audience should ignore the negative messages about the place conveyed by the media, and to feel warmly toward its people for various reasons. Such reasons may lie in common values, history, religion, destiny, world outlook, or indeed enemies.

Emphasis on Similarities and Relevance

Here marketers connect a certain place and its values to a specific appreciative target audience. Manheim and Albariton (1984), for example, found that American public relations firms which promoted third world countries in the US tried to associate these countries with human rights and democracy; the marketers knew that human rights and democracy are highly esteemed by Americans, and an association of these values with a third world country would garner much fondness for it. In a way this strategy can be called 'Like me' (Katz, 2008), in that the marketer wishes to demonstrate to a certain audience that the place has similar aspect to their own. Many countries involved in ongoing conflict situations around the world attempt to generate sympathy in the American audience, in the belief that this audience can affect American decision makers and their international policy (Manheim and Albritton, 1984).

Israel has used this strategy too. In the early 1990s the America–Israel Friendship League launched a campaign aimed at reminding Americans of the values common to both nations and their special bond. The campaign highlighted such joint values as democracy, freedom of speech, cultural heritage, scientific and technological research and immigration absorption. The slogan presented on the AIFL website was 'Building friendship based on common values' (www.aifl.org). More recently, Blue Star, an American public relations firm, initiated a campaign which took into account most of the values which considered important for San Francisco residents, such as women's rights and gay rights, technology, freedom of speech, the environment, and multi-culturalism. In a series of ads the PR firm connected Israel to these values by using visuals and slogans like 'Freedom of the press in the Middle East? Only in Israel', 'Where in the Middle East can gay officers serve their country? Only in Israel', and 'Who makes the greenest energy? Israel'. Some of these ads can be categorized also as a 'What have you done for me lately?' strategy, whereby marketers show the target audience how the brand contributes and is relevant to their lives. The Blue Star ran   several ads with the slogan 'Born in Israel. Used in the US/UK', which showed how Israel's innovations 'add value' and contribute to improving the life of Americans or Britain (http://www.bluestarpr.com).

Over the years Israel has tried to show its relevance to the spiritual side of diverse audiences. Usually during wars and series of terror attacks when the flow of general tourism largely ceases, the tendency is to attract more religious tourism, which is considered less sensitive to the question of safety. For example, in a campaign run in the beginning of the 2000s, Jews and Evangelical Christians became prime target audiences (Beirman, 2003). The advertisements centered on the potential tourists' religious identity to persuade them to visit Israel: 'Don't let your soul wait any longer. Come visit Israel' (*Ha'aretz*, June 5, 2003). Later, similar slogans were adopted: 'Visit Israel. You'll never be the same' (Lerer, 2008) and 'No one belongs here more than you'.

Using Familiar Cultural Symbols

With this strategy, marketers connect a certain place to cultural symbols that are relevant and familiar to a specific target audience. Israel found a highly original way to attract tourism from Japan: arranging a traditional Sumo wrestling match in Caesarea, a leading tourist destination in the country. The tour for 15 Sumo wrestlers, included visits to the Old City of Jerusalem, Sumo training on a Mediterranean beach, handing out gifts in hospitals, and of course, floating in the Dead Sea (*Israeli*, 14 May 2006). One of the visit's aims was to draw Japanese media attention to Israel by hosting the Sumo wrestlers, who are considered mega celebrities and enjoy enormous admiration in Japanese culture. A more important aim was to give the Japanese people the feeling that their traditional culture was being embraced by Israel, and that the Israeli and the Japanese people shared similar interests, ideas and values. In this way Israel delivered the message that Japanese people were welcome and would feel very comfortable visiting Israel (Avraham and Ketter, 2008a).

Association with Strong Brands

Another strategy used by marketers of places with problematic images is to associate the place with strong, familiar brands that are appreciated by the target audience. For example, recently South Africa has attempted to market itself by means of different strategies; one of them is association with familiar world magazines like *Vogue* and *Cosmopolitan*. Israel has used the same strategy. The British *Conde Nast Traveller* carried in its April 2008 issue a 40-page supplement dedicated solely to Israeli tourism. Robert D'Andria, who was involved in this initiative, said: 'It also provides Israel with sense of credibility through brand association. Being linked with *Conde Nast* automatically gives Israel a sense of fashionability and exclusivity' (in Kaufman, 2008: 21). Thus a problematic brand becomes associated with a strong, familiar brand appreciated by the target audience. Marketers hope thereby that the problematic brand will win some of the halo and credibility surrounding the strong brand. The same was achieved when Israel used American celebrities like Madonna, Bill Gates (http://www.youtube.com/watch?v=J3xOqibQ5qI), and Warren Buffet (http://www.youtube.com/watch?v=bV3W_86NTYA) to promote Israel's tourism, economy and technology.

Using the Multi-step Model to Analyse Israel's Strategies

The multi-step model offers several insights regarding the connection between the characteristics of the crisis, the target audience and the place on one hand and the media strategies used by the places on the other hand. Here we would like to use these insights in order to discuss Israel's SAM strategies as presented above.

Sources Strategy

– The intensive coverage of the Israeli-Arab conflict in the international media deprives Israel of the option of ignoring the crisis in its marketing campaigns. In addition, the centrality of the media as primary information source for many audiences about the conflict and the lack of resources to run expensive campaigns to restore Israel's image can explain why the marketers used so many source strategies aiming to affect the coverage of the country in the traditional media. Since Israel is a democracy, it is very hard to block media access (a strategy commonly employed by non-democratic countries) to negative events and this probably explains the highly infrequent use of this strategy by the state. In addition, Israel's decision makers' disappointment with its biased coverage in the international media is likely to explain why the marketers worked hard to find alternatives to the traditional media (such as movies and the Internet). It seems that employing the 'come see by yourself' and 'attracting opinion leaders and celebrities' strategies were in fact the correct choice given that the tourism infrastructure was not damaged during the conflict.

Audience Strategies

The use of the audience strategies to market Israel is interesting. By using these strategies, Israel is promoting its characteristics as a democratic country, that is technologically advanced and central to the world major religions in order to gain sympathy among different audiences around the world. The problem with using this kind of strategy is the cost, which reflects the need to build various campaigns that will be suitable for each different target audience around the world. Therefore it seems that Israeli marketers need to decide on the primary countries in which they want to concentrate their efforts, and to develop a specific campaign for each target audience in those countries.

Message strategies

The multi-step model suggests that there is a connection between the lack of resources and initiating a small number of expensive advertising campaigns. In the Israeli case this insight was proven correct because there was only limited use of these campaigns, which only run for short periods. The lack of resources probably also explain why the marketers did not employ more the strategy 'hosting international events' strategy, such as sport competitions or cultural events, which aims at improving a place's negative image (Avraham and Ketter, 2008b). On one hand, in light of the extensive coverage of the conflict in the international media we can understand the heavy use of strategies aimed at expanding the country's image beyond the conflict and the use of humor in order to soften its image. On the other hand, as mentioned, over the years, several attempts have been made to brand Israel as a sea-and-sun destination, contrary to the country's image. The choice of sea-and-sun branding is inappropriate for countries constantly in crisis, as this branding offers strong competition with much safer destinations. This fruitless branding also resulted in the loss of many resources allocated to it.

Conclusion

Using the multi-step model for altering place image, this article sets out to analyze strategies used by officials and private players to restore Israel's positive image. The results show that over the years, Israel's marketers used strategies with three foci: on the source, on the message, and on the target audience. Because of the severity of the crisis, it has been only natural for Israel to try different strategies, including extreme ones. The Israeli case strongly supports the necessity of the CAP characteristics analysis, illustrating that these characteristics can directly affect the choice of media strategy. On one hand, one can be impressed by the variety of strategies that Israel used in order to restore its positive image; on the other hand, this use of variety of strategies reflects a lack of unity and long-term marketing strategy. Every several years the marketing strategies kept changing, most likely due to the many crises, wars and terror attacks, that constantly created different challenges (Mansfeld, 1994) but also because of many other problems in the country's marketing plan as explained by Gilboa (2006). In any event, our analysis of the Israeli case using the multi-step model shows its relevance to evaluate places' efforts to restore their image after or during a crisis. We believe that many other countries can learn from the Israeli experience.

References

Anholt S. 2005. *Brand New Justice: How Branding Places and Products can Help the Developing World*. Elsevier: Oxford.

Avraham E. 2000. Cities and their news media image. *Cities* 17 (5): 363-270.

Avraham E, Ketter E. 2008. *Media Strategies for Marketing Places in Crises: Improving the Image of Cities, Countries and Tourist Destinations*. Butterworth Heinemann: Oxford.

Avraham E, Ketter E. 2008b. Will we be safe there? Analyzing strategies for altering places' unsafe images. *Place Branding and Public Diplomacy* 4 (3): 196-204.

Bard M. 2005. *The Complete Idiot's Guide to Middle East Conflict*. 3rd edn. Alpha Books: New York.

Beirman D. 2003. *Restoring Tourism Destinations in Crisis: A Strategic Marketing Approach*. CAB International Publishing.

Coaffee J, Rogers P. 2008. Reputational risk and resiliency: The branding of security in place-making. *Place Branding and Public Diplomacy* **4** (3): 205-217.

Denzkin NK, Lincoln YS. 1994. Introduction: Entering the field of qualitative research. In *Handbook of Qualitative Research*. Sage: London.

Dinnie K. 2008. *Nation Branding: Concepts, Issues, Practice*. Butterworth Heinemann: Oxford.

Elizur J. 1987. *National Images*. Hebrew University: Jerusalem.

Galloway C. 2005. Hot bullets, cool media: The Middle East's high stakes media war. *Journal of Communication Management* **9** (3): 233-245.

Gerstenfeld M, Green B. 2004. Watching the pro-Israel media watchers. *Jewish Political Studies Review* **16** (3-4): 1-24.

Gilboa E. 2000. Mass communication and diplomacy. *Communication Theory* **10**: 290-294.

Gilboa E. 2006. Public diplomacy: The missing component in Israeli foreign policy. *Israel Affairs* **12** (4): 715-747.

Hassman R. 2008. *The Israel brand: Nation marketing under constant conflict*. Tel Aviv University: Tel Aviv, Israel.

Ha'aretz, Various dates.

http://www.goIsrael.com; Visited on June 27, 2008.

http://www.mfa.gov.il; Visited on June 2, 2008.

http://www.tourism.gov.il; Visited on May 10, 2008.

http://www.aifl.org; Visited on July 27, 2008.

http://www. Israel21c.net; Visited on July 5, 2008.

http://www.ynet.org.il; Visited on April 4, 2008.

Israeli. 2006. Japanese Sumo wrestlers will promote tourism to Israel. May 14.

Katz M. 2008. The re-branding of Israel. *Moment* May-June.

Kaufman D. 2008. Best face forward. *Adweek*. 17 March.

Kunczik M. 1997. *Images of Nations and International Public Relations*. LEA: Mahwah, NJ.

Lerer I. 2008. Putting Israel on the map. *Ynet*. 13 April.

Manheim JR, Albritton, RB. 1984. Changing national images: International Public relations and media agenda setting. *American Political Science Review* **78**: 641-657.

Mansfeld Y. 1994. The Middle East conflict and tourism to Israel, 1967-1990. *Middle Eastern Studies* **30** (3): 646-667.

Morgan N, Pritchard A, Pride R. 2002. Introduction. In *Destination Branding: Creating the Unique Destination Proposition*, Morgan N, Pritchard A. and Pride R. (eds). Butterworth-Heinemann: Oxford.

Navon E. 2006. *Soft Powerlessness: Arab Propaganda and the Erosion of Israel's International Standing*. IDC Herzeliya, Institute for Policy and Strategy: Herzeliya.

New York Times. 2002. CNN navigates raw emotions in its coverage from Israel. 1 July.

Nielsen C. 2001. *Tourism and the Media*. Hospitality Press: Melbourne.

Pauly J. 1991. A beginner's guide to doing qualitative research in mass communication. *Journalism Monographs* **125**: 1-29.

Ritchie B, Dorrell H, Miller D, Miller GH. 2003. Crisis communication and recovery for the tourism industry: Lessons from the 2001 foot and mouth disease outbreak in the UK. *Journal of Travel and Tourism Marketing* **15**: 199-216.

Short JR, Breitbach S, Buckman S, Essex J. 2000. From world cities to gateway c i t i e s. *City* **4** (3), 317-340.

Tuchman G. 1991. Qualitative methods in the study of news. In A *Handbook of Qualitative Methodologies for Mass Communication Research*. Jensen KB, Jankowski NW (eds). Routledge: London.

van Dijk TA. 1988. *News as Discourse*. Lawrence Erlbaum: Hillsdale, NJ.

Wolfsfeld G. 1997. *Media and Political Conflict: News from the Middle East*. Cambridge University Press: Cambridge, England.

20 Is the Strategy of Becoming the Las Vegas of Asia Working for Macau? A Co-Branding Perspective

Leonardo (Don) A.N. Dioko, Institute for Tourism Studies, Macau; **Siu-Ian (Amy) So,** University of Macau

Introduction

> I am transforming Macau into an Asian Las Vegas.
>
> Sheldon Adelson [1]

With more money now received in betting revenues annually than Las Vegas, the Special Administrative Region of Macau in China has become the gambling center of the world. The tremendous increase in betting revenues is partly attributable to the innovation introduced by the entry of Las Vegas style casino hotels and resorts into what was then a highly regulated gambling monopoly in the formerly sleepy Portuguese territory. Since being granted their licenses to operate casinos in 2002 and the subsequent opening in late 2004 of the first Las Vegas style gaming property in Macau (with several other projects having been established or currently under development), the new Las Vegas operators have radically transformed the product mix of tourism attractions, combining gambling with novel concepts of entertainment and leisure activities. But is the dramatic increase in tourism and gambling activity attributable to new visitor-gambler markets attracted by the new Las Vegas operators or are they simply bringing in more of the same visitor–gambler mix similar to those that came prior to the liberalization of the gaming industry? In other words, have the new Las Vegas casino-resorts truly made Macau into an Asian Las Vegas? Such a question is vital from the point of view of tourism planners and policy makers in Macau whose aim it is to diversify and transform the once sleepy and sleazy territory of Macau into a dynamic destination for international and regional visitors with a 'world-class gaming industry' (Ho, 2002). The burden of expectation for the new Las Vegas operators is immense given their successful reputation for transforming Las Vegas from a mere gambling destination to a major and highly diverse entertainment and business tourism center in the United States.

---

1 Sheldon Adelson is the head of Las Vegas Sands Corporation, one of the sub-concession recipients of three gaming licenses granted by open tender in 2002 to liberalize the industry in Macau. Quoted statement is from Schuman M, Neil G. 2005. The Great Game Macau is in the middle of a building spree that will turn the former colony into Asia's Las Vegas--or maybe something even bigger. Time International 165 (5): 30.

The effectiveness of any tourism development strategy is best evaluated using as many relevant criteria, framework and performance metrics as possible. Often, however, limited time and availability of resources preclude this. This chapter submits the above questions to a limited yet more focused examination using the framework of a nascent but significantly growing field in tourism that consider the choice of destinations by tourists within the context of brand marketing. This developing area of study – destination branding and marketing – considers tourism destinations as branded products to which concepts developed in the brand marketing literature – brand equity, awareness, loyalty, among others – can therefore be applied. More important, the conceptual elements of branding incorporate image, perception, performance and attitudinal criteria that make it more a broader metric with which to judge marketing performance.

This chapter is principally anchored on two brand marketing related presuppositions. The first is that tourists consider their choice of destinations and hotels as a brand selection problem. Second, because destinations and hotels are often chosen by consumers simultaneously in one buying situation, they can be regarded as co-branded products, albeit belonging to different product classes. As separate yet co-branded products, the combined choice (or rejection) of a destination-hotel can be considered as the interactive outcome of consumers' separate evaluation of each brand element whereby such interaction can be additive, subtractive or combinative. These premises are explained briefly as follows.

Branding Destinations

Kotler (1997) defines a brand as 'a name, term, sign, symbol, or design or combination of them which is intended to identify the goods and services of one seller or group of sellers and to differentiate them from those of competitors (p. 443).' A brand serves to distinguish a product or service by enveloping and connecting it with a unique identity. In so doing, a brand serves to enhance product awareness, recognition, memory and image which are postulated to be the effects of the branding process, a conception based on the 'hierarchy of effects' model of advertising communication (Lavidge and Steiner, 1961). What makes a brand valuable to marketers is the equity it generates among consumers, a construct (brand equity) which Keller (1993) defined as 'the marketing effects uniquely attributable to the brand…outcomes resulting because of [its] brand name that would not occur if the same product or service did not have that name.' Because tourism destinations are generally regarded as a form of leisure consumption not far removed from consumption of traditional consumer goods and services, scholars and destination marketers consider the general principles of consumer branding to be applicable in the context of destination marketing. Indeed there has been an increased academic and practical interest of late in branding tourism destinations (Gnoth,1998, 2002; Pritchard and Morgan, 2001). Branding has become an important part of marketing tourism destinations and destination marketers now recognize how they can anchor their marketing programs by capitalizing on the underlying images and associative knowledge that visitors use to identify, distinguish and evaluate destinations (Blain et al., 2005). Ritchie and Ritchie (1998) reinforced the utility of destination branding by defining it and its core components as 'the marketing activities that (1) support the creation of a name, symbol, logo, word mark or other graphic that both identifies and differentiates a destination; (2) that convey the promise of a memorable travel experience that is uniquely associated with the destination; and (3) that serve to consolidate and reinforce the recollection of pleasurable memories of the destination experience, all with the intent purpose of creating an image that influences consumers' decisions to visit the destination in question as opposed to an alternative one.' Recently, Hosany, Ekinci et al. (2006) found that a destination's image and personality are related concepts, a finding that lends support and efficacy to the need for branding destinations.

Destinations and Hotels as Co-branded Choices

Despite the number of recent studies covering destination and hotel branding, it remains unclear what independent or interactive effects branding efforts conducted separately by tourism or destination marketing agencies (DMOs) and hotels have on the overall psychology of visitors' preference. This ignores the likely behavior of many travelers that consider and destinations and hotels as a joint decision. This knowledge gap is surprising considering the substantial amount spent separately by DMOs and hotels on marketing and brand-development activities and undermines tourism competitiveness (Cai, 2002; Ritchie and Ritchie, 1998). If, for example, visitors rate a destination low in brand equity, will the prompt of a hotel rated high in brand equity improve their likelihood of choosing such a combination if both are considered jointly? Conversely, if visitors hypothetically rate a destination high in brand equity but find that few acceptable or no high brand equity hotels exist, will the introduction of new internationally renowned chains of hotel make them more likely to visit? The paucity of studies addressing destination branding in relation to hotel branding is also astonishing when one considers the abundance and progress of knowledge archived in the co-branding literature of the marketing field (Boone, 1997; Grossman, 1997; Hadjicharalambous, 2006; Park et al., 1996; Rao and Ruekert, 1994; Swaminathan, 1999; Washburn et al., 2000; Washburn et al., 2000).

This study utilizes the conceptual elements of co-branding, the pairing of two or more constituent brands (Park et al., 1996) in marketing a product offering, and applies it in the context of a combined destination-hotel choice. Though Park et al. (1996) base their study on consumer goods, in this case the two co-branded objects are considered to be the combination of the destination marketed (Macau) and visitors' preferred (or chosen) hotel (also in Macau). There is ample evidence from the literature that co-branding influences trial and purchase and that the pairing of two constituent brands enhances the likelihood of consumers adopting the co-branded offering than they would if each were marketed separately (Swaminathan, 1999; Washburn et al., 2000; Washburn et al., 2000). The hypothesized mechanism for this occurrence is based on transference (Keller, 2003), in which positively associated attributes of one brand are transferred or extended to the co-branded product, thereby signaling greater product quality overall (Washburn et al., 2000). Washburn et al., (2000) cite Park et al. (1996) and Rao and Ruekert (1994) in utilizing economics of information theory as well as consumer search, experience and credence (SEC) framework to hypothesize that co-branding should produce an overall positive effect for constituents of a co-branded effort.

In this study, however, the constituent elements of the co-branded product include both the hotel and destination (in this case, Macau). Essentially, the aim is to examine whether the new Las Vegas style casino-resorts in Macau – as a group – are able to attract entirely new segments of visitors that are distinguishable from those already attracted by existing 'locally branded and international branded chains of hotels (i.e. non-Las Vegas style casino resorts). This question is reasonable considering that the new Las Vegas style casino-resorts have promised a superior quality of experience compared to existing Macau operators and aim to bring a new kind of gaming and entertainment never before seen prior to the liberalization of industry. These promises have so far been materialized in the style, architecture, diverse product offerings and scale provided by a few of the new properties already in operation. Among these is the Venetian, thus far the biggest hotel in the world complete with the architectural motif and mall 'streetscape' that mimics the streets and canals of old Venice. The complex is similar in every respect to the original one in Las Vegas, including an arena for concerts and events and tie-ups with theatrical companies such as Cirque du Soleil. There is also the high end Wynn Resort and MGM Grand with casino services and gaming atmospherics of a kind never before experienced by Chinese gamblers in Macau. Given such a radical product-market offering introduced in Macau, the study posits that as an entirely new category of hotels in Macau, Las Vegas branded operators should attract a visitor segment mix that exhibit (a) higher perceived hotel brand equity (relative to visitors staying in non-Las Vegas hotels in Macau), (b) higher perceived brand equity for Macau as a destination (due to transference), and (c) exhibit a more varied set of purposes for visiting Macau (as opposed to a more uniform purpose such as gambling).

Methodology

The study uses data from a cross-sectional survey of international visitors in Macau. Analysis employed logistic regression in which the dependent variable was the category of hotel survey respondents indicated they stayed in (Las Vegas brand casino-resort, international brand chain hotel, and local brand hotel). Three independent variables included (a) perceived continuous measures of destination brand equity (or DBE, in this case, Macau), (b) hotel brand equity (or HBE) and (c) a categorical measure of primary purpose or activity for coming to Macau. As a logit form of multiway frequency analysis, logistic regression is often used to predict discrete outcome of group membership. In this study however, it is utilized more for distinguishing and profiling (or discriminating) the segments of visitors that stayed in each of the three types of branded accommodation in Macau as operationalized in the dependent measure. Though the same objective can be achieved by the use of discriminant analysis, the inclusion of a categorical measure for primary activity or purpose for coming to Macau precluded this since the assumptions for parametric testing required by discriminant analysis cannot be met. Logistic regression, on the other hand, provides parametric estimates for predictor variables even if these don't adhere to assumptions of normally distributed data.

Continuous measures for DBE and HBE utilized the brand equity scale developed by (Lassar et al., 1995). This scale incorporates five dimensions of brand equity (performance, social image, value, trustworthiness of communication, and attachment) and is measured by 17 item statements to which respondents indicated their agreement on a seven-point scale. Developed primarily in the context of marketing consumer goods, Lassar et al. (1995) report good validity and reliability features of the scale. Wordings of the 17 item statements were adapted separately for use in the context of destination choice (Macau) and in the choice of hotels. A recent study (reference withheld pending review) utilized the Lassar et al. scale (1995) in the context of destination branding and showed consistency and reliability of factor structures with the original scale. Separate measures of brand equity for DBE and HBE were computed by summating and averaging scale item scores. The DBE measure applied only to Macau while HBE scores were computed for respondents grouped in each of the three categories of hotels (Las Vegas brand casino-resort, international brand chain hotel, and local brand hotel). Respondents in the survey were prompted to indicate which hotel they were staying which was then coded into the three categories of the dependent measure. Coding identified Las Vegas branded casinos hotels or resorts to include properties such as the Venetian and the Sands, the MGM Grand and Wynn Resorts. Hotels coded as international brand chain hotels included, for example, the Mandarin, Westin, Holiday Inn and Crown. Remaining hotels were coded as locally branded hotels even if these included newer concept properties but could not be categorized in the first two groups.

Data for this study were obtained from a survey of international visitors conducted in Macau in March 2008. A total of 494 randomly selected visitors were personally interviewed using structured questionnaires. Interviews were conducted at various attraction sites and major ports of entry into Macau.

Results

Descriptive means for DBE and HBE for respondents in each of the three categories of the dependent variable, as well as frequency counts for the categorical variable measuring primary purpose for visiting, are shown in Table 20.1.

Table 20.1: Descriptive statistics for DBE and HBE as well as frequency counts for each of the three categories of branded hotels

	Local branded hotels		Las Vegas branded hotels		International brand chain hotels	
	Mean	(s.d.)	Mean	(s.d.)	Mean	(s.d.)
Destination Brand Equity* (DBE)	5.10	(.87)	5.17	(.82)	5.01	(.63)
Hotel Brand Equity* (HBE)	4.94	(.98)	5.64	(2.23)	5.16	(.96)
Primary purpose for visiting	Count	%	Count	%	Count	%
Shopping	119	23	45	21	18	25
Gambling	103	20	30	14	4	6
Visit World Heritage Sites	75	14	38	17	12	17
To dine or see cultural shows	66	13	27	12	10	14
Stay at/visit new casinos	59	11	31	14	10	14
Visiting friends or relatives	49	9	11	5	5	7
Business**	28	5	30	14	9	13
Other, unspecified	23	4	6	3	3	4

* Seven-point agreement scale   **Attending conferences, meetings or exhibitions.

To test the validity and consistency of the brand equity scale used in the study, exploratory factor analysis (EFA) was performed. Examination of the factor structure that emerged from a principal components extraction and utilizing a varimax rotation revealed a five-factor structuring that – in the case of destination brand equity (DBE) for Macau – very much conforms to the (Lassar et al., 1995) study, with all the 17 revised scale items loading consistently onto each of the five hypothesized dimensions of the scale (performance, image, value, trust and attachment). Together, these five factors accounted for 71.6% of total variance.

Table 20.2 shows the item loadings as well as the percent of variance accounted for by each factor. In the case of the hotel brand equity (HBE) measure, a five-factor structure also emerged that showed good consistency with the original (Lassar et al., 1995) scale dimensions and altogether accounted for 76.2% of total variance. However, one item out of the 17, 'The hotel where I am currently staying is good value' (V1), originally belonging to the value dimension of the Lassar scale, unexpectedly loaded onto the image dimension for this sample. This can be seen in Table 20.3.

Table 20.2: Factor structure and scale item loadings of destination brand equity (Macau) measures (adapted from Lassar, et al., 1995)

	Component				
	1	2	3	4	5
One can characterize visiting Macao as trouble-free. (P3)	.748				
Visitors to Macao can expect a superior quality of experience than other destination. (P2)	.747				
You can expect an excellent experience when visiting Macao. (P1)	.738				
As a tourism destination, Macao performs very well. (P4)	.665				
The companies and people that market Macao care about visitors' interests. (T2)		.882			
The companies and people that market Macao to visitors are very trustworthy. (T1)		.840			
The companies and people that market Macao to visitors do not take advantage of visitors. (T3)		.822			
Compared to the benefits one receives, visiting Macao is a bargain. (V3)			.740		
Visitors to Macao get much more than what they pay for. (V2)			.739		
The cost of visiting Macao is good value. (V1)			.713		
I am proud to be able to visit Macao. (I2)				.804	
Visiting Macao is something that is regarded highly by my friends, family or colleagues. (I3)				.743	
Macao is a destination that fits my style and status in life. (I4)				.614	
Visiting Macao is something that matches my personality. (I1)				.531	
I have positive personal feeling of Macao as a destination. (A2)					.781
I am likely to grow fond of Macao as a destination. (A1)					.753
I will develop warm feelings of Macao as a destination. (A3)					.644
Percent of variance accounted for	15.7%	14.9%	14.2%	14.1%	12.8%
Factor label	Performance	Trust	Value	Image	Attachment

N.B. Items with loadings of less than .50 suppressed and not shown. Letters and numbers in parentheses i ndicate corresponding item in the Lassar et al. (1995) scale.

Table 20.3: Factor structure and scale item loadings of hotel brand equity measures (adapted from Lassar, et al., 1995)

	Component				
	1	2	3	4	5
I am proud to stay in the hotel where I am currently staying (I2)	.808				
The hotel where I am currently staying is regarded highly by my friends, family or colleagues. (I3)	.726				
The hotel that I am currently staying fits my personality (I1)	.686				
The hotel where I am currently staying fits my style and status in life. (I4)	.676				
The hotel where I am currently staying is good value (V1)	.575				
I choose the hotel where I am currently staying in order to be trouble-free (P3)		.827			
The hotel where I am currently staying provides a superior quality of experience than other hotels (P2)		.700			
From the hotel where I am currently staying, I expect superior performance (P1)		.622			
The hotel that I am currently staying performs very well (P4)		.598			
The staff in the hotel where I am currently staying cares about guest's interests (T2)			.799		
The staff in the hotel where I am currently staying is very trustworthy (T1)			.721		
The staff in the hotel where I am currently staying does not take advantage of visitors (T3)			.714		
For the hotel where I am currently staying, with time, I will develop warm feelings towards the hotel. (A3)				.769	
For the hotel where I am currently staying, I have positive personal feelings (A2)				.721	
I am likely to grow fond of the hotel where I am currently staying (A1)				.612	
For the hotel where I am currently staying, I will be able to get much more than my money worth (V2)					.731
Compared to the benefits one receives, the hotel where I am currently staying is a bargain (V3)					.717
Percent of variance accounted for	20.2	15.6	15.1	13.5	11.9
Factor label	Image	Performance	Trust	Attachment	Value

N.B. Items with loadings of less than .50 suppressed and not shown. Letters and numbers in parentheses indicate corresponding item in the Lassar et al. (1995) scale.

Results of the direct logistic regression analysis indicated good discrimination among the three segments of visitors staying at different branded hotel categories on the basis of all predictors considered together (DBE, HBE and primary purpose for visiting), χ^2 (18, $N=410$) = 71.81, $p < .000$. Among the three predictors, however, only HBE, χ^2 (2, $N=410$) = 38.52, $p < .000$, and primary purpose for visiting, χ^2 (14, $N=410$) = 29.12, $p = .01$, showed significant influence on the dependent variable. DBE exhibited a weak overall relationship with hotel brand category, χ^2 (2, $N=410$) = 5.02, $p = .081$. Table

20.4 shows the regression coefficients, Wald statistics, odds ratios and 95% confidence intervals for odds ratios for predictors in the model comparing respondents staying in Las Vegas brand hotels and international brand chain hotels with local branded hotels as the base reference category. Results indicate that DBE (z=4.710, p = .03) and HBE (z=31.701, p < .001) significantly discriminated visitors staying at the Las Vegas branded hotels from local branded hotels (the reference category) but not between visitors staying at international brand chain hotels and local branded hotels.[2]

Table 20.4: Logistic regression analysis (parameter estimates): Category of hotel as a function of destination brand equity (DBE), hotel brand equity (HBE) and primary purpose for visiting

	B	Wald	Sig.	Odds ratio	95% C.I. for odds ratio	
					L. Bound	U. Bound
Las Vegas branded hotels [a]						
Intercept	-4.981	15.813	.000			
Destination Brand Equity (DBE)	-.428	4.710	.030	.652	.443	.959
Hotel Brand Equity (HBE)	1.063	31.701	.000	2.896	2.000	4.193
Primary purpose for visiting:						
Gambling	.572	.440	.507	1.772	.326	9.625
Stay at/visit new casinos	.652	.546	.460	1.919	.340	10.820
Shopping	.937	1.211	.271	2.551	.481	13.530
Business*	1.846	4.149	.042	6.333	1.072	37.405
Visiting friends or relatives	.106	.013	.911	1.112	.173	7.152
To dine and/or watch cultural shows	1.214	1.888	.169	3.366	.596	19.009
Visit World Heritage Sites	1.337	2.447	.118	3.808	.713	20.337
Other, unspecified	0[b]					
International brand chain hotels [a]						
Intercept	-2.893	3.081	.079			
Destination Brand Equity (DBE)	-.009	.001	.975	.991	.565	1.740
Hotel Brand Equity (HBE)	.280	1.154	.283	1.323	.794	2.204
Primary purpose for visiting:						
Gambling	-2.359	3.394	.065	.095	.008	1.163
Stay at/visit new casinos	-.057	.004	.949	.944	.165	5.405
Shopping	-.075	.008	.930	.928	.173	4.971
Business*	.818	.774	.379	2.266	.366	14.020
Visiting friends or relatives	-1.102	1.048	.306	.332	.040	2.740
To dine and/or watch cultural shows	-.923	.733	.392	.397	.048	3.290
Visit World Heritage Sites	-.705	.549	.459	.494	.076	3.190
Other, unspecified	0[b]					

[a] Reference category is local branded hotels   *Attending conferences, meetings or exhibitions.
[b] Parameter set to zero because it is redundant

---

2   The result for DBE as a significant predictor between Las Vegas brand hotels and local brand hotels contradicts the lack of overall significance of DBE as a predictor in the general model reported (unless α is set at .90). The overall model suggests that DBE be ignored in predicting brand hotel category. But since the purpose of the study is to discriminate visitors attracted by the new Las Vegas brand hotels compared to those attracted by existing hotel brands in Macau (the reference category) then results of the between-category analysis would be more instructive.

In addition, the data suggest that business as a primary purpose of visiting Macau significantly distinguished visitors staying at Las Vegas branded hotels from those staying at local branded ones (z=4.149, p = .042). When interpreted together with the odds ratio provided in the table, it seems that visitors who tend to have higher perceived hotel brand equity ratings, *lower* perceived brand equity ratings for Macau as a destination, and predominantly visiting Macau for business purposes (attending conferences, meetings or exhibitions) are more likely to stay at the new Las Vegas branded hotels in Macau rather than local branded hotels. Results of the logistic regression analysis did not reveal any variable that significantly discriminated between visitors staying at international brand chain hotels and those staying at the reference category of local brand hotels, with the exception of gambling as the primary purpose for visiting Macau which showed marginal significance, z = 3.394, p =.065. Here, the data suggest that international brand chain hotels in Macau distinguish themselves from locally branded hotels in the sense of attracting *fewer* gamblers as clients. The predictive power of the overall model as measured by successful classification rates was 66.6%, which is better than the naïve rate of 50% and statistically significant, $Z^*=6.91$, $p < .05$ (Sharma, 1996).[3] To summarize, analysis of survey data using logistic regression suggests the following:

1.   Visitors attracted to stay at the new Las Vegas brand of casino hotels and resorts in Macau are principally distinct from visitors staying at locally branded hotels principally in terms of having a higher perception of hotel brand equity (of their chosen hotels) and by their primary purpose of visiting (i.e., business related activity such as attending conferences, meetings or exhibitions).There is a slight hint in the data that clients of new Las Vegas hotels in Macau have higher perceived ratings for Macau as a destination brand, but only in so far as this group is compared with clients of locally branded hotels. Generally, however, the logistic regression model indicates destination brand equity (DBE) as an irrelevant factor that does not distinguish between visitors attracted by the different categories of branded hotels.

2.   There is almost no factor significantly distinguishing visitors staying at international brand chain hotels compared to locally branded hotels in Macau, with the possible exception of one purpose for visiting, gambling, whereby analysis indicates a slightly higher chance for visitors *not* to stay at international brand chain hotels if they visit primarily for gambling.

The same analysis was replicated in various steps controlling for demographic variables, visitor characteristics, level of familiarity with Macau and frequency of repeat visits but this supplementary analysis yielded no results that significantly changed the findings described above. In terms of the generalizability of results, the study's sample yielded a mix of visitor nationality normally expected in Macau wherein the majority were of Mainland Chinese (56%), Hong Kong (11%), and Taiwan (7%) origin, with the rest consisting of visitors from other countries.

Conclusion

We interpret the above findings as partial evidence that four years since the establishment of the first Las Vegas branded casino hotels, limited success has thus far been achieved in Macau's long-term strategy of introducing new and diverse segments of visitors through the liberalization of the hospitality industry and introduction of Las Vegas style hotel brands in the market. The findings show that the new Las Vegas brand hotels in Macau,

---

3   Where, as a statistical measure of successful classification, $$Z^* = \frac{(o_i - e_i)\sqrt{n_i}}{\sqrt{e(n-e)}}$$

to some extent, are attracting visitors with perceived levels of brand equity significantly higher than those found among visitors staying at international brand chain hotels and local Macau hotels. This implies that such visitors are probably more sophisticated and cosmopolitan than those that would have been attracted had the new Las Vegas operators not entered Macau. In addition, there is strong evidence from the data that – true to their promise and pledged strategy to bring in more business tourism to Macau – the new Las Vegas operators seem to be attracting more business visitors compared to those staying at locally branded hotels and even long-established international branded hotel chains in Macau. Overall, visitors staying at the three hotel categories are indistinguishable in terms of the level of their perceived brand equity for Macau as a destination, implying that whatever new visitor segment is being attracted to Macau by the new Las Vegas hotels is likely drawn more by the prospect of experiencing what new entertainment concept they have to offer than by the characteristics of the destination. In a narrow sense this is somewhat disappointing given that the literature on co-branding suggest that whenever two product offerings are co-branded, they tend to confer positive evaluations in terms of consumer choice, preference, trial, and even repeat patronage (Park et al., 1996; Swaminathan, 1999) on both constituent elements of the co-branded offering. Data from overall logistic regression analysis indicate, however, that the new Las Vegas hotel operators attract neither those who have perceived low brand equity for Macau (perhaps to 'convert' or pull them into visiting) nor those who have perceived high BE for Macau (perhaps to increase repeat visits from them).

It is possible, however, that the lack of overall relationship between perceived DBE and the kind of hotel patronized by visitors belies an as yet undetectable but developing influence (though it has been some five years since the first of the Las Vegas operators started operating). This can be gleaned from the data in which specific comparison between Las Vegas hotels and locally branded hotels indicate a slight hint of significance for this variable as a predictor between the two categories in the logistic regression analysis. Perhaps transference of brand knowledge (Keller, 2003) and attributes will take more time in this particular case involving the co-branding of a destination with an entirely new category of branded hotel experience introduced by the new Las Vegas operators.

The ultimate outcome of any tourism development strategy is of course judged and measured on many other factors beyond those examined within the limited scope of this study. However, the study demonstrates that brand equity perceptions in the context of a joint destination-hotel choice are relevant in determining and assessing the kind of visitor segments that a new tourism development project attracts, and whether they are consistent with strategy. At a more fundamental level, the findings suggest that the efficacy of any tourism development project – however advanced by the introduction of novel hotel and leisure concepts – should be judged by its overall effects on the destination brand. After all, hotels and destinations are ultimately co-branded products.

References

Blain C, Levy SE et al. 2005. Destination branding: insights and practices from destination management organizations. *Journal of Travel Research* **43** (4): 328-338.

Boone JM. 1997. Hotel-restaurant co-branding – a preliminary study. *Cornell Hotel and Restaurant Administration Quarterly* **38** (5): 34.

Cai LA 2002. Cooperative branding for rural destinations. *Annals of Tourism Research* **29** (3): 720-742.

Gnoth J. 1998. Branding tourism destinations. *Annals of Tourism Research* **25** (3): 758-

760.

Gnoth J. 2002. Leveraging export brands through a tourism destination brand. *Journal of Brand Management* **9** (4): 262-280.

Grossman RP. 1997. Co-branding in advertising: developing effective associations. *Journal of Product and Brand Management* **6** (3): 191.

Hadjicharalambous C. 2006. A typology of brand extensions: positioning cobranding as a sub-case of brand extensions. *Journal of American Academy of Business, Cambridge* **10** (1): 372.

Ho HW. 2002. Policy address by Macao's Chief Executive for the Fiscal Year 2003 of the Macao Special Administrative Region (MSAR) of the People's Republic of China, 20 November 2002. Macao, Macao Government Information Service.

Hosany S, Ekinci Y et al. 2006. Destination image and destination personality: An application of branding theories to tourism places. *Journal of Business Research* **59** (5): 638-642.

Keller KL. 1993. Conceptualizing, measuring, and managing customer-based brand equity. *Journal of Marketing* **57** (1): 1.

Keller KL. 2003. Brand synthesis: The multidimensionality of brand knowledge. *Journal of Consumer Research* **29** (4): 595.

Kotler P. 1997. *Marketing Management: Analysis, Planning, Implementation, and Control.* Prentice Hall: Upper Saddle River, NJ.

Lassar W, Mittal B et al. 1995. Measuring customer-based brand equity. *Journal of Consumer Marketing* **12** (4): 11.

Lavidge RJ, Steiner A. 1961. A model for predictive measurements of advertising effectiveness. *Journal of Marketing (pre-1986)* **25** (6): 59.

Park CW, Jun SY et al. 1996. Composite branding alliances: An investigation of extension and feedback effects. *Journal of Marketing Research* **33** (4): 453.

Pritchard A, Morgan MJ. 2001. Culture, identity and tourism representation: marketing Cymru or Wales? *Tourism Management* **22** (2): 167-179.

Rao AR, Ruekert RW. 1994. Brand alliances as signals of product quality. *Sloan Management Review* **36** (1): 87.

Ritchie BJR, Ritchie RJB. 1998. The branding of tourism destinations: past achievements and future challenges. *1998 Annual Congress of the International Association of Scientific Experts in Tourism, Destination Marketing: Scopes and Limitations*. P. Keller. (ed.) Marrakech, Morocco, International Association of Scientific Experts in Tourism: 89–116.

Schuman M, Neil G. 2005. The Great Game Macau is in the middle of a building spree that will turn the former colony into Asia's Las Vegas - or maybe something even bigger. *Time International* **165** (5): 30.

Sharma S. 1996. *Applied Multivariate Techniques*. John Wiley and Sons: Chichester.

Swaminathan V. 1999. Do cobranding strategies influence brand choice? An empirical analysis. *American Marketing Association. Conference Proceedings* **10**: 73.

Washburn JH, Till BD, et al. 2000. Co-branding: brand equity and trial effects. *Journal of Consumer Marketing* **17** (7): 591.

Washburn JH, Till BD, et al. 2000. The effect of co-branding on search, experience, and credence attribute performance ratings before and after product trial. *American Market-

21 Towards A Tourism Brand Personality Taxonomy: A Survey Of Practices

Rosária Pereira, Antónia Correia, Ronaldo Schutz, University of the Algarve

Introduction

The five-factor model applied to studies on personality emerged after several studies from the early 1930s (Allport and Odbert, 1936) and developed into a reliable and valid model to assess the construct personality. The 'big-five' model has been the basis of several studies in the field of marketing, especially on brand personality (BP) research. Most studies that can be found about tourism BP are focused on the seminal work of Aaker (1997), namely tourism destinations in general (Ekinci and Hosany, 2006); rural tourism destinations (Cai, 2002); the establishment of the difference between brand image and brand personality (Hosany et al., 2006); the comparison between the development of a product/service brand and the development of a destination brand (Cai, 2002; Gnoth, 2002); and comparisons between the development of a brand and (re)positioning (Gilmore, 2002). Furthermore, the characteristics and concepts related to destination brands (importance of destinations' 'identity', and the use of brand elements) were studied by Cai (2002), and Morgan et al. (2004), whereas the role of emotional relationship with consumers was approached by Gilmore (2002).

Studies on brand personality tend to reduce the psychometric scales used to measure human personality by rewording the items and changing the filling form instructions in an attempt to adapt human traits to product traits. In this context, and according to Milas and Mlačič (2007), a taxonomy of brand personality traits is still missing from the literature. Additionally, constructs such as brand, image and personality are often mixed and often misunderstood (Ekinci and Hosany, 2006). Recent studies recommend that researchers should adopt a stricter definition of the concept of brand personality in order to reach a more exact measurement of the concept.

This chapter offers a survey of practices that serves to clarify constructs such as personality, personality traits, personality taxonomy and the 'big-five' model of personality, hence it aims to provide a conceptual framework in which the main personality descriptors can be identified in order to be adapted to the context of a tourism destination. Subsequently a measurement scale can be developed in order to assess destinations' brand personality.

Personality

The theoretical framework of personality emerged in the field of psychology. Personality is one of the most central matters of human psychology. This is due to the fact that personality is a multidimensional concept which deals with individuals in contrast with other domains that deal with particular aspects of the individual. Although its importance is recognized, various definitions can be found in the literature. The main differences in the definitions are related to the scope, nature and development of the concept. When dealing with the concept of personality there is usually an emphasis on wholeness, focusing on what is unique about a person, and his/her behaviour. There are various theories that have emerged in psychology that seek to explain human behaviour and attitudes considering knowledge about the genetic and environmental influence and seeking to predict behaviour in typical situations.

In the field of personology, it is possible to find a conflict known as 'traits versus situationism' between:

> those who assume that the determinants of behaviour are tendencies characteristic of the individual, being traits, roles, motives, predispositions, etc., and those who believe that the determinants of behaviour are environmental stimuli.
>
> (Kreitler and Kreitler, 1993b: 66)

A different approach is supported by the relational theory of motivation, whose dynamic perspective aims to combine factors that are inherent to organism–environment interaction, and is based on an expectation/value model (Nuttin, 1984). Both research trends aim to examine factors that will enable researchers to predict, modify and control human behaviour.

Looking at the origin of the word, which comes from the Greek word *Persona*, meaning 'theatre mask', we define personality as the role performed by an individual, within a certain context, and in front of an audience (Bernaud, 1998). Reuchlin (1992) suggests that personality is a relatively stable and general characteristic of a human being concerning the way s/he reacts to different situations. However, this definition does not include the view that the cognitive determinants, such as emotions, motivations, and traits are central to individuals' reactions.

The Relational Approach to Personality

The relational approach views personality as the relationship between the subject and its life experience, objects and people that make up the subject's own world and maintain essential exchanges that shape its own development. To be able to comprehend personality development, it is important to understand the crucial exchanges taking place between the subject and the world. These relationships are named 'motives' in dynamic-relational theory. Nuttin (1984) argues that 'personality is a network of actual and potential interaction between the individual and the environment' (1984: 58). Relationships are the fundamental dynamic factors of personality, working as functional structure for the subject-situation (Abreu, 1998). Within this model, both the personality and the behavioural world are the products of experience. They are so integral to one another that the behavioural world of a subject is part of the content of its personality. According to this perspective, personality is:

> a set of potential and actual relationships with the behavioural world, which itself, develops gradually through this interactional process and from physical reality. The structural elements, that, in the course of the development, became part of personality – e.g. traits, abilities, dispositions – must also be considered as outcomes of this same interaction process.
>
> (Nuttin, 1984: 73)

As a result, human personality must be conceptualized as a modality of relational functioning and as a coordinating centre of information processing and dynamic decision making. Furthermore, the objects perceived and experienced as well as all the thoughts, feelings and actions, including their motivation, are stored as the content of our personality. An individual is formed and identified, not only by the formal characteristics of his/her intelligence and character but also by the opinions, feelings and motivational objects he is concerned with. (Nuttin, 1984:: 74).

Consumer Behaviour and Personality

Another perspective of personality comes from consumer behaviour researchers. The whole concept of personality and its relationships to how consumers respond has always been very appealing to them. However, researchers from this field find it a very difficult concept to define. It is often described as 'the way individuals react fairly consistently to a variety of environmental situations' (Plummer, 1985: 27). This definition does not seems to consider the dynamic factors of personality, since not all the personality traits are stable over time.

A tourism destination is a complex set of multidimensional services (Ritchie, 1993). Accordingly, and since products do not have genetic characteristics, our claim here is that a taxonomy for a destination brand personality should be based on two different types of traits: (1) stable traits which can be found on the macro-environment attributes and on services infrastructures of the destination (Mo et al., 1993). The stable traits are those perceived similarly in different contexts; and (2) on the traits resulting from the outcomes of the interaction between a subject and the destination.

Personality Traits

Conceptions of personality based on traits have been an extremely rich field of research since the early beginnings of psychology, although there is little agreement about what they are, how they function, how many there are or how they are related to behaviour. Kreitler and Kreitler (1993a) presented a definition of personality traits based on over 20 studies in which 115 of the commonly used personality traits were examined. According to the authors:

> a trait is a unique pattern of meaning assignment tendencies; these tendencies are within a limited numerical range, represent specific kinds of meaning variables, are partly applied by the individual frequently and partly infrequently, constitute together a specific structure and reflect a characteristic grouping of perceptual, cognitive, emotional and attitudinal manifestations.
>
> (Kreitler and Kreitler,1993a: 48)

As the concept of 'meaning' is the central issue in Kreitler and Kreitler's definition, it is necessary to stress that meaning is defined as a referent-centred pattern of cognitive contents. The authors further explained that the referent is the input, the carrier of meaning, anything that meaning can be assigned to (objects, words, concepts, poems, events, amongst others) and the cognitive contents can be expressed verbally or non-verbally, and may differ in veridicality and interpersonal sharedness.

Later on, Bornaud (1998) suggested that traits correspond to an elemental view of personality: each trait refers to a component of personality, each component being independent and characterizing a very precise facet of the individual. Traits are not synonymous with conduct – they only express the probability that the conduct will be manifested in a certain moment or in a certain situation. Traits are characterized as a *continuum* which means that each individual can be described by a level in the trait (Bornaud, 1998). 'Traits theory' is based on two assumptions: on the one hand, traits are relatively stable over time, and on the other hand, they have a certain level of trans-situational coherence, verified when people manifest similar modes of conduct in different situations. Examples of applications of this theory that appear to be most sustainable are those carried out by Allport and Odbert (1936), Fiske (1949) Eysenck (1974, 1970), Cattell (1957), and Goldberg (1981, 1983, 1992, 1999).

Personality Taxonomy

Historical Background

Attempts to create an adequate taxonomy of personality attributes that could provide a common framework for personality research began with the systematic work of Cattell (1943a, b, 1945a, 1946, 1947, and 1957) (cited by Digman, 1990: 419), considered by many the pioneering geometer of the personality realm. His contributions were essential for the development of a quantitative approach to personality assessment. His system reduced the number of personality terms first listed by Allport and Odbert (1936) who had constructed a list of personality-relevant terms, including adjectives and participles. Allport and Odbert's (1936) study resulted in a final list of almost 18 000 words. The terms were divided in four categories. The first was defined as 'stable traits' (internal and casual tendencies) and included terms like: aggressive, introverted and sociable. The second category, described as 'temporary moods or activities' comprised words such as abashed, gibbering, rejoicing and frantic. The third category was dedicated to terms conveying 'social evaluation', examples are: insignificant or worthy. Finally, the fourth category was considered a miscellaneous category including four subcategories, and was named 'metaphorical and doubtful terms'. Within the fourth category, the first subset referred to physical qualities: lean, redhead, amongst others. The second was reserved for capabilities and talents such as gifted and prolific. In this category, one could also find terms that seem to have scarce relevance to personality as well as those that could not be assigned to any of the other three categories. In order to limit the arbitrariness of their classification, Allport and Odbert (1936) submitted it to three independent judges which edited the entire list. The mean agreement among the judges was 47% on a final list of 300 items (John et al., 1988).

Cattell (1943) developed his multidimensional model of personality structure based on Allport and Odbert's list but reducing the number of personality terms to a more manageable size. First, he grouped the semantically similar terms as synonyms under a key word. Within each group he added an opposite for each term (bipolar traits), except for terms describing dynamic traits, and ability traits (unipolar traits).The grouping of antonym pairs eliminated several clusters and permitted a classification of about 4500 terms into 160 bipolar clusters. Then, Cattell selected around 13 terms from each cluster and summarized them with a key term. He found that only an emotionally factor and two or three traits related to neurotic and psychotic disorders were missing and concluded that his selections was completed. However, to achieve a more elaborate representation of the behavioural domains captured by his clusters, Cattel supplemented some of his clusters with terms from the psychological literature; he added the previously missing neurotic and psychotic terms (John et al., 1988: 179). This preliminary work was a relevant starting point for Cattell's system of personality description and provided the initial item selection for other researchers. Later on in his work, he used the Sixteen Personality Factors Questionnaire (16PF) consisting of 16 primary factors and 8 second-order factors to describe individual differences. Fiske (1949) replicated the studies using the 21 Cattell's bipolar scales and found a five factor model. Tupes and Christal (1961) reanalysed Cattell's and Fiske's correlations: finding all of them in rather good agreement in terms of five factors' (Digman, 1990: 419). They labelled their factors: 1-Surgency (talkative, assertive, energetic), 2-Agreeableness (good-natured, cooperative, trustful), 3-Dependability (consciousness, responsible, orderly), 4-Emotional Stability (calm, not neurotic, not easily upset) and 5-Culture (intellectual/cultured, polished, independent-minded).

Other studies corroborating the research of Fiske (1949), and Tupes and Christal (1961) were those of Borgotta (1964), who found five stable factors: Assertiveness, Likeability, Emotionality, Intelligence and Responsibility.

The 'Big-Five' Model of Personality: Hierarchical Structures

In 1963, Norman developed a preliminary hierarchical structure for the entire domain of trait terms. He understood traits as the central concepts internal to the individual and casually affective, excluding traits related to physique and health. He was guided by his interpretation of the big five-factors and later by the semantic similarity among the terms in each of the domains defined by the factors in a total of 75 categories. His main contribution was to create a middle level for factor 5 (Culture), with the following categories: Formality (pompous), Grace (dignified), Vanity (affected), Sophistication (urbane), Maturity (mature), Wisdom (intelligent, philosophical), Originality (creative), Knowledge (informed) and Art (artistic) vs Provinciality (unrefined, earthy), Imperceptiveness (ignorant, narrow) and Immaturity (naïve or superstitious). At the top level, his classification is constrained by a selection from Cattell's limited variable selection and at the lower level, it contains a comprehensive sample of traits descriptors grouped by semantic similarity. 'This view of factor five represents that of a single investigator, and others will disagree with some or most of the specifics' (John et al., 1988:189).

The work of Eysenck (1970) introduced the 'big-two' model: Neuroticism and Extroversion/introversion. Later on, the author added a Psychoticism dimension, and the set was then named the 'three superfactors: P (psychoticism), E (extroversion/introversion) and N (neuroticism)'. He considered, like Guilford (1975), intelligence or intellect to be something apart from temperament. His suggestion was to blend dimensions II and III into the P factor which he called Psychopathy dimension. Table 21.1 presents the various five-factors solutions that have been found in studies for more than 50 years.

Several other researchers noted the robustness of the five-factor model (Digman and Takemoto-Chock, 1981; Goldberg, 1981) concluding that the five factors 'represented an impressive theoretical structure' (Digman, 1990). In the early eighties, Wiggins developed a circular/circumplex model. He divided the 1710 trait adjectives into 6 subdomains: interpersonal traits, material traits, temperamental traits, social roles, character, and mental predicates. He limited his taxonomy to the first subdomain. The axis was status and love (dimensions 1 and 2). The terms were assigned to 16 categories which led to 16 scales with eight single adjectives. His taxonomy differs from Norman's (1963) and Golberg's (1981) in its inclusiveness and in the strategies used to structure the domain.

Goldberg (1981) continued the work of Norman and when analysing the correlations among 75 categories-scale scores formed on the basis of the terms included in each category, the 'big-five' emerged across a variety of different methods of factor extraction and

Table 21.1: The five robust dimensions of personality

Dimension / Author	Dimension I (Extroversion/ Introversion)	Dimension II (Agreeableness)	Dimension III (Conscientiousness)	Dimension IV Neuroticism/ Emotional Stability)	Dimension V Intellect or Openness)
Fiske (1949)	Social adaptability	Conformity	Will to achieve	Emotional control	Inquiring intellect
Cattell (1957)	*Exvia*	*Cortertia*	*Superego strength*	*Anxiety*	*Intelligence*
Tupes & Christal (1961)	*Surgency*	*Agreeableness*	Dependability	Emotionality	Culture
Norman (1963)	Surgency	Agreeableness	Conscientiousness	Emotional	Culture
Borgatta (1964)	Assertiveness	Likeability	Task interest	Emotionality	Intelligence
Esysenck (1970)	Extroversion	Psychoticism		Neuroticism	
Guilford (1975)	Social activity	Paranoid disposition	Thinking introversion	Emotional stability	
Wiggins (1980)	Power	Love			
Goldberg (1981)	Extraversion	Agreeableness	Conscientiousness	Emotional stability	Openness
Buss & Plomin (1984)	Activity	Sociability	Impulsivity	Emotionality	
Costa & McCrae (1985)	Extroversion	Agreeableness	Conscientiousness	Neuroticism	Openness
Tellegen (1985)	Positive emotionality		Constraint	Negative emotionality	
Hogan (1986)	Sociability and ambition	Likeability	Prudence	Adjustment	Intellectance
Lorr (1986)	Interpersonal involvement	Level of socialization	Self-control	Emotional stability	Independent
Peabody & Goldberg (1987)	Power	Love	Work	Affect	Intellect
Digman (1988)	Extroversion	Friendly compliance	Will to achieve	Neuroticism	Intellect
Saucier (1994)	Extroversion	Agreeableness	Conscientiousness	Neuroticism	Openness

Adapted and extended from Digman (1990: 417–440)

rotation. However, when more then five factors were rotated, additional factors were found. When six factors were rotated, the categories, identified by Norman into factor 5, slip into Ability factor and Culture factor. In a seven-factor option, categories such as religiosity, evangelism, passionless and honesty versus irreverence formed a small factor. These two additional dimensions find some parallels in other studies (Digman and Takemoto-Chock, 1981) who interpret factor 5 as Intellect and a less stable factor as Culture.

Later on, Goldberg (1992) also empirically examined Norman's preliminary classification and noted some deficiencies in the middle level categories. He decided to exclude 232 nouns and 25 adjectives and to add 44 new terms. Using bipolar categories, the 'big-five' emerged based on scores on a large number of single adjectives. He then found more factors when the five factors were rotated: 'ability' and 'culture' which encompasses the middle level categories of Norman. From the final version with 42 categories, 4 were not considered strictly personality traits: religion and political attitudes, social roles, effects and sexuality. However, this 'big-five plus little two seems limited to provide an adequately differentiated description of an individual' (John et al., 1988: 190).

In the last three decades, there has been a trend in personality psychology to regard the 'big-five' as a crucial model. The 'big-five' that have been generally accepted as encapsulating the five factor model are those defined by Goldberg (1981), Costa and McCrae (1985) and Saucier (1994): openness to experience, conscientiousness, extraversion, agreeableness and neuroticism – easily remembered as the acronym OCEAN. This model has been tested and/or used in several other studies in the field of psychology (Akrami et al., 2007; Bourdage et al., 2007; Edwards and Woehr, 2007; Gow et al., 2005; John and Rammstedt, 2006; Kulas et al., 2008; Lee et al., 2005; Smith and Snell, 1996); branding (Aaker, 1997, Azoulay and Kapferer, 2003); consumer psychology (Sung and Tinkham, 2005; Whelan and Davies, 2006); economic psychology (Campara et al., 2001; Milas and Mlačić, 2007) to name just a few.

Critical Aspects of the 'Big-Five' Model of Personality

Critique of the 'big-five' has addressed the legitimacy of this approach and whether or not the 'big-five' are theoretically sound. Digman (1990) agrees with Hogan's (1986) argument that the 'big-five' has given a useful set of very broad dimensions that characterize individual differences and that can be measured with high levels of reliability and validity. However, John et al. (1988) considered it to be too broad to satisfy many purposes of personality assessment, for instance when dealing with different languages and/or cultures 'The construction of a taxonomy of personality descriptive terms that is generally accepted in the field will require a substantial effort by personality psychologists working in different languages and cultures' (John et al. , 1988: 199).

The same authors (Goldberg, 1983; Digman and Inouye, 1986; John, 1989) have wondered: why five? Although the 'big-five' taxonomy has not been universally accepted, there is 'a general agreement that it serves as a useful integrative framework for thinking individual differences … and as an organizing principle to hierarchically structure the multitude of domain-specific traits relevant to consumer behaviour' (Baumgartner, 2002: 287).

Further developments included those of Peabody and Goldberg (1987). When trying to achieve an adequate representation of common English trait adjectives, they found what they called the 'small sixth factor': values. Similarly, Lee and Aston (2004) suggested a six dimensional framework, the so-called 'the hexaco model', which added a six factor to the 'big-five': honesty-humility. Goldberg (1999) developed the IPIP 'big-five' scales, which is a psychometrically sound instrument that covered closely other markers of the same construct. In parallel, Mowen (2000) developed the metathoretic model of motivation personality (3M), providing an organized structure for understanding the inter-relations among personality constructs. Reductions from the original inventory BFI- 44 to a ten-item inventory (BFI-10) were made by Gosling et al. (2003) and by Rammstedt and John (2006).

The 'big-five' model has been debated over the years, especially concerning dimension 5, where terms related to culture (artistic, sophisticated), intelligence (intelligent, complicated, sharp-witted), and creativity (imaginative, original, inventive) have been tested in, at least, five different languages, mainly because there are different interpretations of this dimension.

Interpretation of the Dimensions

While consensus was achieved concerning the number of necessary dimensions, the same did not happen concerning their meaning. There is a general agreement that dimension 1 is Eysenck's (1947) '*extroversion/introversion*', extroversion being a characteristic of an individual who is environmental-oriented, and introversion the main trait of a person who tends to be more closed to the external world. Dimension 2 is generally interpreted as 'agreeableness' (Costa and McCrae, 1985; Goldberg, 1981; Norman, 1963; Saucier, 1994; Tupes and Christal, 1961). It refers to the more human aspects, such as altruism, nurturance, caring and emotional support at one end of the dimension and hostility, indifference to others, self-centeredness, spitefulness and jealousy at the other (Digman, 1990). The essence of dimension 3 is linked to educational achievement (Digman, 1972b; Smith, 1967; Wiggins et al., 1969) or 'will to achieve' as suggested by Fiske (1949) and Digman (1988) or Goldberg (1981), Costa and McCrae (1985) and Saucier (1994) 'conscientiousness'. Dimension 4 refers to strong tendency to 'neuroticism' (Costa and McCrae, 1985; Digman, 1988; Saucier, 1994) and to extreme anxiety (Cattell, 1957; Lorr, 1986). It also represents the presence and effects of negative affect, or Tallegen´s (1985) 'negative emotionality'. Finally, dimension 5 has been interpreted by many as 'intellect' (Digman, 1988; Fiske, 1949; Hogan, 1983; Peabody and Goldberg, 1987), Intelligence (Borgotta, 1964; Cattell, 1957) and 'openness' (Costa and McCrae, 1985; Goldberg, 1981; Saucier, 1994). The latter relates to feelings, new ideas, flexibility of thought and readiness to indulgence in fantasy.

In the literature other trait names have been used to refer to the different dimensions: 1–'introversion/extraversion' or 'surgency'; 2–'friendliness/hostility' or 'agreeableness'; 3–'conscientiousness' or 'will'; 4–'neuroticism/emotional stability'; and 5–'intellect' or 'openness'. Each dimension is thus a set of smaller traits, called facets that are statistically linked as (summarized in Table 21.2).

As stated earlier in this chapter, marketing researchers have frequently applied the methodologies that led to the 'big-five' model, because brands, like individuals, can be described with adjectives. The approach used in psychology can be relevant to brand personality as perceived by consumers. In the same way, a personality of an individual is perceived by his/her behaviour, consumers can attribute personality to a brand according to its perceived communication and 'behaviours'. However, the crucial issue is to what extent can the terms (traits) used in human personality be applied to brands.

Table 21.2: Psychological five factors versus brand personality scale

Brand personality scale Aaker (1997)		Psychological five factors Saucier (1994)	
Traits	Dimensions	Traits	Dimensions
Down to earth, honest, wholesome and cheerful	Sincerity	Kind, sympathetic, warm, cooperative, cold, unsympathetic, harsh and rude	Agreeableness
Daring, spirited, imaginative and up-to-date	Excitement	Bold, extraverted, talkative, bashful, quiet, shy, withdrawn and energetic	Extroversion
Reliable, intelligent and successful	Competence	Efficient, organized, systematic, practical, disorganised, inefficient, sloppy and careless	Conscientiousness
Upper-class and charming	Sophistication	Creative, imaginative, intellectual, philosophical, deep, complex, uncreative and unintellectual	Openness
Outdoorsy and tough	Ruggedness	Unenvious, relaxed, fretful, envious, jealous, moody, touchy, temperamental	Neuroticism

Adapted from Azoulay A and Kapferer J N. (2003:149)

Personality Applied to the Brand Personality Concept

The definition proposed by Azoulay and Kapferer (2003: 151) is 'brand personality is the set of human personality traits that are both applicable and relevant for brands'. This concept of BP has become an important topic as it allows the distinguishing of brands (Crask and Laskey, 1990), helping to create a set of unique and favourable associations in consumer memory, builds brand equity (Jonhson et al., 2000; Keller, 1993; Phau and Lau, 2000), it evokes the emotional aspects of the brand (Gilmore, 2002; Morgan et al. 2004) and raises the personal meaning of the brand to the consumer (Levy, 1959). This leads to a fourfold definition of destination BP: (1) brand value (the destination code of behaviour); (2) brand attributes (the character traits of the destination); (3) brand personality (the sum of attributes which gives the destination its own unique brand personality); and (4) brand image (the impressions, beliefs and expectations tourists have about the destination). In the field of tourism research, these type of studies are more difficult as destinations join different interests and stakeholders (Young and Petrick, 2005). Consequently, objectives and research design need to take into account the multidimensionality of the construct and the number of stakeholders involved in the design of the tourism product.

The existing literature about the relationship between an individual and a brand leads to the conclusion that, 'since brands can be personified, human personality descriptors can be used to describe them' (Azoulay and Kapferer, 2003: 149), but the adjectives used to describe human personality may not be relevant to all brands: adaptation is required. Table 21.2 compares the two scales highlighting the factors derived from personality that should be used to measure brand personality. Adaptation was suggested by Aaker (1997) who tried to clarify the concept and build a scale to measure it. The scale was based on the 'big-five model' of personality. She explored brand personality on the basis of 114 adjectives (traits) across 37 brands of various product categories. She reached a five-factor solution: 'sincerity', 'excitement', 'competence', 'sophistication' and 'ruggedness'. Only three of those five factors correspond to elements of the five factors of psychology: Agreeableness and Sincerity capture the idea of warmth and acceptance; Extroversion and Excitement, both connote the notions of sociability, energy and activity; Conscientiousness and Competence both encapsulate responsibility, dependability and security (Aaker, 1997).

Conclusion

The characteristics found in the 'big-five' model of personality are a synthesis of the trait theories of personality developed by Cattell (1957) (comprehensive list of personality traits) and Eysenck (1947) (concise list of personality traits). Those theories seek to describe a person with as few adjectives as possible. Nowadays they are used in a corporate setting, in job interviews or in any situation where personality needs to be assessed. Psychologists claim that factor analysis detects five trait clusters as being strongly internally correlated and not strongly correlated with one another, generating a personality structure generally accepted.

The scale found for brand personality merges all the human characteristics applicable to brands under one word – personality, but it includes dimensions conceptually different from the pure concept of personality, for instance, sophistication and ruggedness. Competence refers to know-how i.e. abilities or cognitive capacities (dynamic factors), which is an item excluded from the definition of personality. Aaker (1997) also added some items related to gender (feminine/masculine), social class (upper-class) and age (youth) creating confusion between the brand itself (product) and the personality of the receiver or consumer. The brand personality scale also fails to include the traits related to the outcomes from the relationship between the receiver and the product (Azoulay and Kapferer, 2003).

Although some of the dimensions, in both scales, have the same connotations and some of the traits are similar, depending on the product (brand) to be assessed, the scale should be adapted to its specific characteristics. This issue is crucial when managers seek to adjust or change the positioning of their brands. Therefore, to establish a unique positioning, the brand should focus on the enhancement of its key brand personality dimensions.

Finally, even if the scale serves brand personality assessment purposes it will always reflect the personality of the respondents/receivers, as consumers seek to find in products their own identity. It can be concluded that a scale designed to measure brand personality can, ultimately, become a potential and useful market segmentation tool; it is therefore, an issue to be further consolidated in brand personality taxonomy.

Future Research

This chapter reviews the literature on lexical approaches to human personality structure and acknowledges the 'big-five' as the most general accepted model of personality. It also analyses how researchers have applied the 'big-five' model to assess brand personality and compares both scales. However, further research will be necessary to explore how this model could be applied to destination brand personality. Specific adaptations will be required to validate a measurement instrument able to assess tourism destination brand personality, than find its key dimensions and facets within each dimension. Other developments should include a cross-cultural study in several different destinations to test and validate the scale.

References

Aaker JL. 1997. Dimensions of brand personality. *Journal of Marketing Research* **34** (3): 347-356.

Abreu, MV. 1998. *Cinco ensaios sobre motivação*. Almedina: Coimbra.

Akrami N, Hedlund LE, Ekehammar B. 2007. Personality scale response latencies as self-schema indicators: the inverted–U effect revisited. *Personality and Individual Differences* **43**: 611-618.Allport GW, Odbert HS. 1936. Trait-names: A psycho-lexical study. *Psychological Monographs* **47**: no.211.

Azoulay A, Kapferer J. 2003. Do brand personality scales really measure brand personality? *Journal of Brand Management* **2** (2): 143-155.

Baumgartner H. 2002. Towards a personology of the consumer. *Journal of Consumer Research* **29**: 286-292.

Bernaud JL. 1998. *Métodos de avaliação da personalidade*. Climepsi Editores: Lisbon.

Borgotta EF. 1964. The structure of personality characteristics. *Behaviour Sciences* **12**: 8-17.

Bourdage JS, Lee K, Ashton MC, Perry A. 2007. Big five and hexaco model personality correlates of sexuality. *Personality and Individual Differences* **43**: 1506-1516.

Cai LA. 2002. Cooperative branding for rural destinations. *Annals of Tourism Research* **29** (3): 720-742.

Caprara GV, Barbaranellu C, Guido G. 2001. Brand personality: How to make the metaphor fit?. *Journal of Economic Psychology* **22** (3): 377-395.

Cattell RB. 1943a. The description of personality II. Basic traits resolved into clusters. *Journal of Abnormal and Social Psychology* **38**: 476-607.

Cattell RB. 1943b. The description of personality I. Foundations of trait measurement. *Psychological Review* **50**: 559-594.

Cattell RB. 1957. *Personality and motivation structure and measurement*. World Book: New York.

Costa PT Jr, McCrae RR. 1985. The NEO personality inventory. *Psychology Assessment Recourses*: Odessa FL.Costa PT Jr, McCrae RR. 1992. NEO Personality Inventory – Revised (NEO-PI-R) and NEO five factor inventory (NEO-FFI) professional manual. *European Journal of Personality* **8**: 357-369.

Crask MR, Laskey HA. 1990. A positioning-based decision model for selecting advertising messages. *Journal of Advertising Research*. August/September: 32-38.

Digman JM. 1972. High school academic achievement as seen in the context of a longitudinal study of personality. Presented at the Annual Meeting American Psychology Association: Honolulu.

Digman JM. 1990. Personality structure: emergence of the five-factor model. *Annual Review of Psychology* **41**: 417-440.

Digman JM, Takemoto-Chock N K. 1981. Factors en the natural language of personality: re-analysis, comparison and interpretation of six major studies. *Multivariate Behavioural Research* **16**: 149-170.

Digman J, Inouye J. 1986. Further specification on the five robust factors of personality. *Journal of Personality and Social Psychology* **50**: 116-123.

Edwuards B, Woehr DJ. 2007. An examination and evaluation of frequency-based personality measurement. *Personality and Individual Differences* **43**: 803-814.

Ekinci Y, Hosany S. 2006. Destination personality: an application of brand personality to tourism destinations. *Journal of Travel Research* **45**: 127-139.

Eysenck HJ. 1947. *Dimensions of Personality.* Praeger: New York.

Eysenck HJ. 1970. *The Structure of Human Personality.* Methuen. 3rd edn: London.

Fiske DW. 1949. Consistency of the factorial structures of personality ratings from different sources *Journal of Abnormal and Social Psychology* **44**: 329-44.

Gilford JP. 1975. Factors and factors of personality. *Psychology Bulletin* **82**: 802-814.

Gilmore F. 2002. Branding for success. In *Destination Branding: Creating a Unique Destination Proposition*, Morgan N, Pritchard A, Pride R (eds). Butterworth Heinemann: Oxford; 57-65.

Gnoth JC. 2002. Leverenging export brands through a tourism destination brand. *Journal of Brand Management* **9**: 262-280.

Goldberg LR. 1981. Language and individual differences: the search for universals in personality lexicons. In *Review of Personality and Social Psychology*, Wheeler L (ed.). Sage: Beverly Hills; 141-165.

Goldberg LR. 1983. The magical number five, plus or minus two: some conjectures on the dimensionality of personality descriptors. Paper presented at a Research Seminar, Gerentology Research Center, Baltimore City Hospitals.

Goldberg LR. 1992. The development of markers for the big five factor structure. *Psychological Assessment* **4** (1): 26-42.

Goldberg LR. 1999. A broad-bandwidth, public-domain, personality inventory measuring the lower level facets of several five factors models. In *Personality Psychology in Europe*, Mervielde I, Deary IJ, de Fruyt F, Ostendorf F (eds). Tilburg University Press: Tilburg; 7-28.

Gosling SD, Rentfrow PJ, Swann WB. 2003. A very brief measure of the big-five personality domains. *Journal of Research in Personality* **37**: 504-528.

Gow AJ, Whitemam MC, Pattie A, Deary IJ. 2005. Goldberg's 'IPIP' Big-Five factor makers: internal consistency and current validation in Scotland. *Personality and Individual Differences* **39** (2): 317-329.

Hogan R. 1983. Socioanalytic theory of personality. In *1982 Nebraska Symposium on Motivation: Personality – Current Theory and Research*, Page MM (ed). University Nebraska Press: Lincoln; 55-89.

Hogan R. 1986. *Hogan Personality Inventory*. National Computer Systems: Minneapolis MS.

Hosany S, Ekinci Y, Uysal M. 2006. Destination image and destination personality: an pplication of branding theories to tourism places. *Journal of Business Research* **59** (5): 638-642.

John OP. 1989. Towards a taxonomy of personality descriptors. In *Personality Psychology: Recent Trends and Emerging Directions*, Buss D, Cantor N (eds). Springer-Verlag: New York.

John OP, Angleitner A, Ostendorf F. 1988. The lexical approach to personality: a historical review of trait taxonomic research. *European Journal of Personality* 2: 171-205.

Jonhson LW, Soutar GN, Sweeney JC. 2000. Moderators of the brand image/perceived roduct quality relationship. *Journal of Brand Management* 7 (6): 425-433.

Keller L. 1993. Conceptualizing measuring and managing consumer-based brand equity. *Journal of Marketing* 57: 1-22.

Kreitler H, Kreitler S. 1993a. Personality traits: the cognitive revolution, in *Modern Trends in Personality, Theory and Research*, Perenzuela D, Barros A (eds). Associação dos Psicólogos Portugueses: Lisbon; 47-63.

Kreitler H, Kreitler S. 1993b. Personality and behaviour: the perspective of cognitive orientation. In *Modern Trends in Personality, Theory and Research*, Perenzuela D, Barros A (eds). Associação dos Psicólogos Portugueses: Lisbon; 65-85.

Kulas JT, Marriam J, Onama Y. 2008. Item-trait association, scale multidimensionality, and diferential item functioning identification in personality assessment. *Journal of Research in Personality.*

Lee K, Ashton MC. 2004. Psychometric properties of the hexaco personality inventory. *Multivarate Behavioural Research* 39: 329-358.

Lee K, Ogunfowora B, Ashton MC. 2005. Personality traits beyond the big five: are they within the hexaco space?. *Journal of Personality* 73 (5): 1437-1463.

Levy S. 1959. Symbols for sales. *Harvard Business Review* 37 (4): 117-1124.

Milas G, Mlačić B. 2007. Brand personality and human personality: findings from ratings of familiar Croatian brands. *Journal of Business Research* 60: 620-626.

Mo C, Howard D, Havitz M. 1993. Testing an international tourist role typology. *Annals of Tourism Research* 20 (2): 319-335.

Morgan N, Pritchard A, Pride R. 2004. *Destination Branding: Creating a Unique Destination Proposition*. Butterworth Heinemann: Oxford.

Mowen JC. 2000. The 3M model of motivation and personality: theory and empirical applications to consumer behaviour. Kluwer Academic Publishers.

Norman WT. 1963. Towards an adequate taxonomy of personality attributes: Replicated factor structure in peer nomination personality ratings. *Journal of Abnormal and Social Psychology* 66: 574-583.

Nuttin J. 1984. *Motivation, Planning and Action: a Relational Theory of Behaviour dynamics*. Louvain University Press and Lawrence Erlbaum Associates: Louvain.

Peabody D, Goldberg LR. 1987. *Variance and Invariance in Personality Structures Determinants of Factors Derived from Trait Adjectives*. Oregon Research Institute: Eugene.

Phau I, Lau KC. 2000. Conceptualizing brand personality: a review and research propositions. *Journal of Targeting, Measurement and Analysis of Marketing* 9 (1): 52-69.

Plummer JT. 1985. How personality makes a difference. *Journal of Advertising Research* 24 (6): 27-31.

Rammstedt B, John O. 2006. Measuring personality in one minute or less: a 10-item short version of the Big Five Inventory in English and German. *Journal of Research in Personality* 41 (1): 203-212.

Reuchlin M. 1992. *Introduction à la recherché en psychologie*. Éditions Nathan: Paris.

Ritchie J. 1993. Crafting a destination vision: Putting the concept of resident responsive tourism into practice. *Tourism Management* 14 (5): 379-389.

Smith JM. 1967. Usefulness of peer ratings of personality in educational research. *Educational Psychological Measurement* **27**: 967-84.

Smith DR, Snell WE Jr. 1996. Goldberg's bipolar measure of the big-five personality dimensions: reliability and validity. *European Journal of Personality* **10**: 283-299.

Sung Y, Tinkham SP. 2005. Brand personality structures in the United States and Corea: common and culture-specific factors. *Journal of Consumer Psychology* **15** (4): 334-350.

Tupes EC, Christal RE. 1961. Recurrent personality factors based on trait ratings, technical report ASD-TR 61-97 US Force, Lackland Air Force Base, TX; (1992) *Journal of Personality* **60**: 225-251.

Young S, Petrick JF. 2005. Destinations' perspectives of branding. *Annals of Tourism Research* **33** (1): 262-265.

Whelan S, Davies G. 2006. Profiling consumers of own brands and national brands using human personality. *Journal of Retailing and Consumer Services* **13**: 393-402.

Wiggins N, Blackburn M, Hackman JR. 1969. The prediction of first-year success in psychology: peer ratings. *Journal of Educational Research* **63**: 81-85.

Part III:

Destination Stakeholders and Networks

22 The Role of Brands in Dialectical Relationships between Destination and Tourist Products

Tonino Pencarelli, Simone Splendiani, University of Urbino

Introduction

The term 'tourist destination' has different meanings, often conflicting, both in the literature and among practitioners. Sometimes *destination* is understood as a geographical area, as a place.[1] In other circumstances, the perceptual dimension is preferred – that is, the tourists' point of view. In other cases, the two perspectives overlap, considering destination in terms of both producers and consumers. Tourist destination definitions can be placed into two fundamental perspectives – the demand and the supply points of view (Franch, 2002). The first group of definitions tends to qualify and assimilate tourist destinations as a set of attractiveness factors, both natural and artificial, able to pull in tourists. Therefore, the destination and the tourist product concepts tend to converge (Answorth and Goodall, 1990; Bieger, 2000; Buhalis, 2000; Davidson and Maitland, 1997). The second group of definitions tends to identify destinations as including producers – assimilating the destination into the territory and supply system (Brunetti, 2002; Martini, 2002; Tamma, 2002).

Some contributions have assumed, more or less explicitly, an overlapping perspective with regard to the destination concept, trying to combine a demand and supply points of view (Casarin, 2002; Della Corte, 2000; Furlan, 2007). It is in this conceptual framework that we introduce the tourist destination concept. The destination can be qualified:

> as a place populated by a combination of businesses and tourism resources able to attract significant inbound tourist numbers, building products capable of meeting visitors' needs. The destination is a relatively homogeneous area from a territorial, social, economic and cultural point of view. In the overlapping perspective, it must tend to have the same connotations also in terms of demand, to be holistically perceived by current and potential tourists.

Following the 'experience economy model' developed by Pine and Gilmore (2000), the tourist destination is the place where the offer is made up of a bundle of commodities, goods, service and experiences, both assembled by producers and self-composed by tourists. These offers progressively increase in value. Tourists can be considered to

---

1 Cf. Hanna and Rowley, 2008. The identification of a tourist destination from a geographical point of view is complicated in itself. As the authors emphasise, this 'is complicated by the fact that a destination may include several towns, cities or municipalities, other government provinces or even an island archipelago may be the entire country'. This depends on the definition of the 'hierarchy of destinations' (Martini, 2002), anticipating the need for strict connection with demand.

be indifferent addressees of undifferentiated economic proposals, or as active subjects, heavily involved in the production and consumption process of the tourist product with a high immateriality content (services and experiences), until they themselves become a sort of 'product', in the case of 'product/transformations'. Tourists become:

> the result of the transformation process put in place by tourism producers to meet their expectations of change and needs at the physical, emotional, psychological and social levels.[2]

It follows that although the tourist product sometimes converges with the resort (the destination):

> it should be more appropriately considered as a result, an output from the activities carried out by the destination actors.

As such, it is a:

> package composed of many elements bundled by one or more producers or by tourists searching for a global tourism product.
>
> (Casarin, 2002; Rispoli, 2001; Rispoli and Tamma, 1995)

A destination is a 'stage', where various tourism products can be arranged in order to satisfy the desires of different market segments. When this stage is able to satisfy the needs of a unique market segment (through one type of product), the destination and tourism product concepts tend to overlap, at least in the perception of intermediaries and users. Assuming, however, that the supply point of view cannot escape the fact that the product is the result of activities performed by destination producers and that although the two concepts are dialectic (the tourist experience is strongly linked to the place in which it occurs), there is a strong distinction between them.

If from the demand-side tourist experiences may qualify as: 'personal and engaging events that involve moving in space and with a time duration that includes one night', from the supply-side *the tourist product is the result of systemic offer of goods, services, information, tourist attractions, environment, etc.*(Pencarelli and Forlani, 2002). This offer is arranged in a tourism production system in order to provide customers with some economic proposals that, going beyond the simple mix of goods and services, is more decidedly and deliberately directed towards providing *products with strong experiential content*. Products offering a strong experiential content also imply the involvement of a variety of actors and resources on the supply-side, including public and private actors, entrepreneurs, information agents, environmental, financial and technological resources, intangible assets, etc.

Consequently, important and strategically relevant competition in the tourist market occurs *among tourist destinations* rather than among individual firms. Whether the destination reveals a shared strategic intent or the activities are spontaneously produced by actors, tourists enjoy and perceive a *comprehensive experience* containing all attractions, goods, services, experiences and transformations during their stay (Keller, 2000; Manente and Cerato, 2000).

Synthetically:

---

2   Here we refer to cases in which tourists who purchase vacations and vacation packages in health spas, instructional retreats, training schools, etc. in which the client pays to be transformed or undergo transformations, the results of which depend on both the supplier's ability and the activities applied by the client.

1. A tourist destination is a geographical area with a block/basin of resources and companies producing commodities, goods, services, experiences and transformations coherent to an emerging and/or deliberate logic;

2. A tourist product is a bundle of commodities, goods, services, experiences and transformations assembled by actors internal or external to the destination or directly by tourists, through needs, motivations and personal cognitive system.

Tourists have the opportunity to use more or less organised resources, commodities, goods, services, experiences and transformations that actors offer them in the destination. What they experience from the point of choosing a destination to the point of returning home represents the comprehensive tourist experience. Depending on how it is perceived, the experience may have created more or less value, influencing customer satisfaction, his/her willingness to return to the destination or to provide positive or negative word-of-mouth, with important consequences for the image of the destination (Figure 22.1).

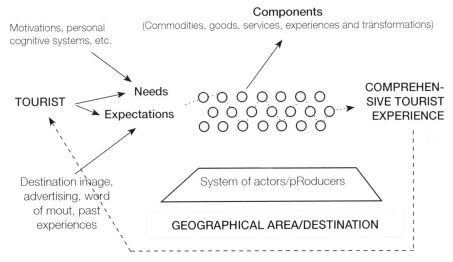

Figure 22.1: Tourists, destination and tourist products

From 'Traditional' Destination Management to Innovative Forms Encountered in Practice

Destination management literature has produced several hypotheses for managing tourist destinations. Some studies suggest spontaneous forms of self-regulation, others consider the presence of a strategic leader essential.[3] From our point of view, tourist destinations

---

3   A semi-hierarchical model was proposed by Brunetti (2002), which argues that before talking about strategic government of tourist destinations we must specify the limits, indicating that is necessary to maintain a proper balance between strict management and spontaneity. Tamma (2002) highlights that the characteristics of each destination can bring to the fore several key figures and that there is no single subject which in theory could act as an authority to regulate and coordinate the development of the destination. On the other hand, there are those like Martini (2005; Martini and Ejarque, 2008), who suggest that in order to develop a Destination Management project the destination must have an organization so as to improve coordination between (and within) sub-systems involved. Buhalis (2000) also affirms that destinations should be managed by a 'destination management organization' (DMO) responsible for destination designing and marketing and having the power and resources to undertake actions aimed at achieving strategic objectives.

need to identify an entity capable of exercising highly complex and articulated functions (planning, coordination, support, advice, monitoring, marketing, promotion, etc.) and which all the destination actors hold to be legitimate. This role could be played by management representatives of public and private members and underpinned by private legal rules in order to facilitate the opening up of ownership (Pencarelli, 2001). The process of creating strategic leadership is very important in terms of its legitimacy. It may take two forms: top-down or bottom-up (Golinelli, 2002; Martini, 2002;).

However, the context strongly influences both organizational solutions and the pertinence of Destination Management principles and tools. Where resources and tourist activities are poorly integrated (fragmentation model), it is extremely difficult to design Destination Management strategies that express a strong and unified supply management (Sciarelli, 2007; Tamma, 2002). Conversely, where there are players who take on a leadership role in organizing and controlling supply (leadership model), or there is a good degree of cooperation between operators (cooperation model), it is easier to build a negotiation board and to identify key players.

Other scholars (Flagestad and Hope, 2001; Martini, 2005) argue that in 'corporate' destinations management is not dissimilar to managing a multi-unit enterprise. The management of 'community' destinations is more problematic because resources are owned by several independent subjects. In this case, management must address many conflicting interests which becomes extremely difficult, but it is necessary for long-term destination success (Buhalis, 2000).

Finally, we must consider the destination's geographical extension and its cultural homogeneity. The territory must have a shared identity that allows the leader to activate relationship systems based on trust among actors (cf Fyall et al. 2003).

Tourist destination strategic management primarily involves the territorial government. Second, it involves resources activated through projects able to promote cooperative systems and to create tourism products capable of addressing competitive challenges. Practice has not always followed this approach. We have found some empirical cases that offered a new interpretation of destination management philosophy – uniting resources, businesses and public actors not necessarily connected to the territory, but related by their capacity to offer value propositions (products) directed toward specific market segments:

> They have pursued strategies not based on valuation of areas on the whole, but focused on resources and attraction groups linked by the same thematic characteristics, such that we can speak more appropriately in terms of product management instead of destination management.

We refer to the case of the Emilia Romagna region, analysed in empirical research carried out in a comparison with the Marche region model (Pencarelli and Splendiani, 2008).

Emilia Romagna is a region in central Italy that faces the Adriatic Sea to the east and borders the Marche region to the south. Both of these regions extend from the Adriatic coast to the Apennine mountain chain, offering a rich territorial geography that encapsulates all of the geographical features of Italy. These regions enjoy important historical and artistic heritage resources and contain numerous cities of art and important spiritual and religious sites (for example, Loreto in Marche). In terms of tourism, Emilia Romagna receives approximately four times the number of trips recorded for the Marche region (8 million to 2 million) and approximately three times the number of overnight stays. This is due to the greater average length of stay in the Marche region (more than 6 days) – the highest in Italy. Both regions are characterized by a concentration of arrivals and overnight stays in their coastal areas, particularly in some areas so well known that they overshadow even the regional brand (for example, Rimini in Emilia Romagna).

In terms of regional organization, while the Marche region has opted for the STL model (local tourism system – *sistemi turistici locali*), in accordance with national laws and in line with the Destination Management approach,[4] the Emilia Romagna region has instead opted for organizational solutions defined as product unions (*Unioni di Prodotto*[55]) and product clubs (*Club di Prodotto*). Emilia Romagna has focused not so much on the territory (although all resources are located within the region), as on the so-called 'tourism sector' to which it belongs (*The Adriatic Coast, Spa and Fitness, Appennines and Nature, Art Cities*).

Both *STLs* and product unions are public and private actor networks aimed at tourism development: the difference is in the location of the players.

In *STLs* they operate in a specific and bounded sub-regional geographical area and have the task of designing and marketing tourism products, produced and consumed inside the area (Figure 22.2). In the Product Unions, however, the players are dispersed throughout the entire region (Figure 22.3)

Figure 22.2: Case sub-region

4   According to Regional legislation, Local Tourism Systems "are the instrument through which the public and private sectors cooperate to manage activities of tourist product formation. The creation of Local Tourism Systems follows a "bottom-up" process, while the creation and dissemination of criteria for formal recognition and the administrative act of recognition remains with the regional government. According to the Regional Law of 2006 (Art.8, comma 4), which draws from National Law n.135 of 29 March 2001, the Systems:
a) indentify tourist products appropriate for the territory in question, also to the point of putting them out on the market, and create a total picture of the value of local resources with particular attention to the specific characteristics of hinterland, mountain and coastal zones;
b) organize reception activities, integrating and harmonizing these with other activities present in the territory in question. (translated from Italian)

5 Product unions are governed by art 13 (Aggregazioni di prodotto di interesse regionale) of Emilia-Romagna's Regional Law n. 7 of 4 March 1998, comma 1 , which states "The Region favours the process of aggregation between public and private operators for the coordination, integration and implementation of tourism sale and promotion projects so as to reward joint actions taken to develop the regional tourist economy, to strengthen and integrate tourism products as well as to increase and improve available resources". The following identifies priority tourism areas around which product unions may be created – in this case, Adriatic Coast, Green Apennines, City of Art/Culture and Business as well as spas.
Cf. Art.12 Regional Law 6 March 2007, n.2.

Figure 22.3: Product unions in Emilia Romagna Region.
(Source: www.emiliaromagnaturismo.it)

3a): Product Union 'The Adriatic Coast'

3b): Product Union 'Spa and Fitness '

3c): Product Union 'Appenines and Nature'

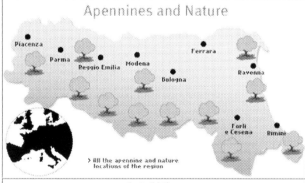

3d): Product Union 'Art Cities'

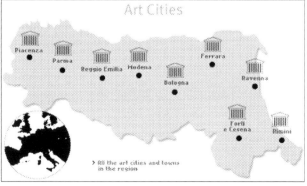

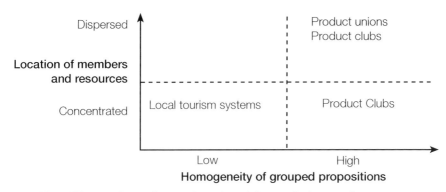

Figure 22.4: STLs, product unions and product clubs postioning matrix.

Similarly, product clubs are networks linked to projects aimed at creating value proposi-tions for specific market segments. They are associated with different legal forms and their members may have different locations.[6] All Clubs formed in the Emilia Romagna region are potential members of Product Unions,[7] just as other associations of tourism operators can participate in the STLs in the Marche region. The matrix in Figure 22.4 distinguishes STLs, product unions and product clubs – on one hand considering the location of members and resources (concentrated or dispersed), and on the other hand the homogeneity of grouped propositions (low or high).

The STLs analysed (Pencarelli and Forlani, 2006; Pencarelli and Splendiani, 2008), however, show more shadow than light, particularly regarding marketing policies, fi-nancial sustainability and entrepreneurial commitment. The latter, in particular, is often weakened by the sometimes excessive public component as well as the lack of coop-eration between players. The study suggests that the success of a destination requires that management understand the perspective of the customer and know how to create, communicate and deliver value through a wide portfolio of offerings with a strong ex-periential content.

Product clubs, instead, have been shown to possess a strong entrepreneurial drive that has enabled effective marketing actions such as bundling, communications and com-mercialization. This is facilitated by a better focus on the mission, and members (nu-merically lower than those of STLs) are able to organize themselves for specific projects, with faster and more readily identifiable feedback. Research on product clubs (Pencarelli and Splendiani, 2008), however, reveals that creating mono-thematic offers may fail to generate acceptable performance, both for buyers (tourists and intermediaries looking for multi-thematic and multi-experienti al travel) and for local stakeholders. In the cases analysed, there was a noticeable tendency to diversify offerings towards segments other than the main one, focusing on all territorial resources and attractions considered to be important attractiveness factors for external stakeholders and cohesive forces for all the members involved.

We believe the different philosophies and approaches tested in the Marche and Emilia Romagna regions represent additional models which can coexist within destinations. The challenge for local tourism policies is to identify the best mix of organizational

6   The geographic extent of the territory is varied. Some Clubs operate nationally, like the 'Borghi più Belli d'Italia', others at the regional or interregional level, others at the sub-regional level or in single cities.

7   The admissibility of members in Product Union statutes is conditioned by their business activities within the specific 'tourism sector' to which they belong.

solutions and paths aimed at exploiting resources and attractions through market-driven strategies. Destinations need to have leaders capable of setting, promoting and marketing tourist products with a strong experiential content, bringing together and balancing components of different economic value (commodities, goods, services, experiences and transformations, following Pine and Gilmore's model).

Destination Brands and Destination Branding

After highlighting the possibilities and approaches for managing destinations, it is useful to clarify the key points for putting in place effective marketing and branding policies. Pencarelli (2001) and Pencarelli and Splendiani (2008) argue that there is a need for the person responsible for managing destinations to adopt an *integrated and holistic marketing management approach*. To meet new features of the tourist market, we believe it is necessary to combine the classic paradigm (through the use of traditional marketing management methods) with both relationship marketing (cf. Fyall et al., 2003) with the aim of creating lasting and interactive relationships with customers and other stakeholders, and *internal marketing*, that builds and maintains a strong service culture among subjects involved in tourist product production and delivery. *Destination branding policies* fall into this framework. The topic of *destination branding*, moreover, cannot be addressed by simple application and transfer of management paradigms and issues designed for businesses. It takes on specific characteristics compared to traditional branding, because it is strongly linked to public communication. This requires integration of all community outputs (not only regarding tourism) as well as communication to all audiences, not only tourists.[8]

It should be noted that destination branding always operates on two levels: *externally*, encouraging the creation of cognitive and affective relationships with current and potential tourists; and *internally*, increasing the sense of belonging, socio-cultural identity of businesses and local community and acting as a powerful internal marketing instrument for building cultural values that inspire collective behaviour with regard to tourism.[9]

While the concept of *destination brand* has been defined by Ritchie et al. (1998) as 'name, symbol, logo, word or other graphic that both identifies and differentiates the destination', Cai (2002) defines *destination branding*[10] 'as selecting a consistent element mix to

---

8   Hanna S., Rowley J. (2008) point out that various "outputs" of a geographical area can be promoted and sold individually, even if they tend to be perceived as a "whole": "the components of nations, such as tourism, agriculture and entertainment, can be individually promoted and sold, but by definition, nations are unlikely to have a single target market or offering". Therefore, in the context of tourism we are focused on destination brand and destination branding, but within the wider strategy of location branding (Morgan, 2006, cited in Hanna et al, 2008) or place branding (Cf. Anholt, 2008). On this, Kerr (2006) claims that "destination marketing and the destination brand have the limitation of being tourism focused only and often preclude major stakeholders in a location". He believes that a more holistic approach of location or place brand management is necessary.

9   As Konecnik (2007) argues "Within such context – tourist destination … which is based on a myriad of different products, services and experiences, managed by different stakeholders with a variety of ownership forms and often without an appropriate hierarchy with a set of rules for stakeholders to adhere to – a brand identity can serve as a network picture, which draws, in turn on historical, national and cultural relationships to develop a common view, which becomes the basis for joint action for and/or against change".

10 There are two different approaches in the literature to the study of destination branding: static and dynamic. The first observes relationships between image and consumer behaviour, such as consumer satisfaction and the process of destination choice. The second (our focus), concentrates on image

identify and distinguish it (destination) through positive image building.[…]Consistent brand elements reinforce each other and serve to unify the entire process of image formation and building, which in turn contributes to the strength and uniqueness of brand identity'. The author's view (which we share) tends to distinguish *destination branding activities* from *the image formation process*: 'image formation plays only a partial role in branding a destination, and total practice should involve actively and methodologically building a consistent image by integrating a variety of marketing activities'.

This approach is consistent with the difference emphasized by Grönroos (2002) between 'brand identity' and 'brand image'. 'Identity' is what marketers wants to create,[11] while 'image' is formed in the customer's mind.[12] The brand creator's goal, therefore, often does not match the image being formed in the customer's mind. It is highly risky to think that marketers can create a brand on their own. As Grönroos argues, if there is anyone who can build a brand it is the customer; the role of marketing is to create structures for brand development in the customers' minds, and planned communication must be considered only as an element of support. This is particularly true in tourism economies, where 'destination image formation' has a strong experiential nature and:

> destination branding activities must guide this process in order to impress a positive destination image in tourists' minds in order to influence their decision-making process.[13]

Destination image, as well as representing the set of values and beliefs that current and potential tourists and all other stakeholders connect with the destination:[14]

---

structure and formation itself (Gallarza et al., 2002). For research on factors that influence destination image, see Beerli and Martin, 2004.

11 Cf. Konecnik et al., 2008. The authors claims that "Brand identity clearly specifies what the brand aspires to stand for and has multiple roles. First, it is a set of associations that the brand strategist seeks to create and maintain. Secondly, it represents a vision of how a particular brand should be perceived by its target audience. Thirdly, upon its projection the brand identity should help establish a relationship between a particular brand and its clientele by generating a value proposition potentially either involving benefits or providing credibility, which endorses the brand in question".

12 For a summary of the concept of destination image, see Konecnik, 2004 and Cai, 2002. On the relationship between destination image and destination personality, see Hosany et al., 2006. On concepts of brand equity applied to destinations, see Konecnik and Gartner, 2007. The latter in particular propose measuring the economic value of the destination brand (brand equity) across four dimensions: image, awareness, quality and loyalty. The managerial implications of this "broad" view of brand are significant: "proper marketing strategies – the authors suggest – should increase tourists' destination awareness, appeal to their image or quality perceptions, or influence their loyalty dimension. It is reasonable to employ different marketing strategies for different foreign markets, but all marketing strategies should be prepared in consideration of the destination's brand identity". Cf. Hankinson, 2004; Prebensen, 2007; Tasci et al., 2007.

13 Cai (2002) also highlights the importance of destination image within the destination choice process: "The challenge of branding destinations lies with the complexity of the decision process on the part of tourists. … Unlike other tangible products, tourists are not able to "test drive" and try the destinations before making a choice. Therefore, the decision involves greater risk and extensive information search, and depends on tourists' mental construct of what a potential destination has to offer relative to their needs. As a result, destination image is a critical stimulus in motivating the tourist".

14 Cf. Gronroos, 2002. Hankinson (2007) claims that "Typically, these brand associations" – held in consumer memory about brand - "have been classified into two categories: functional attributes, which are the tangible features of a product or service; and emotional/symbolic attributes, which are the intangible features that meet consumer needs for social approval, personal expression or self-esteem. Other authors add a third category: experiential attributes, which relate to how it feels to use a product or service and satisfy internally generated needs for stimulation and variety".

♦   *Communicates expectations* through external marketing activities to the tourist, but also to other stakeholders, helping assess information, advertising messages and word-of-mouth;

♦   *Is a filter that influences perceptions* and perceived quality and value;

♦   *Is linked to expectations as much as the experiences*: quality tested in experience can strengthen or weaken the image;

♦   *Has an impact on a destination's actors (internal) as well on tourists (external).*

From the point of view of tourists, the image formation process and value perception can be considered in parallel.[15] Both are dynamic concepts, developing as the tourist experience comes to fruition and beyond, that involve a long-term relationship between tourists and destinations.

Branding policies should be aimed at creating a brand identity that matches the reality experienced in the destination. This is very complex because *destination branding* involves many stakeholders (Laws et al., 2002) including local people (cf. Freire, 2007) Moreover, several brands coexist within the same destination, but they are, often introduced by various actors without a common strategy. Actually, this influences tourists' image perception, and risks confusing them.

It may be useful to analyse different *categories of brand* found in the same destination. Depending on the object to which the brand is linked, these categories may be:

♦   *Territorial*, referring to a specific geographical area. This may be *institutional*, linked to administrative boundaries (nation, region, province, town, mountain community, protected area, etc.) or *natural* (lakes, rivers, mountains, etc.);

♦   *Resource*, referring to single resources (natural or artificial). This becomes increasingly important in proportion to the attractiveness of the resource and, therefore, is able to influence the destination choice process. Brand becomes a means of communicating information between tourists and resources;

♦   *Network*, referring to a supply system based on shared projects. Following the definition of destination used here, 'network brand' identifies a group of businesses and tourist resources operating together in a project and sharing a common aim. In reality this is not always true. Brand may be the only element that unites the players. Network brands focus on tourism 'producers', and therefore belong to the supply-side. Examples of brands are those of STLs, product clubs and unions, franchising networks, tourism boards and other type of networks;

♦   *Product*, referring to a bundle of commodities, goods, services, experiences and transformations created to respond to a particular need. Product brands focus on tourists' perceptual dimension, communicating the value proposition rather than the players that provide it;

♦   *Enterprise*, referring to tourism businesses that provide goods, services and tourist experiences (tour operator, travel agencies, hotels, etc.).

---

15 Pencarelli and Splendiani (2008) state that analysis of the perception of quality (and therefore value) of the tourist experience may be carried out by referring to traditional principles of service management – particularly to the perceived service quality model (Grönroos, 2002; Gummenson, 1979), according to which the quality of a service is equal to that which the client perceives it to be (Grönroos, 2002). In the case of tourist experiences, value is perceived globally and holistically over the course of interaction with the destination through various and varied contacts with the territory and tourism operators as they make use of the single components of the comprehensive tourist experience. On the management and evaluation of quality in tourist destinations, see Woods and Deegan, 2003.

From the marketing management perspective, a brand may be *emerging* or *deliberate* (cf. Anholt, 2008). It is emerging if has its own identity and reputation, developed over time or because of special circumstances (cf. Yeoman et al., 2005), it has no need for promotional activities (territorial brands are certainly emerging because the territory has a name and is located on maps). The brand may be considered deliberate if created from scratch, as the result of planned marketing activities (from design to definition of the brand concept and its positioning). Both emerging and deliberate brands may be the object of branding activities. This requires understanding of the target-segments, brand element definition (name, logo, pay-off, etc.) and support through proper communication policies.

All brand types influence tourists' image formation. Tourists receive a multitude of messages related to different brands but, as with quality perception, they are unable to distinguish providers of goods and services and tend to generate an overall destination image in their minds (cf. Pencarelli and Splendiani, 2008; Buhalis, 2000). Managing and branding destination need to cope with a constant dialectic among brands and brand activities, according to the classification proposed above. Territorial branding activities are oriented towards expressing uniformity of values and symbols. Territorial brands 'should be indicative of the location's vision for the future and receive wide stakeholder support: it is aligned to the 'corporate brand' (Kerr, 2006).[16] Branding activities involving network and business brands, instead, focus on the providers and resources that produce tourist services, focusing on characteristics like quality and professionalism, aiming to improve tourists' loyalty. Finally, product branding activities aim at stimulating purchase of a specific value proposition.

The interweaving and overlapping of different activities make the roles of key-players very complex. It is responsible for coordinating and giving coherency to various paths, seeking a shared mission aimed at the valorization of territorial identity.[17]

---

16 The author argues that "the application of brand management practices to the location or place brand may well address some of the structural and strategic dilemmas facing destination marketing organisations and the destination brand. It is first necessary to address some of the brand concepts that are important when applying brand practices to a location — brand architecture, brand portfolio and the corporate brand".... A destination brand may be seen to be more closely aligned to a product brand defining the 'tourism product', while a location brand should be more aligned to the corporate brand model and be managed more strategically 'from the top', with a strong emphasis on relationships within its architecture and portfolio As with a corporation, a location has a number of options when considering its brand architecture. Should there be a 'branded house' or a 'house of brands'? Should the brand focus only on tourism? The destination brand could be part of the location brand architecture". In his work where he applied corporate brand theories to destination brand management, Hankinson (2007) argued: "While it is acknowledged that there are evident differences both in the character and in the management of these two categories of brand, it is argued that there are sufficient similarities between the two types of brand to allow useful lessons to be drawn..... In particular ... destination brand management requires strong, visionary leadership and organisation-wide commitment from the highest level downwards to a set of brand values which encapsulate the destination's brand promise. This process begins with the top management of the DMO and a strategic vision which can form the basis for a brand-oriented culture manifested in the alignment of processes and departmental coordination around the brand. Then, through a process of dialogue and discussion, a brand strategy must be refined by the organisations forming the network of alliances and partnerships who will eventually communicate and deliver the destination brand experience. The role of the DMO throughout this process is to ensure consistent communications, both collectively and individually with all stakeholders: partners, visitors and residents".

17 Similar, in this sense, to Morgan et al. (2002), who, in reference to NTOs (National Tourism Organization) role, argued that "Destination marketing requires foresight and planning, but it is not an

Conclusion

What does the term 'tourist destination' mean? What about 'tourist product'? Can we consider the two concepts to be synonyms? This chapter has attempted to provide answers to these questions through a critical analysis of the literature which, we believe, has often underestimated the importance of these points.

We then analysed two different organizational solutions adopted by two Italian regions for managing tourism at the regional level. We observed different ways of creating networks which should be considered complementary and the challenge for tourism policies is to find the proper mix of paths and organizational solutions.

We pointed out that any attempt at destination management needs to cope with the dialectical relationship between destination and tourist product. This relationship must be analysed in order to understand the problems intrinsic to branding tourist destinations and to understand role of destination leader, which is very complex since it must coordinate and make consistent different branding paths and different brand levels (destination, products, network, resource), and find a shared mission aimed at the valorization of territorial identity.

This mission needs both a legitimate leader and a collaborative relationship – based on trust – between network members. Consequently, we can assert that fragmentation is a huge barrier to destination promotion, communication and branding. On the other hand, brand creation may represent an opportunity for fragmented contexts because it favours a growing sense of belonging around the social and cultural identity of economic actors and the local community. In this sense, great attention must be paid to the design phase of brand identity, which should be the synthesis of belief and meanings and must be realistic with respect to those of the territory. At the same time, it must be able to transmit personality and emotional values affecting tourist choice processes (cf. Morgan et al., 2002). The same attention should be paid to subsequent stages when introducing a new brand. Very often brand proliferation suffers from inadequate follow-up. This not only refers to financial support for traditional promotion, but, above all, requires the definition of a path aimed at exploiting strategic assets such as destination brands – once they are created. In this sense, it is advisable to encourage brand discipline and to set out clear rules for using the brand by members, as well as a description of brand identity.

In conclusion, the critical factors of communication and branding mainly regard the complexity of the 'destination' entity, in which multiple interests tend to overlap, and application of Destination Management tools becomes very problematic. Seizing the challenge of this application is essential, in our opinion, to meet the increasing need to create and communicate a unique identity and compete successfully in the *global arena* of tourist destination markets.

---

exact science and branding offers destination marketers an opportunity to communicate key place attributes to their intended audience.... The role of the NTO is to take these and construct a singular point of differentiation from its competitors, but destinations operate in a global marketplace where many countries try to deliver a multitude of messages about what their country represents. In this, branding can help bridge any gaps between a destination's strengths and potential visitors' perceptions. Place reputations are not made in a vacuum and neither are tourist choices, so place marketers must establish how their destination's image compares with those of its key competitors. It takes patience to establish brand reputations, and building a powerful destination brand is a long-term effort which more often than not yields incremental and not exponential results".

References

Anholt S. 2008. Place branding: Is it marketing, or isn't it? *Place Branding and Public Diplomacy* **4**: 1-6

Ashworth G, Goodball B. 1990. *Marketing Tourism Places*. Routledge: London.

Beerli A, Martin JD. 2004. Factors influencing destination image. *Annals of Tourism Research* **31** (3): 657-681.

Bieger T. 2000. Destination Management e finanziamenti. In *Destination Management. Fondamenti di marketing e gestione delle destinazioni turistiche*, Pechlaner H, Weiermair K (eds). TUP: Milan.

Brunetti F. 2002. Il Destination Management: aspetti problematici, significato e percorsi alla ricerca di una qualità ad effetto prolungato. In *Destination Management. Governare il turismo fra locale e globale*, Franch M (ed.). Giappichelli: Turin.

Buhalis D. 2000. Marketing the competitive destination of the future. *Tourism Management* **21**: 97-116.

Cai LA. 2002. Cooperative branding for rural destinations. *Annals of Tourism Research* **29** (3): 720-742.

Casarin F. 2002. *Il marketing dei prodotti turistici*. Giappichelli: Turin.

Davidson R, Maitland R. 1997. *Tourism Destination*. Hodder & Stoughton: London.

Della Corte V. 2000. *La gestione dei sistemi locali di offerta turistica*. Cedam: Padua.

Flagestad A, Hope CA. 2001. Strategic success in winter sport destination: A sustainable value creation perspective. *Tourism Management* **22**: 445-461.

Franch M (ed.). 2002. *Destination Management. Governare il turismo fra locale e globale*. Giappichelli: Turin.

Freire JR. 2007. 'Local people' a critical dimension for place brands. *Journal of Brand Management*: 1-19.

Furlan MC. 2007. Il marketing della destinazione turistica. In *Il marketing dei prodotti turistici. Specificità e varietà. Vol.II*, Casarin F (ed.). Giappichelli: Turin.

Fyall A, Callod C, Edwards B. 2003. Relationship marketing. The challenge for destination. *Annals of Tourism Research* **30** (3): 644-659.

Gallarza MG, Saura IG, Garcia HC. 2002. Destination image. Towards a conceptual framework. *Annals of Tourism Reseach* **29** (1): 56-78.

Golinelli CM. 2002. *Il territorio sistema vitale*. Giappichelli: Turin.

Grönroos C. 2002. *Management e Marketing dei Servizi. Un approccio al management dei rapporti con la clientela*. ISEDI: Turin.

Gummenson E. 1979. *Models of Professional Service Marketing*. Liber/Marketing Technique Center: Stockholm.

Hanna S, Rowley J. 2008. An analysis of terminology use in place branding. *Place Branding and Public Diplomacy* **4** (1): 61-75.

Hankinson G. 2004. Repertory grid analysis: An application to the measurement of destination images. *International Journal of Non-profit and Voluntary Sector Marketing* **9** (2): 145–153.

Hankinson G. 2007. The management of destination brands: Five guiding principles based on recent developments in corporate branding theory. *Brand Management* **14** (3): 240-254.

Hosany S, Ekinci Y, Uysal M. 2006. Destination image and destination personality: an application of branding theories to tourism places. *Journal of Business Research* **59**: 638-642.

Keller P. 2000. Le organizzazioni turistiche nazionali a una svolta. In *Destination Management*, Pechlaner H, Weiermair K (eds). Touring University Press:

Milan.Kerr G. 2006. From destination brand to location brand. *Brand Management* **13** (4/5): 276-283.

Konecnik M. 2004. Evaluating Slovenia's image as a tourism destination: A self-analysis process towards building a destination brand. *Brand Management* **11** (4): 307-316.

Konecnik M, Gartner WC. 2007. Customer-based brand equity for a destination. *Annals of Tourism Research* **34** (2): 400-421.

Konecnik M, Go F. 2008. Tourism destination brand identity: the case of Slovenia. *Brand Management* **15** (3): 177-189.

Laws E, Scott N, Parfitt N. 2002. Synergies in destination image management: a case study and conceptualisation. *International Journal of Tourism Research* **4**: 39-55.

Manente M, Cerato M. 2000. *From Destination to Destination Marketing and Management*. Ciset: Venice.

Martini U. 2002. Da luoghi a destinazioni turistiche. Ipotesi di destination management nel turismo alpino. In *Destination Management. Governare il turismo fra locale e globale*, Franch M (ed.). Giappichelli: Turin.

Martini U. 2005. *Management dei sistemi territoriali. Gestione e marketing delle destinazioni turistiche.* Giappichelli: Turin.

Martini U, Ejarque J (eds). 2008. *Le nuove strategie di destination marketing. Come rafforzare la competitività delle regioni turistiche italiane.* Franco Angeli: Milan.

Morgan N, Pritchard A, Piggott R. 2002. New Zealand, 100% Pure. The creation of a powerful niche destination brand. *Brand Management* **9** (4-5): 335-354.

Morgan N. 2006. Opinion pieces: How has place branding developed during the year that *Place Branding* has been in publication. *Place Branding* **2** (1): 6 – 17.

Pencarelli T. 2001. *Marketing e performance dell'industria turistica.* Quattro Venti: Urbino.

Pencarelli T, Forlani F. 2002. Il marketing dei distretti turistici-sistemi vitali nell'economia delle esperienze. *Sinergie* (58).

Pencarelli T, Forlani F. 2006. Il marketing dei prodotti tipici nella prospettiva dell'economia delle esperienze. In *Marketing Trends*, International Congress, Venice.

Pencarelli T, Splendiani S. 2008. Il governo delle destinazioni e dei prodotti turistici: analisi di alcune esperienze. *Mercati e Competitività* (2). Pine J, Gilmore J. 2000. *L'Economia delle esperienze, oltre il servizio.* ETAS: Milan.

Prebensen NK. 2007. Exploring tourists' images of a distant destination. *Tourism Management* (28): 747-756. Rispoli M (ed). 2001. *Prodotti turistici evoluti. Casi ed esperienze in Italia.* Giappichelli Editore: Turin.

Rispoli M, Tamma M. 1995. *Risposte strategiche alla complessità: le forme di offerta dei prodotti alberghieri.* Giappichelli: Turin.

Ritchie JR, Ritchie JB. 1998. The branding of tourism destinations. In *Annual Congress of the International Association of Scientific Experts in Tourism*, Morocco, September.

Sciarelli S (ed). 2007. *Il management dei Sistemi Turistici Locali. Strategie e strumenti per la governance*. Giappichelli: Turin.

Tamma M. 2002. Destination Management: gestire prodotti e sistemi locali di offerta. In *Destination Management. Governare il turismo fra locale e globale*, Franch M (ed.). Giappichelli: Turin.

Tasci ADA, Gartner WC, Cavusgil ST. 2007. Measurement of destination brand bias using a quasi-experimental design. *Tourism Management* **28**: 1529-1540.

Woods M, Deegan J. 2003. A Warm Welcome for Destination Quality Brands: the Example of the Pays Cathare Region. *International Journal of Tourism Research* **5**: 269-282.

Yeoman I, Durie A, McMahon-Beattie U, Palmer A. 2005. Capturing the essence of a brand from its history: the case of Scottish tourism marketing. *Brand Management* **13** (2): 134-147.

www.emiliaromagnaturismo.it, accessed 28 January 2009

www.ambiente.regione.marche.it, accessed 28 January 2009

23 The Power of Loose Ties – Networking for Market Diversification in Remote Australia

Doris Schmallegger, James Cook University

Introduction

Tourism in remote Outback areas of Australia has become increasingly homogenous in terms of products and markets over the last decade and is currently suffering substantial declines in visitor numbers (Carson and Taylor, 2009). As a result, calls have been mounting for more innovative approaches to market diversification and product development in remote Australia. Much of the literature on innovation suggests that one of the most effective ways to create innovations is by operating as a 'system of innovation' in which individual businesses, public organisations and institutions interact and influence each other (Carlsson and Stankiewicz, 1991; Edquist, 1997; Iammarino, 2005). Having strong institutional arrangements that encourage strong networks and clusters is a key factor in the development of regional systems of innovation (Doloreux and Parto, 2005; Storper, 1995). Remote regions appear to be fundamentally constrained in the pursuit of networks and clusters by a lack of critical mass, the geographic dispersal and isolation of firms, and limited resources and preparedness to engage in networks and collaboration (Doloreux and Dionne, 2008; Virkkala, 2006).

How remote areas can still succeed in the marketplace, despite their structural weaknesses, remains a big question. This research investigates whether more flexible approaches to networking and clustering can provide a way for remote regions to overcome their weaknesses. The chapter looks at the case of the Flinders Ranges, a remote tourism destination in South Australia. It examines the strategies that the region has used to diversify its tourism market and analyses the different forms of networks and collaboration that have evolved around these initiatives. The chapter discusses the potential value of 'institutional thinness' and argues that a lack of strong ties in networks and clusters can have advantages for remote regions. Having only thin ties and flexible relationships with other players in the system can encourage multiple initiatives with different network constellations that can lead to market diversification. Limited support for all-of-destination networks can, in turn, increase commitment to individual projects as operators can choose where to participate and do not feel constrained to contribute to non-priority projects.

Background

Tourism in Outback Australia has been struggling over at least the past decade to keep pace with the performance of the Australian tourism industry as a whole and has experienced a steady decline in visitor numbers since the year 2000 (Desert Knowledge Australia, 2005). Major markets, including the backpacker market and the coach tourism market, have been declining and other performance indicators, such as visitor expenditure, length of stay or repeat visitor rates, have remained flat or continued to decrease (Carson and Schmallegger, in press). One reason for this might be the increasing homogenisation of tourism products and experiences in remote Australia. Previous research has identified a substantial decline in the diversity of product types and marketing strategies across remote parts of Australia. A recent review of the online marketing of Outback destinations (Carson and Taylor, 2009) revealed that there is limited variety in terms of the images and experiences promoted in the Outback. Most remote destinations tend to rely on their natural environment and a limited number of iconic attractions to draw tourists to the region (Hohl and Tisdell, 1995; Prideaux, 2002). As a result, tourism products tend to be extensively clustered around these attractions and are dominated by large-scale (mostly external) resort-type operators who promote similar types of 'sight-seeing packages' for the mass tourism market (Carson and Schmallegger, in press). This has reduced the involvement of local populations in tourism (also evidenced by decreasing employment in the sector (Carson and Taylor, 2009)) and has hampered the development of a more diversified tourism industry in remote destinations.

This lack of product diversity has stifled tourism growth in remote regions, especially among higher yield or special interest niche markets. The need for innovative product development and market diversification has often been recognised as central to stimulating tourism growth in peripheral or remote areas (Hohl and Tisdell, 1995; Sharpley, 2002). Researchers have increasingly suggested that peripheral regions must seek to attract different markets to those that frequent the respective core destinations (Blackman et al., 2004; Sharpley, 2002). Breaking out of the prevailing mass market strategies, identifying new potential markets and developing commercial products for these markets is required to create a more diversified image of the destination.

For such marketing innovation to happen, tourism destinations cannot rely on individuals but have to operate as a 'system of innovation' (Carson and Macbeth, 2005). 'Systems of innovation' theory suggests that innovation rarely happens in isolation but rather through continuous interactions between a whole range of stakeholders in the marketplace, including private entrepreneurs, public organisations and regulatory institutions (Carlsson and Stankiewicz, 1991; Edquist, 1997; Iammarino, 2005). The role of interactions and interdependence between firms and organisations has repeatedly been described as critical in the innovation process (Doloreux, 2003). This process is particularly encouraged through physical proximity between firms, trust-based networks and common institutional arrangements within the system which can contribute to the formation of regional clusters and 'creative milieus' (Doloreux and Parto, 2005; Storper, 1995). Regions with strong institutional arrangements – also referred to as 'institutional thickness' – tend to have strong networks and high levels of regional interaction. Networks based on 'institutional thickness' typically emerge as a result of historically embedded relations, reciprocal trust and a set of common values and goals (Amin and Thrift, 1995; Markey et al., 2006). Such arrangements often develop as an evolutionary process over time and as such naturally form the borders within which system stakeholders choose to operate.

More recent research has found that peripheral regions face considerable challenges in developing systems of innovation due to a number of inherent limitations and structural impediments (Doloreux, 2003; Malecki and Oinas, 1999; Virkkala, 2006). Peripheral areas are characterised by a lack of critical mass, a limited number of entrepreneurs, a lack of economic competence, and an insufficient density of businesses and resources due to the enormous distances and isolated locations of settlements in remote areas (Botterill et al., 2000). Doloreux (2003) argued that these factors make it less likely for peripheral firms to engage in collaboration and form strong network relationships. Firms are mostly small-scale and family-owned who compete amongst each other with similar products for small markets. They tend to lack a tradition of cooperation and trust, which leads more often than not to structures of 'institutional thinness' rather than 'institutional thickness' (Doloreux and Dionne, 2008).

What adds to the problem in remote areas is that they are politically and economically dependent on core areas as their main markets, as well as their main sources of funding and investment (Nelson and Mackinnon, 2004; Wellstead, 2007). Hence, important decisions and policies tend to be dictated from the core. In tourism, small local operators often lack influence on decision-making because the industry is ultimately controlled by bigger external operators, multinational wholesalers, or centralised government bodies (Botterill et al., 2000; Hohl and Tisdell, 1995; Keller, 1987). In Australia, regional tourism boundaries are defined by the respective state tourism organisation (STO). Even though regional tourism organisations (RTOs) do exist, they are largely controlled and funded by the STO so that decisions regarding regional tourism marketing and development are mainly coordinated from outside. This artifical top-down creation of tourism regions can potentially stifle innovation because it pre-defines the region's institutional arrangements and discourages the formation of more organic linkages and of 'creative milieus' (Dredge and Jenkins, 2003). This is even worse in the case of remote regions in Australia. In order to absorb expected 'market failures' at the destination level, centralised government agencies tend to be made responsible for destination marketing in remote areas. For administration and cost-saving reasons, the sparsely populated Outback regions are often simply 'lumped together' and forced within the boundaries of one big tourism region (Carson and Taylor, 2009). A limited sense of cohesion among remote operators and a rather disjoint and fragmented tourism industry have been the consequences (Cartan and Carson, 2009).

It has been argued that remote tourism destinations, *because* of their inherent limitations, must place more emphasis on collaboration in order to compete with non-remote destinations and to overcome limited resources and knowledge of individuals (Buhalis and Main, 1998; McAdam et al., 2004). It has been common practice to encourage (or even expect) tourism operators to sign up to local and regional tourism organisations or industry associations in the area to get the best possible support for regional marketing strategies and maximise the outcome of the limited resources available for marketing and development. However, this push for collaboration and 'artificial cohesion' around a set of pre-defined institutional arrangements can also put barriers to innovation within a region. The relative absence of local competition through extensive networking and clustering might mean that firms are less likely to come up with innovative marketing strategies and that product and market structures get more homogenous because of the tendency to agree with and copy from each other (Ioannides and Petersen, 2003; Virkkala, 2006). As a result, researchers have argued that firms in peripheral locations need to establish networks with external stakeholders to get access to new ideas, knowledge or technologies (Oinas and Malecki, 1999).

Finding the right mix of networking partners and the right level of collaboration and interaction seems to be critical to develop innovative marketing strategies. However, the research available to date indicates that remote regions are fundamentally constrained to form such meaningful connections. The lack of critical mass and entrepreneurship, as well as a sense of 'not belonging together' (indicating a lack of 'institutional thickness') in vast and sparsely populated regions, will most likely mean that efficient intra-regional networking remains wishful thinking. Similarly, the isolated location of remote firms and the huge distances to external players might naturally limit the propensity to establish external networks. Networking as such can be extremely time intensive and costly for remote operators, especially for small businesses with limited staff and resources (Cross et al., 2007).

It is very unlikely that these limitations will change in the future. The question, then, is how remote regions, despite these inherent limitations, can succeed in the marketplace. Developing alternative and more flexible approaches to collaboration and networking might be a potential way to stimulate innovative development. This chapter looks at the case of the Flinders Ranges, a peripheral tourism destination in South Australia that has experienced a substantial market decrease in the early 2000s (Tourism Research Australia, 2008) and has responded by developing a range of new initiatives to diversify its tourism market. The research investigated what attempts have been made in the past five years to diversify the Flinders Ranges tourism product and what sort of network structures evolved around each of these initiatives. Specifically, the research identified the number and type of stakeholders involved in these projects, the ways in which stakeholders were relating to each other, their reasons for participating in new projects, and the perceived benefits of their 'networking behaviour'.

Methodology

Data were drawn from 45 semi-structured in-depth interviews which were conducted from February to November 2008. Interview participants included a diverse range of stakeholders in the Flinder Ranges tourism system, including owners/managers of accommodation businesses (resorts, hotels, caravan parks, B&Bs, and farmstay operators), owners/managers of restaurants and cafés, local tour operators, four-wheel-drive track operators, local government members of the various council districts, local visitor centres, economic development officers, members of the regional tourism organisation (FROSAT) and the state tourism organisation (SATC), and tourism consultants working in the region.

The Flinders Ranges are part of the largest tourism region in South Australia – the Flinders Ranges and Outback South Australia Tourism Region – which comprises almost two-thirds of the state (Figure 23.1). The Flinders Ranges are a range of mountains stretching some 400 km in length, commencing around 200 km north of Adelaide. The destination is divided into three major regions: the Southern, Central and Northern Flinders Ranges. The Southern Flinders Ranges are more densely populated and include the towns of Port Augusta and Quorn in the West, Port Pirie and Port Germein on the shore of Spencer Gulf, Wilmington, Orroroo and Peterborough in the East, and Jamestown and Crystal Brook in the South. The Central Flinders Ranges stretch from Hawker in the South to the Parachilna and Blinman in the North. A considerable amount of this area is encompassed by the Flinders Ranges National Park, which includes Wilpena Pound as its most iconic attraction. The rugged and very remote Northern Flinders Ranges reach from Parachilna to the northern mining towns of Leigh Creek and Lyndhurst and through to Arkaroola and the Gammon Ranges National Park. Access to many locations in the National Parks is by unsealed roads only (Port Augusta City Council, 2008).

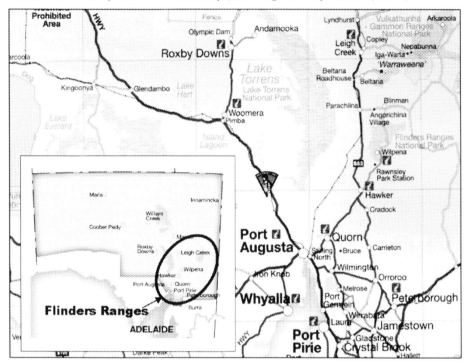

Figure 23.1: Map of the Flinders Ranges
Source: adapted from Flinders Ranges and Outback SA Tourism, 2007

Increased tourism activity in the Flinders Ranges began in the 1970s when it became a popular camping holiday destination for families from the state capital city Adelaide (Delforce et al., 1986). Non-commercial activities such as bushwalking and sightseeing, mainly around the iconic rock formation Wilpena Pound in the central Flinders Ranges, were dominating tourists' itineraries. In addition, the Flinders Ranges were a popular transit destination for coach tours on their way up from Adelaide to Alice Springs. Tourist products along the way, including accommodation, restaurants or guided tours, were limited to a few bigger resorts around Wilpena Pound and further north at Arkaroola. The main economic sectors in the Flinders Ranges have traditionally been mining, pastoralism and agriculture. However, economic restructuring, fluctuating commodity prices and a long-term period of drought have forced many locals, particularly pastoralists, to diversify their incomes and develop tourism operations on their properties (Northern Regional Development Board, 2008).

Data from the National and International Visitor Surveys suggest that the Flinders Ranges received around 439,000 overnight visitors in 2007, generating about a total of 1.3 million visitor nights (South Australian Tourist Commission, 2008). Domestic travellers accounted for well over 80% of all visitors. There is, however, a growing segment of international visitors, mainly from Germany, the UK, other central Europe and North America. The traditional market segment of families has shifted to older age groups, including an increasing group of retired and semi-retired couples of the 'baby boomer generation'.

Even though the region has officially been united with the rest of Outback South Australia to form the 'Flinders Ranges and Outback South Australia' tourism region, there have been a number of attempts on behalf of Flinders Ranges operators and organisations to diversify their product portfolio and differentiate the destination from the larger Outback South Australia region. This chapter reports on five of the most recent initiatives in the Flinders Ranges: the Geotourism Strategy, the development of the four-wheel-drive (4WD) and Repeater Tower brochure, the Quorn Adventures marketing group, the development of cycle tourism strategies, and the Tastes of the Outback Festival.

Results

The Geotourism Branding Strategy

In 2005, operators in the Flinders Ranges decided to exploit the region's unique geological formations by developing a geotourism strategy. This initiative was driven and managed by the Flinders Ranges Tourism Operator Association (FRTOA), which consists of about 45 (mostly small-scale) operator members. The network was set up in the early 2000s as a parallel group to FROSAT, mainly to advocate for and represent the interests of local and small-scale operators. This was following general discontent with STO and RTO marketing initiatives that were perceived to be supporting only the bigger operators. Participation in the network is voluntary and involves a small annual membership fee. In turn, the organising committee arranges quarterly forums for local operators to exchange ideas and organises guest speakers and training sessions with external experts.

Funding from a federal government development programme was sourced to develop a new geotourism branding strategy, a communications and marketing plan, an interpretation and merchandise strategy, and a training programme for operators to educate them about how to use the outcome of these strategies. In the course of the project the number of operators joining the network increased substantially, mainly because operators felt that the project was gaining more momentum as an operator-driven initiative rather than a project dominated from outside. Operators were keen to redefine the image of the Flinders Ranges as being substantially different from the overall Outback destination image promoted by FROSAT and SATC. They also got the impression that they could personally benefit from this project, particularly from training sessions and forums. Even operators from the Southern Flinders Ranges, who had until then somewhat isolated themselves from tourism development in the central and northern parts, joined the project. Group members valued the flexible structure of the network group and the fact that they did not feel compelled to participate and commit to group activities all the time. It is acknowledged within the group that, because of the long distances between individual operators and the limited time resources of small owner-manager businesses, members can often not show up personally or contribute actively. Members who cannot come to meetings are kept in the loop by circulating minutes of meetings, project updates and newsletters.

The 4WD and Repeater Tower Brochure

The increasing number of both four-wheel-drive club members and private four-wheel-drive vehicle owners, especially in south-eastern Australia, has led more and more station owners in the Flinders Ranges to open extensive tracts of their pastoral properties for 4WD exploration. Although many station owners are not entirely committed to tourism they have decided to tap into this growing market by developing a range of self-guided 4WD tracks, tag-along routes, and alternative accommodation options along the way, including camp sites and converted shearers' quarters. This provided them with the opportunity to complement their marginal farm incomes without having to invest too much into new tourism infrastructure.

In response to the increased demand for off-road 4WD experiences, FROSAT in collaboration with a range of other public organisations in the Flinders Ranges, including the Outback Areas Community Development Trust, the Department for Environment and Heritage, and the Department of Water, Land, and Biodiversity, developed a destination-wide '4WD Tracks & Repeater Towers' brochure. What was initially thought of as a safety guide for 4WD travellers with detailed maps indicating the location of radio repeater towers, soon developed into one of the main marketing tools for 4WD tourism. Operators were given the chance to buy in and provide information about the tracks and complementary services available on their properties. At present, the brochure features eighteen 4WD track operators scattered over several hundred kilometres from the southern to the northern Flinders Ranges. Most participating operators still have pastoralism as their main source of income and therefore are not too concerned about keeping close collaborative ties with other station owners for tourism development and marketing. Only very few participating operators have close relationships with other (mainly neighbouring) station owners. However, they all appreciated the brochure as a useful tool to establish the region's reputation as a 4WD destination and promote their tracks under this umbrella.

Quorn Adventures

In 2004, operators within the council district of Quorn, south of Wilpena Pound, decided to form their own marketing network – the Quorn Adventures group. The reason for this initiative was that operators in and around Quorn felt somewhat neglected by the marketing efforts of FROSAT and SATC compared to the bigger and more well established tourist hotspots around Wilpena Pound and Parachilna. The main objectives of the network were to create more market exposure for the area as an adventure tourism destination, to establish a cluster of complementary products to keep tourists longer within the council area, and to get some more recognition from the RTO and STO as a competitive tourist region. The group consists of about twelve operators, including accommodation operators, 4WD track operators, and other local tour operators specialised in activities such as camel safaris, water cruises, steam train rides and hot air ballooning. Some members of the group work together very closely and meet fairly regularly to prepare common marketing initiatives, such as joint participation in 4WD and camping shows. They also try and make business referrals to other members of the group or combine individual products to smaller packages. On the other hand, some members are only loosely involved and joined the network to be part of a local industry association that represents their general interests and to get some additional market exposure that they would not get on their own.

Cycle Tourism in the Flinders Ranges

In 2001, the Southern Flinders Regional Tourism Authority (SFRTA), a network between the southern district councils, the Southern Flinders Ranges Development Board, SATC,

National Parks and the Southern Flinders Ranges tourism operators association, started with the development of a cycle tourism strategy for the Southern Flinders Ranges. At the beginning, the initiative was mainly driven by a consortium of public organisations, represented by a few proactive councillors, regional tourism development officers and key contacts within the state cycling organisation, Bicycle SA. In addition, the group sought external advice from cycle tourism experts in the United States. The network obtained funding for the development of mountain bike trails and cycling infrastructure, the development of a ten-year master plan, and for marketing the Southern Flinders as a cycle tourism destination. Active participation of private operators in this network was initially only very sporadic and limited to some minor input from local accommodation operators and local landowners. In 2008, a bike shop was opened in Melrose, the main centre of mountain biking in the Southern Flinders Ranges, which has since taken over a leading role in promoting and organising cycle tourism in and around Melrose. A major part of the initiative is the organisation of an annual mountain bike event, the Melrose Fat Tyre Festival. The event was initially facilitated by Bicycle SA but has now been taken over by the local bike shop and community representatives, who team up once a year for this particular event.

Another form of cycle tourism development took place almost simultaneously in the central-northern Flinders Ranges. Again through the initiative of Bicycle SA, five local station owners in the area between Hawker and Blinman joined together to form the group 'Flinders by Bike' to stimulate cycle tourism as an alternative form of tourism in the remoter northern parts of the Flinders Ranges. The idea was to establish a 200km roundtrip cycle trail leading through private pastoralist properties and parts of the Flinders Ranges National Park. The project was essentially set up as a public–private partnership and collaboration between individual land owners was facilitated by Bicycle SA. As the participating pastoralists are all on neighbouring properties, most station owners knew each other well before and had worked together on previous occasions, either for pastoralist work or for tourism related projects.

Tastes of the Outback

As part of the Australian 'Year of the Outback' in 2002, a handful of tourism operators had the idea to host a regional food and wine festival in the Flinders Ranges focusing on local produce and regional Outback cuisine. Since then, the festival has been organised annually as a collective of individual events being held at different locations in the Flinders Ranges and Outback SA over the period of one week in April. It is coordinated by participating local tourism operators, the FRTOA group, and has gained marketing support from FROSAT and SATC's Regional Events and Festivals program. Participating operators can join the festival group by contributing to the marketing budget. Since its inception in 2002, the festival attracted between 10 and 15 participants, although the type and composition of participants changed from year to year. Interestingly, the festival was also joined by a number of operators who refused to be part of other regional networks. The majority of operators were usually from the Flinders Ranges, with only very few participants being operators from Outback SA. Even though the name of the festival suggests a focus on 'Outback' the festival has recently started to create a reputation for the Flinders Ranges as being a destination for 'quality food experiences'. Local produce, including bush foods, products of native plants and animals, as well as local wines are now increasingly being promoted in hotels, restaurants and visitor information centres as a fixed component of the Flinders Ranges tourism product.

Conclusion

The results of this research show that recent marketing and product development initiatives in the Flinders Ranges are based on the creation of a number of different network structures. Some networks, particularly those formed around the organisation and marketing of events (e.g. the Tastes of the Outback Festival or the Fat Tyre Festival), were characterised by their temporariness, while others (e.g. Quorn Adventures or FRTOA) were set up as more permanent ventures. Some projects were characterised by very loose networks of participants who did not show any signs of strong connectedness. Again the event-based projects but also the 4WD track cluster are examples of this category. Conversely, some networks exhibited signs of stronger cohesion. For example, the Quorn Adventures and FRTOA networks had a number of participants who were trying to actively work together for a set of common objectives. Nevertheless, both groups also had quite a few formal participants who did not make any active contributions. Another substantial difference could be identified in the composition of network participants. Some networks emerged among private operators only (e.g. Quorn Adventures or FRTOA), whereas others involved active participation of public organisations. The latter was the case in the cycle tourism strategies, the 4WD track cluster, or the Tastes of the Outback Festival. Some networks were confined to local participation (e.g. Quorn Adventures Group, FRTOA, 4WD cluster), while others had a number of links to external stakeholders (e.g. the cycle tourism strategies, Tastes of the Outback Festival).

What all these network constellations have in common, though, is that they were formed around a particular product development or marketing initiative. Projects did not emerge as a result of strong collaborative ties and pre-existing networks; on the contrary, it was the projects that stimulated the formation of individual new networks. They involved participants who were not otherwise engaged in collaborative strategies but joined the network because of a particular project. Another common characteristic was that all networks had some sort of pre-defined limitation that participants agreed to. They were either based around temporal limitations, such as participation in the organisation and marketing of events, or limited by a specific outcome, such as the creation of a particular brochure, participation in a trade show, or the implementation of a new branding strategy. A third common characteristic was that the expected level of engagement and commitment to the group was deliberately kept flexible, respecting the limited resources (both time and financial) that operators in remote regions have available for collaborative activities.

The reasons for participating in the various projects and joining the respective networks were very diverse, too. For many small-scale operators who were part of the FRTOA or Quorn Adventures groups, it was important to create a counterforce to the dominating big operators in the region and to have some sort of lobbying group against local and state government organisations. Other reasons were to get access to internal and external market knowledge, to learn from other operators in the region, and/or to get business referrals and keep tourists within the region. Getting recognition in the area as a new tourism operator was a very common motive among newcomers who had moved into the area from outside to open up a tourism business. Many of them tried to join as many networks as possible in order to get established and make a name for themselves in the region. It appears that, exactly for these reasons, some of the bigger operators have avoided these common projects and networks. As they were already relatively successful in the marketplace the perceived benefits of these sorts of relationships were very low.

Many operators were simultaneously participating in several projects according to their own personal interests and business priorities at the time. At first sight, it might seem that the average Flinders Ranges operator is well connected and actively seeks networking and clustering opportunities in the region. It appears to be common practice that 'you have to be part of something to be somebody' in the region. On closer examination, however, it becomes obvious that links within the networks discussed above are often rather superficial, temporally limited, and lack any sense of strong connectedness. Even networks which appear to have stronger ties between members, for example in the Quorn Adventures or the FRTOA groups, turned out to be only strong at the core between organising leaders and key members. Most of the remaining members prefer to be only loosely involved, as they cannot devote too much time and effort to maintaining close relationships. This is largely in line with findings from previous research that found that networking and clustering tend to be very limited in remote regions due to a lack of 'institutional thickness' (Doloreux and Dionne, 2008).

The lack of 'institutional thickness' in remote areas does not mean that businesses do not have any strong ties at all, rather that they are spatially more limited to the immediate surrounding region where business links have emerged and are consolidated through historic family or neighbourhood relationships and as such do not go much beyond such local boundaries. In turn, the level of involvement in regional (or even external) networks is deliberately kept flexible to participate only in selected group activities that are perceived to have an immediate benefit for the participant. This way, having only thin and flexible ties is not necessarily a disadvantage for a remote region. Networks can become more powerful when participants can choose when and where they want to participate and the level of resources they want to contribute. This might ultimately result in a higher level of individual commitment than in generic all-of-destination networks that are often enforced by external institutional organisations (see, for example, Dredge, 2003) and where operators almost as a matter of dogma 'have to participate' to demonstrate good will and regional cohesion.

The research in the Flinders Ranges suggests that having mainly thin ties among multiple networks can stimulate greater diversity of projects and encourage the formation of multiple development blocs in a remote region. Institutional thickness could pose a barrier to such innovative development in remote regions, as expected protocols and an increased level of bureaucracy involved in coordinating big networks with multiple strong links would slow down the innovation process substantially. Having networks characterised by 'institutional thinness' could actually mean that project related decisions within a group are processed faster as extensive bureaucratic protocols can be avoided. In addition, both financial and time resources can be used more effectively within the various individual groups to focus on one specific purpose instead of having to satisfy a collective of different interests within a larger destination-wide network.

Since not everybody is participating in every initiative and not everybody feels obliged to maintain strong relations among participants, a reasonable level of competition is maintained within the destination. This can stimulate product diversity and help remote regions to avoid falling into the trap of product homogenisation as a result of excessive networking and clustering (Ioannides and Petersen, 2003; Virkkala, 2006). In addition, it appears that loose networks, especially those initiated by public organisations or those formed around temporary ventures, can facilitate increased participation by operators as the perceived risks and ultimate responsibilities for the project are either temporally limited or remain within the public organisation. It is possible that such temporary and loose networks might grow into more permanent and stronger networks and become institutionalised over time, as participants get used to working with each other and gain mutual trust.

There are still a number of questions remaining in terms of how remote destinations can manage 'institutional thinness' to encourage innovative development. While it seems that having thin and flexible ties supported the formation of multiple tourism development projects and so contributed to greater product diversity in the Flinders Ranges, it has to be acknowledged that the success of most projects ultimately also relied on a range of other factors. Having some sort of champion or leader (be it a private operator or a public organisation) who has the required entrepreneurial skills and economic competence to initiate and guide the whole innovation process, was in most cases essential. Such entrepreneurial leaders are undoubtedly a crucial factor in the whole innovation process (Carlsson and Stankiewicz, 1991). How remote destinations can deal with a natural lack of entrepreneurial leaders, however, goes beyond the scope of this research and merits further investigation.

This chapter proposed a new way of looking at the capacity for innovation in remote destination systems from a different angle and concludes that 'institutional thinness' might have a number of benefits for innovative development in remote regions. Previous research into economic systems of innovation (Doloreux, 2003; Edquist, 1997) suggested that some of the fundamental components of innovation lie in a system's institutional infrastructure and the resulting formation of strong networks and clusters. Remote regions are unlikely to ever reach such a stage of 'institutional thickness' as they simply lack the critical mass and geographic proximity of entrepreneurs and resources that are necessary to form such strong connections. Instead of focusing on the idea of how remote regions can change or improve their inherent limitations (e.g. how to increase critical mass or to create a strong institutional infrastructure), future research should look at potential ways to use these weaknesses to their advantage.

Acknowledgment

The work reported in this publication was supported by funding from the Australian Government Cooperative Research Centres Programme through the Desert Knowledge CRC; the views expressed herein do not necessarily represent the views of Desert Knowledge CRC or its participants.

References

Amin A, Thrift N. 1995. Globalisation, institutional 'thickness' and the local economy. In *Managing Cities: The New Urban Context*, Healey P, Cameron S, Davoudi S, Graham S, Madani-Pour A (eds). John Wiley: Chichester; 92–108.

Blackman A, Foster F, Hyvonen T, Kuilboer A, Moscardo G. 2004. Tourism development in peripheral regions. *Journal of Tourism Studies* 15 (1): 59-70.

Botterill D, Owen RE, Emanuel L, Foster N, Gale T, Nelson C, Selby M. 2000. Perceptions from the periphery: The experience of Wales. In *Tourism in Peripheral Areas: Case Studies*, Brown F, Hall D (eds). Channel View Publications: Clevedon; 7-38.

Buhalis D, Main H. 1998. Information technology in peripheral small and medium hospitality enterprises: Strategic analysis and critical factors. *International Journal of Contemporary Hospitality Management* 10 (5): 198-202.

Carlsson B, Stankiewicz R. 1991. On the nature, function and composition of technological systems. *Journal of Evolutionary Economics* **1** (2): 93-118.

Carson D, Macbeth J. 2005. *Regional Tourism Cases: Innovation in Regional Tourism.* Common Ground: Melbourne.

Carson D, Schmallegger D. In press. The declining value of icon attractions in the Northern Territory: Lessons for regional Australia. *Tourism Review International.*

Carson D, Taylor A. 2009. 'We'll all go down together': The marketing response of Australia's Outback destinations to recent declines in performance. 3rd Advances in Tourism Marketing Conference, 6-9 September 2009, Bournemouth.

Cartan G, Carson D. (2009, in press). Local engagement in economic development and Industrial Collaboration around Australia's Gunbarrel Highway. *Tourism Geographies.*

Delforce RJ, Sinden JA, Young MD. 1986. An economic analysis of relationships between pastoralism and tourism in the Flinders Ranges of South Australia. CSIRO (Division of Wildlife and Rangelands Research): Melbourne.

Desert Knowledge Australia. 2005. *Our Outback: Partnerships and Pathways to Success in Tourism.* Desert Knowledge Australia: Alice Springs.

Stark D. 2009. *The Sense of Dissonance: Accounts of Worth in Economic Life.* Princeton University Press: Princeton, NJ.

Doloreux D, Dionne S. 2008. Is regional innovation system development possible in peripheral regions? Some evidence from the case of La Pocatière, Canada. *Entrepreneurship and Regional Development* 20 **May**: 259-283.

Doloreux D, Parto S. 2005. Regional innovation systems: Current discourse and unresolved issues. *Technology in Society* 27: 133-153.

Dredge D, Jenkins J. 2003. Destination place identity and regional tourism policy. *Tourism Geographies* 5 (4): 383-407.

Edquist C. 1997. Systems of innovation approaches – their emergence and characteristics. In *Systems of Innovation: Technologies, Institutions and Organisations*, Edquist C (ed.). Pinter: London; 1-35.

Flinders Ranges and Outback SA Tourism. 2007. *South Australia: Flinders Ranges & Outback: Visitor Guide.* South Australian Tourist Commission: Adelaide.

Hohl AE, Tisdell CA. 1995. Peripheral tourism: development and management. *Annals of Tourism Research* 22 (3): 517-534.

Iammarino S. 2005. An evolutionary integrated view of regional systems of innovation: concepts, measures and historical perspectives. *European Planning Studies* 13 (4): 497-519.

Ioannides D, Petersen T. 2003. Tourism 'non-entrepreneurship' in peripheral destinations: a case study of small and medium tourism enterprises on Bornholm, Denmark. *Tourism Geographies* 5 (4): 408-435.

Keller CP. 1987. Stages of peripheral tourism development: Canada's Northwest Territories. *Tourism Management* 8: 20-32.

Malecki E, Oinas P. 1999. *Making Connections: Technological Learning and Regional Economic Change.* Ashgate: Aldershot.

Markey S, Halseth G, Manson D. 2006. The struggle to compete: From comparative to competitive advantage in Northern British Columbia. *International Planning Studies* 11 (1): 19-39.

McAdam R, McConvery T, Armstrong G. 2004. Barriers to innovation within small firms in a peripheral location. *International Journal of Entrepreneurial Behaviour & Research* **10** (3): 206-221.

Nelson R, Mackinnon R. 2004. The peripheries of British Columbia: Patterns of migration and economic structure, 1976-2002. *Canadian Journal of Regional Science* **27** (3): 353-394.

Northern Regional Development Board. 2008. Flinders Ranges: investing in an icon. Investment Brief. Available online: http://www.nrdb.com.au/content/docs/Investment_Briefs/Flinders_Ranges_Investment_Brief.pdf.

Port Augusta City Council (2008). Flinders Ranges. Available on: http://www.portaugusta.sa.gov.au/site/page.cfm?u=825

Prideaux B. 2002. Building visitor attractions in peripheral areas – can uniqueness overcome isolation to produce viability? *International Journal of Tourism Research* **4**: 379-389.

Sharpley R. 2002. Rural tourism and the challenge of tourism diversification: the case of Cyprus. *Tourism Management* **23**: 233-244.

South Australian Tourist Commission. 2008. Flinders Ranges & Outback: Regional Tourism Profile 2007. Available online: http://www.tourism.sa.gov.au/WebFiles/publications/ResearchReports-RegionalProfiles/PDFDocument/FlindersOB_Profile07.pdf

Storper M. 1995. Territorial development in the global learning economy: The challenge to developed countries. *Review of International Political Economy* **2**: 394–424.

Tourism Research Australia. 2008. National and International Visitor Survey, 1999-2007. Available online: http://www.tourism.australia.com/Research.asp?sub=0390.

Virkkala S. 2006. What is the role of peripheral areas in a knowledge economy? A study of the innovation processes and networks of rural firms. Paper presented at the conference Innovation Pressure, 15-17 March 2006, Tampere, Finland. Available online: www.proact2006.fi/index.phtml?menu_id=16&lang=1.

Wellstead A. 2007. The (post) staples economy and the (post) staples state in historical perspective. *Canadian Political Science Review* **1** (1): 8-25.

24 From Marketing to Market Practices: Assembling the Ruin Bars of Budapest

Peter Lugosi and Peter Erdélyi, Bournemouth University

Introduction

In a recent special issue of *Marketing Theory*, Araujo et al. (2008) call on the marketing discipline to embrace the insights of the social study of markets in economic sociology as a promising avenue for revitalising the classical concepts of marketing. Drawing on the research programme launched by Michel Callon's 1998 volume, *The Laws of the Markets*, they suggest that one traditional disciplinary distinction be abandoned in particular: 'Although convenient, a distinction between market-making practices – defined as activities that shape the overall market structure – and market*ing* practices – defined as firm-based activities aimed at developing an actor's position within a structure – is misleading' (Araujo et al., 2008: 8). In this chapter, we take up Araujo et al.'s (2008) call to deploy such a constructivist economic sociology perspective in the study of an empirical case. The case study concerns the emergence of a particular type of hospitality establishment in Budapest between 1999 and 2009. A *romkert* or *romkocsma* (meaning ruin garden and ruin pub respectively), referred to hereafter as a *rom* bar, is a venue that incorporates its ruinous surroundings (such as dilapidated courtyards and other distressed material goods) as part of its service concept and consumer experience (see Lugosi and Lugosi, 2008). We re-describe the evolution of the rom phenomenon using the actor–network theory (ANT) perspective of Callon and colleagues. A small but growing body of work has begun to apply ANT in tourism research (cf., Jóhannesson, 2005; van der Duim, 2007), but attempts to engage with ANT in studies of hospitality have been limited (e.g. Grit and Lynch, 2008). This chapter demonstrates the applicability of ANT to hospitality by providing a nuanced, processual approach to understanding how hospitality venues draw upon, incorporate, and contribute to a range of social and spatial practices. By doing so, it contributes to an emerging body of work that seeks to understand the complex relationships between hospitality and space (see Bell, 2007; Lugosi, 2009). However, beyond contributing to debates in hospitality research, we are interested in exploring what the case of Budapest's rom bars can contribute to debates on market practices. Implicit in our discussion is the assumption that traditional marketing concepts such as segmentation, positioning and targeting through integrated marketing communications offer a simplistic understanding of the emergence and existence of rom bars. Our work therefore offers an alternative way to conceptualise marketing and market practices.

The chapter demonstrates how the owners-managers of the rom bars had to painstakingly assemble the marketplace for their service concept. The bars' operators found that they had to struggle to establish their ventures' legitimacy because they could not slot into any pre-existing categories that were available to the relevant authorities and other stakeholders. The rom bars of Budapest managed to survive thanks to a most curious inversion and reflexivity: in their struggle to create a marketplace for their new service, they themselves became a marketplace of sort, by providing a space for the outputs of cultural and creative industries. This enabled the rom bars not only to enrol an important set of allies but, in their quest for legitimacy, also to ask to be considered cultural institutions by the authorities. The multiple blurring of distinctions, between marketing and market-making practices, marketplaces and services, the bars and their ruinous surroundings, commercial ventures and cultural spaces, is a key outcome of this study, and it highlights the need for new ways to conceptualise some of the most fundamental notions of marketing and economics.

From Marketing to Market Theory: Learning from Economic Sociology

Michel Callon's (1998c) *The Laws of the Markets* marks the moment when actor–network theory, which he (1980; 1986a; 1986b), together with Bruno Latour (1986; 1987; 1988) and John Law (1986; 1988), had developed in the 1980s within science and technology studies (STS), had turned toward the study of the economy and the markets. Despite what the name might suggest, ANT is not a theory of actors and networks, and as its main proponents insist, it is not a theory at all (Callon, 1999; Law 2004; Latour, 2005b). Rather, it is a social science research approach, which is based on a set of arguably radical and much contested ontological assumptions in order to bypass some of the most fundamental problems of modern social theory. The most prominent of these issues that ANT was meant to ignore, rather than overcome, read like chapter headings in an introductory social theory textbook: the subject–object distinction, the agency–structure problem, the micro–macro problem, or the local vs. global dualism.

Actor-network theory can be described as a constructivist approach. According to Latour (2003: 40) this type of constructivism is concerned with 'something which (a) has not always been around, (b) which is of humble origin, (c) which is composed of heterogeneous parts, (d) which was never fully under the control of its makers, (e) which could have failed to come into existence, (f) which now provides occasions as well as obligations, and (g) which needs for this reason to be protected and maintained if it is to continue to exist.' However, ANT is not to be confused with social constructivism. While they share some characteristics, ANT departs from social constructivism on one fundamental point: it is not the social that does the constructing; on the contrary, it is the social that is in need of construction. To put it differently, the social is not an *explanans* but rather the *explanandum* (Latour, 2005b).

Latour (2005b) offers the following advice as methodological steps in order to conduct an actor–network theory analysis. There are two aspects to the analysis: the deployment of controversies and the tracing of associations between entities. The deployment of controversies refers to the implementation of five key ontological assumptions of actor–network theory: (1) the existence of entities is the result of performance; (2) action is distributed: actors are networks, and networks are actors; (3) objects too have agency and they take part in the construction of the world; (4) facts and things are socio-materially constructed; and (5), description is experimental, writing accounts down is risky: they may or may not work and there are no formulas to follow, no frameworks to implement.

Absorbing these principles should allow the researcher to embark on the task of description, the tracing of associations, by following three moves (Latour, 2005b), which are aimed at keeping a flat perspective of the world. Flatness here refers to the avoidance of resorting to external theories or categories that would be imposed upon the empirical situation being described and thus introducing a depth or hierarchy that is not part of the empirical reality. The first move is concerned with localising the global, i.e. finding local or micro-level manifestations or mechanisms for effects that appear to be global or macro-phenomena. The next move is aimed at redistributing the local, focusing on the tracing of mechanisms that produce sites as local, as micro-phenomena. Once a flat perspective has been achieved, the third move becomes possible: the connection of various sites. These manoeuvres should give rise to a reassembled view of the world where the circulation of entities can be observed and where complex formations come into view.

These complex formations have been described by various terms over the years, such as actor–networks (Callon, 1986a), quasi-objects (Latour, 1993), assemblages (Latour, 2005b), things (Latour, 2005a), arrangements (Barry, 2001) or agencements (Callon, 2005). Whatever the term, it is meant to convey the composite and heterogeneous nature of these complex formations that are in continuous need to be sustained. Within the domain of economic sociology, actor–network theory is deployed to provide a fresh description of the complex mechanisms (Callon et al., 2007) that make markets and the economy possible. Callon and Çalışkan (unpublished, 23) define a market as a sociotechnical agencement that 'can be described and analysed as an arrangement or assemblage of heterogeneous elements which include, in particular: rules and conventions; technical devices; metrological systems; logistical infrastructures; texts, discourses and narratives ...; technical and scientific knowledge ...; and competencies and skills embodied in living beings.'

Economic markets as sociotechnical arrangements are 'calculative collective devices' (Callon and Muniesa, 2005), the purpose of which is to facilitate the articulation, valuation and distribution of goods, whether they are products or services. Indeed, given the heterogeneous socio-material nature of things, drawing a sharp distinction between products and services no longer makes sense: Callon (2007) proposes the terms 'service-products' and 'product-services' instead. The calculations that markets facilitate are not simply quantitative operations but also qualitative ones. After Cochoy (2002), Callon and Muniesa (2005) introduce the neologism 'qualculation' to account for the continuum between calculation and qualitative judgement that characterises market practices. Markets are arrangements of qualification tests or trials in which (1) economic goods become detached from their providers and are sorted out; (2) then they undergo associations, manipulations and transformations; and (3) finally a result, a new entity, is extracted, including its value (Callon and Muniesa, 2005).

An important aspect of a market is the way it is set up or framed, so that it can serve as a frame within which the above-described process of qualculation can take place (Callon, 1998a). This framing inevitably leads to overflowing, i.e. to excluding entities from this process of qualification and affecting them in various other ways (what is described in economics as a positive or negative externality) (Callon, 1998a; 1998b). Markets therefore contribute to the 'proliferation of the social' (Callon, 2007), the production of groups that emerge around matters of concern that result from the way the particular markets are framed and maintained.

In the following we will deploy actor–network theory in order to assemble a narrative of the emergence of the rom bars of Budapest. We will focus on describing both how the framing of the marketplace for these rom bars has come to be accomplished and how the bars came to be qualified as services. It is a story of a series of trials of strength through which the arrangements gradually take form.

The Case of the Rom Bars of Budapest

The data gathering for this chapter originally began within a study of entrepreneurship and organisation (see Lugosi and Bray, 2008). That study utilised interviews with owners, guides and tourists as well as participant observation of guided tours in Budapest, during which a number of licensed venues were visited. The emergence of rom bars during the period of the study warranted focused research into this phenomenon. The study of the rom bars utilised a mixture of secondary and primary data collection methods. The venues were visited repeatedly from 1999 onwards, during which photographic evidence was gathered. In addition, a review was conducted of commentary and representations of the venues in printed and electronic media between 2001 and 2008. This included Hungarian and English language newspapers and magazines, online forums and blogs.

Repeat visits to the venues and reviews of the media helped to identify eight owner/managers who, between them, have been partly responsible for the operation of 15 venues in Budapest. That number rises even higher if it includes those venues that have reopened under the same name in different locations. Two of the individuals were part of teams that operated the longest running and most established venues, Szimpla Kert and Szoda Udvar, which in various guises have reopened in several locations in the city. These operators have also opened further venues in Budapest as well as Berlin. The remaining six have been part of teams that opened a number of venues between 1997 and 2008, some of which have moved and others that closed during this period. These venues were prominent in media discussions of the rom phenomenon and the bar scene of the city.

Semi-structured interviews were conducted with the eight bar operators, which were later transcribed. The interviews focused, among other things, on the owners' personal and professional motivations, the history of the venues, the clientele, including changes in consumer profile, relationships with stakeholders, operational challenges, perceptions of the rom phenomenon and their expectations for the future.

The analysis for this chapter of the interview material, photographic data, observations and the literature was directly informed by the ANT approach (cf., Latour 2005b). Fundamental was the assumption of symmetry, and in analysing our data we tried to avoid distinguishing between, and thus privileging, human or non-human actors. We focused on identifying the different actors, mapping the networks of relationships between them, including the various processes of qualification and qualculation (Callon and Muniesa, 2005) and uncovering the externalities or overflows (Callon, 1998a) resulting from their relationships.

The Emergence of the Rom Bar Assemblage

Arguably the lineage of the rom bar phenomenon can be traced further, but cultural commentators claim it started in 1999 with the opening of Pótkulcs (meaning latch key) – a bar/restaurant located in a gap between two buildings in the VI district of Budapest (Lakos, 2003). The Pótkulcs subsequently closed, but has since reopened permanently.

One of the distinguishing features of the venue was and remains its inconspicuousness. The entrance is an unmarked rusty door, which opens into a courtyard leading to the bar. The majority of the dimly-lit bar space is in the basement of the residential building. The bare walls are painted and it is furnished with an eclectic collection of distressed tables, chairs and sofas. The venue regularly hosts photography and other art exhibitions as well as musical performances and DJ-selected music.

The marking of the Pótkulcs in media commentary as a foundational time/space represents a framing of the rom phenomenon as a distinct service format, which is drawn on and subsequently reproduced in other venues. However, a second and more substantial moment in the emergence of the rom phenomenon was the opening of the Szimpla kert in 2002. The Szimpla kert was an extension of the Szimpla café – an indoor venue, which opened in 2001 and was patronised, in part at least, by people involved in the creative sectors. The operators found an abandoned residential building in the VII district of the city, which is undergoing a rehabilitation process (Amichay, 2004). The building on Király Utca had gained notoriety because of the long battle between residents and officials over the vacating of the building (Lakos, 2003).

According to one of the Szimpla's operators, the local council could not find an appropriate status for the rental agreement and it was originally rented as a storage space. Like many of the buildings in Budapest, it was made up of several floors of flats located around an inner courtyard. The flats were barricaded off and the inner courtyard was furnished with a makeshift bar, lampions and an assortment of chairs and tables. Customers entered the crumbling building's courtyard through a car park of an adjacent building. Kiss noted that they had to rent several of the parking spaces, which had to be kept vacant to enable free access to the venue. The Király Utca building represents what Groth and Corijn (2005) call 'indeterminate space', which is left out of 'time and space' and subsequently occupied and animated by informal actors. In occupying this space the Szimpla' s operators established a schematic, a template, which was appropriated and translated further in the development of the rom genre in the subsequent two years.

In 2003 the Szimpla was joined by two other venues: the Gozsdu and Szoda Udvar (Soda court), which was an outdoor venue and brand extension of an indoor bar, Szoda. Emulating the Szimpla kert model the Gozsdu and Szoda Udvar both opened in abandoned courtyards. It is interesting to highlight the history of the Gozsdu, which is one of conflicts that created opportunities for the emergence of the rom model. The Gozsdu Udvar is a large building complex built in the early 20th century by a Romanian-born lawyer, and the Hungarian and Romanian authorities have contested its ownership throughout the last century. The rehabilitation of the Gozsdu Udvar complex was delayed partly by arguments about ownership but also because of disagreements about the precise form of the rehabilitation process (Amichay, 2004). Added to this was the resistance by one particular Gozsdu resident, a dentist, who refused to vacate his premises and allow reconstruction to begin (Földes, 2003; sulinet.hu, ND). These disputes destabilised the broader transformation of the physical sites and it is through these emerging conflicts that the Gozsdu' s operators could construct a marketplace for a particular hospitality service and consumer experience. This process of market construction was aided in no small part by the various cultural commentators that included reporters and bloggers, who engaged in representations of these venues, and began to define rom as a distinct process of ordering, which can be read simultaneously as a cultural phenomenon, a service model and an increasingly refined aesthetic model (see e.g. Földes, 2003; palkata.hu, 2003).

In 2004 further groups of entrepreneurs began to engage in these processes of ordering, creating a new set of venues (Földes, 2004; Földes et al., 2004; Mayer, 2004). Alongside the Szoda Udvar and Szimpla kert operators opened the Szimpla kiskert (small garden), Mumus, Tetthely, Kuplung and West Balkan. However, this expansion was halted in 2005, when the mayoral office of the VII district refused to lease premises and withheld licences from several of the venues, despite appeals by operators that they were actually cultural institutions rather than bars (Dudás and Földes, 2005; Munkácsy, 2005). Part of the problem was the noise generated by the bars, which attracted protests from local residents. Operators attempted to soundproof venues using improvised, low-tech solutions (e.g. padding the doors leading to the inner courtyard), which helped to address noise pollution inside the venues, but patrons walking to and leaving the venues drew negative attention. The operators collaborated to introduce the *bagoly* (owl) initiative: signs were displayed, which asked people in several languages to respect the surrounding residents and to keep the noise down, while security staff stood outside the bars quietening people as they approached and as they left. In Callon's (1998a) parlance, the framing of the marketplace inevitably led to overflows (negative externalities in classical economics), whereby the noise and the public disorder resulting from this service gave rise to some concerned groups. The owl initiative can be understood as a device for stabilising this matter of concern.

Szimpla kert remained open in 2005 and the operators maintained the Kiskert in the neighbouring VI district. Kiss claimed that their survival was helped by the fact that the Kazinczy Utca building was privately owned – unlike the others which were owned and leased by the state. Szimpla's operators also took a calculative decision to redefine themselves as a cultural institute rather than a bar: they organised various cultural events and the venue had an outdoor cinema. In an earlier interview Kiss had claimed that the cinema placed it above the status of a *romkocsma* (Balogh, 2005), and the sign outside the Szimpla still states that it is a cinema rather than a bar. Self definition as cultural institutes was a strategy subsequently adopted by other venues. For example, the perpetuation of this framing by operators and cultural commentators in the media has subsequently helped operators in 2008 to reoccupy the Tetthely and for operators of venues to occupy other abandoned buildings with the approval of the local authorities without incurring rental costs. The qualitative process of classification and category formation was intertwined with the calculative processes aimed at reducing the operating costs and ensuring both the legitimacy of the service concept and the viability of the business model.

In 2005 the Tűzraktár (fire warehouse) opened in a disused medical supplies building in the IX district. The Tűzraktár emulated the design features of the earlier rom venues, but it was an overt attempt to develop a cultural institute and to bring together the hospitality industry with art and culture. The Tűzraktár continued to construct the market by engaging with increasingly disparate networks of actors, which ranged from artists and members of the creative industries to regular patrons. More significantly, the rom bar itself has become a marketplace for cultural goods, by bringing together producers from the creative industries with consumers of cultural products and services. As well as having the usual features of rom venues such as the bar space and table football, the venue hosted fashion shows, literature evenings, concerts, theatre shows and exhibited work by artists in the empty rooms in the building.

In 2007 the rom bar model was transformed yet again: several new venues were opened by the operators of previous ones by enrolling a whole new set of actors, such as department stores and swimming pools. The most significant was the Corvintető (Corvin roof) on the top two floors of a department store in Pest. On the other side of the river Danube in Buda, a terrace bar, Fecske (swallow), opened on the roof of a swimming pool. The Corvintető and Fecske continue to incorporate the features of the rom bars: both occupy and reuse unusual and dilapidated spaces and both venues are decorated with graffiti and other art. This occupation of terraces was extended further in 2008 by the opening of the Kópé Terrace on top of another iconic department store in the centre of Pest.

The rom bars were a particular type of spatial arrangement that enrolled the existing ordering of space through material and performative practices. Rom venues have in the past hosted intellectual debates, book launches, exhibitions, fashion shows with local art college students, and musical concerts – particularly jazz or blues and contemporary electronic music, which represent alternative experiences to mainstream, popular culture. Many of the venues have incorporated graffiti, poetry extracts, paintings and artistic collages into the decoration and projected artistic images on to the walls of the dilapidated venues. Even in the Corvintető and Fecske, which emerged in part at least from the rom model but have reinterpreted the model, art and artistry re-emerge in the design and operation. The walls of the entranceway leading to the Fecske were adorned with elaborate graffiti works and large prints. The Kópé Terrace's design incorporates visual collages and Corvintető uses comic inspired graphics throughout the venue. This is not to suggest that all the venues have the same musical policies or are equally keen to champion art. Nevertheless, all the venues attempted to utilise some aspects of art or the creative industries, albeit in often subversive or non-institutionalised forms of art, such as graffiti.

As already noted, a key aspect of the rom phenomenon was the celebration of the urban decay that characterised these venues, with their crumbling facades and interiors, exposed brick walls covered in stickers and scratched messages, the ramshackle collection of beaten-up chairs and tables, and exposed cabling and lampions. The eclectic and distressed state of the fixtures and fittings in the rom venues is a purposeful inversion that communicates and reinforces the bohemian credentials of the owners, operators and consumers. Moreover, the establishment of the rom venues in the crumbling buildings weaves together the manifestations of ruin and marginality reflected in the urban fabric with feelings of marginality and dissent of people involved in the creative sectors who originally patronised these venues. In other words, the service concept and the consumer experience offered by the venue is inseparable from the urban milieu in which it is located.

Finally, it is important to stress the role of networking in these spatial arrangements. Kiss, for example, noted that information dissemination about the Szimpla kert often utilised their own email lists of people who then spread word about the venue and thereby brought in other selected patrons. Several of the venues, and the Szoda in particular, organised events for cycle couriers who patronised the bars. Gozsdu was decorated at least in part by students from a local art college and the operator of the new Mumus, which opened in 2008, enrolled several artists who produced bespoke designs and sculptures for the venue. Within these advocacy networks, loosely connected groups of individuals were called upon and mobilised to support the venue's operation and to build the consumer experience. Local residents and patrons were also enrolled by the Szimpla's owners who mobilised them to sign a petition in support of the venue when the local authorities threatened to shut it (Munkácsy, 2005). In Callon's (1998a) terminology this can be characterised as a market overflow that is considered a positive externality by the local residents: namely, the provision of cultural services to the local community. These advocacy networks also involved other cultural entrepreneurs, such as the producers of the Budapest City Spy map, who included the venues on small colour maps that are distributed freely in and around the city. Also engaged in the creation of the hospitality offering in the Fecske and Corvintető is 'Ági Mama' – a toilet attendant who decorates the facilities, and sells copies of her book alongside other items such as chewing gum, contraceptives and spare clothing.

Conclusion

Figure 24.1 summarises the key components of the assemblage that constituted the framing of the marketplace for rom bars and the qualification processes of their services. It is important to keep in mind that this orderly and static image is an abstraction of a highly heterogeneous and emergent gathering of actors which, to paraphrase the earlier cited Latour (2003: 40) quote, has not always been around, is of humble origin, is composed of heterogeneous parts, was never fully under the control of its makers, could have failed to come into existence, provides occasions as well as obligations, and needs to be protected and maintained if it is to continue to exist. This fragile entity, the marketplace for rom bars, is framed by a number of key actors.

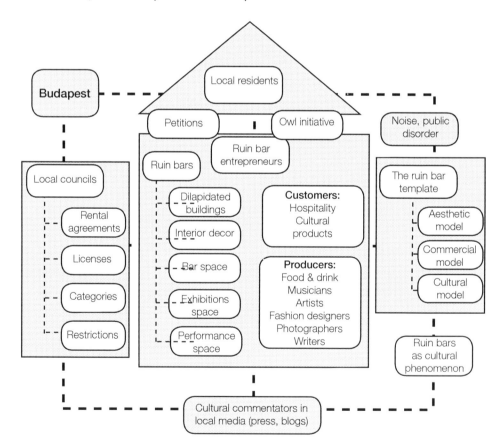

Figure 24.1: Assemblage components

The local government is one main actor, which, through the use of its framing devices, such as rental agreements, licences, categories for classifying businesses and various restrictions, participates actively in the assembly of the marketplace and the qualification of services, by granting them legitimacy in the eye of the law. Cultural commentators – through their interventions in the local media – help construct the frame which identifies rom bars as significant cultural institutions. Local residents, lending support with their petitions, similarly contribute to propping up the scaffolding that allows for the rom bars to be constituted as their own classificatory category in the hospitality and cultural scene of Budapest. The rom bar entrepreneurs themselves take part in co-constructing the frame with the above actors to ensure that their ventures can be properly assessed and qualified.

At the same time the entrepreneurs are also busy assembling the rom bars as centres of calculation (Latour, 1987) and qualification (Callon and Muniesa, 2005), by turning them into business ventures that are also marketplaces for cultural products. A most curious double-inversion takes place here. In order to qualify as a cultural institution (and stay alive as a business concern), the rom bar becomes a place where cultural goods themselves are qualified. In order to become a place that produces worth (both in the sense of economic value and social values (Stark, 2009), the rom bar becomes an arrangement of things that may initially seem worthless: dilapidated buildings and discarded objects. The rom bars can be understood as ingenious mechanisms for translating the worthless into something worthy.

This translation mechanism of the worthless into worthy however also needs a method of transporting. The rom bar schematic (as a commercial, cultural, and aesthetic model) emerges as the mediating device that enables the transportation of this assemblage from site to site as new rom bars are launched. With each new opening, the schematic itself transforms and evolves, as it responds to both positive and negative overflows that the rom bar market generates. The rom bar schematic therefore can be also considered as an important actor that lends coherence to the overall framing of the market.

Following Araujo et al. (2008) and Callon (1998), this chapter has attempted to challenge the existing divide between marketing and market-making practices, thereby contributing to knowledge in several academic areas. First, it advances emerging debates that have encouraged further engagement with social rather than managerial science in conceptualisations of hospitality management (see Lashley et al., 2007; Lugosi, 2008, 2009). The rom bar case helps to show how different actors interact and are enrolled in the creation of hospitality services and spaces. In adopting an ANT approach, we have avoided viewing venues as distinct organisational entities that are separated from the market environments in which they emerge and where they operate. By doing so, this chapter has also responded to contemporary calls among academics to engage with ANT and to provide contextually nuanced accounts of how tourism, leisure and hospitality emerge and are constructed (cf., van der Duim, 2007).

The chapter has also demonstrated how markets are assembled. Rather than adopting a narrow marketing management approach, focusing on organisational attempts to segment the market and position and target their services, we have interrogated the complex interaction of actors as they engage in the ongoing construction of markets. Utilising an ANT approach helps to convey the interactive, processual nature of market making, which relies on the ongoing calculative practices of various actors and agencies – in this case operators, patrons and local authorities alongside artists, cultural commentators and entrepreneurs who shape the operational offerings, the physical servicescapes as well as the consumer experiences possible in these venues. The ANT perspective also helps to stress the importance of discontinuity and conflict, which provide opportunities for assessing and articulating the components in the construction and rearrangements of markets.

References

Amichay EM. 2004. A valódi rehabilitáció esélye. *Múlt és Jövő* 3: 100-133.

Araujo L, Kjellberg H, Spencer R. 2008. Market practices and forms: Introduction to the special issue. *Marketing Theory* 8 (1): 5-14.

Balogh G. 2005. Sem nem rom, sem nem kocsma. *UFI* VII(7) July: 24-25. http://szimpla.hu/press/2007/ufi.html, accessed 28 February 2008).

Barry A. 2001. *Political Machines: Governing a Technological Society*. Athlone: London.

Bell D. 2007. The hospitable city: Social relations in commercial settings. *Progress in Human Geography* 31: 7-22.

Callon M. 1980. Struggles and negotiations to define what is problematic and what is not: The sociology of translation. In *The Social Process of Scientific Investigation: Sociology of The Sciences Yearbook*, Knorr WR, Krohn R and Whitley RD (eds). Reidel: Dordrecht and Boston, MA; 197-219.

Callon M. 1986a. The sociology of an actor–network: The case of the electric vehicle. In *Mapping the Dynamics of Science and Technology: Sociology of Science in the Real World*, Callon M, Law J and Rip A (eds). Macmillan: London; 19-34.

Callon M. 1986b. Some elements of a sociology of translation: Domestication of the scallops and the fishermen of St. Brieuc Bay. In *Power, Action, and Belief: A New Sociology of Knowledge?*, Law J (ed.). Routledge and Kegan Paul: London; 196-233.

Callon M. 1998a. An essay on framing and overflowing: Economic externalities revisited by sociology. In *The Laws of the Markets*, Callon M (ed.). Oxford: Blackwell; 244-269.

Callon M. 1998b. Introduction. The embeddedness of economic markets in economics. In *The Laws of the Markets*, Callon M (ed.). Blackwell: Oxford; 1-57.

Callon M. 1998c. *The Laws of the Markets*. Oxford: Blackwell.

Callon M. 1999. Actor–network theory: The market test. In *Actor Network Theory and After*, Law J and Hassard J (eds). Blackwell for Sociological Review: Oxford; 181-195.

Callon M. 2005. Why virtualism paves the way to political impotence: A reply to Daniel Miller's critique of *The Laws of the Markets*. *Economic Sociology: European Electronic Newsletter* 6 (2): 3-20.

Callon M. 2007. An essay on the growing contribution of economic markets to the proliferation of the social. *Theory, Culture Society* 24 (7-8): 139-163.

Callon M, Muniesa F. 2005. Economic markets as calculative collective devices. *Organization Studies* 26 (8): 1229-1250.

Callon M, Millo Y, Muniesa F. 2007. *Market Devices*. Blackwell: Oxford.

Cochoy F. 2002. *Une sociologie du packaging ou L' âne De Buridan Face Au Marché*. Presses Universitaires de France: Paris.

Dudás G, Földes A. 2005. Leáldozott a romkocsmáknak. *Index* May 13, http://index.hu/kultur/eletmod/rom0511/ , accessed 28 February 2008.

Földes A. 2003. 'Láthatatlan' alternatív szórakozónegyed, belső udvarokban. *Index* June 10, http://index.hu/politika/bulvar/alter0608/, accessed 20 February 2008.

Földes A. 2004. Versenyfutás a romházakért. *Index* April 16, http://index.hu/kultur/eletmod/rom0409/ (last accessed 20 February 2008.

Földes A, Rácz J, Szabó Z. 2004. Kerthelyiség-kalauz igényeseknek és igényteleneknek. *Index* July 20, http://index.hu/kultur/eletmod/kert0717/, accessed 20 February 2008.

Grit A, Lynch P. 2008. Home exchange experiences and the evaluation of network approaches for conceptualising spaces of hospitality in which home exchanges happen. In *Proceedings of the 17th Annual CHME Research Conference*. Department of Hospitality and Tourism Management, University of Strathclyde: Glasgow; 754-758.

Groth J, Corijn E. 2005. Reclaiming urbanity: Indeterminate spaces, informal actor and urban agenda setting. *Urban Studies* **42** (3): 503-526.

Jóhannesson GT. 2005. Tourism translations: Actor–network theory and tourism research. *Tourist Studies* **5** (2): 133-150.

Lakos N. 2003. Festive courtyards: Budapest's ruins are summer playground for youth. *Diplomacy and Trade*, June, http://www.dteurope.com/junius/english/11_perspectives.html, accessed 20 February 2008.

Lashley C, Lynch P, Morrison A (eds). 2007. *Hospitality: A Social Lens*. Elsevier: Oxford.

Latour B. 1986. The powers of association. In *Power, Action and Belief: A New Sociology of Knowledge?*, Law J (ed.). Routledge and Kegan Paul: London; 264-280.

Latour B. 1987. *Science in Action: How to Follow Scientists and Engineers through Society*. Open University Press: Milton Keynes.

Latour B. 1988. *The Pasteurization of France*. Harvard University Press: Cambridge, MA.

Latour B. 1993. *We Have Never Been Modern*. Harvard University Press: Cambridge, MA.

Latour B. 2003. The promises of constructivism. In *Chasing Technoscience: Matrix for Materiality*. Ihde D and Selinger E (eds). Indiana University Press: Bloomington and Indianapolis; 27-46.

Latour B. 2005a. From realpolitik to dingpolitik or how to make things public. Available from http://www.bruno-latour.fr/articles/article/96-MTP-DING.pdf. (last accessed 24 March 2007).

Latour B. 2005b. *Reassembling the Social: An Introduction to Actor-Network-Theory*. Oxford University Press: Oxford/New York.

Law J. 1986. On the methods of long distance control: Vessels, navigation and the Portuguese route to India. In *Power, Action and Belief: A New Sociology of Knowledge?* Sociological Review Monograph 32. Law J (ed.). Routledge and Kegan Paul: London; 234-263.

Law J. 1988. The anatomy of a sociotechnical struggle: The design of the TSR2. In *Technology and Social Process*. Elliott B (ed.). Edinburgh University Press: Edinburgh; 44-69.

Law J. 2004. *After Method: Mess in Social Science Research*. Routledge: London.

Lugosi P. 2008. Hospitality spaces, hospitable moments: Consumer encounters and affective experiences in commercial settings. *Journal of Foodservice* **19** (2): 139-149.

Lugosi P. 2009. The production of hospitable space: Commercial propositions and consumer co-creation in a bar operation. *Space and Culture* (in press).

Lugosi P, Bray J. 2008. Tour guiding, organisational culture and learning: Lessons from an entrepreneurial company. *International Journal of Tourism Research* **10** (5): 467-479.

Lugosi P, Lugosi K. 2008. Guerrilla hospitality: Urban decay, entrepreneurship and the 'ruin' bars of Budapest. *Hospitality Review* **10** (2): 36-44.

Mayer A. 2004. Víg élet a romokon. *Múlt és Jövö* **3**: 134-136.

Munkácsy M. 2005. Érdekvédelem a romkocsmákért. *Magyar Hírlap* May 12, http://szimpla.hu/press/closeing/MH.htm (last accessed 28.02.08).

palkata.hu. 2003. Jelszó: udvarok. http://www.palkata.hu/03junius.htm (last accessed 20.02.08).

Stark D. 2009. *The Sense of Dissonance: Accounts of Worth in Economic Life.* Princeton University Press: Princeton, NJ.

sulinet.hu. ND. Múlatni az időt - a Gozsdu-udvarban. http://www.sulinet.hu/tart/fcikk/Kgc/0/16022/1 (last accessed 20 February 2008.

van der Duim R. 2007. Tourismscapes: An actor-network perspective. *Annals of Tourism Research* **34**: 961-976.

25 Determinants of Hotel Performance: Continental or Worldwide Style?

Ruggero Sainaghi, Università IULM

Introduction

Performance is the time test of any strategy and performance improvement is at the heart of firm strategy (Chakravarthy, 1986). Researchers into management agree in considering performances a polyhydric, complex issue which, to be suitably measured, requires the joint use of several dimensions (Venkatraman and Ramanujam, 1986), the integration of financial and non-financial measures (Eccles, 1991), and the broadening of survey perspectives, involving the main business stakeholders (Kaplan and Norton, 1992).

These observations have certainly been stimulated by the tendency on the part of many managers and entrepreneurs to use financial, profit-based, accounting-based, non-'balanced' and excessively firm-oriented measurements.

This observation did not remain confined to strategic management studies, but also influenced researchers dealing with tourism businesses with particular attention to the lodging industry (Okumus, 2002). In a previous study, starting from the analysis of papers published in the leading journals in the last twenty years, we identified two research streams: one devoted to the analysis of performance measurement systems and one to investigating performance determinants.

The present chapter focuses exclusively on this second area of research, which is quantitatively more important, and sets out to present the state of the art on the basis of the descriptive variables identified in the methodological section.

The focal point of the article is however on the 'research styles' which emerge after segmenting the studies above all on the (continental) geographic basis of the empirical evidence employed and in particular according to their European , American or Asiatic origin.

Methodology

The databases for the observations proposed are composed of the main studies published in international journals in the last twenty years dealing with hospitality management, tourism and service management despite having strategic management or special business functions as their focus, and using the hotel industry as their empirical basis.

To identify articles we used hotel or similar words like hospitality or lodging industry to define the sector and performance or specific indicators (e.g. occupancy, Revpar) to identify dependent variables. This approach was integrated with the analysis of references. The reviews are the main tourism and hospitality journals. In addition, some articles were found in the management literature, primarily related to the work of Ingram and Baum.

The collected papers, with various emphases, develop the theme of performance determinants. All the studies therefore use performances as a dependent variable, while researchers have identified some determinants (independent variables) when considering mainly business functions or some external primary causes (sector, market, destination, macro-economic variables). Bibliographical research made it possible to identify 67 articles. A complete reference list is available on request from the author.

Variables

Each paper was inserted into a database whose main fields are a series of information relating to: (1) the paper (year of publication and type of journal), (2) dependent variables, (3) independent variables, (4) research design.

Concerning the *dependent variables* (performance), we distinguished between: (1) the dimensions used to assess results and (2) the operating indices employed to measure the selected dimensions.

The dimensions were identified by using the well-known classification worked out by Venkatraman and Ramanujan (1986). The authors propose a tri-partition of performances, distinguishing between a financial, operational and organisational dimension.

Regarding the indices, the researchers had very wide choices in the field, but tended to favour financial ratios to measure the financial dimension; occupancy, average daily rate (ADR) and revenues per available room (revpar), customer satisfaction, repeat visit and word of mouth, product development for the operational dimension; customer and employee satisfaction or the failure rate for the organisational dimension.

The *independent variables* were segmented by distinguishing the articles according to whether the performance determinants were sought inside or outside the firm or in both directions.

Lastly, concerning *research design*, information relating to the sample and information sources was highlighted – all the papers, with one exception, are empirical in nature.

The sample was analysed by describing the country or, more rarely, the countries from which the empirical evidence was taken, the numerousness of the sample itself (usually in hotel units), the distinction between samples constructed on the observation of a country or a specific destination or region, seen as a sum of destinations.

The information sources were segmented by mainly distinguishing between data collected through questionnaires and archival records, to which a residual category of other sources is added. Regarding the papers using quantitative data, the length in years of the historic series used was analysed.

Results

Journals and Years of Publication

The number of articles published dealing with performance determinants (Table 25.1) is growing and reached its peak in the three-year period 2003-05 (31.3%). The three-year period 2006-08, not yet ended when the data collection was completed, seems to confirm the peak in the previous three years.

Table 25.1: Periods and type of journals.

Type of journals	before 1997	1997-1999	2000-2002	2003-2005	2006-2008	Total
Total						
#	10	10	9	21	17	67
%	14.9%	14.9%	13.4%	31.3%	25.4%	100.0%
Journals (%)						
Hospitality management	70.0%	50.0%	44.4%	42.9%	52.9%	50.7%
Tourism	0.0%	10.0%	33.3%	57.1%	41.2%	34.3%
Strategic management	30.0%	40.0%	11.1%	0.0%	0.0%	11.9%
Other	0.0%	0.0%	11.1%	0.0%	5.9%	3.0%
Total	100.0%	100.0%	100.0%	100.0%	100.0%	100.0%
Journals (papers)						
Hospitality management	1, 2, 4, 5, 6, 9, 26	11, 14, 16, 17, 19	20, 22, 24, 27	33, 34, 39, 41, 42, 45, 47, 49, 50	51, 52, 57, 60, 61, 62, 63, 64, 65	
Tourism		18	21, 23, 29	30, 31, 32, 35, 36, 37, 38, 40, 43, 44, 46, 48	53, 54, 55, 58, 59, 66, 67	
Strategic management	3, 7, 8	10, 12, 13, 15	25			
Other			28		56	

Legend (for all tables)

1 Umbreit and Eder (1987); 2 Tse and Olsen (1988); 3 Baum and Mezias (1992); 4 Baker and Riley (1994); 5 Barrows and Naka (1994); 6 Harrington and Akehurst (1996); 7 Ingram (1996); 8 Ingram and Inman (1996); 9 Phillips (1996); 10 Baum and Haveman (1997); 11 Damonte et al. (1997); 12 Ingram and Baum (1997a); 13 Ingram and Baum (1997b); 14 Johns, Howcroft and Drake (1997); 15 Baum and Ingram (1998); 16 Anderson et al. (1999); 17 Brown and Dev (1999); 18 Davies (1999); 19 Worsfold (1999); 20 Camison (2000); 21 Chung (2000); 22 Gray, Matear and Matheson (2000); 23 Jeffrey and Barden (2000a); 24 Jeffrey and Barden (2000b); 25 Chung and Kalnins (2001); 26 Enz, Canina and Walsh (2001); 27 Israeli (2002); 28 Jeffrey et al. (2002); 29 Nicolau (2002); 30 Hwang and Chang (2003); 31 Barros (2004); 32 Chiang, Tsai and Wang (2004); 33 Espino-Rodríguez and Padrón-Robaina (2004); 34 Harrington (2004); 35 Hu and Cai (2004); 36 Koenig and Bischoff (2004); 37 Sigala (2004); 38 Barros (2005); 39 Chen, Kim and Kim (2005)

40 Espino-Rodríguez and Padrón-Robaina (2005); 41 Garrigós-Simon et al. (2005); 42 Ham, Kim and Jeong (2005); 43 Kim and Kim (2005); 44 Pan (2005); 45 Pine and Phillips (2005); 46 Reichel and Haber (2005); 47 Sin et al. (2005); 48 Tse et al. (2005); 49 Winata and Mia (2005); 50 Yeung and Lau (2005); 51 Alleyne, Doherty and Greenidge (2006); 52 Claver, Tarí and Pereira (2006); 53 Claver-Cortés et al. (2006); 54 Urtasun and Gutiérrez (2006); 55 Capó, Riera and Rosselló (2007); 56 Chand and Katou (2007); 57 Chathoth and Olsen (2007); 58 Chen C.F. (2007); 59 Chen M.H. (2007); 60 Claver-Cortés et al. (2007); 61 Gursoy and Swanger (2007); 62 Lee and Jang (2007); 63 Madan (2007); 64 Namasivayam, Miao and Zhao (2007); 65 Rodríguez, Cruz (2007); 66 Hu, Horng and Sun (2008); 67 Øgaard, Marnburg and Larsen (2008)

This is not surprising. Apart from the specific independent variables used, many papers underline in their introduction that growing competition, uncertainty and complexity mark the hotel sector. In this scenario, the attention needed to identify performance determinants becomes a crucial issue not only to improve business results, but also to ensure the survival of the firm. As widely documented in several longitudinal papers, failure rates in the hotel industry are fairly high and, of course, significantly increase in periods of recession or uncertainty (Ingram, 1996).

The journals publishing this growing stream of research mainly specialise in hospitality management (50.7%) and tourism (34.3%), although the space devoted to it by leading strategic management journals is not negligible (11.9%).

Dependent Variables

We pick up the previously introduced distinction between dimensions and indicators (Table 25.2).

Table 25.2: Table Dependent variables: Dimensions and indicators.

Type of journals	before 1997	1997-1999	2000-2002	2003-2005	2006-2008	Total
A (percentages)						
Operational perf.	20,0%	30,0%	66,7%	14,3%	23,5%	**26,9%**
Occupancy and prices						61,1%
Other						38,9%
Financial perf.	30,0%	20,0%	11,1%	23,8%	35,3%	**25,4%**
Financial ratios						64,7%
Other						35,3%
Oper. & Financ. perf.	10,0%	20,0%	11,1%	47,6%	35,3%	**29,9%**
Organisational perf.	30,0%	30,0%	11,1%	0,0%	5,9%	**11,9%**
All three dimensions	10,0%	0,0%	0,0%	14,3%	0,0%	**6,0%**
B (papers)						
Operational perf.	4, 26	10, 11, 19	21, 23, 24, 25, 27, 28	36, 43, 45	54, 55, 64, 66	
Financial perf.	2, 5, 6	16, 18	29	31, 34, 39, 44, 49	57, 59, 61, 62, 63, 65	
Oper. & Financ. erf.	9	14, 17	22	30, 32, 35, 37, 38, 42, 46, 47, 48, 50	51, 52, 53, 56, 58, 60	
Organisational perf.	3, 7, 8	12, 13, 15	20		67	
All three dimensions	1			33, 40, 41		

The operational and financial dimension, used both stand alone (respectively 26.9% and 25.4%) or jointly (29.9%), are those most commonly employed by researchers (81.1%). The organisational dimension, though not marginal, is less important (11.9%), while the joint use of all three dimensions is rare (6.0%). These data show the importance and spread of non-financial indices, which are normally constructed by using the operational dimension.

If we divide this analysis into periods, we see a progressive growth in the last six years of the importance of the financial dimension (23.8%, 35.3%), while, although falling, the joint use of the financial and operational dimension remains important (47.6%, 35.3%).

On the other hand, lower percentages are seen in those studies using the operational dimension alone (14.3%, 23.5%), especially if compared with the three-year period 2000-02 (66.7%). The organisational dimension has been progressively abandoned, although it was important at the beginning of the period examined (30.0% before 1997, 1997-99).

We will now examine the *indicators* used to measure the selected dimensions. Generally speaking, the *financial* dimension is seen in several financial ratios (64.7%), to which are added stock prices (23.5%) or efficiency indices constructed by using accounting data. This confirms the central importance of synthetic measurements borrowed from financial statements and therefore accounting based.

The *operational* dimension is mainly expressed through indices relating to occupancy, prices (typically per room) or their combination through revpar (61.1%). A residual item was also identified (38.9%); the high percentage of this category shows the greater freedom with which researchers analyse the operational dimension.

The *operational and financial* dimension is measured jointly through synthetic profitability measurements and operational indices which often go beyond occupancy and prices to include service innovation, customer retention and satisfaction, repeat visit and word of mouth and product development. Given the greater complexity and variability of these indices, it was not possible to contain them in categories as was previously done.

Lastly, the *organisational dimension* is expressed through indices aimed at measuring the satisfaction of some stakeholders, mainly customers and employees, or by the failure rate of hotel businesses in specific destinations or countries.

Independent Variables

An initial segmentation divides the articles according to whether the performance determinants were researched inside or outside the business or in both directions (Table 25.3).

Table 25.3: Independent variables

Kind of independent variables	Number of paper	%	%	Papers
External	6	9.0%		5, 18, 39, 44, 46, 59
Internal and external	11	16.4%		2, 3, 8, 10, 13, 15, 21, 25, 34, 54, 57
Internal	50	74.6%		1, 4, 6, 7, 9, 11, 12, 14, 16, 17, 19, 20, 22, 23, 24, 26, 27, 28, 29, 30, 31, 32, 33, 35, 36, 37, 38, 40, 41, 42, 43, 45, 47, 48, 49, 50, 51, 52, 53, 55, 56, 58, 60, 61, 62, 63, 64, 65, 66, 67
1. Strategy	15	**30.0%**	100.0%	
Hotel traits	9		60.0%	7, 11, 12, 26, 27, 45, 53, 55, 60
Competitive strategy	6		40.0%	9, 41, 50, 61, 62, 65
2. Production	12	**24.0%**	100.0%	
Efficiency and productivity	10		83.3%	14, 16, 17, 30, 31, 32, 35, 37, 38, 58
Other	2		16.7%	33, 40
3. Marketing	10	**20.0%**	100.0%	
Seasonality	4		40.0%	23, 24, 28, 36
Market orientation	3		30.0%	22, 47, 48
Quality & brand manag.	3		30.0%	6, 52, 43
4. Other	13	**26.0%**	100.0%	1, 4, 19, 20, 29, 42, 49, 51, 56, 63, 64, 66, 67

Among the papers focusing on *external causes* (9.0%), a small number examined the effect of the economic environment, level of concentration of the market and the sectors and the type of destination on economic performances.

The studies making joint use of *internal and external variables* are also small in number (16.4%), although not marginal. These articles generally place particular emphasis on external variables, typically proxy of the intensity of competition in the sector or of the specific destination in which a structure operates; the importance of some internal choices is however recognised to explain the impact on dependent variables.

The number of studies focusing on *internal variables* is the highest (74.6%). Given the large number of articles, we decided to classify the papers in relation to the specific theme on which the independent variables hinge. We thus identified three main streams represented by: (1) strategy, (2) production and (3) marketing (Table 25.3).

Strategy is the area of greatest research (30.0%) and in it two distinct, although correlated sub-fields are identified: hotel traits (60.0%) and competitive strategies (40.0%).

Hotel traits include a series of often structural features linked to dimension, location, the range of services, category, quality level, the decision to join a chain, resource commitment and activity scope, reputation. These are primary strategic decisions, many of which must be taken on founding, and which will influence company strategy for a long time, giving content to 'what' and 'where' (Baum and Mezias, 1992).

The high number of articles examining this field of research thus appears in line with the managerial importance of these decisions. Moreover, they are independent variables which are generally simple to monitor, since they constitute 'non-sensitive' information and generally published in the guides of the reception department. A second stream of enquiry was identified in studies exploring the link between performances and competitive strategies. The latter issue was dealt with by highlighting the importance of diversification (Lee and Jang, 2007) and the business portfolio (Yeung and Lau, 2005), applying the framework of Miles and Snow (1978) (Garrigós-Simon et al., 2005), identifying some critical success factors (Gursoy and Swanger, 2007) and developing the links with planning (Phillips, 1996).

A second important theme is the use of independent variables variously linked to the *production* function, in which a central importance is seen in the studies devoted to the analysis of efficiency and productivity (83.3%).

The growing interest in this type of study is definitely related to the growing competition to which firms are exposed. The oligopolist features of the market (Barros, 2004) have caused the search for efficiency to become 'essential not only for profitability, but also for a hotel's survival' (Chen, 2007, p. 696).

Efficiency and productivity may be measured at the level of single chains, by constructing indices for their units (Barros, 2005), destination (Chiang et al., 2004), country (Hwang and Chang, 2003) or category (Sigala, 2004), and by constructing rankings to assess the relative efficiency of the single firms. The indices may be synthetic measurements at business level or regarding single departments. Output is mainly measured for room department (sold rooms, number of guests or, more rarely, overnights, yielding index, room revenues) and F&B area (primarily covers and F&B revenues). Inputs are generally represented by: full time equivalents; room or covers available; room or F&B costs; utilities, labour, materials, operating or external costs; surface; capital (usually book capital).

The findings of this stream are not univocal, but more recent studies underline a progressive growth in productivity, the symptom of a real increase in competitive pressure.

A third dominant theme is dealt with in articles exploring *marketing* issues as an independent variable. They particularly concern the management of seasonality (40.0%), market orientation (30.0%) and quality and brand management (30.0%).

The use of seasonality as an independent variable appears a promising area for research, above all when, instead of being divided on a monthly basis, as generally happens (Koenig and Bischoff, 2004), the data used have a daily basis. The explorative study carried out by Jeffrey and Barden (2000a, 2000b), for example, highlighted a strong correlation between the segments of customers served by reception structures and location, described by the type of destination. Seasonality is definitely a research approach to better understand the mechanisms of price formation, as in part emerged from the exploratory work by Chung (2000). Seasonality ought to be inserted as a control variable in many studies devoted to performance.

The importance of market orientation is grasped by simply comparing the contrasting findings of the study carried out by Au and Tse (1995) with research by Sin et al. (2005). In the mid-1990s, the first study reveals a negative correlation between market orientation and performance, while the second finds a positive, significant link. Both studies have a sufficiently homogeneous research design. The apparent paradox of the empirical findings is explained by Sin et al. as a consequence of the new competitive climate: 'during periods of economic downturn, the orientation of a property to the market becomes a deciding factor on its survival and profitability, because the market is considerably smaller and customers more carefully differentiate between the values of competing hotel services before making a final decision' (2005, p. 1146).

Research Design

The sample was explored by analysing the geographic element and the number of firms.

In geographic terms (Table 25.4), empirical studies show a focus on countries (68.7%), compared with a decidedly smaller number of destinations (26.9%); there is, however, a small use of tourism regions (sets of destinations) (3.0%).

Of the articles, 92.5% concentrate on three continents: Europe (35.8%), Northern and Central America (32.8%) and Asia (23.9%); in terms of countries, three nations have a predominant importance: the USA (28.4%), Spain (6.4%) and the UK (13.4%). It is interesting to note that major countries for international tourism, like France and Italy, do not appear in the list.

The time spread shows a growing interest in Asiatic destinations (10 papers published between 2003-05), mainly headed by studies dealing with China and Taiwan.

Regarding the number of the sample, some dimensional groups were subjectively outlined. Most of the articles are broad samples, made up of a number of observations – normally hotel units – equal to or over 200 units (37.3%) or small samples (1-49; 34.3%) or medium-small (50-99, 20.9%).

The *collected data* were classified, in the case of the empirical papers, by distinguishing between data collected through questionnaires, archival records or both and documentation. 53.7% use archival records, while 38.8% of the articles use data collected

Table 25.4: Research design

Kind of independent variables	Number of paper	%	Papers
Geographic scope	67	100.0%	
Country	46	68.7%	1, 2, 4, 5, 6, 7, 9, 11, 13, 14, 16, 17, 18, 22, 23, 24, 25, 26, 27, 28, 29, 30, 31, 34, 35, 37, 38, 39, 41, 43, 44, 45, 46, 49, 51, 56, 57, 58, 59, 61, 62, 63, 64, 65, 66, 67
Destination	18	26.9%	3, 8, 10, 12, 15, 21, 32, 33, 40, 42, 47, 48, 50, 52, 53, 54, 55, 60
Other	3	4.5%	19, 20, 36
Europe	24	35.8%	4, 6, 9, 14, 18, 20, 23, 24, 28, 29, 31, 33, 36, 37, 38, 40, 41, 52, 53, 54, 55, 60, 65, 67
America	22	32.8%	1, 2, 3, 5, 7, 8, 10, 11, 12, 13, 15, 16, 17, 25, 26, 34, 35, 51, 57, 61, 62, 64
Asia	16	23.9%	21, 30, 32, 39, 42, 43, 44, 45, 47, 48, 50, 56, 58, 59, 63, 66
Other	5	7.5%	19, 22, 27, 46, 49
Sample size (units)	67	100.0%	
1-49	23	34.3%	5, 14, 16, 18, 21, 22, 29, 30, 31, 32, 38, 39, 42, 44, 49, 50, 51, 52, 57, 59, 62, 63, 66
50-99	14	20.9%	1, 4, 9, 20, 23, 33, 34, 37, 40, 47, 48, 58, 65, 67
100-199	5	7.5%	3, 41, 53, 55, 60
>=200	25	37.3%	2, 7, 7, 8, 10, 11, 12, 13, 15, 17, 19, 24, 25, 26, 27, 28, 35, 36, 43, 45, 46, 54, 56, 61, 64
Kind of data	67	100.0%	
Archivial	36	53.7%	3, 4, 5, 7, 8, 10, 11, 12, 13, 14, 15, 16, 18, 21, 23, 24, 25, 26, 27, 30, 31, 32, 36, 38, 49, 44, 45, 50, 54, 55, 57, 58, 59, 62, 63, 64
Questionnaire	26	38.8%	1, 2, 6, 9, 17, 20, 22, 33, 35, 37, 40, 41, 42, 46, 47, 48, 49, 51, 62, 53, 56, 60, 61, 65, 66, 67
Other	5	7.5%	19, 28, 29, 34, 43
Number of year (only archivial data)	36	100.0%	
1-3	17	47.2%	4, 11, 14, 16, 23, 24, 25, 27, 31, 32, 36, 38, 45, 55, 58, 63, 64
4-6	7	19.4%	18, 30, 39, 50, 57, 59, 62

through questionnaires. Only 4.5% of the papers make joint use of the two sources of information.

The papers using archival records generally focus on a small historic series (1-3 years, 47.2%), although giving importance to data covering a higher number of years (>10 years, 30.6%), utilised above all for articles published in strategic management reviews (63.6%). In any case, the development shows a progressive abandoning of long historic series – from 83.3% (before 1997) to 12.5% (2006-2008) – in favour of measures more linked to short and medium term.

Research Styles

Following our synthetic analysis of the four segmentation variables, we will now analyse these variables jointly, using as macro-segmentation the geographic area of origin for the empirical evidence, that in Europe, North and Central America, and Asia. We must state that the continental adjective (e.g. *European* style) is used exclusively to refer to the origin of the evidence and not the nationality of the researchers.

Table 25.5 synthesises the different connotation of the variables previously introduced with reference to the three styles.

European Style

The papers utilising empirical evidence taken from European countries have some recurrent features in their research design (point 4 in Table 25.5). The data are mainly collected through questionnaires (50.0%), the samples are medium-small (50-99, 37.5%) or small (1-49, 25.0%), and the historical series when archival records are used (41.7%) are above all short (1-3 years, 80.0%). As in the other styles, a main focus is seen on countries (62.5%), compared with an importance essentially in line with the overall average of destinations (29.2% against 26.9%).

The performance concept (point 2) is expressed by using the operational dimension stand alone (29.2%) or the financial and operational dimension used jointly (29.2%). Especially if compared with the American style, the use of the financial dimension alone is more limited (20.8% against 31.8%).

The independent variables (point 3) are almost always sought inside the firm (91.7%), by exploring the various business functions, with shares perfectly in line between strategy, production and marketing – always at 27.3%.

The scientific production (point 1) shows a regular development over the years, though with an intensification in the last two periods, with the same percentage share (29.2%). The papers are addressed above all to journals on tourism (50.0%) and hospitality management (45.8%); no article published in strategic management journals was found.

A decisive point to frame the European style is the combination occurring between the performance dimensions (operational, financial and organisational) and the type of evidence used (primarily archival records or questionnaire).

The studies using European evidence tend to favour the operational dimension (29.2%); the operational indices are mainly occupancy and prices (57.1%).

When the financial dimension is added to the operational one (29.2%), the data retrieval shifts significantly towards information collected through questionnaires (71.4%). This datum appears consistent, since information is often sought regarding volumes and prices or financial data on departments (generally not available in official statistics).

Lastly, in dealing with the financial dimension (20.8%), where the indices are mainly financial ratios (60.0%), the use of archival records is minor (40.0%). This is a European approach which is not confirmed in the American and Asiatic styles.

On the whole, these data seem to describe the researchers' difficulty in using European evidence to find already available secondary data. The result is a greater utilisation of data collected directly in house, often with questionnaires. This however tends to limit the size of the sample.

Table 25.2: Research styles

	European style	American style	Asiatic style	Total
1. Paper				
Type of journal				
Hospitality	45.8%	59.1%	37.5%	50.7%
Tourism	50.0%	4.5%	56.3%	34.3%
Strategic management	0.0%	36.4%	0.0%	11.9%
Others	4.2%	0.0%	6.3%	3.0%
Years (periods)				
Before '00	20.8%	63.6%	0.0%	29.9%
2000-'02	20.8%	4.5%	6.3%	13.4%
2003-'05	29.2%	9.1%	62.5%	31.3%
2006-'08	29.2%	22.7%	31.3%	25.4%
2. Dimensions				
Operational perf.	**29.2%**	**22.7%**	**25.0%**	**26.9%**
Occupancy and prices	57.1%	80.0%	50.0%	61.1%
Financial perf.	**20.8%**	**31.8%**	**25.0%**	**25.4%**
Financial ratios	60.0%	71.4%	50.0%	64.7%
Oper. and fin. perf.	**29.2%**	**13.6%**	**50.0%**	**29.9%**
Organizational perf.	**8.3%**	**27.3%**	**0.0%**	**11.9%**
All three dimensions	**12.5%**	**4.5%**	**0.0%**	**6.0%**
3. Indep. Variables				
External	**4.2%**	**4.5%**	**18.8%**	**9.0%**
External and internal	**4.2%**	**40.9%**	**6.3%**	**16.4%**
Internal	**91.7%**	**54.5%**	**75.0%**	**74.6%**
Strategy	27.3%	50.0%	16.7%	30.0%
Production	27.3%	25.0%	25.0%	24.0%
Marketing	27.3%	0.0%	25.0%	20.0%
Other	18.2%	25.0%	33.3%	26.0%
4. Research design				
Geographic scope				
Country	62.5%	77.3%	62.5%	68.7%
Destination	29.2%	22.7%	37.5%	26.9%
Other	8.3%	0.0%	0.0%	4.5%
Weight first 3 countries	91.7%	95.5%	81.3%	59.1%
Names of first 3 countries	Spain (45.8%), UK, Portugal	USA (86.4%), Canada, Barbados	Taiwan (37.5%), China, Korea	USA (28.8%), Spain, UK
Sample size (units)				
1-49	25.0%	22.7%	62.5%	34.3%
50-99	37.5%	9.1%	18.8%	20.9%
100-199	16.7%	4.5%	0.0%	7.5%
>=200	20.8%	63.6%	18.8%	37.3%
Kind of data				
Archivial records	41.7%	68.2%	62.5%	53.7%
Questionnaire	50.0%	27.3%	31.3%	38.8%
Other	8.3%	4.5%	6.3%	7.5%
Number of years (only archivial records)				
1-3	80.0%	26.7%	40.0%	47.2%
4-6	10.0%	13.3%	40.0%	19.4%
7-9	0.0%	0.0%	10.0%	2.8%
>10	10.0%	60.0%	10.0%	30.6%

A second hindering factor, again partly linked to the fragmentation of the supply, may be connected to the smaller spread of information covered by the official statistics for tourism. Apart from specific local exceptions, the European tradition tends to particularly monitor the operational dimension, often limited to volumes. The small size of firms makes the management of data collection of financial information very complex, but also related to prices applied. The restrictions of official statistics might explain the small number of publications which, based on European evidence, use external independent (4.2%) or internal and external variables (4.2%).

On the other hand, the direct collection of in-company information, above all through questionnaires (50.0%), has made it possible to use independent variables taken from the main business functions.

American Style

The American style developed the performance issue especially in the last century (63.6%, point 1), then marked time in the following years to show a considerable recovery in the last three-year period (22.7%). The observations have been mainly published in two scientific channels: hospitality journals (59.1%) and those of strategic management (36.4%). The debate in tourism reviews has been marginal (4.5%).

Research design (point 4) shows a decided orientation for studies carried out at country-level (77.3%), using large-size samples (63.6%). The research approaches favour archival records (68.2%), while questionnaires are less frequently used (27.3%). When quantitative data are used, the historical series tend to have a broad time span: 60.0% of the studies use data with a time spread of over 10 years, while only 26.7% use historical series with a 1-3 year span (80.0% for European style).

The second dimension explored is the organisational one (27.3%). The high percentage (overall average is 11.9%) is due to studies carried out during the 1990s by researchers in the field of population ecology, led by Baum and Ingram. This fact explains the high percentage of archival records with a time span over 10 years (60.0%) previously recorded, on the one hand, and the large number of publications produced before 2000, on the other.

The operational dimension is the third utilised, although with a lower percentage (22.7%). It is interesting to note the considerable use of the typically quantitative indices, of occupancy and prices (80.0%).

Lastly, the joint use of the organisational and financial dimension, an important area for European papers and a feature of the Asiatic style, has a slight importance in the American approach (13.6%).

A distinctive feature in American style is therefore the close link between research design, independent variables and performance dimensions.

The research design favours the use of quantitative data, referring to broad samples and long historical series. The use of broad samples is definitely favoured by the geographic size of the North American states, especially in the USA, the presence of many hotel chains and destinations with large concentrations of receptions.

The decision to explore the joint impact of external and internal causes in performances is a mainly American feature. This choice of field has certainly stimulated researchers to favour the use of quantitative data and information on broad historical series. This need, in turn, encourages the use of archival records, instead of questionnaires. On the other hand, the substantial nature of the papers has made it possible to guide a significant number of publications towards strategic management journals.

Lastly, the use of quantitative data on short horizons, often related not only to single firms but also to the industry and markets, tends to stimulate the use of dependent variables and equally quantitative indices, favouring the stand alone operational and financial dimension and, on the other hand, limiting their joint use. In this latter case, it is difficult to utilise archival records and long time series. The widespread use of quantitative data is also reflected in the utilisation of equally quantitative indicators, such as financial ratios (71.4%), or those of occupancy and prices (80.0%).

Asiatic Style

In some ways, the Asiatic style is a sort of intermediary model between the European and American ones, while showing a specific personality and character of its own.

A first important factor is the relative 'youth' of this style: 62.5% of the articles were published between 2003 and 2005, 31.3% in the last three years (point 1). The scientific papers mainly appeared in tourism reviews (56.3%), the number published in hospitality management journals is the smallest percentage in the three styles (37.5%).

From the point of view of research design (point 3), the Asiatic papers use above all small-sized samples (62.5%), contrasting with the other two styles. The data, however, stem mainly from archival records (62.5%), a fairly similar percentage to the American style (68.2%). The historical series are both short (1-3 years, 40.0%), and medium-term (4-6 years, 40.0%); there is little use of long historical series (>10 years, 10.0%). The main subject of enquiry is again the country (62.5%), whereas destination has the highest percentage (37.5%).

The independent variables are mainly sought inside firms (75.0%), while the highest percentage of studies is seen in those also exploring the impact of external variables (18.8%). Those looking inside business are less interested in strategy (16.7%), which has the lowest percentage, while attention is more focused on marketing (25.0%), production (25.0%) and other issues (33.3%), above all including organisation.

Performances are analysed by making joint use of the operational and financial dimension (50.0%), a value which is unequalled in the previous two styles.

These are followed, with the same percentage, by the stand-alone use of the operational (25.0%) and financial (25.0%) dimensions. While making wide use of quantitative data, the Asiatic papers have the lowest percentage of indices regarding financial ratios (50.0%) and those of occupancy and prices (50.0%).

The features characterising this style are context conditions, often relating to strongly growing countries where the tourism industry has traditionally not enjoted the same importance as that in Europe or America. The average size of the firms is small in many cases and their number is not particularly high, especially in some states.

The spread of international chains is not always large, and there is often a differentiation in supply according to whether the customer target is the international tourist or domestic tourist. Generally speaking, the academic papers are concerned with the former structures, further reducing the size of the sample.

These data easily explain why the samples are often composed of a very small number of firms and enables us to understand why scientific production especially addresses tourism and not hospitality journals. The articles have as their target more the policy makers than managers in the tourism sector.

Having clarified the reason for the smallness of the samples, we might however expect the collected data to be mainly based on questionnaires, in line with the European tradition. On the contrary, the papers using Asiatic evidence make considerable use of archival records (62.5%), a value almost in line with the American tradition (68.2%). This fact is partly linked to the decision to study international companies above all and to the specificity of context.

Regarding the first point, the greater complexity of management together with a sufficiently homogeneous size and service profile tends to favour the exchange of data and information between hotels, in line with the benchmarking services usually present in the main American and European destinations. The result is a greater facility of data access by researchers.

Concerning the second point, in many Asiatic countries studies generally conducted by agencies for local development have been carried out, taking international companies as their target.

The decision to focus attention on international hotels tends to favour the study of certain cities rather than countries. International arrivals, in fact, tend to concentrate in a few towns due to their importance above all in the business segment.

As far as the independent variables are concerned, 75.0% of the articles focus their attention on internal variables. However, the strategy occupies an important percentage (16.7%), but is decidedly lower than the European style (27.3%) and the American one (50.0%). We may recall that the strategy is mainly described by the hotel traits and hence by the choices of 'what' and 'where', with especial attention to the moments of founding. The researchers using Asiatic evidence seem more interested in understanding how, more than strategy, the high competition and variability influences the search for efficiency in production processes (25.0%), management of marketing levers (25.0%) and a residual category of other issues (33.3%). Among the latter, particular importance is given mainly to the management of organisational variables and the use of IT-ICT.

References

Au K, Tse C. 1995. The effect of marketing orientation on company performance in the service sector. A comparative study of the hotel industry in Hong Kong and New Zeland. *Journal of International Consumer Marketing* 8: 77-87.

Barros CPA. 2005. Measuring efficiency in the hotel sector. *Annals of Tourism Research* 32 (2): 456-477.

Baum JAC, Mezias SJ. 1992. Localized competition and organizational failure in the Manhattan hotel industry, 1898-1990. *Administrative Science Quarterly* 37 (4): 580-604.

Chakravarthy B. 1986. Measuring strategic performance. *Strategic Management Journal* 7 (5): 437-458.

Chen CF. 2007. Applying the stochastic frontier approach to measure hotel managerial efficiency in Taiwan. *Tourism Management* 28 (3): 696-702.

Chiang WE, Tsai MH, Wang LSM. 2004. A DEA evaluation of Taipei hotels. *Annals of Tourism Research* **31** (3): 712-715.

Chung KY. 2000. Hotel room rate pricing strategy for market share in oligopolistic competition – eight-year longitudinal study of super deluxe hotels in Seoul. *Tourism Management* **21** (2): 135-145.

Eccles RG. 1991. The performance measurement manifesto. *Harvard Business Review* **69** (1): 131-137.

Garrigós-Simon FJ, Marqués DP, Narangajavana Y. 2005. Competitive strategies and performance in Spanish hospitality firms. *International Journal of Contemporary Hospitality Management* **17** (1): 22-38.

Gursoy D, Swanger J. 2007. Performance-enhancing internal strategic factors and competencies: impacts on financial success. *International Journal of Hospitality Management* **26** (1): 213-227.

Hwang S, Chang T. 2003. Using data envelopment analysis to measure hotel managerial efficiency change in Taiwan. *Tourism Management* **24** (4): 357-369.

Ingram P. 1996. Organizational form as a solution to the problem of credible commitment: the evolution of naming strategies among U.S. hotel chains, 1896-1980. *Strategic Management Journal* **17** (SI): 85-98.

Jeffrey D, Barden RRD. 2000a. An analysis of daily occupancy performance: a basis for effective hotel marketing? *International Journal of Contemporary Hospitality Management* **12** (3): 179-189.

Jeffrey D, Barden RRD. 2000b. Monitoring hotel performance using occupancy time-series analysis: the concept of occupancy performance space. *International Journal of Tourism Research* **2** (6): 383-402.

Kaplan RS, Norton DP. 1992. The balanced scorecard: measures that drive performance. *Harvard Business Review* **33** (7/8): 172-180.

Koenig N, Bischoff EE. 2004. Analyzing seasonality in Welsh room occupancy data. *Annals of Tourism Research* **31** (2): 374-392.

Lee MJ, Jang S 2007. Market diversification and financial performance and stability: a study of hotel companies. *International Journal of Hospitality Management* **26** (2): 362-375.

Miles RE. 1978. Snow CC. *Organisational strategy, structure and process.* McGraw-Hill: New York.

Okumus F. 2002. Can hospitality researchers contribute to the strategic management literature? *International Journal of Hospitality Management* **21** (2): 105-110.

Phillips PA. 1996. Strategic planning and business performance in the quoted UK hotel sector: results of an exploratory study. *International Journal of Hospitality Management* **15** (4): 347-362.

Sigala M. 2004. Using data envelopment analysis for measuring and benchmarking productivity in the hotel sector. *Journal of Travel and Tourism Marketing* **16** (2/3): 39-60.

Sin LYM, Tse ACB, Heung VCS, Yim FHK. 2005. An analysis of the relationship between market orientation and business performance in the hotel industry. *International Journal of Hospitality Management* **24** (4): 555-577.

Venkatraman N, Ramanujam V. 1986. Measurement of business performance in strategy research: a comparison of approaches. *Academy of Management Review* **11** (4): 801-814.

Yeung PK, Lau CM. 2005. Competitive actions and firm performance of hotels in Hong Kong. *International Journal of Hospitality Management* **24** (4): 611-633.

26 An Investigation into the Relationship between Marketability of a Destination and the Long-Term Survival of Hawkers

Christine Harris, Bournemouth University

Introduction

The purpose of this chapter is to explore the relationship between the marketability of a tourist destination and the long-term viability of hawkers, a component of the retail sector. This research is concerned with those traders who operate outside a fixed retail outlet, in the main tourist areas. It is concerned with those that sell products rather than a service, such as car and boat hire, and excludes time share selling. There are a number of terms that could be used to describe these sellers, but for consistency, hawker despite some of its negative overtones, has been used.

It is not the purpose of this chapter to distinguish between the formal economy (those who are monitored in some way by the government) and the informal economy (where no such structure exists). Henry and Sills (2006) give a comprehensive list of the terms that could be applied to the hawker economy. They include terms such as 'hidden', 'underground' and 'subterranean' which might be apt from the government perspective, from a tourist perspective; hawkers on the beach are all too visible and in some cases omnipresent. Hawking is one of the earliest forms of retailing and is likely to remain part of the tourist landscape for the foreseeable future, and shows resistance to government regulation.

Hawkers have not always been popular with shopkeepers who have argued that they take trade away from established shops. However, evidence from the Adriatic coast (Nelken, 2006) does not support the view that they threaten established trades. Groups such as shopkeepers and local officials often call for the removal of hawkers but this is unlikely to be effective despite the introduction of legislation. Although in many countries they are operating illegally, the local police often lack the resources or inclination to prosecute. There is some local sympathy for the hawker who is seen to be trying to scrape a living from the 'rich' overseas visitors. Even in countries where hawking is not permitted by law it is difficult to differentiate between locals and visitors interacting, and those who are broking a sale, if the goods and the monetary exchange are not clearly visible.

Model

A simple model has been constructed which illustrates the relationship between the marketability of the destination and the hawker's long-term future and this is shown in Figure 26.1.

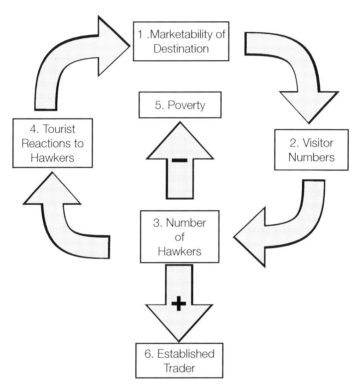

Figure 26.1: The relationship between the marketability of the destination and the hawkers' long-term future.

The marketability of the destination is dependent on a number of factors; this paper concentrates on the relationship with hawkers, which is one part of the mix. Westwood (2006) suggests that the tourism experience is a 'range of intrinsic and extrinsic influences, perceptions and constraints', and hence encounters with hawkers can be one of the range of influences. It is not the contention that the future of a destination is entirely in the hands of the hawkers rather that their long-term future is dependent on their marketability.

The marketability of the destination can have a positive impact on the number of tourists that visit the destination. As tourist numbers increase the level of entrepreneurial activity including hawking increases, due to the enterprise of local people. If the reaction to hawkers is positive, then the image of the destination becomes more marketable and hence there is a positive loop. Cole (2007) argues that tourism can have a 'large multiplier effect which can stimulate the local economy'. Engagement with entrepreneurial activity is encouraged by governments who are keen for tourist expenditure to filter into the local economy. If the hawkers are successful then they can choose to establish entrepreneurial businesses, achieving stability in the long term.

If the tourist reaction is negative then the marketability of the destination declines, which can lead to a fall in tourism and a lack of potential customers for the hawker, creating a negative loop. The hawkers' response to falling demand can either to be more aggressive salesmanship which will increase the negative effect or to try and survive on a reduced income and ultimately maybe slip into poverty.

This is a brief description of the model that is being driven by the consumer reaction, which determines whether this is a positive or negative loop, and hence the long-term options available to the hawkers. The elements of the loop are discussed in detail below.

Marketability of Destination

Tourists are more discerning and more knowledgeable about destinations than ever. The consumer has travelled widely and has a broad range of destinations that can be used as reference points. They are able to access the World Wide Web, where many review based web sites are available for example, www.tripadvisor.com. The influence of online communities in the marketability of any brand or service has been increasingly recognised (Armstrong and Hagel III, 1996; Kozinets, 1999; Muniz and O'Guinn, 2001) and this it true of the tourism industry. Web-based communities can offer unsanitised opinions of destinations, with popular destinations often having in excess of 50 reviews. These reviews are usually not edited or censored unless they are likely to be the subject of legal action, and hence some comments are very negative. These sites can be penetrated by vested interests but the range and volume of reviews enables the customer to evaluate alternative opinions and make an informed choice.

Contrast this with the situation 30 years ago when most destination information was provided by the sanitised glossy brochures from major tour operators and travel guides which may not have been entirely independent. With the inability to control information concerning destinations, it is important that all aspects of the destination have a good marketable image in order not to adversely affect visitor numbers.

Visitor Numbers

In an ever more competitive market where customers have a wide variety of options, it is important that the destination has a marketable image. Tourism has now expanded into most corners of the world, even the poorest, least developed, countries. Tourists are now travelling further afield, due to increasing low airfares, wider availability of destination and the ease of booking services overseas. They are tempted by interesting visual images, that offer new experiences (Harrison, 1995), and it is a positive experience that they seek.

There is a view that all publicity is good publicity as it gets you noticed but there is no evidence to suggest that this is true in the case of tourism. Baker and Coutler (2007) provide details of tourism numbers in Bali before and after the widely publicised terrorist bombings, showing the negative impact this had on visitor numbers. Research undertaken post the attacks on the World Trade Center in New York (Floyd and Pennington-Gray, 2004) showed that visitors are risk averse. Tourists are unlikely to repeat bad experiences, or visit places which they think may be a bad experience (Moutinho, 1987; Sonmez and Graefe, 1998).

As tourism has grown, successive governments have tried to ensure that income passes into the local economy, rather than to tour operators. Many countries positively encourage tourism as a means of stimulating small economies (Brohman, 1996) of which hawking is a part. As the levels of tourism increase then the levels of activity among small entrepreneurs also increases (Dahles, 1999; Go, 1997). Litterell et al. (1994) estimated that shopping accounts for between 30% and 33% of that spend, of which hawkers can take a proportion.

Number of Hawkers

Hawking is a very fluid sector, as the barriers to entry and exit are low. In places where there is no regulation it is easy to move in and out of the industry switching between hawking and alternative sources of income where available. Where licences are required, entry may be more difficult. Whilst to be successful as a hawker, good retail skills are required (Harris, 2009) it is possible to survive in the industry by replacing skills with long hours, low margins and persistence. Goods are readily available, by picking flowers and fruit from the fields, or making simple jewellery from beads and string.

In poor countries with low levels of employment there is likely to be large numbers of hawkers, for lack of alternative sources of income. The fluidity of the industry is aided by the migratory nature of some hawkers. Bali attracts hawkers from all over Indonesia (Cukier and Wall, 1994; De Jonge, 2000), including many ethnic groups (Hitchcock, 2000).

Hawkers operate in a situation close to perfect competition, selling similar products at similar prices with little possibility of differentiation. Economic theory would suggest (Soloman, 1998/1999) that they are unlikely to earn much above subsistence level. If the earnings increase, the situation is likely to attract others into the profession, and unless this is accompanied by an increase in visitor numbers, the effect on profits will be detrimental.

Primary Research

The reaction of tourists to hawkers is an essential element of the model presented in this chapter in determining whether there is a positive or negative loop and hence the long-term outcome. In order to examine this essential element, primary research was undertaken. The intention of this research was to explore a range of opinions, rather than to try to quantify opinions; a qualitative approach was therefore indicated. Internet blogs were chosen as a way of obtaining tourist reactions, as it was important that respondents were not influenced by the enquirer as might be in the case of an interview. It was also important that the information concerning hawking should occur naturally in writing concerning visitor experiences. If interviewing or focus groups had been used in order to maximise the efficiency of the interview the subject might have to have been raised by the interviewer.

The use of blogs for ethnographic research is no longer new and a number of practitioners have advocated it (Grossnickle and Raskin, 2000; Hakken, 1999; Jones, 1995; Kozinets, 2002; Miller and Slater, 2000). Blogs offer a snapshot in time where the hawker may not always be in the centre of the picture, sometimes they are part of the background. Blogs are generally less than 200 words and hence a snapshot, as the blogger has had to be selective about what is to be included and provide the 'best view'. The blogs offer immediacy, many are written on a daily basis although some travellers write one per country visited. Blogs like photographs are used to capture memorable events rather than the mundane and this is ideal from the viewpoint of the researcher. These are the images that are the strongest and hence have the most marketability or not as the case may be. As with all qualitative work, the method involves some element of interpretation. The blogs that have been included are representative of those found through the Internet search engines. The blogs were categorised using approach-avoidance strategies first proposed by Russell and Mehrabian (1978) and those who employed the former strategy were analysed first.

Approach

Many of the tourists had very positive reactions towards hawkers and they were the central theme of their blogs. Hawker centres, where hawkers were drawn together and regulated received positive recommendations for visitors. The hawker centre in Singapore was described as a 'great experience...organised and tidy' (Ladycarmelkent, 2007) and 'fab and dirt cheap' (Boris&Alyssa, 2007). These types of centres offer a degree of permanency but have spaces available for casual hawkers. It was not only hawkers in organised centres who were praised, Jim and his wife were pleased with the outcome of their encounter with a beach hawker. They were celebrating their wedding anniversary and had decided to dress for the occasion:

> ... with clothes Adele had purchased for a beach hawker. Not exactly Vera Wang stuff but we still looked good.
>
> (Jim&Adele, 2007)

This is perhaps one of the extreme examples found but there were many other examples of positive reactions to purchases. Even the stationary tourist on the beach can welcome the arrival of the hawker which enabled them to 'partake of some fresh fruit from a beach hawker with a fantastic smile' (Matt&Amp:Lou, 2005). The previous two examples illustrate that visitors can have a very positive experience that encourages them to tell the world about it.

In other blogs, the hawker is part of the background and helps to paint a picture of a good visitor experience. Akshay uses the image of the hawker in this way:

> Street vendors push food carts piled with steamed dumplings, smoked beef teriyaki sticks, and roasted peanuts along the sidewalk as they begin to set up for another day of business.
>
> (Akshay, 2008)

Another blogger has evocative memories of ' the smell of street vendors' food' (Anon, 2007), which adds depth to the picture by adding the sense of smell. Alternatively sound can be used, 'the beach hawkers cry twists through the Barcelona heat' (Anon, 2008), to add depth. All have happy memories of hawkers viewing them as an integral part of the landscape, and one, which has added value to their experience, although in some instances a purchase was not made.

Some bloggers had carried their approach strategies to extremes and developed personal relationships with the hawkers. Carol (2007) writes fondly of Lalbi, a seller of fruit which she will 'enjoy for dessert'. Besides being on first name terms, tourists can show a positive caring attitude towards the hawkers, as a way of enhancing their own experience. Mimi (Mimi's Musings, 2005) comments that she is actively seeking Mary Bella and Sulee (two hawkers) in order to buy 'some more clothes for their little children'. Klein (2006) developed a relationship with Palani an ex-fisherman who took to hawking when medical problems forced an end to his former employment, a typical route into the profession. He was prepared to compromise the quality of the products for the satisfaction of the purchase and the sense of helping the vendor. Alan (2007) also shows concern for the hawker, he wants to make friends but comments that it is a difficult to build any relationship as you are 'primarily marked out as potential sources of income'. This friendliness can be unwelcome or misunderstood, Pinkowski (2007) worries about the etiquette towards the mango seller who after the sale sits down in close proximity, and the blogger wonders, 'are we supposed to chat under this umbrella?' implying that although the purchase was welcome the blogger did not want to develop a relationship with the vendor but did not 'begrudge someone shade'.

Within these blogs, there is a sense that the visitor wants to approach and help the hawker, even as part of their social responsibility. It was a chance for them to mix with local people and share some experiences, even of seeking novelty (Hirschman, 1980). This was not a view however shared by all as will be discussed in the next section.

Avoidance

Avoidance strategies can be successful as illustrated by Elena and Richard (2007) who write on their blog that there are 'so many quite aggressive hawkers to get past first', illustrating that avoidance can be a problem however what is clear is that they succeed. Richard goes on to propose that 'hawker dodging required so much skill and planning that it should become a recognised sport'. This implies that it was seen as a game with two sides and a definable set of rules. If the encounter cannot be avoided then it can be turned into a game that can be enjoyed.

Other bloggers have made a success of 'hawker dodging', Chris Willetts (2006) whilst searching for the Tourist Information Center in Jerusalem writes, 'after ten minutes of hawker dodging I was outside the little shop'. H is another successful dodger he had been experimenting with the 'blank look' but worries that it might not be:

> ... a healthy nor ethical approach to engaging with humanity, particularily those of the hawker variety, but it has proved extremely effective today. Oh dear the things I do for a bit of peace and quiet.
>
> (H, 2007)

Dodging and pretending not to understand are two common ploys when using the avoidance strategy, and both of these can work despite the view that hawkers are persistent. Hawkers are not without retailing skills and are only likely to be persistent when they sense there is the possibility of a sale. Tourists in most instances are numerous; time is a valuable resource not to be wasted on the unresponsive.

If 'dodging' is not successful then the visitor may try to rationale the purchase and hence change a potentially 'bad' experience into a 'good' one. Burnt Oatmeal (2005) used the term 'hawker dodging' whilst writing about a visit to China but in this instance eventually made a purchase which the writer subsequently discovered was dearer than other competitors. This was rationalised as follows: 'it's hard to complain too much when the 'inflated' price is less than you'd expect to pay in any wealthier nation'. Gado Gado, (2008) also tries to rationalise the experience, after making several purchases from a hawker and paying above the market price 'but I figure I am supporting the locals' and have 'made some people's days'.

An avoidance strategy can be difficult to deploy on the beach where the majority of tourists on the beaches are stationary, relaxing and soaking up the sun. The hawkers in contrast are mobile wandering up and down the beach, searching for customers. If approach is inevitable then the tourist tries to rationale the encounter in order to improve the outcome of the experience. Fortunately tourists have a different attitude to locals, they have a desire to make bad situations into interesting experiences and adventures.

Some however see no value in hawkers; they are to be avoided as they provide no useful purpose. One of their harshest critics writes that they are 'selling junk to pollute the environment' (Travelbaxter2, 2008) then rationalises it by writing that it is an 'easy home industry for villagers'. Others would have preferred avoidance:

> We won't miss hawkers, especially those on the beaches with their god-forsaken drums, maps, stickers and magnets that hassle you every day even though you have told them, 'No!' 493 times…that day
>
> (Anthony&Astrid, 2008)

Negative Loop

If the tourist is unhappy with the hawker encounter to the extent of posting negative blogs on the Internet then this can have serious repercussions for the marketability of the destination. Blogs are increasingly used as a source of information by potential visitors. The lack of a sale to a visitor is likely to encourage the hawker to be more persistent in the future increasing the volume of negative images.

If tourist numbers decline, and there is a decrease in tourist spend, less money will filter into the local economy. Many hawkers are entirely dependent on the trade; their whole family is involved, from children as young as eight years. Unless some hawkers leave the sector, the choices are stark. In the poorer less developed countries, alternative sources of income are few. They could join the ranks of the migrant hawkers, trying to find destinations that are more lucrative, or sink into poverty.

Positive Loop

If the loop is positive and there were many stories of rewarding encounters with hawkers on the Internet, then this increases the marketability of the destination. There is some evidence to suggest that visitors try to make the best of a bad experience, by rationalising the encounter. If a steady income can be achieved, the hawker can look to move into the established retail sector or other areas of the tourist market.

One success story is that of Shiva Mandre from Goa (Goa Unltd, 2008). He came to Goa in 1985 and spent seven years sleeping on the streets. He started by selling newspapers on the beach in 1991. He switched in 2003 due to declining sales to selling 'postcards and books, besides renting bicycles' as well as acting as a tour guide; in addition, his wife runs cookery classes for tourists. His contact with tourists he claims has given him 'mastery over 25 languages'. Whilst on the streets he enrolled in classes and hopes to 'learn more German and French and to complete his graduation in the Arts stream and go on to complete his masters' degree in French language'. This is just one example of what can be achieved through hawking

Conclusion

From a detailed examination of the factors involved, the linkages between the four elements in the model have been established. Each of the elements in the loop are dependent on each other and can have a positive or negative impact.

For hawkers their long-term survival is dependent on a positive loop. This will enable them to grow and possibly move into more established sectors and provide a secure future. If the loop is negative then the marketability falls resulting in less demand for the goods, leading to a decline in the hawking industry. With few other sources of income available especially for the unfit and uneducated, the prospects are poor.

Evidence from the blogs shows that visitors operate both approach and avoidance strategies. The good news from the hawker's viewpoint is that many of those who are reluctant to engage with hawkers but are forced into the situation try to rationalise it, justifying the purchase by stressing other elements of the sale. This chapter has thus proved that the long-term survival of the hawker is dependent on his or her marketability.

References

Akshay 2008. *Good Morning Vietnam*. Available from: http://trivialmatters.blogspot.com/2008/11/good-morning-vietnam.html [Accessed 19 February 2009].

Alan 2007. *Alan Said*. Available from: http://www.blogger.com/comments.g?blogID=5653064720582670163&postID=6427 [Accessed 10 February 2009].

Anon 2007. *Return to Spokane*. Available from: com/spokane-journals-j5399683.html. [Accessed 21 January 2009].

Anon 2008. *Last Days of Summer*. Available from: http://www.minisagas.org/story.php?title=Last days of summer [Accessed 29 January 2009].

Anthony&Astrid 2008. *Anthony&Astrid's India Blog, We came, we saw, we kicked its ass*. Available from: http://indiatraveller.wordpress.com/2008/02/09/what-we-wont-miss-about-india/ [Accessed 29 January 2009].

Armstrong A, Hagel III J. 1996. The Real Value of Online Communities. *Harvard Business Review* **74** (May/June): 131-141.

Baker K, Coutler A. 2007. Terrorism and tourism: The vulnerability of beach vendors' livelihoods in Bali. *Journal of Sustainable Tourism* **15** (3): 249-266.

Boris&Alyssa 2007. *The road to Taumatawhaka tangihangakoau auotamateaturipuka kapikimaungaho rongukapokaiwhen uakitanatahu*. Available from: http://realtravel.com/singapore-journals-j5226845.html [Accessed 21 January 2009].

Brohman, J. 1996. New directions in tourism for Third World development. *Annals of Tourism Research* **23** (1): 48-70.

Burnt Oatmeal 2005. *China Journal*, part 5. Available from: http://burnt-oatmeal.livejournal.com/3331.html [Accessed 10 February 2009].

Carol 2007. *Carol's Kitchen*. Available from: http://insidecarolskitchen.blogspot.com/2007/12/current-events.html [Accessed 29 January 2009].

Cole S. 2007. Entrepreneurship and empowerment: Considering the barriers - a case study from Indonesia. *Tourism Review* **55** (4): 461-473.

Cukier J, Wall G. 1994. Informal tourism employment: Vendors in Bali. *Indonesia. Tourism Management* **15** (6): 464-476.

De Jonge H. 2000. Trade and ethnicity: Street and beach sellers from Raas on Bali. *Pacific Tourism Review* **4**: 75-86.

Elena and Richard 2007. *Elena and Richard's European Adventure*. Available from: http://realtravel.com/paris-journals-j4665213.html [Accessed 21 January 2009].

Floyd M, Pennington-Gray L. 2004. Profiling risk perceptions of tourists. *Annals of Tourism Research* **31** (4): 1051-1054.

Gado Gado 2008. *Shantitour*. Available from: http://shantitour.blogspot.com/2008/04/gado-gado.html [Accessed 29 January 2009].

Goa Unltd 2008. *Newspaper selling changes the course of Shiva Mandre's life*. Available from: http://goaunltd.com/?p=561 [Accessed 29 January 2009].

Grossnickle J, Raskin O. 2000. *The Handbook of Online Marketing Research: Knowing your Customer Using the Net*. McGraw-Hill: New York.

H. 2007. *Hawker Dodging*. Available from: http://tigertigerbb.blogspot.com/2007/09/hawker-dodging.html [Accessed 18 February 2009].

Hakken D. 1999. *Cyborgs@Cyberspace? An Ethnographer Looks to the Future*. Routledge: New York.

Harris C. 2009. An examination into the retail skills of itinerant retailers before 1900. EAERCD Conference. Surrey.

Harrison D. 1995. International tourism and less developed countries: The background. In *International Tourism and Less Developed Countries*, Harrison D (eds). Wiley: New York; 1-19.

Henry S, Sills S. 2006. Informal economic activity: Early thinking, conceptual shifts, continuing patterns and persistent issues – a Michigan study. *Crime Law and Social Change* **45**, 263-284.

Hirschman E. 1980. Innovativeness, novelty seeking, and consumer creativity. *Journal of Consumer Research* **7** (December), 283-295.

Hitchcock M. 2000. Ethnicity and tourism entrepreneurship in Java and Bali. *Current Issues in Tourism* **3** (3): 204-225.

Jim&Adele 2007. *Wedding Anniversary*. Available from: http://jimandadelestrip.blogspot.com/2007/10/wedding-anniversary.html [Accessed 29 January 2009].

Jones S. 1995. Understanding community in the information age. In *Cybersociety: Computer-Mediated Communication and Community*, Jones SE (ed.). Thousand Oaks,CA: Sage Publications.

Klein G. 2006. *My Surface Hippy Adventure*. Available from: http://garyhip.blogspot.com/2006/07/palani.html [Accessed 29 January 2009].

Kozinets RV. 1999. E-tribalized marketing? The strategic implications of virtual communities of consumption. *European Journal of Marketing* **17** (3): 252-264.

Kozinets RV. 2002. The field behind the screen: Using netography for marketing research in online communities. *Journal of Marketing Research* **XXXIX** (February): 61-72.

Ladycarmelkent 2007. *Lady Carmel's Adventures*. Available from: http://realtravel.com/singapore-journals-j5008188.html [Accessed 21 January 2009].

Litterell M, Baizerman S, Kean R, Gahring S, Niemeyer S, Reilly R, Stout JA. 1994. Souvenirs and tourism styles. *Journal of Travel Research* **33** (3): 3-11.

Matt&Amp:Lou 2005. *Samui*. Available from: http://travelspam.blogspot.com/2005/04/last-days-in-koh-samui.html [Accessed 29 January 2009].

Miller D, Slater D. 2000. *The Internet: An Ethnological Approach*. Berg: Oxford.

Mimi's Musings 2005. *Bali-Bound!* Available from: http://rodgersatnjis.blogspot.com/2005/02/goodbye-2004hello-2005.html [Accessed 29 January 2009].

Moutinho L. 1987. Consumer behaviour in tourism. *European Journal of Marketing* **21** (10): 6-11.

Muniz A, O'Guinn T. 2001. Brand community. *Journal of Consumer Research* **27** (March): 412-432.

Nelken D. 2006. Immigrant beach selling along the Italian Adriatic coast: De-constructing a social problem. *Crime Law and Social Change* **45**: 297-313.

Pinkowski J. 2007. *Phantom Husband Goes for a Swim.* Available from: http://www.jenpinkowski.com/blog/?p=213 [Accessed 29 January 2009].

Russell J, Mehrabian, A. 1978. Approach-avoidance and affiliation as functions of the emotion-eliciting quality of an environment. *Environment and Behaviour* **10** (3): 355-387.

Soloman J. 1998/1999. *Economics.* Prentice Hall Europe.

Sonmez S, Graefe A. 1998. Determining future travel behaviour from past travel experience and perceptions of risk. *Journal of Travel Research* **37**: 171-177.

Travelbaxter2 2008. *The Exotic Durian - Explorations in Indonesia.* Available from: http://realtravel.com/tasikmalaya-journals-j6699961.html [Accessed 21 January 2009].

Westwood S. 2006. Shopping in sanitised and un-sanitised spaces: Adding value to tourist experiences. *Journal of Retail and Leisure Property* **5** (4): 281-291.

Willetts C. 2006. *Jerusalem day 2* Available from: http://cwillett.blogspot.com/2006/07/jerusalem-day-2.html [Accessed 12 February 2009].

Contemporary Tourism Reviews

Editor in chief:

Professor Chris Cooper, Dean of the Business School, Oxford Brookes University

Critical, state of the art, authoritative reviews written by leading thinkers and academics in the field providing flexible, current and topical information as an instant download. Students and researchers need information that is fast, current, immediate and flexible.

Contemporary Tourism Reviews offers just that, by providing 'packets' (ie. reviews) of downloadable, searchable and must-have information based on core Tourism topics. Customers can target the exact information they require, on a 'pick and mix' basis, with all information purchased as an fully searchable XML tagged PDF file for immediate download.

Reviews are divided into the following four areas and cover each of the topics therein, and more:

♦ **Discipline-based Reviews** including Economics and Tourism; Sociology and Tourism; and Geography and Tourism.

♦ **Business-themed Reviews** including Service Management and Tourism; ICT and Tourism; and Human Resources and Tourism.

♦ **Issues-based Reviews** including Climate Change and Tourism; Sustainability and Tourism; and Transport and Tourism.

♦ **Essential Tourism Reviews** including Tourism and Event Management; Attractions and Tourism; and Risk/Security and Tourism.

Each review covers:

• The development of the field - the key milestones, literature, events and writers involved.

• Framing the field – the current state of the art/thinking and a clearly legible mapping of the field.

• Emerging issues and a future focussed agenda for the field.

• An extensive reference list.

Contemporary Cases Online **and** *Contemporary Tourism Reviews*
are available for download from www.goodfellowpublishers.com
from Autumn 2009

Tourism and Political Change

Edited by Richard Butler, Professor in the Department of Hospitality and Tourism Management of University of Strathclyde, and Dr Wantanee Suntikul, Assistant Professor in Tourism Planning and Development at the Institute for Tourism Studies in Macao, China

Tourism is a vital tool for political and economic change – the use of tourism to initiate political discussions, increased pressure for fair trade, and tourist boycotts all reflect the huge impact the tourism industry has on political change. With international contributions from an esteemed list of experienced individuals, *Tourism and Political Change* addresses these issues of great current relevance and importance focussing on events and their impacts.

Prov UK prices: Hard copy: £34.99   E-Book: £25   E-Chapter: £3.99

Tourism and Crime: Key Themes

Edited by David Botterill, freelance academic and higher education consultant and Professor Emeritus in the Welsh Centre for Tourism Research, University of Wales Institute Cardiff, and Trevor Jones, Reader in Criminology and Criminal Justice at the School of Social Sciences, University of Cardiff

The tourist as victim or offender? With contributions from international experts *Tourism and Crime: Key Themes* is the first text to addresses the tourism-crime nexus, including issues such as drugs tourism, sex tourism and alcohol-related crime and disorder among holidaymakers, the 'naming and shaming' of specific 'danger travel spots', the governance of safety in 'stateless' spaces, cooperation between justice authorities in different jurisdictions, and much more.

Prov UK prices: Hard copy: £34.99   E-Book: £25   E-Chapter: £3.99

Tourism Research: a 20:20 vision

Edited by Professor Richard Butler, Professor in the Department of Hospitality and Tourism Management of University of Strathclyde and Professor Douglas Pearce, Professor in Tourism Management, Victoria Management School, New Zealand

Tourism research continues to expand at a rapid rate and this explosion in output has meant it is more and more difficult to keep pace with what is being produced, as well as the quality of what is produced. *Tourism Research: a 20:20 vision* examines how research agendas have evolved and might develop in coming years, considers conceptual and methodological advances, discusses obstacles that have been encountered and suggests ways forward.

Prov UK prices: Hard copy: £49.99   E-Book: £39.99   E-Chapter: £2.50